human learning and memory

human learning and memory

An Introduction

ARTHUR WINGFIELD
Brandeis University

HARPER & ROW, PUBLISHERS
New York, Hagerstown, Philadelphia, San Francisco, London

For Mark, Catherine, and Thomas,
who allowed the author a second chance
to discover the magic of discovery.

SCULPTURE AND DETAILS: Henry Moore, *Family Group*.
The Phillips Collection, Washington, D.C.

SPONSORING EDITOR: George A. Middendorf
PROJECT EDITORS: Karla B. Philip/H. Detgen
DESIGNER: Robert Sugar
SENIOR PRODUCTION MANAGER: Kewal K. Sharma
PHOTO RESEARCHER: Myra Schachne
COMPOSITOR: American–Stratford Graphic Services, Inc.
PRINTER AND BINDER: The Maple Press Company
ART STUDIO: Vantage Art, Inc.

Human Learning and Memory: An Introduction
Copyright © 1979 by Harper & Row, Publishers, Inc.

Library of Congress Cataloging in Publication Data

Wingfield, Arthur.
    Human learning and memory.

    Bibliography: p.
    Includes index.
    1. Learning, Psychology of. 2. Memory. I. Title.
BF318.W56   153.1   78–18197
ISBN 0–06–047149–2

contents

The Concept of a Concept 196 / A Concept Is More than a
Composite Picture 196

TYPES OF CONCEPTS   **198**

STRATEGIES IN CONCEPT ATTAINMENT   **201**

SOME PARAMETERS OF CONCEPT ATTAINMENT   **203**

SOME PARAMETERS OF THE CONCEPT ATTAINER   **209**
Motivation and Set in Concept Attainment 209 / Inhibiting
Factors in Concept Formation 210 / Problem Solving by
Children 212

SUMMARY   **214**

Real-World Concept Attainment   **215**

PERCEPTUAL LEARNING   **215**
Attribute Redundancy Revisited 215 / The Role of Distinctive
Features 216 / Perceptual Reorganization 217

NAMES AND CATEGORIES   **218**
Names as Signals 218 / Names as Properties 219 /
Variability of Names 219

OTHER METHODS OF TEACHING CONCEPTS   **220**
Formal Definition 220 / Linguistic Context   220

VERBAL MEDIATION IN CONCEPT LEARNING   **221**

CATEGORIZING WITH PROBABILISTIC CUES   **223**

IS CONCEPT LEARNING UNIQUELY HUMAN?   **226**

SUMMARY AND CONCLUSIONS   **228**

9   Concept Learning II: Rules and Language
     Acquisition   **230**

     Early Language Acquisition   **231**

IS LANGUAGE SPECIES SPECIFIC?   **232**
The Human as a "Smart" Ape 233 / Language as an Innate
Property 233 / Enter Washoe 233

BIOLOGICAL READINESS FOR LANGUAGE   **235**
Requisites for Normal Language Development 237

SUMMARY   **239**

     What Is It the Child Learns When the Child Learns
     Language?   **239**

part four
Human Memory   271

part five
The Biological Basis and Readiness for Learning

preface

The winter months in Copenhagen have a certain stark beauty. The days are short and overcast, and the buildings and landscape take on a gray bleakness only slightly relieved by the bright decorations strung across the roadways in anticipation of the Christmas Goblin, a bearded character strangely reminiscent of that other person in white beard and red suit familiar to so many generations of English and American school children.

It was during such a winter in 1973 that work on this book began in earnest. The University of Copenhagen had offered me a brief respite from the flurry of teaching, research, and endless committee meetings of my American university. It was a chance to think, to write, and to try to consolidate, in my own mind, several disparate "fields" of psychology that clearly had much to say to each other if only they were allowed to speak in a single place: learning theory, studies of human memory, cognitive processes, and studies of conceptual development in children.

All of these fields, it seemed to me, were relevant to any understanding of human learning. Yet the traditions of specialization within each of these fields tended to keep them apart, aided and abetted by the logistics of instruction (and historical tradition) which determined that certain materials, while admittedly important, are necessarily "beyond the scope" of a single one-semester course. At the same time, however, such an integration is overdue in a "young" psychology—one represented by large numbers of students whose interests turn increasingly to understanding conceptions of learning and memory as they apply to human experience, whether in formal education, learning disabilities, or learning in child development. Whether in departments of psychology or schools of education, these are students whose backgrounds in formal psychology might be limited to a one-semester survey course in general psychology, but whose acquaintances with the nature of human learning (and its occasional failures) are surely as great as their own experiences.

Human Learning and Memory is an attempt at such an integration for the beginning student. The reader will find discussions drawn from research on both lower animals and humans, sometimes with a historical, and sometimes a developmental, perspective, as each relates to the current status of a common theoretical question. Our understanding of learning has grown with the historical development of psychology as surely as learning develops within the lifetime of an individual. I have tried to supply a historical perspective at points where this perspective illuminates the modern assessment of a particular problem or issue. Because learning is not simply an accumulative process but is interwoven with the changing competencies and maturation of the individual, *Human Learning and Memory* offers developmental views of the effects of experience when this appears necessary.

To aid the reader in organizing the material, the book is divided into five parts. Part One (Chapter 1) contains a brief survey of the varieties of learning covered in the text, together with a background on the problems and early development of learning theory. Part Two (Chapters 2 and 3) examines two issues necessary for any complete understanding of learning: Chapter 2 looks at the problem of selective attention as people try, not always successfully, to learn in the face of several competing sources of input and distraction; Chapter 3 deals with the general concept of motivation—the necessary "why" of learning upon which the "how" of learning must be understood. Part Three (Chapters 4–9) is devoted to the several varieties of learning, running the range from simple association learning in lower animals to cognitive rule learning in humans, as typified by the acquisition of linguistic skills. Part Four (Chapters 10 and 11) deals specifically with the study of human memory. Chapter 10 describes the general characteristics of human memory; that is, the phenomenon to be explained, while Chapter 11 surveys several attempts to produce a theory of memory. Part Five (Chapters 12 and 13) looks briefly at the biological basis of learning and memory (Chapter 12), and at the factors of conceptual development and mental ability as they relate to the learning process (Chapter 13).

Over the years in which this text developed, the changes in the fields represented have been so immense that, even at this introductory level, the manuscript had to undergo numerous revisions and refinements. In spite of these efforts, many readers may find too much coverage of some findings and theories, and insufficient coverage of others. It is hoped, however, that all readers will find a solid basis of "good psychology" to which the student and professor can bring depth in the areas that uniquely represent their interests.

It would not be possible to acknowledge all those whose teaching, friendship, advice, and personal example found their way into my own "world view" of psychology. As an undergraduate and graduate student, I count myself fortunate to have been exposed to the work and ideas of such persons as Weston Bousfield and David Zeaman at the University of Connecticut; Harold Westlake at Northwestern University; and at Oxford University, Anne Treisman, Nick Mackintosh, Stuart Sutherland, and especially the late Carolus Oldfield. Oxford, by the way, is not only a town of dreaming spires. It is also a place where visits by distinguished scholars from all over the world (and even Cambridge) is a commonplace event. George Miller, B. F. Skinner, A. R. Luria, Sir Frederic Bartlett, Donald Broadbent, and others took the time to visit our laboratory and to share their ideas with us. From this early experience came the realization that very divergent opinion can easily coexist within a common framework of scholarly integrity and respect for ideas.

Professor Franz From, Kristian Moustgaard, Strange Ross, and Lilly Ekner of the Psychological Laboratory, University of Copenhagen, are very special godparents to this book, having been present not at its birth, but at its conception. I thank them, and the other members of the staff, for their hospitality and support.

Several reviewers who offered many helpful comments have my appreciation. Edward S. Cobb of Bronx Community College, C.U.N.Y., read the manuscript from a very special perspective, and I owe much to his careful reading and thoughtful criticisms. Many students, former students, and colleagues also read all or parts of the manuscript. The final copy is richer for their reactions and recommendations. I especially want to thank Helene Intraub, now at M.I.T., and Dennis Byrnes, at the University of Massachusetts, Boston, for invaluable critical comments on the final revision. Brendan Maher at Harvard receives particular thanks for sharing with me his wisdom and greater experience as an author. Finally, I owe the greatest debt of all to my wife, Jill, and our children, Mark, Catherine, and Thomas, whose support, patience, and understanding made the completion of this text possible.

ARTHUR WINGFIELD

part one

Toward an Understanding of Learning

1 Introduction

chapter 1

Introduction

At 3:30 in the afternoon, five days a week, they come crashing through a thousand front doors of a thousand households after yet another day at school. As typical fourth-graders, they have learned a great deal that day. They have learned that subtracting a larger number from a smaller one produces a negative value, that the brontosaurus was a vegetarian (but not necessarily what a brontosaurus was, or what a vegetarian is), that a report on the latter subject is due on Monday, and that their best friend may not be such a friend after all. When asked how school was that day, they answer "fine" (having long ago learned that complaining about school represents a less than rewarding pastime). If asked at that moment what they would *really* like to learn, they would probably say, "to drive a car."

Learning can be defined as *a relatively permanent change in behavior or knowledge brought about by practice or experience.* If we adopt this definition, and it is a good one, it becomes clear that any explanation of learning must be a far-ranging one if it is to include even the kinds of learning present in a single day of a typical fourth-grader. It must include rote memorization, the acquisition of logical concepts, the development of reasoning ability, changes in emotional attitude, and the acquisition of motor skills.

THE DIMENSIONS OF LEARNING

Once we consider learning in any detail, it becomes apparent that there are three identifiably different dimensions to the question. These three dimensions are the *accumulation of knowledge* over a lifetime, the *sequence of learning*, and the *varieties of learning*.

The Accumulation of Knowledge: Meaningful Versus Rote Learning

There is a well-known story about the great American educator, John Dewey, who visited an elementary school classroom and asked the children, "What would happen if you were to dig a deep hole into the earth?" When no answer was forthcoming, the classroom teacher called Dewey aside and explained, with some embarrassment, that he had asked the "wrong" question. The teacher then turned to the class and asked, "What is the state of the center of the earth?" The children replied as with one voice: "Igneous fusion." (Bloom, 1956, pg. 29).

In one sense, the children did know the "right" answer, but they had learned it in rote fashion, without necessarily seeing its full implications. For learning to rise above the level of rote memorization, the material must be meaningful to the learner (Ausubel, 1968). For example, the sentence, "The boy ran quickly home," is far easier to learn than the nonsense string, "The vax wug bigly gim." It is easier, of course, because we already know something of the meaning and structure of English. In most cases, in other words, new learning is built on previous learning and it is this which gives meaning to the learning materials. Interestingly, when we are under too much pressure, as may have been the case with the classroom Dewey visited, we often revert to rote memory as the only way to produce a "right" answer (Ausubel, 1968, pg. 38).

As we think about meaningful learning, we realize that most learning tasks require specific prerequisite skills or the mastery of what Gagné (1965) calls *subordinate knowledge*:

> The acquisition of knowledge is a process in which every new capability builds on a new foundation established by previously learned abilities. . . . A student is ready to learn something new when he has mastered the prerequisites; that is, when he has acquired the necessary capabilities through preceding learning (Gagné, 1965, pg. 25).

To fully understand the learning process we must thus recognize that there exist *hierarchies* of skills, even though they are not always immediately apparent. For example, a child or adult's ability to perform a particular task usually implies that we should be able to demonstrate that he or she can also perform any number of subskills which are prerequisites to it. Conversely, the acquisition of complex skills or concepts should, in principle, be easier if all of the necessary subskills have already been learned. In practice, numerous studies have shown both of these statements to be true (e.g., Gagné, 1969; Gagné & Wiegand, 1970).

In its broadest sense, this first dimension of learning represents the learning of skills and knowledge which build over a lifetime. Learning begins from the moment of birth, as seen when infants begin to associate the comfort of feeding with the presence of the parents, and to distinguish the faces of their parents from among others. Later, children learn the value of communication: a single howl brings that source of parental comfort on the run. As children progress into the first year of life, they begin to learn to name objects, and later, to learn the structure of their language. As school age arrives, they begin to use this language to learn mathematics, history, and philosophy. And in adulthood, they now use this knowledge to fulfill their creative potentials, to understand the world, and perhaps most important, to understand themselves.

The Sequence of Learning

If the accumulation of knowledge over a lifetime represents one "sequence" of learning, there is another sequence of learning which must be understood on a more limited, "microscopic" level. This relates to the sequence of events which occurs in the learning of a single skill. As we will see in the following chapter, this sequence can be roughly divided into three stages. The first stage involves our perception of the material to be learned as we focus our concentration, and attempt to ignore other, potentially distracting, events. Second, the learning material must be practiced or rehearsed until it becomes stabilized in memory. Finally, we must have ready access to this learned material for future reference.

While there are very real limitations to the rate and amount of information that one can be expected to acquire at any one moment, we are equally aware of the amazing speed and flexibility of human learning. Indeed, it is easy to take these abilities for granted until one becomes reminded of them by those individuals who, through accident or disease, have lost some of these powers. One such case was that of a man whose misfortune at the hands of a well-intentioned surgeon reminded a whole generation of psychologists of the importance of this sequence. This was a man who began with a rare and very severe form of epilepsy, and who ended as a person who, in the words of Colin Blakemore, lived a "nightmare world of eternal forgetfulness—a condition that Franz Kafka would have been delighted to describe" (Blakemore, 1976, pg. 705). In a single operation to his brain, this man, known in the literature as "Case H. M.," was robbed of his power to remember.

The injury to H. M.'s brain was deliberate. As a young man, H. M. had gradually developed a form of epilepsy which was so severe that normal home activity and work became impossible. Efficient drugs for the supression of epileptic symptoms were not yet available, and our knowledge of normal brain function was still in a primitive stage. The surgeon treating him decided to remove a part of the brain which he thought was causing the epilepsy. This was the *hippocampus,* a twisted band of nerve fibers which lies under the temporal lobes of the two hemispheres of the brain. (It is called the hippocampus because its twisted shape reminded early anatomists of a sea horse, which is the literal meaning of the term.)

Parts of the hippocampus had been removed many times before for the treatment of epilepsy, but because this particular patient's seizures were especially severe and involved the whole of his brain, the surgeon decided to destroy the hippocampus on both sides. This was the cause of the ultimate tragedy, for we now know that the hippocampus is crucially important for the formation of long-term memories.

Brenda Milner, of the Montreal Neurological Institute, followed Case H. M. for a period of some 20 years after his operation. Here are some of her observations (Milner, 1966).

Fundamentally, H. M.'s world was a limited one which existed for only several minutes at a time. Although his intelligence, and his memory for events prior to the operation were intact, he was unable to remember any new experience for more than a few seconds or minutes. In spite of having spent countless hours with Milner, every meeting with her required a new introduction and he reacted as if they had never before met. He could not remember the names of the hospital staff, the route to the bathroom, or the day-to-day happenings in the hospital. He would do the same jigsaw puzzle time after time without showing the slightest practice effect, and he would read the same magazine over and over without realizing he had read it before, or noticing its familiarity. His favorite uncle had died some three years previously, but each time he was informed of this fact he reacted to it with fresh grief as if learning of it for the first time.

On one occasion Milner asked H. M. to simply try to remember the number 584. He sat quietly for a full 15 minutes and then, much to her surprise, recited it perfectly. (He had, for example, moved some six years earlier, and while he seemed to know that he had moved, he was still unsure of the address.) How did he remember the number? He explained that it was easy. "You just remember the number eight. You see, five, eight and four add up to 17. You remember eight, subtract it from 17 and it leaves nine. Divide nine in half and you get five and four, and there you are: 584. It's easy!" (Milner, 1966, pg. 115).

This is an impressive memory trick, but we must remember why H. M. had to employ it. He could not, on a single glance, store in memory a simple three-digit number. It is no wonder, then, that so much of learning theory has concentrated on simple learning tasks, and the study of the role of practice and rehearsal in the long-term storage of learned material.

The Varieties of Learning

The third dimension to the problem of learning is to realize that there is no single "theory of learning," so much as attempts to understand the many varieties of learning. Gagné (1970), for example, describes some eight types of learning which he views as hierarchical, in the sense that we previously used the term: the more basic types of learning are necessary before the individual can advance to more complex forms of learning. In subsequent chapters we will look at these varieties of learning in terms of six categories, each with its own conditions and characteristics.

1. CLASSICAL CONDITIONING. Classical conditioning, which Gagné considers the most basic form of learning on the hierarchy, describes the primitive associations formed between stimuli which often occur without one's conscious awareness. For example, if a dog barks and then viciously bites a person's leg, that person may, for some time, feel a sense of fright whenever a dog barks, even when it is a friendly one. Sometimes called "Pavlovian conditioning," after its first student, this form of learning deals with often involuntary associations between stimuli and physiological reactions and emotional responses.

2. TRIAL-AND-ERROR LEARNING. Trial-and-error learning goes by many names, such as *instrumental learning, operant conditioning*, or simply, *S-R learning*. In this type of learning individuals are "instrumental" in achieving some goal, and they "operate" on their environment in doing so. It is sometimes called S-R learning because it was originally characterized as the simple learning of a specific response (R) to a particular stimulus (S). If a dog owner says, "Shake hands," lifts the animal's paw, and gives the dog a biscuit, the dog will eventually "learn to shake hands." While it may be hard to say what it is that the dog has actually "learned," we can say that it is a response which requires reward (unlike classical conditioning), and that the learner must first initiate the response for the reward to be delivered.

3. SENSORIMOTOR LEARNING. In many respects, the learning of skilled motor tasks, such as riding a bicycle, writing one's name, or tying one's shoelaces, can be seen as a "chain" of previously learned individual associations. As we shall see later, however, such behavior often looks only superficially like a chain of responses, but in fact involves rather complex, long-term planning of motor sequences.

4. VERBAL LEARNING.   A fourth type of learning was seen by Gagné as a variety of "chaining," but this time on a verbal level. "Verbal learning" refers essentially to "rote" memorization, that well-known chore that occupies so much of the early school years. One thinks, for example, of the learning of foreign language vocabulary, as we learn to associate the French word *alumette*, with the English word *match*. We chose this example especially, as it illustrates one common feature of this form of learning, the way we employ previous associations to facilitate the task. With a bit of imagination, many a student of French has learned the chain: "a *match* illuminates; illuminate—*alumette.*"

5. CONCEPT LEARNING.   Part of the problem in learning is to discriminate the essential features of a stimulus as when, for example, a child must learn that not all four-footed animals are called "doggy." We speak here of the learning of *concepts*, as children learn to categorize objects and events in the environment and to abstract those properties which are essential to category membership. Concept learning is, to be sure, a variety of learning, although it contains its own very special characteristics and pitfalls.

6. RULE LEARNING.   Probably the highest form of learning on any hierarchy must be the acquisition of rules; the formalization of what may previously have been only intuitively appreciated concepts. We can, for example, learn to recognize the letter *b*, versus the letter *d*, long before we can formalize the rule that "the letter *b* has the stem on the left."

It is at this point that we return full circle to John Dewey's discovery that one can know a "rule" without understanding its underlying concept. That is, one can learn the fact that the state of the earth's core is "igneous fusion," even though the full implications of the concept may remain a mystery. Thus, while we may view these varieties of learning as forming a hierarchy, they need not necessarily progress in this order.

As we think of the realities of learning, one is reminded of Glasser's remarks in *Schools Without Failure:*

> While talking to elementary school teachers and asking them whether they allow free discussion in their classes, I have been told hotly by several teachers that they do encourage free discussion. They say, "We discuss everything until we arrive at the right answer" (Glasser, 1969, pg. 37).

THE SEARCH FOR A "THEORY OF LEARNING"

Because of its abstraction, our conceptions of learning have always been rife with analogies and metaphors. For example, according to Plato and his famous student, Aristotle, sensory impressions enter our minds with such force that they leave a physical "inscription" on the brain. It was, they said, rather like the letters a scribe might engrave on a wax tablet. From this analogy later came the idea of the mind as a *tabula rasa*, a blank slate, on which our experiences are literally written.[1]

With such analogies came the *empiricist* view that all human behavior results from simple experience and interaction with the environment. The notion of the mind as a tabula rasa was quite explicit in this extract from John Locke's, *An Essay Concerning Human Understanding*, written in 1690:

> Let us then suppose the mind to be, as we say, white paper, void of all charac-
> ters, without any ideas; how comes it to be furnished? Whence comes it by
> that vast store, which the busy and boundless fancy of man has painted on it
> with an almost endless variety? . . . To this I answer, in one word, from Ex-
> perience (Herrnstein & Boring, 1965, pg. 584).

The empiricists, in extreme or moderate form, largely captured intellectual thought for most of the present century. Their philosophy, in fact,
was a strong reaction to an earlier view of human nature as a consequence
of *inborn*, or *innate*, predispositions. This view, sometimes referred to as *na-
tivism*, held that much of our behavior, from the organization of our per-
ceptions to the early acquisition of language, was built on preestablished
mental structures present at birth. Only relatively recently has the nativist
view again begun to surface, in however tentative a way (cf. Lorenz, 1966;
Ardrey, 1961; Morris, 1967; Lenneberg, 1967; Chomsky, 1968).

The nativist-empiricist controversy had a long and involved history in
the development of psychology. No longer, of course, does one ask whether
all behavior is the product of experience *or* of innate mental properties. We
ask, instead, how much of the total of behavior can be attributed to each or,
more properly, how the two interact. That this question is by no means an
easy one to answer becomes apparent when we consider three aspects related to our understanding of learning: learning versus instinct, learning
versus maturation, and learning versus performance.

Instinct Versus Learning

Our earlier definition of learning emphasized behavior brought about by
practice or *experience*. Many lower animals show extraordinarily complex
behavior patterns which are not primarily a consequence of learning, in the
sense of involving specific practice and reward. For example, many species
of birds mark their territory and defend it against other birds who compete
for the same food sources. (The birds' song only seems like a celebration of

[1] Aristotle, incidentally, had some peculiar notions of physiology, attributing to the
heart many functions, such as memory, which are now known to be located in the brain.
From Aristotle we still have the expression, "learned by heart," with its implication of
having something completely in memory, and available on call (Adams, 1976, pg. 224).

spring. It is in actuality one method they use to signal their territorial boundaries to potential competitors.) Further, the size of the territory they will try to claim depends directly on the availability of food in terms of their needs (Lack, 1965).

We know that behavior patterns are instinctive when (1) they occur in all members of a species, and (2) when they appear even when an animal is raised in isolation without any model on which to base its behavior. For example, the nut-burying pattern of squirrels occurs even when a baby squirrel is raised in isolation from other squirrels and sees a nut for the very first time. When seeing its first nut on a bare wooden floor, the squirrel will make scratching motions as if to dig, tamp the nut with its nose as if to "push" it into the floor, and then make covering movements with its paws. The nut, of course, remains on the surface of the floor as before: the squirrel is exercising an innate, fixed, behavior pattern over which it has no control (Brown, 1965, pg. 23).

The notion of learning versus instinct is not always as clear as it was in this example. First, one occasionally sees unlearned, instinctive behavior patterns which have been modified by experience during an animal's lifetime, as for example, the case of some birds whose songs show regional variation and some influence of hearing other birds' songs (e.g., Thorpe, 1956). Second, instinctive patterns can change over a period of time within a given creature as for example, when mating or nest building begins to emerge only as the organism undergoes a hormonal change associated with the time of year or maturational development.

The study of instinct is a fascinating pursuit in itself, as embodied in the modern field of *ethology*, or the study of "animal behavior." (See Brown, 1965, pp. 3–45 or Tinbergen, 1969, for good introductory discussions.)

Maturation Versus Learning

Very little of human behavior is inherited, in the sense of animal instinct. At the same time, any notion of a tabula rasa on which experience can be "written" is equally wrong. The child of 5 simply cannot learn integral calculus, no matter how innovative the teaching methods, and we cannot expect a child to learn to write until he or she has developed the neuromotor control necessary to grasp a pencil. There is, for all learners, a minimal level of *maturation* which must be present for learning to be possible. We will later address the interaction between maturation and learning in greater detail. For now, let us only exert the warning that the appearance of some skill, such as walking, only after a period of some life, should not lead us to assume that this passage of time was necessary for practice and experience. It could have been required for the nervous system to reach a necessary level of maturational readiness for the behavior to appear.

Figure 1.1 shows the results of a classic study undertaken by Hilgard

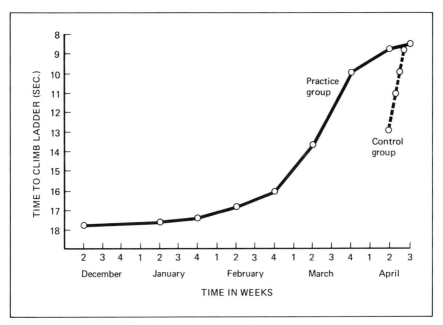

Figure 1.1   Speed of climbing a three-step ladder for one group of 28-month-old children trained for 12 weeks (practice group) and for another group of children who were given only one week of practice at the end of the 12-week study period (control group). (*Source:* J. R. Hilgard, Learning and maturation in preschool children. *Journal of Genetic Psychology*, 1932, 41: fig. 1, pg. 50. By permission of The Journal Press.)

(1932) with sixteen 28-month-old infants. Eight of these children were trained for 12 weeks to climb up and down a short stepladder, while eight were not. The graph shows the gradual increase in the speed of climbing the three-step ladder for the group given daily practice over the 12-week period. On the other hand, the graph also shows the performance of the untrained group who were introduced to the ladder only after, in Hilgard's judgement, they were "ready" to learn to climb. Only one week of practice was necessary for this group to reach the same level of skill.

In most cases, training or practice prior to maturational readiness is an unproductive investment of time. On the other hand, there are some known exceptions to this rule. One of the most intriguing of these, coincidentally, also relates to the leg movements of young children. Zelazo, Zelazo, and Kolb (1972) became curious about the common observation that newborn infants often make walkinglike movements when they are held in an upright position with their feet touching the floor. This is an unlearned reflex which usually disappears after the age of 2 months.

The question Zelazo and his colleagues asked was simply this: could one exploit this early reflex through training and exercise to produce earlier walking? To test this possibility they worked with a group of six infants on a daily basis from the ages of 2 to 8 weeks. For several minutes a day the infants were held in the upright position necessary to elicit the "walking" reflex. At the end of this training period they were compared with another group of six infants who did not have these daily exercise sessions. The results were dramatic. Figure 1.2 shows that by the eighth week, the experienced group were sustaining their walking movements significantly longer than the unexercised control group (approximately 5 "walking" responses per minute, versus approximately 30 per minute). Interestingly, a third group of children who had their legs passively moved by an adult for the same period while they remained prone showed virtually the same absence of change as the control group.

It seemed to these workers that even reflexive responses can, if approached at the right age, be turned into practiced, voluntary movements. The effect of this early exercise later appeared in the average age at which these children eventually learned to walk. While the control group learned

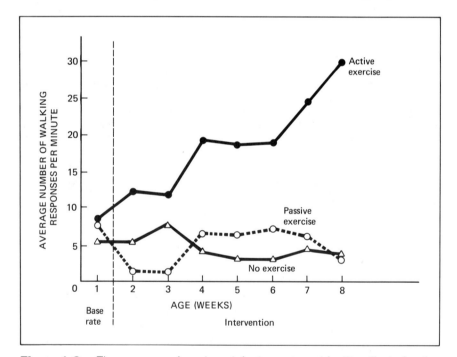

Figure 1.2   Three groups of newborn infants compared for the effect of active exercise of reflexive "walking" movements over an eight-week period. The active exercise group shows a steady increase in the number of "walking" movements when held upright, while a group given no exercise and a group whose legs were only passively exercised do not. (*Source:* P. R. Zelazo, N. A. Zelazo, and S. Kolb, Walking in the newborn. *Science*, 1972, 176: fig. 1, pg. 315. Copyright 1972 by the American Association for the Advancement of Science. Reprinted by permission of the publisher.)

to walk at an average of 11.7 months, the "exercised" group were walking by the age of 10.1 months.

This experiment was offered as an illustration of the notion of maturational readiness periods in skill acquisition, not as an inducement for parents to get their children walking any earlier than they ordinarily would. We are concerned both for the strain on the child's legs which might be caused by early walking, and for the possible strain on the parents who would have to chase their walking infants even sooner than is ordinarily necessary.

Learning Versus Performance

There is a final caution. That is the reminder that we usually cannot measure learning directly, but only the products of the learning. Learning itself is an internal event, which, like the wind, is invisible to the eye and can only be judged by its effects. Like the wind, it can be accurately measured, induced, and inhibited, and from these operations we can form some impressions about its nature.

The distinction we are making is an important one in learning theory. It is a distinction between *learning* and *performance.* In most cases we can only measure a person's level of performance, and from this, infer that learning has taken place. While correct performance invariably implies learning, the absence of correct performance need not imply that no learning has occurred. This point may be obvious to any student who has ever felt that his or her performance on a particular examination was not a true reflection of his or her knowledge of the subject matter. As we shall see later, however, this distinction was so obvious as to have eluded many an early learning theorist, and it was to prompt many an early debate on the nature of learning.

BEHAVIORISM, MENTALISM, AND COGNITIVISM

For many years, the terms *learning theory* and *behaviorism* were used in American psychology as if they were synonymous. The reason for this confusion is both understandable and predictable as one traces the development of psychology's search for an understanding of human behavior in general, and learning in particular.

The early philosopher-psychologists assumed from the very beginning that people think, that they have ideas and sensations, and that they act largely through the power of free will. Their task, as they saw it, was to catalog the nature of these ideas and sensations using the only tool at their command: introspection. To put it bluntly, they did their best to "think about thinking," spending long hours solving problems, noting their sensations, and trying to describe their internal mental activities. Indeed, over the years, introspection became something of an art as, for example, when Wilhelm Wundt, founder of the first psychological laboratory in 1879 in Leipzig, Germany, trained volunteers to "look inside themselves," and to report their internal experiences as they thought, perceived, and learned.

Watson and Early Behaviorism

A vocal opponent of the use of introspection as a research tool was the American psychologist John B. Watson (1878–1958) who, beginning in the early 1900s, began a systematic campaign against what he termed the whole notion of "mentalism" in psychology. First, he defied anyone of his time to define such terms as "ideas," "sensations," or "will." Second, he questioned the validity of individuals' subjective reports of their private, internal, mental events. We are, he argued, notoriously poor judges of our internal goings-on.

With the appearance of his first book in 1914, Watson began to redirect the efforts of American psychology. Our task, he said, should be to deal only with observable and measurable events. In the case of learning, the observable events would be physical *stimuli* which give rise to overt *responses.* In short, Watson argued that the field of psychology should concentrate its efforts on the study of *behavior,* and leave the understanding of our internal mental states for a later date if, indeed, this understanding were ever judged to be necessary. That is, the behavior itself, the specification of laws relating observable stimuli to measurable responses, might not only be necessary for the understanding of human learning, it might be fully sufficient.

In some of its forms, behaviorism grew to extremes within the rarified air of academic psychology. Words such as "mental," "unconscious," and "thinking" began to drop out of the research vocabulary. They were, to the behaviorists, rather vague, unscientific constructs, used only by vague, unscientific people. On one occasion, referring to the notion of mental imagery, Watson was to use the term "ghosts."

In spite of its self-imposed limitations, behaviorist philosophy nevertheless represented an important milestone in the study of learning and attracted such important figures as Hull, Guthrie, Thorndike, and Skinner. It became a milestone in the sense that, for the first time, psychology began to see the critical necessity for measurement and objectivity in experimental research. Milestones, however, can easily turn into millstones when they take on the status of dogma which inhibits the pursuit of legitimate enquiry. This, tragically, was to be the fate of the behaviorist movement in America.

The Growth of Cognitive Psychology

As Watson's behaviorism was a reaction to the earlier "mentalism," so other psychologists, while respecting the importance of measurement and objectivity in research, nevertheless felt that the time had arrived to look more closely at those "internal events" so completely rejected by the behaviorist movement. Names such as Bartlett, Tolman, and Piaget became associated with the argument that we are not just passive receivers of "stimuli" and producers of "responses." Learning, they argued, is an *active process* which involves the use of stategies and the transformation of sensory experience into new categories and organized conceptions.

The term "cognition," which was first used in reference to studies of thinking and reasoning, began to receive wider use throughout experimental psychology. *Cognition* came to be used as a general term to describe those mental processes which transform sensory input in various ways, code it, store it in memory, and retrieve it for later use (Neisser, 1967). Since human learning invariably involves active responding, organizing, and reorganizing material, human learning almost always involves some kind of cognitive activity (cf. Ellis, 1972, pg. 4).

A COGNITIVE APPROACH TO LEARNING

Behaviorism rejected the subjective study of "mental" phenomena in order to make psychology a science and to equip it with the tools of objectivity and measurement. *Cognitive psychology* later rejected the narrowness of this so-called stimulus-response view of human activity, setting as its goal a no less objective and scientific study of behavior, but one which would hope to understand and explain those internal mental states which lie between the "stimuli" and "responses."

Because Watson focused on observable behavior, he called himself a behaviorist. Modern learning theory is, in a sense, no less behaviorist: it too focuses its attention on the study and measurement of behavior. The critical difference lies in the fact that while Watson saw the study of behavior as an end in itself, the modern cognitive-behaviorist sees the study of behavior as only the means to the end of understanding those internal events, strategies, and "cognitive processes" which give rise to this behavior. Our goal in the pages which follow is to describe these operations and processes as they combine to bring about the process of human learning.

part two
Some Preliminaries to Learning

chapter 2

The Sequence of Learning:

SOME LIMITS ON THE ABILITY TO ACQUIRE INFORMATION

There is a degree of magic in the world, but it is available only to those who have the time or the inclination to be aware of it. Young children, of-course, have both. It is they, not the scientist or the poet, who are the true observers of the world. It is a curious thing that the appreciation of the magic of discovery seems to die with adulthood. Little time is spent in the wonder of the touch of snow, watching a spider unerringly build its symmetrical web, or sensing the effects of the wind on trees and grass. Once discovered, we may retain and even utilize the knowledge. Discovery does not cease with childhood. What does, is the magic of discovery.

There is for some of us, a second chance, however. Some of us get this second chance as parents, as we watch our children going through the same almost forgotten experience of newness. For many adults, who again have the time and inclination, one can make the further discovery of the child himself or herself, and wonder (for that is all we can do) at how eager children are for knowledge, and how readily it is acquired. The learning of language, the extraordinary memory for details of events long forgotten by the parents, the development of an individual identity and will—all of these are so often taken for granted. The child's mind seems so ready and able to grasp new information that one can develop the feeling that, given time and available stimulation, there are no limits to children's abilities to learn.

A belief in this open-ended nature of learning, however, does come to an end, and often rather abruptly. It appears to end at about the age of 6 or 7. It appears to end as the child has his or her first experiences with school and formal education. This is understandable.

School represents many "firsts" in the child's acquisition of knowledge. There is the routine and length of the school day which extends the bounds of interest and resistance to fatigue. Information comes faster. It is harder, less natural, less immediately relevant to the child's everyday existence. The nature of the information he or she is expected to acquire is at once both more abstract and more specific than has ever been encountered before. A final "first" is perhaps the most important of all in bringing about this abrupt realization. School represents the first time the child's progress and knowledge is systematically tested and objectively recorded. Perhaps there were just as many failures and difficulties in learning before. Perhaps it is only with school that specific records of achievement are kept, and that we become aware of these difficulties. Whatever the circumstances, there does eventually come a time when we do forcefully appreciate that there are some real and definite limitations on speed or capacity of learning in all individuals. These limitations apply to both children and to adults not only in school, but in any setting where information is expected to arrive and be assimilated with some rapidity and success.

There are limits to learning ability, and these can be divided into two general categories. The first of these, and the one which seems to get the most attention in education, relates to *individual differences*. In this regard we tend to think of the double-edged sword of *intelligence* and *motivation*. Limitations in either can retard learning, limitations in both can be devastating, and limitations in one can sometimes be confused with limitations in the other. Like any double-edged sword, it is often of little immediate advantage to know which side you have been hit with.

Both motivation and intelligence do vary from child to child, and both impose some bounds to the speed with which a particular child can be expected to learn. While the two are clearly separable in a formal sense, they often interact in very important and intimate ways. Even the most gifted child will show poor performance if his or her abilities are not accompanied by an equally high level of desire to succeed. On the other hand, the "slow learning" child can experience more than his or her fair share of failure and frustration, sometimes to the point where motivation becomes a more central problem than limited ability, per se. These factors are important ones to the learning process, and will be treated in some detail later.

Regardless of an individual's level of motivation or of intelligence, there is a second class of limitations on one's ability to acquire information. As distinct from individual differences, this second class seems to represent an invariant property of the human nervous system and the mechanisms of perception and learning in all individuals. Paradoxically, while they mark an upper bound on the speed and quantity of information which can be taken in and assimilated, the very limits they impose play a necessary role in learning. In brief, they protect us from the mental chaos that would most assuredly result from the simultaneous receipt of *too much* information.

THE SEQUENCE OF LEARNING

Let us consider for a moment any learning situation and examine the detailed train of internal events that occur as the information is presented, learned, and finally recalled. We can, for convenience, divide what is in reality a dynamic, ongoing process into three major stages, each consisting of essentially two operations. The three major stages are *input, storage*, and *retrieval*.

1. Stimulus Input

In order for learning to take place, the individual must selectively attend to the source of information (the *stimulus*) and filter out competing stimuli. In the classroom situation we have a child trying to focus his or her attention on what the teacher is saying in the face of a massive bombardment of competing stimulation. These may be extraneous sounds, from the whispering of other children in the classroom, to the noises of street traffic and the ever present crashes and thumps which seem invariably to emanate somehow from empty corridors during class hours. It may also be competition from visual sources too numerous to mention. To a real degree, attention must be focused like the narrow beam of a searchlight. To focus it on one stimulus means the exclusion of others. Stimuli out of the beam have little chance of invading awareness.

The really extraordinary fact is that one can—at least for limited periods—filter out competing stimuli and attend to a selected source. This directed awareness goes by many names, "selective attention," "sensory input," "focal attention," and for some, simply "perception." As a general term for this rather complex process, we might at this point revive a fairly old term in psychology, and refer to it as *apprehension*. (Literally, the amount of information one can "capture" from the environment at any one time.) There is still considerable theoretical disagreement about the details of this first process, from which the venerable age and admitted vagueness of apprehension may offer us some measure of protection.

That limited information which does manage to pass the first hurdle of selective filtering is not necessarily retained with any degree of permanence. Nor, for that matter, would we wish it to be. The second process of the input stage involves a very special form of memory for recently received, or registered, information. It has a limited capacity and is of relatively short duration. Its impermanence, moreover, is underlined by an extreme susceptibility to interference. If one were to recite aloud a series of random numbers just once, how many could you remember without error? For most people this might be six, seven, or eight numbers. How long could you remember them without active rehearsal? Perhaps for a period of 18 to 20 seconds. (This latter point is true, but not intuitively obvious, as it is hard in the ordinary course of events to "not rehearse.") As for susceptibility to interference, even with overt rehearsal of the numbers, the slate is virtually wiped clean or hopelessly confused if someone else loudly recites another set of numbers within your range of hearing.

We should not leave the term rehearsal without qualification since, as we shall see, rehearsal, or "practice," plays a critical role in most theories of learning. Craik and Watkins (1973) distinguished between two separate operations one can perform when one rehearses. The first of these, which they call maintenance rehearsal, represents what most of us think of when we hear the term rehearsal. This is typified by the way we temporarily retain a telephone number for the brief period it takes us to dial the number after finding it in a telephone directory. For most of us, this is accomplished by simple, repetitive rehearsal of the number as we recite it aloud or to ourselves to keep the memory alive.

Craik and Watkins use the term elaborative operations to characterize another method of rehearsing new information which is very different from simple maintenance rehearsal. This form of rehearsal represents the way we frequently keep a memory alive by connecting the new material with past associations, by giving it meaning, using visualization, and so forth.

To illustrate the distinction between maintenance rehearsal and elaborative rehearsal, Bjork and Jongeward (1975) had volunteers learn six-word sequences using either of the two memory strategies. When tested immediately, both types of rehearsal proved to be quite effective, with maintenance rehearsal showing a slight edge. When tested some time later,however, the group using elaborative rehearsal showed significantly better retention. For example, as Norman (1976) notes, each type of rehearsal has its virtues and its weaknesses. These two methods of rehearsal are not mutually exclusive, however, and most of us intuitively use them in a complimentary way for the temporary storage of recently acquired information.

Referred to as short-term memory, and discussed in detail in Chapter 11, this transient storage of new information can be seen as a "buffer" memory which performs the function of temporarily holding recently received information just long enough for it to be analyzed and, if relevant, consolidated into a longer-term memory. Because of its limited capacity and impermanence, it forms a second limitation on the amount of information that can be rapidly acquired by even the most astute and keen student. One result of this is the desire one often feels to ask a rapid speaker to slow down or pause occasionally while speaking. In terms of our own experience, newly registered information needs time to "sink in" or "consolidate" before the arrival of yet more information. In the terms of this model, the rapid input of information is overloading the limited capacity of this short-term, buffer memory.

The system comes into its own, however, in protecting us from the acquisition of too much irrelevant information which would surely interfere with learning and retention. It would be hard to contemplate the results of a student doing large numbers of mathematical problems and going home later with a permanent knowledge of each and every number used in the calculations. One attends to the problem, registers and holds the numbers just long enough to calculate the answer, and then clears this working memory for the intake of new information. The characteristics of short-term memory very definitely do impose limits on the intake of information. But here lies the power of the nervous system to cope with a too rich sensory environment. Limitations there are, but the alternative would be chaos.

2. Storage of Information

Part of the process of registering information in short-term memory is to transform or *encode* it in such a form that it is capable of being rehearsed or practiced. This encoding process is usually thought of as a sorting out of the complex visual or auditory stimulation, and a recognition of their meaningful qualities as letters, speech sounds, or words. Both from our own experience, and from the results of numerous studies, it would appear that short-term memory storage is ordinarily verbal in nature. Regardless of the form of sensory input (auditory, visual, tactile, etc.), we tend to *name* the stimuli and to rehearse these names. It is certainly the case that recognition and categorization are requisites for retention through rehearsal in short-term memory. It is less clear whether the verbal character of this process is obligatory, or whether it is merely the most usual form of encoding for rehearsal (see Chapter 10 for a discussion of "visual" versus "verbal" memory).

The practice or rehearsal of temporarily held information acts to strengthen and preserve it in *long-term memory*, where it can be retained for hours, weeks, or sometimes years. The process of stabilizing this trace is, of course, sometimes referred to simply as "learning." As we will see, however, "simple" is the last word one would prefer to use to describe learning.

For some unique forms of learning such as rote memory of specific facts, long-term storage can be fairly represented as the consolidation of the information in much the same form as it was originally rehearsed. In most cases, however, the transfer of information to long-term memory involves a further process of transformation and encoding of the stimulus input. The information is organized in terms of individual past experience and prior knowledge. In most cases, then, memory is an active process, where we give *meaning* to recent experience and remember it in terms of this meaning. As such, what we remember, and how we remember it, will be heavily influenced by our own conception of the world, our biases, and our beliefs. This characteristic of human memory explains, as we will see in detail later, how it is that two individuals can experience the same event and yet manifest great and often irreconcilable differences in the way in which it is later recalled.

3. Retrieval of Information

The third stage of the learning-retention sequence is represented by the availability and utilization of the learned material. In some cases this takes the form of an overt response. Because overt recall can be readily observed and tested, it is often misleadingly taken to characterize retrieval from memory. More frequently, recall represents a search and retrieval of information for what one might call "internal use only" in the process of problem solving, reasoning, or indeed for the analysis and categorization of new material in memory. It is retrieval and utilization nonetheless, except that in this case the consequences of any failure can be observed only indirectly.

As we shall see later, a failure in memory may result from loss due to the passage of time or, more likely, from the interference of competing memory traces. Since the acquisition and storage of information is a consequence of three processes, however, a failure in recall does not in itself directly imply a failure in memory. Unavailability of material may result from the fact that it was never fully registered in the first place, that it failed in later consolidation, or, more interestingly, that its encoding in memory contained sufficient distortion that its later retrieval was in an unrecognizable form only remotely resembling the character of the original input. It is in the nature of the dynamics of the sequence that it is often difficult either for an observer, or for the person himself or herself, to determine exactly where the loss has occurred.

Figure 2.1 summarizes in a schematic form the essential elements in the flow of information through the three stages of input, storage, and retrieval. (1) *Input:* the first stage involves the apprehension and selective filtering of sensory input, such that only a limited amount of relevant material is perceived and registered in the nervous system. This information is encoded, usually verbally, in the limited capacity short-term memory. (2) *Storage:* the transient store of short-term memory can allow for rehearsal into the more permanent and durable long-term memory. Here storage is now further organized, and the material heavily influenced by its meaning in relation to past experience. (3) *Retrieval:* the final stage is the access of memory for required information, either organized for the output of an overt response or utilized in internal cognitive activity.

Simplification can often be misleading. Two essential points should be made in regard to the sequence of information flow as summarized in Figure 2.1. First, the sequence is not truly spatial as it is shown in the flow diagram or as it might be if information were neatly transferred from one location in the brain to another as it is analyzed and stored. Rather, the sequence outlined here is a *temporal* one, reflecting changes in the character and durability of the material over time. Second, the three stages are by no means independent of each other. For example, selective attention and stimulus recognition logically demand access to information already stored in long-term memory. To recognize an acoustic signal as a word for storage and rehearsal in short-term memory must imply that this input has been matched against information in long-term memory for its recognition. Indeed, the flexible nature of the operations we perform in analyzing and holding newly acquired information has led some writers to emphasize differences in "levels of processing," rather than seeing a set sequence of stages (cf. Craik & Lockhart, 1972). We will have more to say on this issue later.

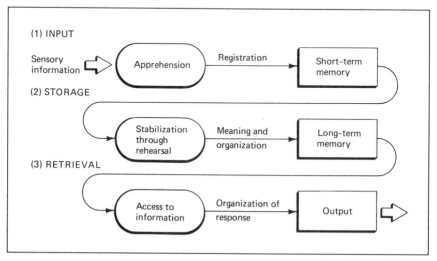

Figure 2.1   Outline of the sequence of learning, showing the sequence of events involved in the three major stages of *input, storage,* and *retrieval.*

THE "BOTTLENECK" OF STIMULUS INPUT

If the ultimate capacities of learning and memory are so large as to defy estimate, the first stage of information processing does have very real and measurable limits. The character of these input limitations brings to mind a rather fanciful image of a large library suddenly besieged by hundreds of generous donors, all eager to donate several books each for permanent storage in the library. The donors with their books are there, and so are the rooms full of empty shelves ready to accommodate them. There is only one problem. At the entrance to the library sits a single desk, and behind it, a single librarian to catalog each and every donation before it is entered on the shelves.

The librarian must be there to prevent the disorganized chaos and loss which would surely ensue if all the donors were allowed to rush simultaneously to place their own books on the first convenient shelves they encountered. And so the donors form an orderly queue at the single desk to wait their turn to singly present their books for cataloging. Being impatient, some donors will leave before their turn comes, and their donations will be lost to the collection. Others' books, however, will get through: limited in number, but correctly indexed and referenced for future availability and use.

It is admittedly artificial to view the donors as a too rich stimulus environment, the library shelves as long-term acquisition and memory, and the easily overloaded librarian as the bottleneck of stimulus input. Nevertheless, the flavor of the two problems is strikingly similar. There is too much stimulus information constantly reaching our senses, and an orderly reduction in input is accomplished by the nervous system in all individuals. It is crucial, then, that we examine this important but frequently overlooked initial stage in the learning sequence before turning to the broader issues of learning.

The Span of Apprehension and Short-Term Memory

Earlier we spoke of a degree of magic in the world. In April, 1955, in an invited address to the Eastern Psychological Association, George Miller brought another bit of magic to the world—or at least to the world of psychology. In this case, the magic was a particular number which Miller observed to occur with peculiar and perhaps important regularity in the results of numerous experimental studies.

> My problem is that I have been persecuted by an integer. . . . This number assumes a variety of disguises, being sometimes a little larger and sometimes a little smaller than usual, but never changing so much as to be unrecognizable.

The persistence with which this number plagues me is far more than a random accident. There is, to quote a famous senator, a design behind it, some pattern governing its appearances. Either there really is something unusual about the number or else I am suffering from delusions of persecution (Miller, 1956, pg. 81).[1]

This "magical number," as Miller referred to it in his paper, was seven, and the small range within which it appeared was seven, plus or minus two. There are, of course, the seven wonders of the world, the seven seas, the seven deadly sins, and seven daughters of Pleiades, the seven ages of man, the seven levels of hell, the seven primary colors, the seven notes of the musical scale, the seven days in the week, and a goodly number of other sevens. But the seven (plus or minus two) to which Miller referred was the answer to a variety of questions in human performance. If a picture is briefly flashed on a screen, on average, how many objects in it can be readily identified? In reading aloud, the reader's eyes typically range some words ahead of the particular words being spoken from moment to moment. How large is this typical "eye-voice span"? How long a list of numbers can be readily remembered without error after only a single hearing? how many letters? how many unrelated words? The answer to all of these questions is a range of values, sometimes as small as five, sometimes as large as nine. The easiest way to summarize it is as Miller did: seven, plus or minus two.

The number seven, plus or minus two, is not just an accidental finding, but occurs whenever one carefully measures the span of apprehension; the number of stimuli normal adults can easily register and identify on a single exposure. It represents a seemingly invariant upper limit on the amount and speed of stimulus input and appears to be fairly uniform across all of the senses. The importance of this finding justifies the lengths to which experimenters have gone to confirm its existence and explore its generality. They have done both, and we might briefly cite some examples if only to give a feeling for the wide range of studies undertaken over the past years.

In studies of *absolute judgments,* subjects are required to categorically identify simple stimuli in the absence of any external standard against which they can be compared. For example, one might be presented with three pure-tone sounds of different pitches. After becoming familiar with the three, one of them is now presented alone as the listener attempts to give the correct identification by saying "1" if it was the lowest tone of the set, "2" if it was the middle one, and "3" if it was the highest. For two, three, four, or five tones this presents no problem, and errors are rare. As the number of tones in a set increases beyond this point, however, so does the

[1] From G. A. Miller, "The Magical Number Seven Plus or Minus Two: Some Limits on Our Capacity for Processing Information," *Psychological Review* (1956), 63:81–97. Copyright 1956 by the American Psychological Association. Reprinted by permission.

confusion. By the time subjects have to judge sets of 14 different tones, the task clearly exceeds their ability. The break-off point between completely error-free performance and the beginning of confusion seems to be about six tones (Pollack, 1952). Parallel studies for absolute judgments of loudness show exactly parallel results: the upper limit on error-free identification is about five or six different intensities (Garner, 1953).

Studies of vision have included absolute category judgments of size (Eriksen & Hake, 1955), spatial position (Hake & Garner, 1951), and brightness and hue (Eriksen, 1954). Vision shows generally better capacity, varying from five to ten categorical judgments without error, depending on the task. What these experiments are doing is systematically plotting the upper limits of the normal span of apprehension. When this is done, such limits appear with surprising abruptness. One group of experimenters had adult volunteers watch a screen while they flashed on it random patterns of anywhere from 1 to 200 dots for $^1/_5$ second. The task was simply to report the correct number of dots seen in this single glance. For up to five or six dots, subjects reported the correct number virtually without error. For seven or more, errors were routine. So different was the character of performance, however, that difffferent terms had to be used to describe their behavior. Above seven the subjects were *estimating*, below seven they were said to be *subitizing* (Kaufman, Lord, Reese & Volkmann, 1949).

Taste seems much less well developed, at least in studies where it is varied along a single dimension such as "saltiness" or "sweetness" (varying the concentration of salt or sugar solution in drinking water). Here, only about four categories of either can be handled without error. Other studies have looked at tactile sensation for various numbers of vibrators on the chest area. The average person can identify about four intensities, five durations, and seven locations without error.

The relative invariance with which this number seven plus or minus two occurs, suggests strongly that we are dealing with some central limitation on both the capacity and speed of stimulus identification and of storage in short-term memory. It is also surprisingly small.

These limitations make themselves felt in a variety of ways and, as Miller pointed out, appear in many disguises. Psychologists and others using rating scales in opinion surveys and attitude questionnaires, for example, typically use no more than a 7-point rating scale, through the trial-and-error discovery that category judgments finer than this number carry little meaning. These limits control the complexity of the sentences we can use in normal conversation; not so much the length of the entire sentence, but the size of the linquistic constituent phrases that serve as "units" of perceptual processing (Wingfield & Klein, 1971). They govern the length of our telephone numbers and postal zip codes, which we expect will be easily memorized and utilized. They show their effect even in the evolution of the most common academic grading scale of A, B, C, D, F. While category placement of grades may conceivably be open to a charge of arbitrariness from time to time, the upper limit on the *number* of categories is not, and must be kept to within some usable limits.

Stimulus Encoding and the Span of Short-Term Memory

The previous sections emphasized two major points. First, the number of different visual and auditory stimuli which constantly bombard the individual far exceed the amount that can be taken in by even the most intelligent and highly motivated person. Second, the upper limit on this span of apprehension and capacity of short-term memory seems to be in the order of seven, plus or minus two stimuli. One of the most fascinating and practically important features of this limitation, however, is that while this capacity may be fixed by the nervous system, we can and routinely do increase its *useful* capacity. This will be true as experience and learning allow us to efficiently classify or categorize stimuli into coherent groups. This general process of transforming sensory information into meaningful groups has already been referred to by the term *stimulus encoding*, and seems to be the likely source of many apparent dramatic differences in input capacity between individuals as a consequence of experience and training. It is also one aspect of *elaborative rehearsal*, as we referred to it earlier.

Some examples of this encoding to increase useful capacity were implicit in our initial discussion of this capacity. Thus, while we can memorize about seven letters easily, we can increase this number to say 35 if the letters in fact form seven 5-letter words. What we are memorizing in the latter case is the words, but knowing their spelling, we can decode them back to the constituent letters if so required. The upper limit of seven plus or minus two still exists, but it will refer either to specific stimuli or, if they can be encoded, to groups of stimuli. It is more correct, then, to say that the upper limit is defined as seven plus or minus two "chunks" (Miller's generic term for such coherent groups). It also points to the way in which training and experience can maximize performance by making the most use of this limited capacity.

In many cases, the normal encoding of stimulus information can be readily understood, even though one may have no conscious awareness that such encoding is taking place. In some few cases the form of encoding is both obvious and conscious, as in the numerous "memory tricks" which serve to delight and amaze the uninitiated. One very well known example is the ease of memorizing the following number on a single glance: 149162536496481. (It can be remembered as the square of each of the numbers from 1 through 9: 1^2, 2^2, 3^2, 4^2 . . .) There are other cases of stimulus encoding which are neither conscious to the encoder, nor easily understood. Earlier we said that, for most people, absolute judgments for identifying pitch without error is limited to about five or so categories. Some musicians with "absolute pitch," however, may be able to identify 50 or 60 pitches without error. There is still a lot to be learned about the interaction between the limitations of our sensory abilities and the role of training and experience.

By far the most common form of encoding is linguistic, where, through experience, we can group a sequence of stimulus inputs, give that group a name, and then remember the name rather than the original sequence. This process of categorizing inputs, naming them, and rehearsing the names, as we suggested earlier, is the characteristic form of rehearsal in short-term memory. This appears to be true not only for inherently linguistic stimuli such as words, but also for memory of objects, events, and perhaps even for colors (cf. Lenneberg, 1961). The role of language in learning and memory is an important one, and it will be treated in detail in subsequent chapters.

FOCAL ATTENTION

Perhaps at this point, we can develop some insight into the child and his or her very natural and expected limitations in the learning environment. The pupil enters the classroom at the beginning of the hour. He walks to his seat, keeping some vague notice of other desks and other pupils if only to avoid collision. As he takes his seat, he monitors a conversation behind him (intermixed with the ringing of the school bell), and wonder whether today's lunch will be worth eating. At the same time, he begins setting out his books and pencils while glancing at the blackboard which contains the outlines of today's lesson and, off to one side, tomorrow's homework assignment. While this is going on, the teacher has entered the room and has appointed someone to pass out yesterday's test papers. As his paper arrives on his desk and he ponders his score, he becomes suddenly aware that somehow the blackboard has become filled with additional writing and the room is filled with the teacher's voice already well into the day's topic. The child's problem is not to "pay attention." His problem is what to pay attention to.

There are times, such as working on a car engine, sewing, or hanging wallpaper, that one wishes humans were octopuslike, with eight arms all able to work simultaneously. There are other times when one could wish for an "octomind," with mental activity similarly equipped for spontaneous and independent analysis of the many simultaneously occurring events in the environment. But, as we have already seen, this is not the case. The bottleneck of the limited resouses of apprehension demand the focusing of attention to a limited area of sensation which can be efficiently handled.

The scanning of the environment, as we normally do to avoid collision and to search for stimuli of potential importance, has been termed *preattentive* activity. The concentrated attention to a single source for detailed analysis is known as *focal attention* (Neisser, 1967). Preattentive activity is primarily a rapid scan of the environment, as one does to detect and avoid an object hazily seen out of the corner of the eye without necessarily recognizing any specific details of the object. Preattentive activity is also the scanning of a cluttered blackboard for the words TOMORROW'S HOMEWORK, without actually registering or identifying the other material scanned in the process. Most important, it seems unlikely that very much learning can occur for material thus encountered in this preattentive activity (cf. Neisser, 1963, 1967). Effective learning necessitates the selection, awareness, and registration of a limited stimulus source, through the narrowed beam of focal attention.

Elements of Focal Attention

If the single act of focal attention is looked at in sufficient detail, it becomes clear that it in fact relies on the existence of two separate but related abilities. The first is the ability to perceptually organized a jumble of complex visual and auditory sensations into a series of separable and identifiable stimuli, and to isolate the source of each. The second ability is that of selecting for attention one or a few of these sources, while excluding the potential distraction of others. These two interrelated abilities operate so spontaneously, and their development from infancy is so gradual, that they are easily taken for granted. Indeed, it is extremely difficult in the ordinary course of events to even imagine what experience would be like without their existence. Such an awareness will be brought home dramatically, however, in the event of a sudden and major change in habitual modes of perception where these abilities now require major readjustment.

One such case can result from a sudden loss of hearing in only one ear through accident or disease, without loss of acuity in the other. While overall acuity is relatively unaffected through the good ear, the immediate effect is of a sudden loss of the primary means of localizing the source of the heard sounds. Cocktail parties and small group discussions cease to be made up of separate voices, some to be attended to, and others ignored. Until adaptation to this loss eventually takes place, what is experienced is a continuous and disconcerting buzz of mixed sounds rather like a badly tuned radio picking up two or three stations at once, each making difficult the perception of the others.

If the sudden loss of a sensory ability supplies one example, so the sudden gain of one supplies another. A particularly striking case was reported some years ago by Richard Gregory (1966), describing the experiences of a blind patient first given sight in adulthood through corneal grafting. Before having sight, this intelligent 52-year-old man led an active and interesting life. He read well in braille, was skillful in the use of tools which he used as a hobby, went for long walks alone, and even rode a bicycle with a friend who rode alongside holding his shoulder to guide him. Although corneal grafting was then new, the operation giving him sight was by all accounts an immediate success and within a few days of the bandages being removed he had learned to recognize the faces of his doctors and nurses, to tell time visually, and to recognize objects heretofore known to him only by touch. Sight, however, now presented an unexpected and disconcerting distraction to his habitual modes of perception. As Gregory, who observed the patient during this period, noted:

> Before the operation, he was undaunted by traffic. He would cross alone, holding his arm or his stick stubbornly before him, when the traffic would subside as the waters before Christ. But after the operation, it took two of us on either side to force him across the road: he was terrified as never before in his life (Gregory, 1966, pg. 197).

Directed Attention

Focal attention is ordinarily an inner-directed activity; one voluntarily chooses to look at one object as opposed to another or to attend to a particular voice in a conversation. At the same time, it is true that some stimuli such as sudden loud sounds, movements, or bright flashes of color seem inherently to attract attention, even against one's will.

Numerous attempts have been made to identify and describe those conditions most likely to ordinarily capture attention. Because of the nature of things, no such list could ever hope to be complete or, to some extent, even be internally consistent. Traditionally, however, certain major factors in attention have been stressed. They can be conveniently summarized under the general headings of *motivation, set, contrast, and novelty.*

1. MOTIVATION.   Personal motivation is perhaps the most important variable in attention but, because motivating factors vary so much between individuals, it is by far the hardest to specify. There is an old myth that a mother will hear her child crying in another room long before others the same distance away will hear it. It often comes as a bit of a surprise when old myths turn out to be objectively true. This, as it happens, is one of those rare cases. Stimuli which affect one's own needs, desires, or concerns will capture attention and thus heighten perceptual sensitivity (cf. Kahneman, 1973). This is true whether we are thinking of a hungry person seeing a sign that says "food" or almost anyone seeing a sign that says "free." Indeed, the goal of much modern advertising is just that: to detect and exploit personal motivation in advertisements in order to attract and hold attention.

2. SET.   The term *set* is usually defined as a readiness to perceive, and is therefore closely related to motivation. The best example of set is the runner who hears the starter's commands, "ready, set . . ."; at "set," the run-

ner is braced, taut, and truly ready to go. He or she is listening only for the
sound of the starter's gun and will indeed often "hear" it before it has gone
off. Set, or readiness to perceive, acts both to increase the likelihood of a
stimulus attracting attention, and often, to decrease it. The so-called proof-
reader's error, for example, occurs when a person misses obvious spelling or
typing errors as he or she tries at the same time to read the material for
meaning. A case in point is the well-known phrase in the triangle below. It
may have to be read several times before anything wrong is noticed.

3. CONTRAST. Size, intensity, and movement are all known to attract attention. This is true whether we are speaking of the bold print of a newspaper headline, bright colors in an advertisement, or a loud shout in an
otherwise quiet room. If an object is bright enough, loud enough, or large
enough, it will most surely capture attention. The question, "How loud is
loud?" however is not an absolute, but depends almost entirely on the
background context against which it occurs. What is loud in a quiet library
will be soft at an outdoor sporting event. The general principle that stimuli
which stand out from the background will be likely to attract attention also
holds true for movement against a stable surrounding.

4. NOVELTY. If set and expectancy will attract attention, so will the totally
unexpected. A lion in the zoo will not attract as much attention as a lion in
your livingroom, and a close friend simply acting out of character will often
attract more attention than if he or she were to shout. Novelty is in reality a
combination of effects of psychological contrast set against a background of
expectancy and, as such, is highly dependent on individual motivation and
experience.

  When we speak of a child as being "distractible," a very common and
real concern in learning, we usually think of one whose attention seems to
wander more than the average child's. Anyone will be drawn away by a
sudden movement, a loud sound, or an unexpected event. The term "distractible," on the other hand, is usually reserved for the person whose focal
concentration can only be maintained for unusually short periods, and for
whom even the slightest sound or the mildest activity is enough to drastically draw his or her attention.

  Since fairly good attentive ability is possessed by most people, and the
"distractible" ones are in the minority, it is tempting to assume that maintained focal attention is the normal state of the interested individual, and
that distraction is some sort of peculiar aberration. In fact, the results of

considerable research puts the emphasis quite the other way around: the real question is not so much why people get distracted, but how it is that they ordinarily can maintain focal attention for so long.

The maintenance of attention to a single source, and the exclusion of possible distractors, is not a passive activity on the observer's part, and the mechanisms of this capacity are not fully understood. This process, aptly known as *selective attention*, has received considerable research effort, however, and a great deal of both theoretical and practical information has been forthcoming in recent years.

SELECTIVE ATTENTION

Let us begin our analysis not with the easiest conditions for selective attention, but with perhaps the most difficult. To do this you will have to place yourself, at least in imagination, in the middle of a large and noisy party with perhaps five or six knots of people all engaged in separate conversation. Let us assume, to make the problem more interesting, that the person with whom you are talking has a fairly soft voice, much softer than those booming from other places in the room. The fact is that you can and do attend easily to the relevant conversation, and can be totally unaware of what is being said in the irrelevant ones. Selective attention at such times seems quite absolute. It feels experientially almost as if the other conversations have been somehow attenuated, tuned out, switched off, or whatever term suits one's intuitions.

So far, so good. The problem for psychologists is now simply (1) to determine how the several conversations are discriminated (they do, after all, all vibrate the same set of ear drums) and sorted into separate "channels" for possible attention, and (2) how one can filter out all of the irrelevant channels and let only the relevant one through to conscious awareness. Before we get too deeply into any explanations along these lines, however, there is a second part to the problem which we have also all experienced. While you are engrossed in your particular conversation, what happens when someone across the room happens to mention your name in the course of a conversation? You not only hear your name, but you also suddenly become very much aware of that hitherto "irrelevant" conversation, with the full force of attention now directed toward it. When you do this, of course, you also lose all track of what is being said in the conversation to which you were supposed to be attending. It is usually at this point that one suddenly becomes aware that the person with whom you have been talking must have asked a direct question, because he or she is now looking at you with perplexed silence. Perhaps your most honest response at this point could be, "I'm sorry. Would you say that again? I wasn't paying attention." Attention does seem to be both limited and absolute. As you switch to the other, previously ignored conversation, you have similarly switched out of the one you were in.

It is at this point that we have the full problem, complete with its logical paradox. If you were not listening to the other conversations in the room, how were you able to hear your name when it was spoken? If in fact you were monitoring the other conversations, how is it that you had no notion of their content or even of hearing them before the moment when your name was mentioned? This situation of the noisy party is almost a model of the essential problems of selective attention, and it explains why the problem is now universally known to people engaged in research as, "the cocktail party problem" (Cherry, 1953).

Cocktail Parties in the Laboratory

Experimental psychologists long ago discovered the advantages of studying everyday phenomena in the controlled environment of the laboratory. (We will leave aside for the moment those skeptics who maintain that psychologists will not even believe a phenomenon exists until they can demonstrate it in those august and austere surroundings.) In any event, it was at least fortuitous that the revival of interest in this very old problem of selective attention coincided with the ready availability of a new piece of research apparatus not necessarily invented for the purpose: the stereophonic tape recorder. The stereophonic recorder in fact proved itself most amenable to selective attention research and allowed for very systematic studies to be performed under ingeniously controlled conditions. Here is how it is done.

The experimenter first records a passage of normal prose, perhaps reading from a magazine or a book, onto one channel of the recorder. He or she then rewinds the tape and now records another, different passage on the second channel. When the tape is now replayed and monitored over stereophonic earphones, a listener hears one message in the left ear and the other one simultaneously in the right ear. This is referred to as *dichotic listening* ("dichotic" is from the Greek *dich* meaning two different, and *otic* referring to the ear).

With these conditions, we can now simulate the cocktail party by instructing the listener to concentrate on, say, the passage in the left ear, and to ignore the one in the right. To make sure this is being done, the listener is usually required to "shadow" what is heard in the left, or relevant ear. "Shadowing" is simply repeating aloud what is heard, as it is heard, on a word-by-word basis. It sounds difficult, but in fact most people can do it with good accuracy after surprisingly little practice (Broadbent, 1952; Treisman, 1964a). By using a script to keep track of the subject's accuracy of shadowing, we can be sure that he or she is attending where required. Any wavering of attention to the other ear will immediately become apparent as he or she falters in shadowing or potentially even produces by accident some words from the supposedly ignored ear.

Under these carefully controlled conditions, a number of our intuitions about selective attention become clarified. The first of these is that attention seems to be even more absolute than it might first appear from everyday experience. When instructed to attend to only one ear, virtually no information seems to get through from the other. Indeed, not only is one unaware of the content of the ignored message, but subjects often will not even notice anything amiss if a male voice beginning in that ear is replaced by a female one, or if the unattended message gradually changes from, say, English to French (Treisman, 1964a). The ignored message, it would seem, truly is ignored.

These results were as surprising to the early researchers in selective attention as they may be to the reader. Under these controlled laboratory conditions it seemed almost as if people could "turn off" an entire source of information as completely as one turns off a kitchen tap. We can, of course, ignore visual information by simply closing our eyes or turning our head. But auditory information, speech from more than one source, cannot be *physically* shut out in any analogous way. Yet, the ability to ignore unattended auditory information seemed just as complete. Numerous studies showed that subjects could attend to speech equally well with or without a distracting message, so long as two different voices were used, or the voices came from different locations (cf. Cherry, 1953; Moray & O'Brien, 1967; Kahneman, 1973, pg. 115). Indeed, under certain conditions, ignoring two potentially distractable messages is no more difficult than ignoring one. Treisman (1964b), for example, found shadowing speech from one ear no more difficult if two messages were spoken simultaneously in the unattended ear than if one message was.

These and other experiments demonstrate our efficiency in ignoring unwanted information and illustrate dramatically the power of our selectivity in attention. On the other hand, how could we hope to hear a warning of fire even when engrossed in conversation or, for that matter, hear our name spoken in another conversation at a cocktail party? Clearly, there must be some way of monitoring irrelevant information, even though we may only become aware that we have been doing so when that "irrelevant" information suddenly becomes relevant.

Moray (1959) was able to simulate the full cocktail party problem by simply prerecording a volunteer's name somewhere in the speech on the ignored channel. His subjects would put on their earphones and begin shadowing the speech in the particular ear Moray indicated. As in previous experiments, attention seemed to be totally focused on that ear only. It seemed focused, in any event, until the voice in the unattended ear said the person's name and told him or her either to stop shadowing or to switch attention to that ear. In about 30 percent of the cases, subjects heard their names and responded appropriately.

One would expect that if anything broke through the barrier of attention, it would be something as relevant as the person's own name. Indeed, even in fairly deep sleep, softly speaking a person's name will—if not wake the individual—then produce a neurological startle response (called a "K-complex") detectable on an electroencephalogram (EEG) (Oswald, Taylor & Treisman, 1960).

One's name is not the only kind of information that will break through from a previously ignored message. For example, when subjects are told that a certain word will occur in the ignored ear they will sometimes respond to it when it occurs, either by noting its presence or by faltering in their shadowing of the attended message (cf. Mowbray, 1964; Shaffer & Hardwick, 1969). Nevertheless, it is equally true that recognition accuracy for critical words from the attended ear is far higher than that for words in the unattended ear (Treisman & Geffen, 1967; Treisman & Riley, 1969).

However selective the attentional process may be, it can also be driven by meaning or contextual set. Treisman (1960), for example, wondered what would happen if at a certain point the messages in the relevant and ignored ears were switched without warning. Let us say, for example, that the subject is to shadow the message in the left ear and ignore the one from the right. Here are extracts from two typical messages to the two ears (Treisman, 1960, pg. 246).

> Left Ear: . . . SITTING AT A MAHOGANY/ three possibilities . . .
> Right Ear: . . . Let us look at these/ TABLE WITH HER HEAD . . .

At a certain moment, idicated by the slashes, the two messages were interchanged between ears. A subject's typical shadowing response might be: ". . . SITTING AT A MAHOGANY table POSSIBILITIES . . ." Studying this response closely, shows the essence of selective attention. First, the word "table" was heard even though it occurred in the to-be-ignored ear because it fit the context of the sentence beginning in the relevant channel. Second, subjects can retain fairly tight control on attention. Even though the left ear's message carried on in the right ear and they followed it, they were quick to realize their error and shifted back to the left ear almost immediately. Third, attention is relatively absolute. When attention did momentarily shift to the wrong ear, the word occurring at that moment in the to-be-attended ear (the word "three") was lost.

The Filter in Selective Attention

Over the past years numerous experiments have been conducted to gain a fuller understanding of the mechanisms of selective attention. Some have employed dichotic listening techniques, and others have had subjects simply attending to two different but discriminable voices heard over a single loudspeaker. The results are virtually the same as found for dichotic listening (cf. Moray, 1960). The task for researchers is not an easy one, since accu-

rate descriptions of the behavior always come more readily than explanations. In this case one is also handicapped by the inability to draw many direct insights from physiological studies of lower animals. Lower animals do
show something comparable to selective attention, but it appears at a lower
level of functioning as a peripheral adjustment of the sensory receptors (cf.
Mackintosh, 1965). In the human, the form of selective attention we have
been referring to is clearly a cognitive phenomenon, largely controlled by
context, meaning, and language.

A number of intriguing descriptive explanations have been developed
over the years either as an extension of, or as a reaction to, the pioneer work
of Donald Broadbent, who took the concept of "filtering" of attention quite
literally (Broadbent, 1954, 1958, 1971). Broadbent's basic postulates as they
developed were simple, logical, and fairly consistent with both results of
empirical research and one's own intuitions about the phenomenon of selective attention. Although we cannot here go into many of the details, or
review all of the evidence on which it was based, we can give a flavor of this
important model and explore some of its implications.

Although information from several sources may arrive at the senses simultaneously, they cannot be attended to simultaneously. The block is a *selective filter* which can pass only one source (*channel*) at a time into what
we have been referring to as the limited capacity short-term memory. It is
this filter which prevents an overloading of short-term memory by switching first to one source and then to another as we try to monitor the activity
around us. The filter might well be looked on as a selective switch and, as
such, it might take a finite time to operate. One estimate puts the time to
switch attention from one source to another at about $1/6$ second (Cherry &
Taylor, 1954).

Let us return to the paradox of how one can be totally unaware of other
conversations, and yet hear one's name when it is spoken. If we had only
this switch, nothing from any but the attended source could be registered. A
possible solution is that information from the blocked channels may be held
for a very short period (estimates put it at something under a second) almost
as an "echo" of the stimulus. This store, or *echoic memory* (Neisser, 1967)
has a very much shorter duration than short-term memory and, unlike the
latter, is held very much as a sensory echo, unanalyzed as to recognition or
meaning. (This "echoic memory," which has a visual counterpart sometimes referred to as "iconic memory," will be discussed more fully in Chapter 11.)

In operation, the filter would admit to short-term memory a single
channel, such as the message in the relevant ear in a dichotic listening experiment or one speaker at a cocktail party. Only this attended channel will
invade awareness and be capable of recognition, understanding, and potentially, of learning. The filter can sample nonattended information in the
echoic memory, and if it contains a fading trace of something relevant, like

one's name, it will switch to that input channel. If the echoic store contains nothing of interest, the filter will sweep back to the primary source of information.

Since the echoic memory holds material unanalyzed for meaning, and then only for some fraction of a second, one is ordinarily unaware either of its content or the fact that it was briefly sampled. Because of its fleeting, preanalytic nature, one admittedly may not have the same intuitive feeling for echoic memory as one potentially can have for the filter. There is nevertheless considerable evidence to argue for its existence.

Broadbent outlined the basic elements of his model in the form of a flow diagram, reminiscent of the one used earlier in this chapter to represent the sequence of learning. Like that one, it is only an attempt to outline a series of events and operations performed by the nervous system without at this point saying how, physiologically, they are actually performed.

Here briefly are the basic elements of Broadbent's model as summarized in Figure 2.2. You may recognize that the first three elements of his model were earlier subsumed under the single heading of "apprehension" in the sequence of learning. (1) *Sense organs and channel separation*: the first element of the model represents the arrival of information from the great variety of usual sources. The irregular arrows entering this element represent the "tangled" form in which they arrive, and the parallel arrows leaving it represent the result of some preliminary analysis which separates the various channels (a voice from location *a*, a voice from location *b*, the hum of an air conditioner in the background, etc.). (2) *Echoic memory*: information from all input channels are held simultaneously in echoic memory but for a very short period of under a second. This storage seems almost an "echo" of the stimulus input and remains unanalyzed as to identification or meaning. (3) *Selective filter*: the filter is the heart of Broadbent's model and operates

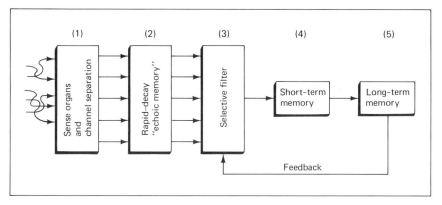

Figure 2.2   Flow diagram of Broadbent's filter theory of selective attention. The heart of the theory is a *selective filter* (3) which allows information from only one channel at a time to pass into short-term memory.

to pass only one channel at a time into short-term memory, while at the same time blocking admission of any others. The rejected channels remain in the echoic store only briefly before they fade and are irretrievably lost. (4) *Short-term memory*: short-term memory represents the previously discussed limited capacity store (7 ± 2 "chunks") which can hold analyzed or identified information for immediate use and/or for rehearsal into long-term memory. The primary function of the filter is to help protect this limited capacity memory from overload. (5) *Long-term memory*: that material which receives rehearsal and is allowed to consolidate without the interference of too rapidly arriving new information will be retained in long-term memory for long and indefinite periods. The arrow going from long-term memory back to the selective filter is included to indicate the influence of information already stored in long-term memory on the operation of the filter. This so-called feedback loop supplies such information as needed for the filter to select the channel of greatest relevance or importance.

Doing Two Things at Once

One of the implications of Broadbent's theory is that attending to more than one source of information at a time is virtually impossible. Our own experience, however, is that we seem to do this constantly: reading a book while listening to the radio or holding a conversation while driving a car. One occasionally even encounters a person writing a letter while talking to someone else on the telephone, although one does wonder whether sufficient justice is being done to either. Is this focal attention to more than one source at a time, or is it a delusion? The answer, like so many others in psychology, is that it is partially both. A rather weak analogy might help to clarify the issue, especially if we show just where the analogy is weak.

The analogy is that of a bored television watcher who from time to time gets curious about what is happening on the other channels. The less interesting the program, the more likely the viewer is to be curious. Given a slow-moving tv program, it is quite possible to switch momentarily to another channel, check that program, and then return to the original one without having lost enough of the plot to be unable to reconstruct what was missed from the preceding and following contexts. If we assume a not atypical evening fare of two dreadful old films, a rerun of a situation comedy out of the 1950s, and a tedious panel quiz program, it is all too possible to spend most of the time on one channel, while every so often sweeping through the others for a few seconds each—just to see if anything interesting is happening (it never is)—and still be quite able to keep track of the essentials of all of them.

The tv channel selector, like Broadbent's filter, can only "attend" to one channel at a time. In both cases, however, the limitation can be partially overcome by brief sampling of alternative channels. The analogy of a tv set is weak, however, in that one would be aware both of monitoring the alternative channels and of the content received during these brief samplings. In human selective attention the duration of a single sampling might be in the order of milliseconds rather than seconds, and awareness of the operation need not be the case. The human brain, we hasten to report, is not a tv set.

The analogy is strong, however, on the important role of redundancy or predictability to the normal operation of selective attention. As we will see in detail later, speech is in fact highly redundant, and often as much as 30 to 50 percent of what is said can be missed without appreciable difficulty in following the train of thought. We take advantage of this redundancy when using a noisy telephone line or holding a conversation in a noisy location. So automatic in this perceptual processing of incomplete stimuli that one is often unaware of how much of the stimuli is being heard and how much is being inferred from the context. One typically becomes aware of this only when a mistake is made—a noticeable, but relatively infrequent occurrence.

Most activities are extraordinarily predictable and free of surprises. This holds true for such things as listening to a typical conversation, driving a car on a clear straight highway, or listening to familiar music on the radio. Occasional sampling of information from these sources while attending primarily to something else is often sufficient not only to allow one to handle both, but to give the illusion that they are being handled simultaneously. When the unexpected does occur, like seeing an accident ahead on the roadway, hearing the radio music interrupted by a special news bulletin, or hearing your name being spoken at a cocktail party, the primary activity is at once halted both abruptly and completely. It is at that point that one is aware of the limited nature of focal attention. In short, one can gain information from more than one source at a time provided (1) that the information available in both sources is highly predictable or redundant, or (2) that one is willing to sacrifice as much as half the potential information available in each if they are not. To assume neither of these facts is a delusion counterproductive to the learning process.

At this point we have a final clear departure from the tv set analogy. The maintenance of focal attention on even the most relevant and important of sources is never a continuous or passive operation. The routine monitoring of alternative channels is necessary for survival in a complex and constantly changing stimulus environment. Perhaps because of this, the maintenance of focal attention for very extended periods is difficult and, as we all know, exhausting when it is attempted. So long as one is awake, one is constantly attending to *something*. "Attentive" behavior, as one hopes to see it in a learning situation, means only that focal attention is directed most of the time to the important source and that routine sampling of other channels is kept to a minimum. To expect complete attention and no sampling (hence brief inattention), no matter how interesting the source or motivated the person, is to expect something other than the nervous system is equipped to produce. When we speak of concentration in studying, or at-

tention to a teacher, we are in reality speaking not of absolutes but of—one
may hope—higher proportions of time being allocated to these stimuli.

FILTERS, "LEAKY" FILTERS, AND NO FILTERS

Broadbent's "filter theory" of selective attention did much to consolidate interest in the problem of attention, and it caused numerous psychologists to look more closely at the "bottleneck" of stimulus input than they
had in the past. As they looked, however, many came to feel that Broadbent's explanation of how one could catch information from "unattended"
sources seemed not to be the complete answer. To them, the chance of just
happening to monitor an irrelevant conversation the instant one's name is
spoken, or some other pertinent message occurs, relied just too much on
chance.

An Attenuating Filter?

Treisman (1969) proposed a modification to Broadbent's original theory;
one which Broadbent (1971) later came to accept. She proposed that the filter does not totally block from perception all unattended channels of information but merely *attenuates* them. If Broadbent's original notion of the
filter in attention was analogous to the channel selector on a television set,
so Treisman's modification was analogous to the tuning of an AM radio at a
point on the dial where several weak stations can all be heard at the same
time. By carefully tuning the dial, one can make one station louder than the
others, but the other stations always continue to be heard softly in the
background. We cannot block them completely, we can only attenuate
them.

In Treisman's view, some information from the unattended channels always does "leak" through the filter, and this accounts for our ability to recognize something as pertinent as our name, but little else. Her explanation
still postulated a perceptual filter similar to Broadbent's original idea, but
her modification seemed to be more congenial with the results of the experiments we have cited to this point.

On the other hand, many theorists have questioned whether a lack of
awareness of irrelevant information need necessarily imply that it has been
blocked (or attenuated) in the process of perception. To these theorists, the
"bottleneck" occurs not at the point of entry of the information at the stage
of perception, but that limited attention is a consequence of limitations on
how much can be retained at once in memory, or limitations on how much
information can simultaneously enter awareness (cf. Deutsch & Deutsch,
1963; 1967; Yntema & Trask, 1963; Norman, 1968; Wingfield & Byrnes,
1972; Keele, 1973).

The question is not whether we can "filter" from awareness irrelevant information, but whether this filtering occurs at the stage of apprehension or at the stage of memory. MacKay (1973), for example, had subjects shadow ambiguous sentences, such as "They threw stones toward the bank yesterday," while either the word "river" or the word "money" was spoken in the unattended ear. When later questioned about the meaning of the shadowed sentence, the influence of the disambiguating word showed a clear influence ("They threw stones toward the side of the river yesterday" versus "They threw stones toward the savings and loan association yesterday"). The meaning of the words in the unattended ear obviously got through, yet the subjects—as we might have expected from the previous experiments—denied conscious awareness of ever hearing the disambiguating words. Other evidence has also come to light to suggest that some meaning is given to apparently unattended information before it is rejected from awareness, a finding quite contrary to Broadbent or Triesman's filter theories (cf. Corteen & Wood, 1972; Lewis, 1970; Von Wright, Anderson & Stenman, 1975).

Could these results be explained by very rapid switching of attention, such that both channels could be almost constantly monitored? This is how filter theory would explain such results. Some theorists, on the other hand, have proposed an explanation which does not rely on the presumed existence of a filter, attenuating or otherwise. This theory in its several versions is sometimes known as a "capacity" model of attention (Kahneman, 1973; Norman & Bobrow, 1975).

A "Capacity" Theory of Attention

The "capacity" explanation of divided attention postulates a limited capacity to one's mental resources which must be allocated between attending to new information, holding recently acquired information in memory, and perhaps thinking about this information. According to this theory, if two or more tasks sharing the same limited resources must be performed simultaneously, then a principle of "complementarity" operates: an increase in the use of resources on one task will result in a decrease in resources available for the others. For example, if one is shadowing a message to one ear, there is limited processing capacity left for other activities, whether it is analyzing a simultaneous message in the other ear, attempting to look simultaneously at a visual stimulus, or whatever.

The notion of resource allocation requires a careful specification of the nature of the tasks involved and the measurement criteria (cf., Kantowitz & Knight, 1976; Norman & Bobrow, 1976). The spirit of the theory, however, can be seen in the results of an experiment in which subjects were required to monitor tape-recorded messages while simultaneously watching a small light bulb which could at any moment change its intensity. Not only did the subjects find doing this extremely difficult, but they were significantly slower in reacting to the light when the monitored speech was an unfamiliar passage than when it was a familiar one (Johnston & Heinz, 1974). One might say that shadowing the unfamiliar passage strained the subjects' processing resources to the point where it interfered with a quick response to the light.

When applied to simultaneous listening, the capacity explanation would not speak of the information from the ear being shadowed as passing an attentional filter and the other being totally blocked from analysis. It would see the shadowed ear as being given *priority* in one's limited capacity for processing information. The so-called unattended ear also receives analysis but only in terms of the now very limited resources still remaining after the allocation to the primary task. For example, as Norman and Bobrow (1975) view the capacity explanation, it is not inconsistent with Treisman's notion of "attentuation." Rather, it sees attenuation, not as a *cause* of a perceptual bottleneck, but as a *consequence* of priorities in a limited capacity cognitive system.

The capacity model of attention is admittedly more abstract, and harder to visualize, than Broadbent's filter theory. It does, however, attempt to bring a unitary concept to the notion of attention.

> A person can direct processing resources in many different ways, concentrating sometimes on some aspect of the sensory input through the sense organs, sometimes on deep processing of internally generated ideas, and sometimes on preparing for a forthcoming activity. Moreover, the processing system is continually attempting to combine all sources of information at its disposal into a unified, understandable picture (Norman, 1976, pp. 79–80).

Broadbent's original filter theory was an important beginning to our understanding of selective attention, and it retains considerable merit as a convenient description of everyday behavior and problems in selective attention. Even more important, it brought about the realization of the fact of very real human limitations on the input of information, and the ways in which the nervous system both copes with and exploits these limitations. Readers especially interested in selective attention and the development of these various theories can find good reviews of the experiments and detailed arguments in, for example, Broadbent (1971), Kahneman (1973), and Norman (1976).

SUMMARY

Although it is common to think of learning as something that "happens," learning is in fact something one does. Learning is an active process, and one not without its problems and pitfalls. Two of these, which will be addressed in subsequent chapters, are the limitations of motivation and intelligence on the speed and quality of learning.

In the present chapter we looked at the limitations on learning from the perspective of learning as a sequence of operations. These were the stages of input, storage, and retrieval.

The input stage included the selective attention to some information and the filtering out of competing stimuli. Once referred to as the span of apprehension, there are upper limits on the amount of information even the most eager learner can take in on a single hearing or in a single glance. We included in the input stage the process of rehearsal in short-term memory, as information is temporarily held either for immediate use or for consolidation in more permanent memory.

The second stage of the sequence of learning was referred to as the storage of information in long-term memory. At this stage the information is given meaning and is assimilated into our more permanent store of knowledge and past experience.

The final stage of the sequence ordinarily represents the retrieval of information, either in the form of an overt response or for "internal" use in reasoning and in giving meaning to newly acquired information.

Selective attention refers to the ability to focus on one source of stimulus information, while "filtering" from awareness other, potentially distracting, stimulus sources. One of the earliest models of selective attention was a so-called filter theory of attention which proposed a perceptual filtering mechanism which only allowed one channel of information at a time to be passed through the input stage. According to this theory, monitoring competing messages could be accomplished only by rapidly switching this perceptual filter from one source to another.

Later theories of selective attention included the notion of an attenuating filter which merely reduces, but does not eliminate, simultaneous input of information. So-called capacity explanations of attention are a major alternative to either of these models, and they attempt to specify the way in which one may allocate one's limited resources by giving priority to one stimulus input or another.

chapter 3

Motivation, Reward, and Arousal

In the previous chapter we spoke of the importance of motivation in human learning. This is not to say that learning cannot occur without conscious awareness, or a desire to learn. In Chapter 5 we will see this topic discussed under the heading of *latent*, or *incidental learning* (Postman, 1964). It is equally true, however, that the more actively involved and goal oriented one is, the more rapid and complete the learning will be. As the previous chapter showed that there are upper limits to the quantity and rate at which information can be assimilated, so the present chapter will examine the role of *motivation* in learning, and the way it can determine the extent to which this limited capacity may be utilized.

Our discussion will take place in three parts. First, we will look at the nature of motivation and reward in human learning. This will include differences between internal and external motivation, and some examples of each. Second, we will examine the historical approaches to the study of motivation, as psychologists with a strong biological orientation tried to derive a single theory of "reward" which would encompass both human and animal learning. In the final sections we will return again to distinctly human motivation in an attempt to put these early theories into perspective, and to offer some current alternatives.

Reward in Human Learning

The expression, *motivated behavior*, is a very broad term in psychology which refers to any behavior or learning which is encouraged by specific needs and is directed toward the attainment of specific goals. While many learning theorists see strong motivation as a precondition for effective learning, still others emphasize that the relationship is often a reciprocal one. This means that one may begin to learn with weak motivation, but as the acquisition of knowledge or skills begins to bring practical gain or feelings of accomplishment, this itself may increase the level of motivation for further learning (cf. Ausubel, 1968).

This potential interaction between the level of motivation and success at learning can be seen more clearly as we distinguish between two general aspects of motivation. One of these is represented by the short-term offer of reward for good performance (or punishment for bad performance). The second refers to rewards which are a natural consequence of the behavior itself. These are referred to respectively as *extrinsic* and *intrinsic* sources of reward.

EXTRINSIC REWARD

Extrinsic incentives for performance are typified by the use of tangible rewards, such as food, candy, special privileges, or, in later years, good school grades or professional advancement. While these may be typical, it would be wrong to think of reward solely in terms of material gain. Social approval and peer group influence are also important sources of extrinsic reward.

The influence of social approval on learning can be illustrated in a variety of ways. In one experiment, for example, a group of psychologists showed how one can guide quite specific behavior by simply saying "good" at the appropriate times. The subjects in this experiment were college students who were shown cards containing a single verb and six pronouns (I, we, he, they, she, you). Their task was simply to make up sentences using the verb and any one of the pronouns they chose. Over the course of the experiment the students were given some 80 different cards. Each card contained a different verb but the same six pronouns (Cohen, Kalish, Thurston & Cohen, 1954).

While the students looked at each of the cards and generaged their sentences, the experimenters remained quietly in the background, only occasionally commenting on the students' performance. Whenever the students produced a sentence beginning with the words *I* or *we*, one of the experimenters quietly said, "good." When a sentence was begun with any of the other four pronouns they said nothing.

The results are summarized in Figure 3.1, which shows the number of times the words *I* or *we* were used in the first 20 sentences, the second 20 sentences, the third 20 sentences, and the fourth 20 sentences. The frequency of use of these words rose from an average of under 9 times per 20 sentences at the beginning of the experiment, to over 12 times per 20 sentences by the end of the experiment. The lower curve is for another group of students, a *control group*, who had nothing said to them as they constructed their sentences. This group was necessary to show that the words *I* and *we* would not ordinarily increase in use if they were not selectively

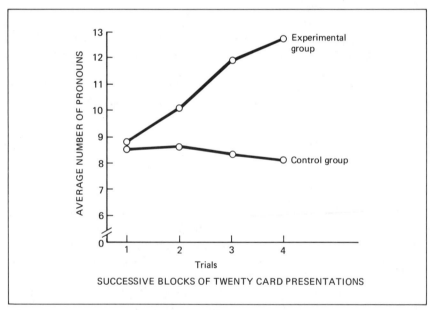

Figure 3.1   The effect of saying "good" to reward students for using the pronouns *I* or *we* in a sentence construction task. (*Source:* B. D. Cohen, H. I. Kalish, J. R. Thurston, and E. Cohen, Experimental manipulation of verbal behavior. *Journal of Experimental Psychology*, 1954, 47: fig. 1, pg. 107. Copyright 1954 by the American Psychological Association. Reprinted by permission.)

rewarded. We can see from the control group's curve that this did not occur.

Reward and Awareness of Reward

An interesting feature of this experiment was not merely the clear influence of mild praise in directing the students' verbal behavior, but the fact that the students later denied any awareness either that they had been selectively rewarded for using certain words, or that their frequency of using these words had steadily increased.

It may be safe to conclude that a reward can have its effect without a person's conscious awareness of the reward. At the same time, learning without such awareness is probably quite rare in human behavior. For example, Levin (1961) repeated the Cohen et al. experiment, but questioned his subjects much more extensively about what they thought might have been happening during the course of the study. Levin concluded not only that many of his subjects were indeed aware of the principle of reward which had been used, but that this awareness may have been important to the learning process.

Support for this latter view has come from a variety of sources. In one experiment, for example, subjects were told simply to speak for several minutes with whatever words came to mind. As one group of subjects spoke, the experimenter simply said "Mmm-hmm" whenever a word classed as a "human noun" was used (e.g., man, woman, boy, girl, and so forth). A control group was also treated to a series of "Mmm-hmm's" as they spoke, but these were said at random intervals (DeNike, 1964; Spielberger & DeNike, 1966).

Figure 3.2 shows three curves. The top curve, which looks very similar to the one in Cohen et al.'s experiment, shows a progressive increase in the use of the "rewarded" nouns over the course of the experiment. This curve, however, is only for those subjects who were rewarded for using this class of words and who, in written comments, implied that they were also aware of the association. Subjects who claimed to be unaware of the connection used the "rewarded" words no more frequently than the control group. This is shown by the lower two curves on the graph.

It is of course difficult to say in all cases that awareness of reward actually facilitates learning. It could be argued that learning can occur without such awareness, and only after the fact does one sometimes realize that a reward had been systematically tied to certain responses. That is, the learning may produce the awareness, rather than the awareness producing the learning. We can find advocates for both positions in the literature (cf. Greenspoon & Brownstein, 1967; Kanfer, 1968; Patty & Page, 1973). There is no argument, however, about the power of verbal praise or social approval as a trigger for learning.

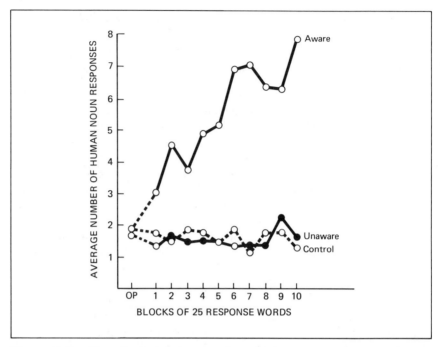

Figure 3.2   The effect of awareness that certain words (human nouns) were being rewarded on the frequency of using those words. (*Source:* L. D. DeNike, The temporal relationship between awareness and performance in verbal conditioning. *Journal of Experimental Psychology,* 1964, 68: fig. 1, pg. 525. Copyright 1964 by the American Psychological Association. Reprinted by permission.)

The Application of Reward

We can illustrate the role of social approval as a source of extrinsic reward in a more realistic setting. This is a study which was conducted in an elementary school classroom which had more than its share of disruptive behavior. ("Disruptive behavior" is a common euphemism in education for chaos in the classroom: fighting, noise, anger at being reprimanded, ignoring the teacher, and so forth.)

Using a carefully controlled plan, the classroom teacher was instructed to adopt two principles of reaction to any behavior. Behavior which facilitated learning was to be rewarded with verbal praise and attention. Behavior which interferred with learning was to be ignored. The verbal praise took the form of comments such as, "I like the way you are working quietly," "Good job. You are doing fine," and so forth. Each child had his or her own behavior for reward. One child, for example, was specifically praised for sitting instead of standing, for paying attention to the teacher, and for not sucking her thumb.

Over an eight-week observation period, there was a 33 percent reduction in the frequency of disruptive behavior in the classroom (Becker, Madsen, Arnold & Thomas, 1967). While the scheme was obviously an effective one, the rewarding of the good behavior may at first seem intuitively more reasonable than the teacher's instructions to ignore the disruptive behavior. Numerous studies, however, have shown this combination to be an effective one (Howe, 1972, pg. 24).

The reason this is so may lie in the nature of the "reward" in this situation. One component of verbal praise is direct approval of the desired behavior. A second component is the attention the child receives along with the verbal praise. If a need for attention was the motivation behind any of the disruptive behavior, which is more than possible, then the attention which would accompany a reprimand might inadvertently serve as a reward for that behavior.

INTRINSIC REWARD

Tangible reward, social approval, and attention are important incentives for human learning. They are, however, situational factors which are not always present in all learning situations. Indeed, it is possible to overestimate their importance in human motivation because of the ease with which their presence can be observed, and the ease with which they can be manipulated in experimental studies. The greater part of human learning may well be based on rewards which are intrinsic to the behavior.

Many writers see *identification* as among the more important sources of internal motivation for learning. *Identification* has a prominent place in theories of socialization, role learning, and the acquisition of internal controls and moral values (Secord & Backman, 1964, pg. 532). Although identification remains one of the most complex and controversial issues in psychology, it can be described as, "The strong human tendency to model one's 'self' and one's aspirations upon some other person. When we feel we have succeeded in 'being like' an identification figure, we derive pleasure from the achievement and conversely, we suffer when we have 'let him down'" (Bruner, 1966, pg. 122).

The development of identification with a model can be attributed to a variety of sources, from love and admiration for a person, to physical dependence and status envy (cf. Sears, 1957; Whiting, 1960; Winch, 1962). The basic elements of identification, however, are first, a desire to *imitate* the behavior and values of the identification object, and second, to *internalize* these values as one's own. As such, not only is much childhood learning derived from a desire to "be like" the parent (or teacher), but identification, a source of instrinsic motivation, also underlies the reward value of such extrinsic sources as social approval and verbal praise.

Learning for Learning's Sake

To this point, we have painted a rather hedonistic picture of motivation, a "what's in it for me?" view of learning. Many writers, however, have emphasized the possibility that young children, as well as adults, may have strong internal drives to fulfill their potential abilities merely for its own sake. This form of intrinsic motivation has been referred to as "a need for task mastery," or simply, as *competence motivation* (White, 1959). In this view, whether the task is learning to ride a bicycle, learning to read, or learning to successfully build a tower of blocks, the child's motivation rests solely on "an intrinsic need to deal with the environment" (White, 1959, pg. 319).

In the view of many, competence motivation, or something like it, may well be an inborn human trait, a view reinforced by its similarity to the "exploratory behavior," or "curiosity," which can often be observed in lower animals (see pg. 63).

A form of intrinsic motivation closely related to a need for competence has been referred to as *achievement motivation*. In this case at least, one can identify a strong component of learning in its development.

Achievement Motivation

The study of achievement motivation arose from the recognition that individuals frequently pursue excellence even when there is no immediate gain in sight. To put it simply, some people appear to have a desire to achieve for achievement's sake. Moreover, while the level of achievement motivation may change from time to time within an individual, there seem to be sufficiently stable individual differences between people to give it the enduring character of a personality trait. It is a trait which is critical for the fulfillment of one's learning potential, and it is one factor underlying the common problem of the "underachiever": a child or adult whose level of performance is clearly below his or her potential capabilities.

Although the full picture of achievement motivation is complex (McClelland, Atkinson, Clark & Lowell, 1953; McClelland, 1955, 1961; Atkinson, 1958), the flavor of the phenomenon can be easily illustrated.

Imagine a drawing of a boy seated at a desk with a book open in front of him. The picture does not make it immediately clear whether he is actually reading the book, or whether he is staring thoughtfully off into space. You are asked to study the picture and then to write a brief statement explaining (1) what you think is happening in the picture, (2) what might have led up to this situation, (3) what the person in the picture may be thinking, and (4) what you think may happen in the future.

You may recognize this situation as similar to the thematic apperception test (TAT), a projective personality test consisting of a series of ambiguous pictures sometimes used in clinical settings. The test assumes that such pictures are open to a sufficient variety of interpretations that one may unconsciously "project" one's feelings, concerns, and motivations into the description of the pictures.

Here are two such descriptions, both given by college students who saw the picture of the seated boy. The first story shows a strong concentration on academic achievement and success. The second does not (Atkinson, 1954, pg. 101).

HIGH MOTIVATION STORY

(1) A boy in a classroom of students being asked to write a scientific thesis. (2) The boy, in his desire to be a writer of important themes, has gone into an advanced English course. (3) He is attempting to correlate and pull together all he knows of the subject. He wants to give it a different twist, the same old story but in a new and different way. (4) He will work . . . and prepare a fine theme with a new twist, and consequently go on writing.

LOW MOTIVATION STORY

(1) The student seems to be perplexed with some problems and then finding no solution appears to daydream. (2) The young student was asked a question about which he didn't know the answer, so he felt rather discouraged and disgusted. (3) The student is wondering whether school work is necessary "stuff" or not. He hopes he were doing something else. (4) He will continue in school and look for adventure somewhere else, perhaps in a trade school.

According to McClelland and his associates, analyses of TAT descriptions, questionnaire responses, and personal interviews, all combine to show some individuals with generally high levels of achievement motivation and others with lower levels. Even when compared with others of equal ability, persons with high achievement needs can be shown to work harder to gain success, and to translate this need into higher grades in school and college, a greater speed in completing learning tasks, and an overall higher level of success in both academic and professional pursuits (cf. Lowell, 1952; French & Thomas, 1958). Furthermore, differences in achievement motivation can be recognized even in young children, and these differences seem to remain fairly stable into adulthood. One study, for example, reported that the level of achievement motivation exhibited by children as young as 6 to 10 can reliably predict their level of achievement needs as adults (Moss & Kagan, 1961).

Figure 3.3 shows actual task performance of two groups of college students who were required to spend 20 minutes solving a lengthy series of anagram problems. The anagrams consisted of sets of scrambled letters, such as WTSE, which had to be quickly rearranged to form English words (e.g., WEST). This task is unquestionably a pointless and trivial one, and

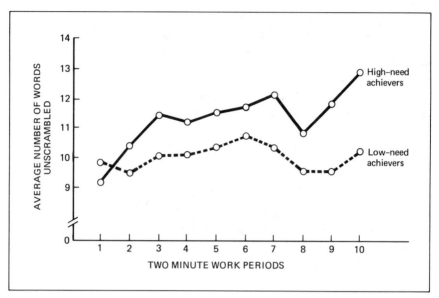

Figure 3.3   Performance on an anagram solution task for students with high and low achievement motivation. (*Source:* E. L. Lowell, The effect of need for achievement on learning and speed of performance. *Journal of Psychology,* 1952, 33: fig. 1, pg. 36. Reprinted by permission of The Journal Press.)

whatever entertainment value it might have at the beginning, it is bound to become lost after the first 50 or 100 problems have been completed. This is precisely why this study is so illustrative (Lowell, 1952).

The results are shown for students rated high or low in achievement needs based on TAT responses. While at the beginning of the task both groups show approximately equal ability, the low achievement need group fails to improve beyond the sixth training session. The high need group continues to work progressively harder with each session and, with the exception of a single reversal, shows an overall trend of continued improvement. As we have seen, the difference between the two groups was not one of initial ability with the task. The sole difference was in their relative "needs to achieve," and hence, the effort they were willing to give to superior performance.

Persons with high achievement needs see success itself as a reward. For persons with low achievement needs, "why bother?" is a question they often ask themselves, and one they often fail to answer. Short-term extrinsic reward may represent their only incentive for achievement.

It would be a mistake to see extremely high achievement motivation, and its attendant aspiration levels, as an automatic key to success. We are all familiar with those individuals who habitually set their goals so high that success, as they define it, is virtually impossible. For them, learning can become a routine of failure and frustration. The defeats they suffer are no less real, simply because they are self-imposed. The opposite side of the coin is represented by those who set their sights too low, defining success at levels far below their true ability. That is to say, the hope of success associated with high achievement motivation may also be accompanied by a strong fear of failure (Atkinson & Feather, 1966).

The Development of Achievement Motivation

The development of achievement motivation can be traced to early childhood, and to the influence of parental attitudes and reactions to achievement by their children. Winterbottom (1958) began one study by selecting children showing either very high or very low achievement needs. She simply asked the children to make up a story about "a little boy in school."

> "Make up a real story with a beginning and an end just like the ones you read. Tell me as much about your story as you can, and I'll write down what you say" (Winterbottom, 1958, pg. 459).

This story-telling task has the same "projective" potential as the TAT and can be scored for evidence of high or low achievement needs in much the same way.

Once these two groups of children were identified, she then interviewed their parents, focusing her questions on (1) their attitudes toward their children's independence, (2) the ages at which they expected their children to have mastered various skills, and (3) how they reacted to their children's mastery when it was achieved.

The results were consistent. Parents of children with low needs for achievement tended to routinely underestimate their children's ability to achieve task independence in a wide variety of skills. Parents of high-need achievers *expected* high achievement from their children from the very beginning. And when they saw it, they reacted with warmth, encouragement, and affection.

One can easily set up the conditions to illustrate the difference. We begin by giving children toy blocks and asking them how tall a tower they think they can build before it will topple over. We then compare their initial aspiration levels with what turns out to be their true ability. Were their expectations too high or too low? The answer to this question will often make certain predictions about what we can expect to see if we now bring their parents into the picture.

We tell the parents how high an "average" child can build a tower, and ask them their expectations for their own child. We can infer from Winterbottom's study that we will probably discover that the children's levels of aspiration closely match those of their parents. We can now develop her picture of the interaction by observing how the parents react as the child begins to build. Do the parents let the child get on with it, occasionally offering approval and encouragement? Or do they watch with uncertainty, and move to "take over" the moment the tower begins to look unsteady? The parent who does this may have the intention of helping the child. It can also serve as a signal to the child that they do not believe that he or she can handle the task alone.

Scenes such as this are a model of children's early experience with attempts at new and daring exercise of their own ability. Continual intervention, with its implied lack of confidence, can lead to strong towers at the expense of self-confidence and high levels of aspiration.

Expectation, Aspiration, and Performance

While achievement motivation establishes itself at an early age, it continues to develop throughout the school years as teacher and peer group expectations begin to show their influence. In one well-known study, elementary school teachers were told that their class had been given a special test, and that some of the children had scores indicating that they had unusual potential which was about to "bloom" shortly. (None of this was true, and no such test even exists.) The teachers later claimed that they did not treat these children any differently, nor that they could even recall who was on the "bloomers" list. Tracing the performance of the two groups, however, showed startling differences. Among the differences was an increase in the IQ test scores for the children in the "blooming" group!

Rosenthal and Jacobsen (1968), who conducted this study, interpreted these results as showing that the erroneous information led the teachers to higher expectations for the "blooming" children. This was unconsciously translated into a feeling of greater respect for them, and the feeling that more could be expected from them. The children, equally without awareness, fell into this role and worked to live up to these expectations. Although not without criticism (cf. Snow, 1969; Rosenthal, 1970), this study illustrates well the important influence of expectations on level of aspiration and performance. This is an important issue, and one which we will pursue further in Chapter 13.

The study of achievement motivation, its influence on performance, and the history of its development, is still a subject of ongoing research. Many questions remain to be answered. Among them are important investigations into the possibility of culturally determined differences between the achievement histories of male and female children, and their later attitudes toward success (Stein & Bailey, 1973; Alper, 1973). We can add to this the puzzling tendency of parents to show generally higher achievement expectations for firstborn children than for later ones, with a concomitant effect on actual later school achievement (Adams & Phillips, 1972).

Achievement motivation, however, like those needs which are satisfied by the short-term external rewards of food and special privileges, remains an important source of motivation. In the following section we will look at the history of psychology's search for a single "theory of reward" which might, in principle, encompass all forms of motivation for learning.

SUMMARY

Motivated behavior was defined as any behavior or learning which is encouraged by specific needs, and is directed toward the attainment of specific goals. Two general sources of incentive were described.

Extrinsic reward refers to systems of reward or sanctions imposed by others to motivate performance. Such sources would include tangible rewards, social approval, and peer group influence.

Intrinsic reward refers to the satisfaction of more enduring sources of motivation which come from within the individual. These include identification, competence needs, and achievement motivation.

Achievement motivation has had good success in predicting individuals' rate of learning, level of performance, and levels of aspiration. Low levels of achievement motivation can result in poor performance even in persons of superior ability. On the other hand, very high achievement needs can cause persons to set their goals too high, such that quite successful performance is perceived by them as a failure.

Toward a Theory of Reward: The Biological Perspective

We have pointed to the very different character of extrinsic rewards such as gaining food or money for good performance, versus intrinsic reward, such as the satisfaction of achievement needs, where success is its own reward. Extrinsic rewards are short-term and situational; intrinsic rewards come from within the individual and represent the satisfaction of sustaining drives independent of any outward signs of material gain.

On the outer hand, both sources of reward have much in common. They both result from individual needs, and both reward learning to the extent that the learning produces a satisfaction of these needs. For this reason, psychologists from the very beginning began an inevitable search for a single theory of reward which would hopefully capture the essense of all forms of motivation.

Some of the earliest attempts to understand motivation for learning were delightfully circular. Learning, it was said, occurs whenever it results in a desirable outcome. For example, food, money, and "achievement" are all desirable outcomes, and hence they serve as rewards for learning. How does one define a desirable outcome? A "desirable outcome" is anything which motivates learning.

On one level, this is obviously true. As an explanation of reward and motivation for learning, however, it begins to mean progressively less the more one looks at it. First, we have the problem of defining a reward, or "desirable outcome," beyond the circularity of "anything which produces learning." Second, we must ask whether all intrinsic and extrinsic sources of reward are separable, or whether some sources of reward derive from others. (A third question will be postponed until Chapter 5: the question of whether reward is necessary for the learning itself, or whether its value lies in motivating the individual to perform the correct response once it is learned.)

THE PRINCIPLE OF HOMEOSTASIS

Theories are inevitably a product of the theoretician, and it happened, perhaps as nothing more than a historical accident, that the early students of motivation were drawn from the biological sciences. Psychology and sociology did not exist with the influence they have today, and whatever contributions philosophy could have made to the subject went largely unappreciated. The study of motivation, in other words, began with a distinctly "biological" perspective, and one which colored the thinking and research in the field for decades.

The experimental analysis of motivation began in the 1920s with Richter's (1922, 1927) view that all behavior, animal and human, was "driven" by various biological needs. Motivation, he believed, could be best understood as a "homeostatic" process (Gross, 1968, pg. 91).

Homeostasis refers to any physiological process which maintains the organism in internal balance. Examples in biology are numerous. When body temperature drops, blood vessels on the skin surface contract, which produces a warming effect. Similarly, a rise in body temperature causes a dilation of blood vessels which increases heat loss. Reflexive shivering and perspiration also respectively raise and lower body temperature to follow changing conditions.

Richter saw motivation as a homeostatic process in the sense that the body's drives for food, water, sleep, and other biological necessities also came and went to satisfy the organism's need for internal balance. When hungry, we must eat until the hunger drive is satisfied. During this period, motivation is high. Once the hunger drive has been reduced, motivation drops and remains low until the organism is again in need of food. At this point the hunger drive returns in full strength, and the level of motivation is again high. Motivation could thus be seen in terms of biological needs, and "reward" could be defined in terms of their satisfaction.

The budding field of psychology began to speak increasingly of the *motivation cycle*. Deprivation of a biological need, such as food or water, would lead to a *drive-state* (hunger or thirst) which, in turn, "motivated" activity directed toward attaining the appropriate *goal* (food or water). Goal attainment, and the *drive-reduction* which followed, seemed an adequate definition of reward. At this point the organism's level of motivation would diminish until a period of food or water deprivation caused the cycle to begin anew. The basic elements of the motivation cycle are diagrammed in Figure 3.4.

It remained only for psychology to translate human needs into various "drives," and to define "reward" as drive-reduction.

THE DRIVE-REDUCTION THEORY OF REINFORCEMENT

At the time the homeostatic theory of motivation began to attract increasing interest, the field of learning theory was largely mired in the circularity of the "reward-as-pleasure" view of motivation. E. L. Thorndike (1911), one of the pioneers of learning theory, had already published some of the first studies of trial-and-error learning in lower animals. In a view sometimes referred to as "behavioral hedonism," Thorndike proposed that any response followed by "pleasurable" or "satisfying" consequences would be repeatedly performed, while those which were not would diminish.

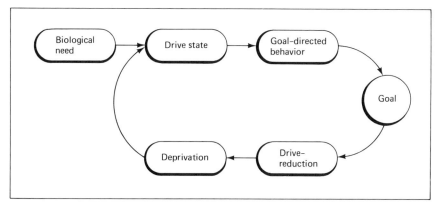

Figure 3.4   The Motivation Cycle. The sequence begins with some basic need (e.g. food). Deprivation leads to a state of drive (hunger) in the organism who then performs some response to obtain the goal (food). After some period of deprivation, the cycle begins again.

Thorndike saw such "satisfying consequences" as indispensible to the learning process, referring to it as the *law of effect:* reward, technically referred to as *reinforcement,* was defined as a "pleasurable consequence," and only rewarded events would be learned. (See Chapter 5 for a fuller discussion of Thorndike's ideas.)

The basic elements for a unified theory of motivation and reward thus seemed to be at hand. From Thorndike's work came the importance of reward (reinforcement) for learning, and from the homeostatic theory came the definition of reward as the reduction of biological drives, or, by analogy, the satisfaction of learned drives. It fell to Clark Hull (1943), a Yale psychologist, to unite the two views in his *drive-reduction theory of reinforcement.* These were its main principles:

1. Reinforcement, would be substituted for "reward," and would include both positive consequences, such as food (positive reinforcement), or learning motivated by a desire to avoid negative consequences, such as pain (negative reinforcement).
2. Stimuli will act as a reward (positive reinforcement) to the extent that they satisfy biological needs, thus reducing their attendant drive-states.
3. Learned drives, such as the desire for money or status, draw their reinforcing properties from their association with the reduction of biological drives in the indiviual's past experience.
4. The presence of drive-reducing reinforcement, whether biological or learned, is necessary for initial learning, and later, to motivate performance of the learned behavior.
5. The stronger the motivating drive (e.g., hours of deprivation from food or water), the greater will be the reward value of the drive-reducing stimuli.

Throughout the 1940s and 1950s, lower animals, such as rats, became the primary test vehicles for the study of motivation and learning. There were two understandable reasons for this. First, the biological orientation of the drive-reduction theory assumed that the ultimate explanation of motivation and drive would lie in principles so basic as to encompass all living organisms. Thus, finding parallels between man and rat would only serve to strengthen the theory. The second reason was more pragmatic. A lower animal, such as a rat, it was argued, is no more or less driven by its various motivational states than the human. It is just that the rat's drives are easier to see. If a hungry rat is given a choice between eating and attending a psychology lecture, it will always choose to eat. The behavior of the hungry student is less predictable. Thus, principles derived from studies of lower animals might serve as a simplified model of human motivation whose complexities made it difficult to study.

There was an obvious risk in this approach. No one would doubt that both rats and humans can be "driven" by hunger or thirst, or that these drives are fundamentally similar in both. The risk did not center on the possibility that animals and humans do not share many of the same drives. It centered on the possibility that homeostatic drives form only a very small part of human motivation. Thus, the facts might be correct, but the entire weight of the emphasis might be wrong.

A typical experiment of the 1940s, however, illustrates the ease with which motivational studies can be conducted with lower animals, and the intuitive reasonableness of most of their findings. This particular study was conducted to investigate the effects of the strength of a hunger drive on behavior by depriving animals of food for various lengths of time (Perin, 1942).

In the initial stage of the experiment, a group of rats were taught to press a lever in their cage by being rewarded with food every time they accidentally pressed it. This, incidentally, is a very easy task for rats to learn, especially when they are hungry. The test came when the trained rats were now removed from the cage and kept in isolation without food for either 3 hours or 22 hours. Following this deprivation period they were then returned to the cage for the main part of the experiment. The lever was still there, but this time no food would be delivered when it was pressed. The question Perin asked, was how long the hungry rats, and the very hungry rats, would continue to press the lever even though it brought them no food.

Figure 3.5 shows the results for hungry rats (3 hours of deprivation) and for very hungry rats (22 hours of deprivation) who had received various numbers of rewarded training sessions in the initial stage of the experiment. The results were clear. Regardless of the number of initial training sessions, the hungrier rats continued to work at pressing the lever far longer before giving up than the less hungry rats.

The hunger drive in rats is an important one, and without it food offers virtually no incentive for performance. For example, when Koch and Daniel (1945) repeated Perin's experiment with well-fed, satiated rats, some ignored the lever completely when returned to the cage, while others gave the lever only a few desultory taps before quitting. These general findings on drive-strength and motivation have been confirmed with lower animals in a variety of learning tasks (cf. Brown, 1961).

Classification of Drives

Before we turn to various tests of the drive-reduction theory, we should briefly remind ourselves of the categories of human and animal drives. Some drives are obviously learned, such as the motivating value of money, while others are just as obviously innate, such as the need for food. Indeed, the initial attempts to classify drives were built on just this obvious a level. All human and animal drives were classified either as *primary drives*, which were unlearned drives related to biological tissue needs (such as hunger or thirst), or as *secondary drives*, which might potentially have very strong

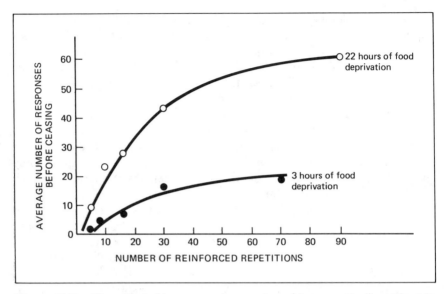

Figure 3.5   The effect of hunger on the number of times a rat will continue to press a lever even though food is no longer delivered when the lever is pressed. (*Source:* C. T. Perin, Behavior potentiality as a joint function of the amount of training and the degree of hunger at the time of extinction. *Journal of Experimental Psychology*, 1942, 30: fig. 4, pg. 101. Copyright 1942 by the American Psychological Association. Reprinted by permission.)

motivating value, but which were, themselves, a product of learning (Hull, 1943). A drive was usually assumed to be learned if it differed from culture to culture, or if it varied in strength from one person to another. The variable "drive" for membership in a country club, for example, perfectly fits this picture.

This simple dichotomy between primary and secondary drives became somewhat complicated over the years when psychologists began to study motivations which did not appear to fall unambiguously into either category. Some psychologists said they were learned, others said they were surely innate. In no way, however, did they directly satisfy the tissue needs of the body. Two notable examples were the drives of love or affection (cf. Bowlby, 1958; Harlow & Zimmerman, 1959) and of aggression (cf. Lorenz, 1966; Berkowitz, 1969).

A Tripartite Classification of Drives

The trend today is toward a three part classification of human and animal drives. These are (1) the unlearned, *biological drives*, (2) unlearned *general drives*, and (3) purely *learned drives*.

1. THE BIOLOGICAL DRIVES. The classification of the biological drives has changed little since the days of Hull. These remain drives which are thought to be unlearned, inborn needs necessary for the biological survival of the organism. Although there are many of them, the most noticeable ones for human and animal motivation are the drives of *hunger, thirst, sex, sleep,* and *pain avoidance.* All of these can be used as effective rewards for learning in deprived animals.

2. THE GENERAL DRIVES. The general drives are also thought to be inborn needs common to many animals and to humans. They differ from the biological drives in that they do not relate directly to bodily tissue needs as do the biological drives. Two examples of commonly accepted general drives should illustrate their character.

Curiosity. Numerous studies have postulated *curiosity,* or a need to explore the environment, as one example of a general drive. Exploratory behavior can be observed in many animals (and children) as they probe and poke the environment, manipulate objects they encounter, and show special interest in novel or unexpected stimuli (Berlyne, 1966; Halliday, 1968). Monkeys, for example, will spend hours manipulating puzzles, peering through windows, and looking into corner cupboards very much in the manner of human children. Furthermore, this "curiosity" drive can be used effectively to motivate learning, as when Butler (1953) showed that rhesus monkeys will learn to press a correctly colored lever for the sole reward of gaining a 30-second peek through a window at the activity outside their cages (the activity being psychologists peeking in at the monkeys). Indeed, many writers have argued that curiosity, or the need to explore the environment, may alone account for much of the motivation for learning in both baby monkeys and baby humans (cf. Butler, 1954).

Affection and contact-comfort. The world of psychology was rudely shaken some years ago when research with primates suggested that "love," or something like it, may be an unlearned, unborn, general drive. For the reader who has always assumed this to be so, we hasten to explain that learning theory had traditionally viewed love, affection, or the comfort of human contact, as a *learned* drive which arises through the infant's association of the feelings of comfort after being fed with the presence of the parent who is always there during feeding. That is, the satisfaction of the hunger drive became associated with the mother (or father) who was the instrument of this satisfaction.

Exactly how this early form of "love" might in turn develop into other, more subtle forms of love, remained something of a mystery. The basic principle of affection as a learned drive, however, was taken as a firm article of faith. Over the years, more careful studies of infants' interactions with their parents and other adults has placed a greater emphasis on the availability of stimulation and attention to affectional attachment, and less of an emphasis on the satisfaction of purely biological needs. In other words, there may be a general need on the part of infants to be near other people, regardless of the presence or absence of feeding care (cf. Schaffer & Emerson, 1964).

This research was largely instigated by a series of studies conducted in the 1950s which showed that infant monkeys raised in isolation would spend hours clinging to a soft, padded dummy in favor of a stiff wire frame that was fitted with a nursing bottle. Although the monkeys would go to the wire frame for feeding, when frightened, it was to the soft, cuddly form that they would run (Harlow & Zimmerman, 1959). To Harlow and his colleagues, the "contact-comfort" supplied by the padded, more monkeylike form, satisfied an unlearned drive which was equal in strength to the need for food.

Among the other general drives which have been postulated over the years are a need for physical activity (Gross, 1968), the previously mentioned need for "task mastery" or "competence" (White, 1959), and a need for sensory stimulation and variety in sensory experience (Bexton, Heron & Scott, 1954; Heron, Doane & Scott, 1956; Brownfield, 1965).

3. LEARNED DRIVES. From the very beginning, learning theory distinguished between stimuli which satisfy the primary biological drives and stimuli which satisfy learned drives. These two forms of reward were referred to respectively as *primary reinforcement* and *secondary reinforcement.*

The use of the term *secondary* was not intended to imply that learned drives are necessarily weaker than unlearned ones, or that secondary reinforcers have less motivational value than primary reinforcers. In human learning, it is frequently just the opposite. Learned drives were called secondary drives only because of the traditional belief that they derived either directly or indirectly from their past association with primary drives and primary reinforcement.

For example, at some point in the lifetime of an individual, money (secondary reinforcement) may have acquired its motivational value through direct association with the food or physical security (primary reinforcement) it can be used to obtain. Often, however, such secondary rewards begin to acquire reinforcing properties quite independent of these early associations. Indeed, they can appear to transcend them. The often misquoted, "Money is the root of all evil," which should read, "The *love* of money is the root of all evil," tells the story.

Secondary reinforcement can be defined as the acquisition by a neutral stimulus of reward value through learning. While more typical of humans than of lower animals, it is certainly not a uniquely human trait. Secondary reinforcement can be demonstrated in rats, pigeons, and a host of other creatures.

In a classic study of its kind, Wolfe (1936) exposed to the world a chimpanzee who had been taught the value of money. The essential feature of secondary reinforcement is the repeated association of a neutral stimulus with some primary goal. In this case, the chimp was given poker chips and taught, through trial and error, to insert them into the slot of a mechanical vending machine which produced a supply of grapes from a chute at the bottom. This was learning through primary reinforcement.

Once this operation became routine, Wolfe found that the poker chips themselves seemed to have acquired a reward value of their own. The chimp could now be given a variety of learning tasks which he would perform for the sole reward of poker chips, even when they could not immediately be exchanged for food. To further the analogy, poker chips of different colors could be exchanged, or "spent," to obtain different primary reinforcers: a red chip could be exchanged for food, a blue chip for water, and a white one to gain exercise. While the chimp continued to revere all of the chips, at any one time he worked the hardest to obtain a chip which could be exchanged for the satisfaction of his most pressing immediate need.

Many writers have viewed more and more abstract rewards as reflecting chains of more and more remote associations to the primary drives. Sources of motivation as abstract as achievement motivation, they argue, might be traceable in principle back through their association with status to security, to food, or to some other biological need.

This notion of a continuity in motivation theory remained as much a statement of belief as an established fact. Somehow, the concept of reinforcement seems to take a quantum leap when we move from animals to humans, and from primary to secondary motivations. The link between primary and secondary reinforcement, as argued in Hull's drive-reduction theory, may underlie all human motivation. But if it does, the links are surely tenuous ones. Thorndike's law of effect defined reinforcement in terms of pleasure, and Hull defined pleasure in terms of drive reduction. We need only look to some of the more exotic forms of human behavior, such as sadomasochism, to know that we will be in serious trouble with any too naive or simplistic notion of "pleasure."

SOME WRINKLES IN DRIVE-REDUCTION

The drive-reduction theory of reinforcement has lost much of the freshness it once had, and it has had more than its share of criticism. To some, the theory is not so much incorrect as limited in its applicability to human motivation. To others, the theory itself has flaws, even when applied to primary drives in lower animals.

When Is a Reward Not a Reward?: Distributive Justice

There is a peril in ignoring individual differences in human motivation. Here is just one example, cited by Lefrancois (1972, pg. 98). Imagine a child who is ordinarily very poor at spelling and who, in spite of considerable effort, rarely passes classroom spelling tests. One day the teacher advises the child to try something special, such as using mnemonics, or taking a series of practice tests at home.[1] On the day of the next spelling test the child receives an unusually high test score of 80 percent. The good test score supplies positive reinforcement and we can expect the child to continue trying these special exercises.

Now contrast this pupil with another one who ordinarily gets scores of 95 or 100 percent with minimal effort. This child also decides to take the special steps outlined by the teacher. Although these are good procedures for even a good speller, something goes wrong on the day of the next test, and this child receives an unusually low score: the same 80 percent as the first child. For one child, 80 percent is a reward; for the other, it is not. The principle here is a simple one, which relates to differences in aspiration level and expectation: the value of a reward is determined as much by past experience and future expectation, as it is by any absolute value in an objective sense.

The subjective nature of reward appears in the general principle of *distributive justice* in personal satisfaction (Homans, 1961). The value of a reward is ordinarily determined by its magnitude relative to what a person expects to receive, or relative to what he or she perceives others as receiving. Viewed in this light, many seemingly inconsistent findings become understandable.[2]

A very well-known study many years ago produced the surprising finding that military policemen had generally greater satisfaction with their system of promotion than air force personnel, even though the rate of promotion was much higher in the air force. Homans saw this apparent paradox in terms of distributive justice.

Now if there is much promotion in a particular branch of the service, some men will see many of their fellows promoted while they themselves are passed over, and this will lead them to ask whether the promotions are just and whether sufficient attention has been paid to their own abilities. It will raise the question of distributive justice—justice in the distribution of rewards among men and justice . . . is a principle ingredient of satisfaction.

[1] *Mnemonics* are specially constructed memory aids, such as the use of rhymes, associations, or imagery. These techniques will be more fully discussed in Chapter 11.
[2] Something analogous to distributive justice can also be observed in lower animals when a reward is suddenly reduced in the course of a learning experiment. Performance invariably drops precipitously, suggesting that expectations play no less a role in rat motivation than in human motivation. This will be discussed in Chapter 5 under the topic of *reinforcement contrast*.

In a branch like the Military Police, on the other hand, where there has been very little promotion, the soldiers are much less apt to compare their fate with that of others and so to raise the question of justice (Homans, 1961, pg. 270).

Distributive justice, for example, may account for unexpected anger in an employee who is informed of a generous salary increase as a reward for his or her good service. The employer may never discover that the lack of enthusiasm rested on the employee's expectation of an even larger raise or on a perhaps erroneous belief that less capable people were receiving the same raise. It is at this point that one can sympathize with those pragmatic psychologists who, from time to time, have defined reward—not totally in jest—as "anything that is rewarding."

Cognitive Control of Biological States

Another problem facing an easy extension of the drive-reduction theory to human motivation is the fact that biological drives are subject to strong psychological control. There are numerous obvious instances of this, such as persons who will miss a meal in spite of hunger or go without sleep even though tired. It is the less obvious cases of cognitive control of biological states, however, that raise the greatest problems in generalizing from any theory based too heavily on biological needs.

Zimbardo (1969, pg. 5) has observed with some humor that the *placebo* (an inactive substance having only the appearance of being medicine) may be one of the more effective drugs ever produced by modern pharmaceutical laboratories. While this may be an exaggeration, Zimbardo is able to cite numerous studies which have shown the administration of a placebo, thought by the patient to be medication, to bring about a significant reduction in pain in as many as 27 percent of patients suffering from symptoms as varied as multiple sclerosis, migraine headaches, colds, postoperative pain, rheumatism, and constipation.

Not only can suggestion cause an inert substance to have physical effects, it can also reverse the ordinary pharmacological effects of some medicines. Many women in about the fourth week of pregnancy suffer from a tendency to early morning nausea, sometimes called "morning sickness." Ipecac is a mixture which is ordinarily used to induce vomiting after accidental poisoning. Hard as it may be to believe, when a group of women were given ipecac, and told it was a medicine to settle their stomachs, some actually reported it to help overcome their early morning nausea! (Zimbardo, 1969).

Although the ipecac study is an extreme case, there have been numerous systematic demonstrations of strong subjective components to the primary drives of hunger (Schachter, 1971a), thirst (Brehm, 1962), and pain (Zimbardo, Cohen, Weisenberg, Dworkin & Firestone, 1969).

The principle of drive-reduction, in other words, may be on stronger footings than its application in practice to human needs.

Primary Drives in Animals

Drive-reduction theory may have been a good beginning to the study of reinforcement and motivation, but it has had its critics even from within the ranks of students of animal behavior.

One implication of Hull's concept of drive was that it was a generalized state of tension, such that a hungry rat should more actively press a lever if, for example, it is also thirsty or frightened. While studies such as Perin's (1942) did support the notion of a generalized drive-state, more recent studies have shown that the summation of different sources of drives does not always occur (Bolles, 1975a). This criticism of Hull's theory is perhaps a subtle one. The most convincing attack on drive-reduction theory, however, came with demonstrations of reinforcement in the absence of drive-reduction.

It is fairly simple to teach a rat to run down the length of a *T*-shaped maze and to turn either to the right or to the left to find food. Like lever pressing, it is especially easy if the rat is especially hungry. This simple apparatus became one of the common testing grounds for the drive-reduction theory.

In one study which offered partial support for the theory, rats were taught to choose one arm of the maze with a very peculiar form of "reward." This study amply illustrates why learning theorists tended to use the neutral term "reinforcement" instead of the word "reward" with its everyday connotation of a desirable object.

In this experiment, conducted by Miller and Kessen (1952), rats choosing the correct goal arm of the maze did not receive food in the ordinary manner. Instead, each correct response was followed by an injection of milk directly into the rats' stomachs. The milk would, of course, reduce the hunger drive, even though the rats could not taste the milk or have any other sensation of being fed. Consistent with Hull's drive-reduction theory, the rats nevertheless learned to take the correct path through the maze for this reinforcement. A control group of rats receiving identical injections of nonnutritive saline into the stomach, which did not reduce the hunger drive, failed to learn the maze.

There was a wrinkle to the Miller and Kessen experiment, however; one which suggested that biological drive-reduction alone is not the complete answer to reinforcement. The fastest learning was accomplished by a third group of rats who were allowed to drink milk in the ordinary way when they chose the correct goal arm.

Clearly, drive-reduction alone can reinforce learning. At the same time, the activity of drinking—the taste of the milk, the feeling of the milk in the mouth, and so forth—seemed to have an additional reinforcing property of its own. It could be that drive-reduction was still the basis of reinforcement, and that the activity of drinking had acquired some reward value because of its past association with drive-reduction. This would fit the traditional picture of secondary reinforcement.

On the other hand, many psychologists came to question whether some stimuli or activities might not be inherently reinforcing even when they are unrelated to the reduction of the primary drives. Sheffield and Roby (1950), for example, found that rats will readily learn a maze if allowed to drink only a sweet-tasting, nonnutritive saccharine solution as a reward. Subsequent studies showed that the taste of a liquid reward can be quite important to a rat: the sweeter the taste, the faster will be the learning (Kraeling, 1961).

The results of these and other experiments gave rise to the *stimulus theory* of reinforcement, which suggests that some stimuli may be inherently reinforcing even though they are not directly involved in drive-reduction (Guttman, 1953). To complete the picture, other psychologists proposed a *response theory* of reinforcement which suggested that strong response tendencies in organisms can themselves reinforce the performance of still other responses (Premack, 1965; Sawisch & Denny, 1973).

"Pleasure Centers" in the Brain?

Motivation research took an interesting turn some years ago with the accidental discovery that direct electrical stimulation to certain parts of a rat's brain (such as the lateral hypothalamus) seems to mimic the effects ordinarily associated with reward. At least it was the case that rats would learn to press a lever, and to keep pressing it, so long as it was followed by such electrical stimulation delivered through electrodes planted deep within the brain (Olds & Milner, 1954; Olds, 1962; Olds & Olds, 1965).

The *hypothalamus* is a structure located in the central portion of the interior of the brain, and we have known for some time that it is important to the regulation of food intake (see Figure 3.9 for its location). For example, patients whose hypothalamus has been disturbed because of a brain tumor or accidental injury frequently overeat to the point where their general health becomes threatened. Similarly, in research with lower animals, electrical stimulation of different areas of the hypothalamus can cause an animal to stop eating even though it is still hungry or to begin eating even though it is already satiated with food (Hoebel & Teitelbaum, 1962).

Although the complete function of the hypothalamus is not yet fully known, more recent work has suggested its critical importance to motivation in general, beyond simply the regulation of feeding behavior (cf. Valenstein, Cox & Kakolewski, 1970; Bergquist, 1972).

The accidental discovery referred to above occurred when Olds and his colleagues were using electrical stimulation to explore the functions of various areas of rats' brains. The general technique involves surgically implanting a microscopically fine wire electrode into an animal's brain and delivering a low voltage electric current to stimulate the general area in which the electrode is located. By inserting the electrode into different brain areas, and observing the effects on behavior, one can attempt to "map" the functional areas of the brain. (See Chapter 12 for a further discussion of this and other "mapping" techniques.)

It was in the course of this work that Olds observed that rats seemed to derive some "pleasure" from stimulation to certain areas in and around the hypothalamus; he noticed that the rats seemed to want to stay in that area of the cage they happened to be in when the hypothalamus was stimulated. This discovery led to a series of more controlled experiments to investigate the hypothalamus as a possible "pleasure center" in the brain.

In the early experiments, a rat was placed in a small, isolated chamber with bare walls and no visual or sound distractions. The only noticeable feature of the rat-sized room was a small lever protruding from one wall. This miniature environment is a favorite one for the study of animal learning, except that a food reward is usually delivered whenever the animal happens to press the lever. In this case, however, Olds had the lever connected to a power source which delivered mild electrical stimulation through an electrode surgically implanted in the hypothalamic region of the rat's brain. Whenever the rat pressed the lever, it automatically supplied self-stimulation to its own brain (see Figure 3.6).

The apparatus may sound complicated, but the results were straightforward. Not only will a rat quickly learn to press the lever to receive the electrical stimulation, but it will do so with extraordinary incentive. Under these conditions, rats have been known to continually press a lever at rates exceeding several thousand per hour for periods as long as 24 hours, until they drop from exhaustion (Olds, 1958; Olds, Travis & Schwing, 1960). Indeed, so rewarding is stimulation to this one part of the animal's brain, that they will cross an electrified grid in order to reach the lever (Olds, 1961), and, given a choice between brain stimulation and food, even very hungry rats will often choose the brain stimulation (Routtenberg & Lindy, 1965).

We should emphasize that this effect is found only with stimulation to this one area of the brain. Repeating these experiments with electrodes implanted in other areas fails to produce any incentive for learning, while stimulation to some areas seems to be actively aversive; animals will learn to press a lever if it terminates the stimulation (Delgado, Roberts & Miller, 1954).

Have we discovered the "pleasure center" of the brain, that part of the brain which is normally activated when drive-reducing reinforcement is present? In most respects, the results of these studies do correspond with the normal effects of reinforcement. In one important respect, however,

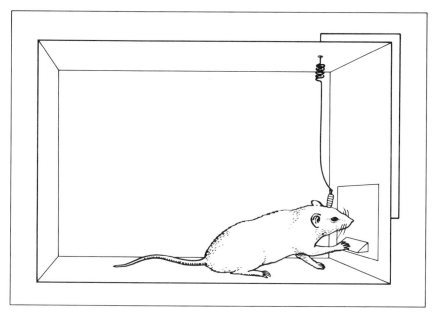

Figure 3.6   Self-stimulation of electric current to the *hypothalamus* serving as a reinforcement for bar pressing by a rat.

they do not. As we know, a hungry animal will eat until it is satiated, and then it will stop eating. When the hunger drive is eliminated, food ceases to be reinforcing, and it will not be reinforcing again until some period of deprivation has elapsed and the animal is again hungry.

The studies of self-stimulation in which animals will press a lever until exhausted suggested that this "pleasure center" does not seem to satiate! If pressing the lever for electrical stimulation was motivated by a drive, it was a drive which did not, as it were, seem to "reduce." To Olds, these results were inconsistent with the drive-reduction theory, at least as it was presented by Hull. At the same time, such studies have brought us closer to understanding the physiological basis of motivation, and they have added to our general knowledge of brain function in learning.

We might close this discussion by mentioning that similar effects are occasionally reported following electrical stimulation to the human brain (Sem-Jacobson, 1959; Heath & Mickle, 1960; Delgado & Hamlin, 1960). One such report involved patients who had received electrical stimulation to the brain in the course of neurosurgery for Parkinson's disease. Although the patients found it difficult to describe their subjective feelings following their brain stimulation, it seemed to be definitely "pleasurable." What they described were unspecifiable "good feelings" which they found intriguingly difficult to relate to ordinary mental experiences (Sem-Jacobson & Torkildsen, 1960).

THE STATUS OF PRIMARY DRIVES IN MOTIVATION

The body's need for the reduction of its primary, biological drives is not in question. On the contrary, we become increasingly impressed with how well the body can "know" its biological needs. In a classic study of its kind, Davis (1939) allowed human infants from the ages of 6 to 11 months free access to a variety of different raw and cooked foods without controlling their choice of what they would eat. While the short-run choices of the infants were often horrifying, over the long run their self-selected diet was virtually as good as any which might have been scientifically planned by a dietician.

At the same time, the drive-reduction theory cannot explain all human (or animal) motivation. We know, for example, how a hunger drive can be aroused in an otherwise satiated person by the sight or smell of a favorite food, not to mention our common penchant for sweet-tasting "junk" foods which have minimal nutritive value. In this regard, we should mention that the foods made available to the infants in Davis' study were all high-nutrition wholesome foods. Repeating that experiment with artifically flavored, low-nutritional foods, such as those available to children today, as possible selections might have produced very different, and very disastrous, results.

We are also aware that, at least for many adults, the desire for food is often determined as much by contextual factors, such as the mere presence of food, or the time of the day (even when the clock is made to be purposely incorrect), as it is on the basis of true tissue needs. Indeed, this is especially true of persons who are already overweight and should, for their biological well-being, eat even less (cf. Nisbett, 1968; Schachter, 1971b).

Expert opinion on Hull's early theory of drive-reduction is mixed. On the one hand, virtually every specific prediction about behavior and drive made by Hull has now been shown to be wrong (cf. Bolles, 1975b, pg. 14). On the other hand, the general principle of drive-reduction continues to have much to say, provided, as Miller (1957) has suggested, that "drive" is not tied as closely to purely biological needs as Hull envisaged it. For example, the concept of drive, and drive-reduction, can remain valuable to the description of motivation for learning, provided one extends the notion of "drive" to include learned sources of motivation, and motivation as abstract as achievement needs (cf. Brown, 1961).

Thus, the basic concept of drive-reduction, with all its flaws and wrinkles, does capture at least the essence of motivation, and it began as a good foundation on which to build our modern notions of reward. As we return again to uniquely human motivation, however, the role of learned drives and motives takes on increasing importance. As the picture becomes more complex, it also becomes more interesting.

SUMMARY

The motivation cycle is a common way of describing the continual influence of drive-reducing stimuli as sources of motivation for learning. The cycle begins with an unfulfilled biological need. A period of deprivation produces a drive-state within the organism which will only be satisfied by a response which results in the attainment of the needed goal. This, in turn, leads to the rewarding state of drive-reduction. After a period of deprivation, the drive is again aroused, and the cycle begins anew.

The notions underlying the motivation cycle were embodied in the drive-reduction theory of reinforcement, which defined "reward" in learning as the reduction of a biological drive (or, potentially, a learned drive). Later research offered alternatives and supplements to the drive-reduction theory, such as the possibility that some stimuli or responses may be inherently rewarding even though they fail to satisfy any biological needs.

Studies of electrical stimulation of the brains of lower animals, primarily in the area of the hypothalamus, have raised the possibility of a "pleasure center" of the brain which may be that part of the brain which is activated following ordinary drive-reduction, and which might control the "pleasurable feelings" associated with their satisfaction.

As one moves from animal to human behavior, learned drives begin to play an increasingly important role relative to the reduction of biological drives.

Human Needs and Human Motivation

We have seen how the drive-reduction theory postulated that particular needs both goad us into action and guide our activities. These needs, it was said, create a "tension" within us that persists until the needs have been satisfied and the tension subsides. This was the basis of reward in learning, and the basis of both human and animal motivation.

While biological drives are universal, they seem to account for a small proportion of human motivation. Further, human needs are always varied, only sometimes predictable, and almost never easy to define. Thus, to the extent that the drive-reduction theory can still serve as a viable base for understanding human motivation, it is only a base on which one must build.

MOTIVATION HIERARCHIES

The attempts to understand distinctly human motivation have been as varied as Freud's psychoanalytic concept of the libido, to Murray (1938), who rejected the relevance of biological drives in human behavior, compiling instead an exhaustive list of social needs which he believed to motivate our activity (e.g., needs for achievement, orderliness, affiliation, endurance, change, helpfulness, and so forth). A critic of both the views of Murray and of Freud was Abraham Maslow (1968, 1970), a psychologist at Brandeis University. While recognizing the diminished role of biological motivation in humans, Maslow also objected to the compilation of long lists of human motives, the length of which would vary simply with the specificity of one's definitions.

To Maslow, the goal of a theory of motivation should be to unite the biological perspective of early motivation theory, with a more "humanistic" appraisal of social motives. To accomplish this goal, he suggested that human motivations are hierarchically based: he argued that some motivations are more basic than others, and that the more basic ones must be satisfied before other forms of motivation begin to operate. In this way, he hoped not merely to classify biological and social needs, but to show how each relates to the others.

In Maslow's view, human needs can be arranged on a *hierarchy*, an ordered sequence in which "higher," more abstract needs, emerge only when the more basic ones have been either fully or partially met. A person's progression up through such a hierarchy can be likened to the experience of a mountain climber negotiating a series of lower-level peaks which increase in height as they approach the summit. The climber becomes aware of each successive peak only when, and if, the previous peaks have been climbed. In Maslow's formulation, the primary, biological needs represented the base of the "mountain," and "self-actualization" represented its summit. Specifically, Maslow envisaged a five-tiered progression as shown in Figure 3.7.

1. Basic Physiological Needs

In common with earlier writers such as Hull, Maslow saw the basic needs as the primary biological drives as we discussed them previously (hunger, thirst, and so forth). He also accepted these as universal drives which are equally present in fundamentally the same form in both humans and lower animals.

If a person is without food, he or she does not think of social power, status, or building memorial monuments. Until this drive is satisfied, all thought is concentrated on food and nothing else. The reason these primary drives seem so unimportant in human behavior, he suggested, is not because they do not exist, but because they are ordinarily already satisfied at least to

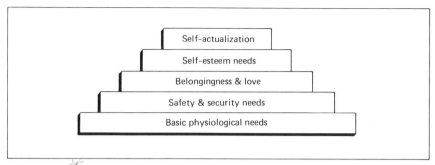

Figure 3.7 Maslow's hierarchy of human motivation shown schematically in the form of a pyramid. The needs at any one level of the pyramid will not come into play until there has been some prior satisfaction of the lower-level needs.

some minimal level. With these needs met, it is only the higher motives on the hierarchy which appear with regularity.

2. Safety and Security Needs

The next higher need on the hierarchy is the drive for security and safety from physical harm and danger. This includes the need for both physical and psychological security. *Safety* was seen as a fundamental need, only one step removed from the biological drives: we need to feel safe from wild animals, extremes of temperature, criminal assault, and so forth. For the child, the safety needs relate to a secure environment which has some degree of predictability and order.

3. Belongingness and Love

Satisfaction of the need for safety and security brings with it the emergence of the need for, and the reward value of, affiliation, love, and a sense of belonging. To Maslow, the need for friendship and group membership was a higher form of security need which, in turn, formed a base from which to pursue even higher goals.

4. Self-esteem Needs

Progression to the fourth level on the hierarchy brings a need for personal achievement and a sense of recognition and approval from others. The rewards at this level are represented by the internal satisfaction which accompanies feelings of self-respect and a feeling of self-worth.

5. Self-actualization

In Maslow's hierarchy, the need for self-actualization was the highest form of human motivation, and it appeared only when and if the more basic needs had been satisfied. The notion of self-actualization is one of the more controversial of Maslow's formulations, and it is certainly the most abstract: "the desire to become more and more what one is, to become everything that one is capable of becoming" (Maslow, 1954, pg. 92).

Interestingly, Maslow came to believe that not all persons will extend themselves to this ultimate search for personal fulfillment, even when their other needs have been met. For some, he felt, the achievement of self-esteem represents the pinnacle of their hierarchy, with perhaps no more than one or two dozen out of three thousand persons showing the signs of independence, self-acceptance, spontaneity, and a sense of purpose, which promises the hope for future self-actualization (Maslow, 1970).

Although Maslow sometimes referred to this hierarchy as a developmental sequence, he did not mean to imply that once the lower needs have been met they are forever replaced by the higher ones. For example, one can think of a recent college graduate who leaves his or her university with ambitions, ideals, and the beginnings of a search for true self-fulfillment. Then comes marriage, children, taxes, and a mortgage. Too easily, one's perspectives can shift to a preoccupation with the basic and security needs, and a loss by default of the higher needs which once seemed so important. "When hunger enters through the door, love flies out the window."

Maslow's theory captured considerable attention, but not because it is easy to prove, or, for that matter, to disprove. Students of management and organizational behavior saw immediate value in his hierarchical view of human motivation (Schein, 1965; Argyris, 1964), and some attempts have been made to apply his notion of self-actualization to the concept of mental health (cf. Knapp, 1965). In Maslow's own mind, however, his hierarchy, and the notion of self-actualization, was only that of a "first stage" investigation, not yet with a "full set of teeth" (Maslow, 1972, pg. 75).

Without this complete "set of teeth," Maslow's hierarchy lacks the specificity necessary for any hope of empirical proof or disproof. It's value lies in the attempt to *organize* human motivation, rather than to simply catalog its varieties. In some ways, it is surprisingly consistent with the earlier thoughts of Thorndike and Hull: individuals will perform in a positive way if that performance leads to the satisfaction of their needs. Perhaps more important, however, is its implication that the traditional studies of learning theory, on the one hand, and personality theory, on the other hand, should no longer continue on separate paths, each ignoring the presence of the other. The future development of motivation theory may well see a productive joining of the two.

PUNISHMENT AND BEHAVIOR

There is a particular reason why our discussion to this point has dealt almost exclusively with the effects of pleasurable or "rewarding" stimuli (*positive reinforcement*). Learning can also be motivated by the desire to escape from some painful or unpleasant stimulus. Technically, we distinguish between two ways in which an aversive stimulus can be used. *Punishment* refers to the application of an aversive stimulus when an undesired behavior is exhibited. *Negative reinforcement* refers to the withdrawal of an aversive stimulus when a desired behavior is exhibited (see Chapter 5 for further discussion).

As we will see later, punishment for incorrect responses often produces faster, and longer lasting, learning than reward for correct responses. This seeming advantage to the use of punishment, however, is far outweighed by its disadvantages and potential for problems.

Punishment can be effective only in those limited situations where all of the alternative behaviors are both readily apparent and readily available to the individual. This is because punishment tells a person only what *not* to do; it does not directly indicate to the person what it is he or she *should* be doing. There are at least three specific consequences of this fact. (1) As noted in our discussion of verbal praise as reinforcement in the classroom, punishment may less indicate the desired behavior than draw attention to the undesired behavior. (2) Punishment for error when the correct solution is not readily apparent can result in levels of emotional upset and stress which are counterproductive to learning. (3) The learning situation can be contaminated by the creation of an unwanted association between the punishment and the punisher, rather than between the punishment and the punished behavior.

Too much anxiety or stress, whatever the cause, can be detrimental to effective learning. One aspect of this is considered in the following section.

MOTIVATION AND AROUSAL

There are many ways to describe the state of a highly motivated learner, as opposed to one who is bored and indifferent. We could speak of the person as being more "alert," as showing better "concentration," or as being more "attentive." All of these terms are in fact different ways to describe a state which is technically known as high arousal. The concept of arousal, a combined interplay between the psychological and physiological state of an individual, has a central place in human motivation, and it plays a critical role in learning efficiency.

Levels of Arousal

Arousal has been defined as the level of awareness or attention of the individual to the environment (Mackworth, 1970, pg. 80). It has also been defined in terms of a dimension of activation of the nervous system, running the range from delirium and coma at the lower end to frenzy and excitement at the upper end. The first definition stresses the psychological state of the individual, while the second one stresses the person's physiological state. The two notions were combined by the British neurologist, Sir Henry Head (1926), who related arousal to "vigilance." "When vigilance is high, mind and body are poised in readiness to respond to any event, external or internal" (Mackworth, 1970).

The terms "boredom" to "excitement" typically define the normal range of wakeful arousal. While ordinarily determined by motivational factors from within the individual, arousal levels are also affected by the physical environment. Arousal is reduced when the temperature is too warm, after long periods devoted to repetitive activities, or following a loss of sleep. Arousal is typically increased with fear, work overload, and noise (Poulton, 1971). It can also be raised and lowered by a bewildering array of modern drugs (see Chapter 12).

Along with each psychological state of mental alertness, there exist concomitant changes in body physiology. The increasing alertness and excitement of high arousal is accompanied by systematic changes in cortical brain wave patterns, blood pressure, pulse rate, respiration rate, skin conductance, and even the diameter of the pupil of the eye (which enlarges with higher levels of arousal) (Mackworth, 1970; Kahneman, 1973).

One cannot maintain high levels of arousal indefinitely, especially in the face of repetitive, tedious activity. A good illustration can be seen in the testing procedures used in research on visual sensitivity for brightness. A volunteer sits alone in a dark room for periods as long as several hours, concentrating on two dim lights. The volunteer's task is to judge the comparative brightness of the two lights by saying whether their intensities are the same or different as their intensities are varied, and the gap between the two is gradually closed. In this way, the experimenter can measure discrimination sensitivity of the human visual system.

One unfortunate byproduct of this technique is the common finding of an apparent deterioration in visual sensitivity over the course of the testing procedure. The cause is fatigue and boredom. The effect is lowered arousal and decreased alertness. In this case, however, the cure is as obvious as the cause. A high level of performance can be maintained over surprisingly long periods simply by giving frequent rest periods, offers of reward, telling the volunteers at intervals how they are performing, or just allowing them to chat with the experimenter between tests (Zwislocki, Maire, Feldman & Rubin, 1958). The effectiveness of these measures illustrates, in a very simple way, the effect of motivation on arousal, and of arousal on levels of performance.

Arousal and Learning

As we saw earlier, the motivation cycle and drive-reduction theory were based on the biological principle of homeostasis: the tendency of all living organisms to maintain an ideal physiological balance in the face of changing conditions. Physical exertion is followed by an increase in heart rate to replenish a weakened system with oxygen. Excessive heat causes perspiration which evaporates on the skin surface to produce a cooling effect. The need-drive-satisfaction model of motivation was homeostatic in exactly the same sense: a way of maintaining an ideal balance in the organism.

There is also an analogous optimal level of arousal for maximally effective and alert functioning, and one which cannot be continuously maintained for extensive periods. A sustained high level of alertness in physically impossible for an entire day, or even for a typical school class period, no matter how interesting the subject matter. We function as well as we do because of three interrelated factors.

The first of these is that the nervous system is constantly in the process of maintaining a balance between our moment-to-moment level of arousal and that which is minimally necessary for effective functioning in the environment. For example, the level of arousal can be adjusted for different forms of activity, such as reading a novel for one's own pleasure versus taking an examination. Each of these can be effectively handled with different levels of arousal and alertness. Second, there is the possibility of motivational control over arousal through the presence of reward, novelty, or our degree of interest in a particular activity. Finally, we can purposely and consciously vary our activities to suit our existing level of arousal. For example, the experienced student will choose different times of the day for different activities and will recognize when it is time to temporarily quit one task which requires maximum alertness for another one which does not.

The Yerkes-Dodson Law

As the individual's state of arousal varies, so too will his or her level of learning efficiency. At the lower end of the arousal continuum is sleep or boredom where little learning is possible. As arousal steadily increases to the middle ranges of mental alertness, we can begin to see a significant improvement in learning performance. Further increases in arousal beyond this point, however, can produce stress, anxiety, and tension. This upper extreme, like the lower one, represents an equally poor condition for learning. It is the condition commonly associated with "blocking" or "going

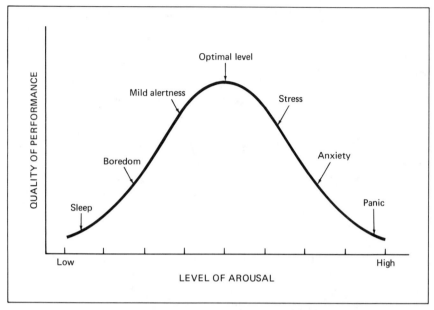

Figure 3.8 Diagrammatic illustration of the Yerkes-Dodson law. The curve shows the theoretical relationship between level of arousal and expected quality of performance.

cold" during an examination when one feels that too much is at stake, or when the fear of failure is too great.

This general relationship between level of arousal and quality of performance is known as the *Yerkes-Dodson law,* which can be described as an inverted U-shaped function such as shown in Figure 3.8 (Yerkes & Dodson, 1908). The principles embodied in the Yerkes-Dodson law can explain the variable effects one often observes with performance under stress.

For example, studies have shown that while a stressful background noise tends to reduce performance when subjects are already working under high incentive, subjects who are initially bored or unmotivated often show better performance under noisy than under quiet conditions (cf. Hockey, 1969). One way to explain such findings is to see the effect of the noise as producing an equal right-hand shift along the arousal scale in Figure 3.8 for both groups. For the unmotivated subjects, starting from a level of low arousal, the noise-induced stress raised their level to that associated with optimal performance. For those already working under high incentive, who began at that position, the same incremental shift produced by the stressful noise raised their arousal level to the point marked by "stress" and "anxiety." The result for this group was a loss in efficiency.

Interestingly, the Yerkes-Dodson law was initially derived from simple experiments with mice, in which it was found that their learning was facilitated when they were "excited" by mild electric shock, but that it began to deteriorate as the intensity of the shock was further increased. While perhaps a modest beginning, the principle was subsequently shown to hold for a variety of learning situations when humans were substituted for mice, and emotional tension and anxiety was substituted for electric shock (cf. Broadhurst, 1957; Stennett, 1957; Kahneman, 1973).

The Reticular Activating System

The regulation of arousal can be seen as analogous to the homeostatic principle of an ordinary home central heating system, where the thermostat operates to "excite" the furnace when the temperature drops and to "suppress" the furnace when the temperature rises above the desired level. The result is the maintenace of a fairly constant, optimal temperature level.

If arousal operates on a similar homeostatic principle, we are bound to ask first, what mechanism in the brain corresponds to the "thermostat," and second, what factors regulate its optimal setting?

There is considerable evidence that the *reticular formation*, sometimes called the *reticular activating system* (RAS), located in the lower portions of the interior of the brain, has the function of regulating arousal level of the cortex (French, 1957; Berlyne, 1960; Hebron, 1966). Figure 3.9 shows a sketch of the interior of the brain indicating the location of the RAS. Also shown is the previously mentioned hypothalamus, with its important function for motivation and drive-satisfaction.

Current views see the brain as ordinarily in a low state of arousal until it is activated by nerve impulses from the RAS. Whether or not this activation occurs depends on, among other things, the novelty or interest of the stimulus. That is, if the stimulus is novel or unexpected, the RAS activates the cortex to a level of alertness and attention which produces that "readiness to respond" we referred to earlier. If the information is of low interest, the impulses from the RAS are blocked from reaching the cortex and the brain remains unaroused (Sokolov, 1963).

If the RAS is analogous to the "thermostat," what regulates its setting to the optimal level? As we have seen, novelty of a stimulus is one factor. To this we must also add the presence of external reward and the operation of intrinsic motivation. With each observable, behavioral difference in level of arousal, there are corresponding changes throughout the nervous system that produce the previously mentioned effects on heart rate, blood pressure, and so forth. It is when the brain is in a high state of arousal that perception is heightened, and clarity of thought and rapidity of learning are at their greatest. This produces an increase in the ability to concentrate and to "take in" new information, which, in turn, can potentially further increase the level of motivation and arousal. Readers interested in the physiology of

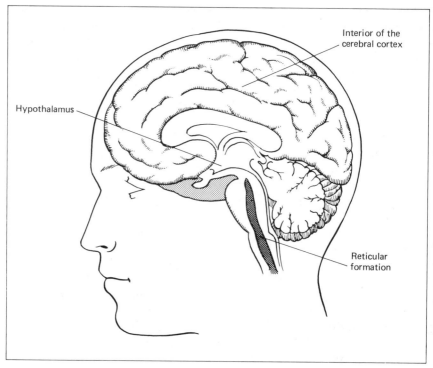

Figure 3.9   Interior cross-section of the human brain showing the location of the *reticular formation,* important to cortical arousal, and the *hypothalamus,* which is critically important to motivation and drive-satisfaction.

arousal and the function of the RAS can find a good discussion and review of the literature in Kahneman (1973) and in Malmo (1975).

LEARNING: WHERE DO WE GO FROM HERE?

Our intention in this chapter and the previous one has been to lay the groundwork for the systematic study of the varieties of learning which is to follow. The previous chapter discussed the limits of human attention and the ways in which active involvement with the environment can exploit and extend these limits. In the present chapter we expanded this notion of active involvement in the learning process through motivation. As we have seen, the sources of motivation may vary from the basic ones of the satisfaction of biological needs, to the higher, more abstract ones, such as the desire for "achievement" for its own sake, and ultimately, for self-actualization.

As we will see in subsequent chapters, some primitive forms of learning, such as *classical conditioning,* can take place without reliance on "motivation" and "reward" as we commonly use the terms. In still others, such as *concept learning,* the motivation is only implicit in an assumed need for competence and understanding of the environment. The principle still holds: the motivation to explore the environment, to receive sensory stimulation, and to manipulate objects, drives the organism to acquire those skills which ultimately lead to their satisfaction. In short, motivation addresses the "why" of learning. We now turn our attention to the "how."

SUMMARY

The drive-reduction theory saw reinforcement in human and animal learning in terms of the satisfaction of either learned or innate needs. In a later formulation, Maslow postulated a hierarchy of needs, ranging from basic, physiological drives, to the need for "self-actualization." This latter need was thought to be the highest level of human motivation, representing the need to express one's true potentials in their most creative and complete form.

Not yet in a form amenable to experimental test, Maslow's hierarchy should be seen as one attempt to recognize both biological and social drives within a single theory, with an emphasis on showing how the motives might be related to each other as they serve to motivate behavior.

One result of high motivation is a heightened sensitivity to sensory stimulation, which is referred to as an individual's level of arousal. Although the physiological basis of arousal is complex, the major points made were: (1) learning is facilitated by the appropriate level of arousal, and different tasks have different arousal levels minimally necessary for their satisfactory performance. (2) Levels of arousal run on a continuum from sleep and boredom, to excitement, stress, anxiety, and panic. Maintenance of high arousal levels for sustained periods for even the most "motivated" of learners is virtually impossible. Regular arousal shifts from one level to another are a necessary component of the homeostatic operation of the nervous system. (3) One of the effects of motivation on learning is to raise the individual's level of arousal, with its resultant effects on efficiency of learning, concentration, alertness, and the intake of information.

part three
The Varieties of Learning

chapter 4

Learning Without Understanding?:
CLASSICAL CONDITIONING

It is probably fair to say that when most people think of human learning, especially those of us concerned with education, we tend to think of learning where there is a very real involvement of insight or understanding in the learning process. This, for most of us, is "real" learning, to be contrasted with that darker, subterranean world of "habits," "reflexes," and "uncontrollable responses."

You are riding down the road at too high a speed. You glance at your watch and realize you are already half an hour late. You are preoccupied with your thoughts and find it difficult to keep your mind from wandering. RED LIGHT: A sudden stab of panic, and your foot slams down hard on the floor for the brake pedal. If you are driving, we call these "good reflexes." If you are a passenger in the back seat, there is nothing left to do but to apologize to the person next to you who had the misfortune of having his or her foot where the brake pedal should have been.

You might want to call this an unconscious or automatic learned reflex.

Indeed, there are many forms of learning where the learner not only has little control over his or her responses but may also have little control over the learning process itself. He or she may even be unaware that the learning has in fact taken place.

There is one type of learning, however, which has a special place in the history of learning theory. It is sometimes called *classical conditioning*, or "Pavlovian conditioning," after its first student. In this form of learning, no active, self-initiated motor response (such as pressing a brake pedal) is involved. There is also no "reward" in the sense that we used the term previously. Classical conditioning represents circumstances whereby the occurrence of one stimulus simply leads the organism to anticipate the later occurrence of another. Typically, this anticipation manifests itself by the two stimuli coming to elicit the same or a similar response. If you break out into a cold sweat merely at the sound of a dentist's drill, are you aware of when you first learned to associate that sound with the process of drilling, and thus be made uncomfortable by the sound alone? If you are among those for whom the sound of thunder causes embarrassing distress, do you remember when you first learned to react to that sound with fear? You may respond to these questions with some uncertainty: was learning really involved?

In fact, learning was very much involved. The last two examples cited are typical of associations acquired through classical conditioning. This form of learning is probably the simplest, most primitive of all types of learning. It can occur without any understanding on the part of the learner, without his or her necessary cooperation in the learning process, and often—as in the cited cases—without any knowledge on the learner's part that learning has even taken place. While the same could be said of some forms of instrumental learning (see Chapter 5), classical conditioning has a number of unique features.

Briefly, the simplest form of classical conditioning relies on some preexisting physiological reflex in the individual. In one of the previous examples, it would be the stimulus of the dentist's drill striking the nerve of an unanesthetized tooth which causes an automatic physical pain response. This preexisting stimulus and response connection (S→R) represents half of the elements necessary for the conditioning process. All that remains is for some other event (in this case, the *sound* of the drill, or perhaps even the sight of the dentist) to co-occur with the unlearned stimulus (the drilling). Should these two stimuli be experienced together a sufficient number of times, the sound of the drill alone will be sufficient to cause the person, if not the pain itself, then at least the same psychological discomfort and nervousness associated with it. This association, if well enough established, may also *generalize* to the sound of other drills. Our victim of conditioning may equally feel a strange discomfort when hearing a carpenter use an electric drill on a construction site.

Classical conditioning is admittedly a very special type of learning. It is special not so much for the simplicity of the conditions necessary for its occurrence, but because this type of learning is restricted primarily to the acquisition of involuntary associations involving diffuse emotional responses. This is of course an important component of human learning. It would not, however, account for the acquisition of skills involving voluntary motor or intellectual responses such as learning to talk, learning to write, and so forth.

Classical conditioning stands apart from other forms of learning for other reasons as well. Because of its primitive nature, the conditions surrounding its occurrence in humans and in lower animals are extraordinarily similar, in spite of the complexities of human intelligence which often tend to obscure or complicate such similarities in other forms of learning. Historically, it was the first type of learning to attract serious scientific attention, and as such had a very strong influence on later studies of more complex learning.

A consequence of this early attention was the gradual realization that as simple as conditioning appeared to be, it was in fact quite complex and intriguing.

AN APPLICATION OF CLASSICAL CONDITIONING

The basic elements of classical conditioning can be illustrated by its use in a technique for testing hearing under certain special circumstances where a person may be unable (or unwilling) to actively cooperate in the testing procedures. At the same time, we can take the opportunity to further introduce some of the conditions and standard terminology of classical conditioning.

The ordinary hearing test makes use of an *audiometer,* a simple device which electronically produces pure tone sounds at controlled frequencies and intensities. The subject wears a set of earphones and is instructed to raise his or her hand or press a signal button when a sound is heard. The examiner begins the test by presenting a tone of a particular pitch at a loudness level well below the sensitivity of normal hearing. The loudness is then steadily increased in set steps until the subject signals that it has become just audible. This is technically referred to as an *ascending threshold:* the loudness level that marks the precise lower boundary of hearing acuity. This process is then systematically repeated for tones of other pitches, first in one ear, then in the other, until there is a complete mapping of the person's acuity across the range of important frequencies in human hearing.

This standard audiometric technique is ordinarily quite effective and can produce a complete hearing test in a matter of minutes. The problem arises in exceptional cases where the simple command to signal when a tone is heard cannot be followed. This might be the case for a severely retarded child or, we must painfully admit, a malingering adult who for one reason or another wishes to give the impression of a hearing loss.

As any regular moviegoer knows, Hollywood's standard solution would seem to be to suddenly drop a book to the floor behind the person, or, perhaps more spectacularly, to fire a revolver to see if the subject in question is startled by hearing the noise. Leaving aside the wear and tear on dropped books, or the routine replastering of a bullet-ridden ceiling, there are serious problems with this approach. One is that such a "test" would fail to detect mild-to-moderate losses which make up the vast majority of hearing problems. The second is that it would fail to detect losses for the higher pitched sounds where hearing problems very often begin.

The question, then, is one of determining when a sound is heard in those cases where a person cannot be relied upon to tell you. The answer is a special use of classical conditioning.

The first element needed is some preexisting reflex, preferably one which is easy to elicit and easy to measure. There is a wide range of potential possibilities available: the pupil of the eye will contract when a bright light is turned on, the smell of food will produce salivation if the person is hungry, the eye will blink if we blow a puff of air in it, and so forth. In addition to these rather obvious reflexes, there is a wide range of more subtle responses generally known as *orienting responses*. These are typically unnoticed physiological changes in the body in response to any sudden, surprising, or novel stimulus. If you are quietly listening to the radio at home when suddenly the announcer mentions your name in connection with a news story, your sudden alertness will be marked by an equally abrupt change in your heart rate and breathing rate. The blood capillaries in your fingers will contract, and those in the temporalis muscle on the side of your head will dilate. There will also be an increase in sweat activity. In extreme cases we may in fact see beads of perspiration on your forehead. In less extreme cases it may be restricted to a very slight and unnoticeable increase in sweating under the skin (subdermal sweating). Many children and some adults can experience these bodily reactions on just hearing their name called by a teacher in an ordinary classroom situation.

These orienting responses represent a physiological alerting reaction of the body to novelty or threat (Sokolov, 1960; Weiskrantz, 1968, pp. 249–252; Siddle & Heron, 1976). The latter feature of threat is admittedly mentioned only as they undoubtedly must have had some survival function, however vestigial.

The orienting response ordinarily used in this context is the last one mentioned; subdermal sweating, which is detected as a *galvanic skin response* (GSR). Although these changes in sweat activity under the skin are slight and cannot actually be seen, they can be detected by measuring changes in electrical conductivity characteristics of the skin which are a consequence of the subdermal sweating. These measurements are usually taken by taping small metal strips (electrodes) to the palm and back of the hands or on the fingers. (Some of these measures are also used on the *polygraph* or "lie detector," as they also respond to sudden changes in arousal, stress, or anxiety which sometimes accompany the telling of a falsehood.)

One easy-to-apply stimulus which will reliably produce the GSR is a slight tingle of electric shock. It need not be a strong shock, and indeed it should not be if we anticipate its use with children. It is the novelty of the stimulus, not the pain, which is all that is necessary to produce the response.

We now have our preexisting reflex, the GSR, a stimulus to produce it, and an appropriate device for its measurement. The latter is a meter which measures changes in electrical characteristics of the skin caused by the subdermal sweating. It is appropriately called a *psychogalvanometer*.

We are now ready to employ classical conditioning of the GSR to test hearing through the technique known as *GSR audiometry* (Steer & Hanley, 1957).

The conditioning procedure is begun by first giving the child a pure tone through the headphones at a loudness level sufficiently high to insure that anyone but the most profoundly deaf would hear it. (We would probably already know from parents' reports that the child can hear very loud sounds. We are interested in the child's ability to hear very soft ones, and sounds of various frequencies.) As the tone is presented, we give the child a small tingle of shock on the fingers and monitor our psychogalvanometer. It will show the needle on the meter to deflect as a result of the automatic GSR response to the shock. This procedure is now repeated a number of times: the tone, the shock, the tone, the shock . . . etc. After sufficient paired presentations of the two stimuli, the conditioning process will be completed. We can check this by now giving the tone alone, without the accompanying shock. The paired presentation of the two stimuli will cause the person to react to the tone in a similar manner as he or she originally did to the shock. The tone alone now produces a change in the GSR. At this point we know of course that the loud tone must have been heard.

Once the response of the GSR is reliably elicited by the tone, the hearing test proper is now begun by presenting a series of softer tones and increasing their loudness until a GSR reaction is first observed. Even though the child may be unable to voluntarily tell us that he or she can hear the soft sounds, the involuntary *conditioned response*, the GSR, will tell us instead.

To be sure, this test is more time consuming and cumbersome than ordinary hearing testing. One reason for this is the problem of continued strengthening or *reinforcing* of the relationship between the tone and the GSR throughout the course of the test. Initially, the relationship will be strong and at the beginning of the testing phase we can be sure of a reliable GSR whenever a tone is heard. Continued presentation of the tones without the accompanying reinforcement of the shock, however, will cause a weakening, or *extinction*, of the response. When this happens a GSR may not be produced even though the tone is heard. For this reason, during the course of testing we must occasionally strengthen or reinforce the relationship by reintroducing the loud sound and shock together to keep the conditioned response alive. However time consuming this technique of GSR audiometry may be, it is, nevertheless, an extremely useful tool in testing the very young or retarded child.

We have to this point outlined the major elements involved in classical conditioning. It can also be seen how relatively passive a form of learning classical conditioning can be. While the person being tested might well understand what is going on, and the nature of the association being formed, this understanding need not interfere with, nor may it be necessary for, the success of the conditioning process. It may well be this "1984" quality of classical conditioning that has attracted the attention of the novelist and the popular press with attendent fears of some "big brother" out to control our lives and behavior.

CLASSICAL CONDITIONING IN HUMAN LEARNING

The previous example shows a rather unique application of classical conditioning in a very formal setting. It was introduced primarily to illustrate the basic elements and terminology of the conditioning process. In ordinary human behavior, however, classical conditioning is mainly involved in the attachment of many emotional responses to originally neutral stimuli. One such example already mentioned is a person's fear of thunder (probably resulting from an association of the sound of thunder with the feelings of emotional upset induced by experiencing the fright of a parent already frightened by thunder).

Classical conditioning is also involved in the development of many other involuntary emotional responses. A person who has on several occasions received upsetting news on the telephone may for some time feel his or her "heart skip a beat" whenever the telephone rings, even though rationally he or she knows that it is probably a very harmless call. Many, perhaps most of these conditioned responses, however, are difficult to identify in real life since the circumstances surrounding the acquisition of the association may be unknown.

We could imagine, for example, a young child who must walk to school every day on a route which passes a fierce dog tied up in someone's yard. The fear induced by the association between going to school and the barking, growling dog, may be sufficient to cause the child to become upset whenever he or she approaches school, even though a different route is taken which no longer passes the dog. (An analogous emotional response to school induced by early encounters with a fierce teacher is an example which perhaps should not be pursued.)

One of the first systematic demonstrations of the way in which classical conditioning might operate in human learning was an early study by Watson and Rayner (1920). It was a very simple experiment in which a young child, now immortalized in the folklore of psychology as "Little Albert," was conditioned to temporarily fear a specific class of objects. As Albert (about 11 months old) was quietly playing, he was casually shown a small white rat which he initially took to with glee and curiosity. Just as Albert reached for the animal, however, one of the experimenters sneaked up behind him and loudly banged an iron bar with a hammer. The sudden loud noise startled the poor child to the point of tears. When Albert recovered, he nevertheless returned to the rat to again play with it. Again, the loud noise was suddenly sounded behind his back. With this pattern repeated a number of times, the mere sight of the inoffensive little animal was sufficient to frighten the child to the point where he would begin to cry whenever the rat was brought near him.

What these experimenters had done was to take a preexisting reflex, a child's natural fear response to a sudden loud noise, couple this noise with the sight of a rat, and thus condition a fear of rats.

Once this conditioned fear had been established, they also found that it had *generalized* to other stimuli similar in appearance to the rat. Albert not only bust into tears when shown a fluffy white rabbit, but he also showed fear at the sight of a white woolen sweater and a ball of white cotton. How long could we expect this conditioned fear of rats, rabbits, and other cuddly white objects to last? Had little Albert been doomed to a life of rabbit-phobia (or, indeed, sweater-phobia), for the cause of science? Fortunately, the answer is that such associations will not last very long provided there is later contact with these objects (without the startling noise), and perhaps some soothing words of comfort whenever they are seen. The passage of time and this additional care will overcome the initial conditioning and *extinguish* the conditioned response.

THE EARLY STUDIES OF PAVLOV

There is no doubt that the principles of classical conditioning were at least intuitively appreciated long before man first turned any scientific attention toward learning and human behavior. Nevertheless, it was not until early in this century that the Russian physiologist I. P. Pavlov (1849–1936) investigated this form of learning with scientific rigor, isolated its essential elements, and tried in some way to understand the mechanisms underlying this learning process. It is for this reason that the terms classical conditioning and "Pavlovian conditioning" are often used interchangeably. In fact,

Pavlov's use of the experimental method in studying learning, and his concentration on quantifiable observations, had an immense impact not only on the study of conditioning, but also on the philosophy of psychological research for decades to come.

In order to understand the processes underlying classical conditioning, a good place to begin is with Pavlov's own early experiments. These experiments developed both a conceptual framework and a terminology which are still in use today.

The Conditioned Reflex

The use of lower animals in behavioral research has a long tradition, and has been of proven usefulness provided one generalizes from results with appropriate caution. It is always a matter of interest, however, as to why a particular behavioral or biological scientist chooses a particular animal for his or her studies. For Pavlov, it was the dog. As it happens, Pavlov did not initially select the dog as the best animal for the study of simple learning. On the contrary, it was his experience with dogs in the laboratory in the first place which caused him to turn his attention to learning.

Prior to his studies of conditioning, Pavlov was engaged in physiological studies of the digestive system in dogs, including the automatic reflex of salivation in response to the smell of food. This work was quite fruitful and saw Pavlov honored in 1904 with a Nobel Prize in Medicine.

Occasionally it takes the true expert to be excited by a blinding flash of the obvious or, perhaps, to realize that what he or she has seen is in fact not really "obvious" at all. In this case Pavlov wondered as he observed that his dogs salivated not only when they were fed, or smelled food, but that they would also salivate whenever they simply saw the man who usually fed them. Since his dogs were often connected to an apparatus for measuring salivation when this event occurred, it could hardly go unnoticed. What intrigued Pavlov, who we must remember was a physiologist studying innate reflexes, was the degree to which he saw the animals having come to associate the food-handler with the food itself. Pavlov was struck by the fact that the dogs' salivation at the sight of the food-handler (something obviously learned) seemed no less "automatic" or "reflexive" than salivation for the food itself. It was in this context that Pavlov began a systematic study of what he later referred to as learned or *conditioned* reflexes (Pavlov, 1927).

When a hungry dog salivates at the sight of the man who usually brings him his food, many factors might conceivably be operating. It might be the sight of the man himself, some characteristic motion he usually makes before feeding the dog, or perhaps even some lingering smell of food on his stained laboratory coat. Pavlov's training as a physiologist suggested the need for a very tightly controlled experiment to carefully isolate the minimum necessary conditions for such an association to be created. To meet these demands, Pavlov arranged a typical experiment in the following way.

A dog was fixed in a special apparatus which included a harness to restrict its movements and a device to accurately measure the extent of any salivation the dog might produce. This apparatus, which he had used in his earlier studies of the salivation reflex per se, consisted of a tube inserted into the animal's mouth which would draw off saliva and allow its measurement in terms either of the quantity of saliva produced or the rate of production in drops per minute.

Pavlov began with what we have referred to as the first element necessary for the conditioning process: an innate, preexisting reflex that occurs in the animal prior to any learning. In this case it was the salivation response of a hungry dog to the presence of food. Since this association already exists in the animal prior to any conditioning, Pavlov referred to the food as the *unconditioned stimulus* (UCS), and to the salivation response as the *unconditioned response* (UCR). This preexisting connection is usually diagrammed as

$$\text{UCS} \longrightarrow \text{UCR}$$
$$\text{(food)} \quad \text{(salivation)}$$

Pavlov then selected what we would today consider the second element for the conditioning process. This would be some "neutral" stimulus which initially has no connection whatsoever with the particular UCR under study. In the event that stimulated Pavlov's initial interest, it was the food-handler. A much simpler stimulus, such as a bell, however, proved quite adequate as another "neutral" stimulus. When a bell is rung near a dog a variety of responses are produced. These, however, are typically alerting or "orienting" responses, such as ear twitching, changes in body posture, etc. The bell qualifies as a "neutral" stimulus in the sense that it does not produce the UCR of salivation.

The third element of the conditioning procedure was now initiated as Pavlov repeatedly rang the bell together with injecting a small quantity of meat powder into the animal's mouth. Each time this happened, the meat powder (UCS) reliably elicited the UCR of salivation. After about 10 or 20 presentations of the bell and the meat powder together, Pavlov found that ringing the bell alone without the presence of the food was sufficient to reliably elicit the UCR of salivation. As the association became established, the bell could be viewed as a *signal*, with the salivation produced in *anticipation* of the actual taste of the food. At this point, Pavlov referred to the bell as the *conditioned stimulus* (CS), and the salivation it produced as the *conditioned response* (CR). We would commonly diagram this conditioned association as

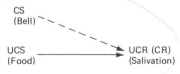

This basic diagram can be used to formally restate the events of two previous examples: GSR audiometry, and the conditioned fear of the rat in little Albert.

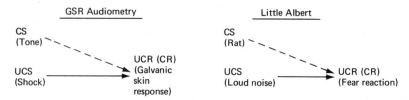

One of the important features of the conditioning process to Pavlov was the gradualness of the developing association. Beginning with a total absence of salivation to the bell, the amount of salivation that ringing the bell elicited increased smoothly and gradually until the association was fully formed and the bell elicited salivation every time it was heard. There was no hint of a lack of association followed by a single point where one could suddenly say, "the association has just occurred." One might expect to see this if some degree of understanding or insight were involved in the conditioning process. It was the gradualness in the building up of the connection that suggested to Pavlov that the conditioning process represents a slowly developing association in the nervous system not at all mediated by intelligent understanding. This view of conditioning as a low-level, primitive category of learning is still held by many, even when applied to its occurrence in the human child or adult. It is precisely because it can take place at a fairly low level of nervous system function that gives classical conditioning its passive, involuntary characteristics noted earlier. The shape of a typical acquisition curved is shown in Figure 4.1.

Reinforcement

Pavlov spoke of the UCS as reinforcing the association in the sense that it was necessary first to establish, and then to strengthen (reinforce), the conditioned response. The term "reinforcement" for the UCS in classical conditioning has a very different character from its use when referring to "reward" in more complex forms of learning. The use of Pavlov's term reinforcement for reward in other forms of learning came very much later, and was largely an attempt by others to develop a common terminology which could be used for all forms of learning. In fact, the UCS and reward have in common only that they are both viewed as necessary for the learning of an association. *In classical conditioning, reinforcement refers specifically to the UCS which elicits the UCR.*

Virtually any preexisting reflex can serve as the basis of classical conditioning, and any stimulus as the CS. All that is needed is their frequent co-

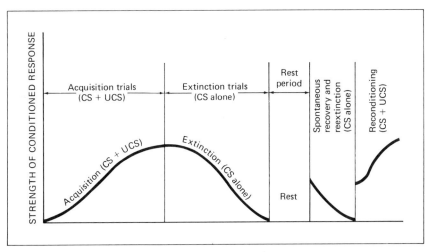

Figure 4.1   The effects of reinforcement and withdrawal of reinforcement over time in classical conditioning. The gradual rise and fall in the strength of the conditioned response is shown in idealized form for the processes of *acquisition, extinction, spontaneous recovery,* and *reconditioning.*

occurrence in time. In the ordinary course of events, classical or Pavlovian conditioning is far more subtle but often no less inevitable. One of the tragic comedies of early conditioning in children is seeing a terrified parent telling his or her child not be afraid of the thunder (or a spider, or an insect . . .) when the parent's own fear reaction is being detected by the child and is simultaneously reinforcing that conditioned response.

Pseudoconditioning

Armed with the knowledge of the conditioning paradigm, early psychologists began to see examples of classical conditioning everywhere, even where it was not. One of the best known cases was that of *pseudoconditioning,* a term coined by Grether (1938). Pavlov's work had been published (in English) some 11 years earlier, and numerous workers such as Grether were eager to explore its implications. Grether had decided to see whether he could condition a fright response in an animal using a brilliant flash of light as the UCS and the sound of a bell as the CS.

Before beginning the experiment, Grether rang the bell several times to verify that it would not initially frighten the animal. It did not. Next, he flashed the brilliant light to make sure that this would produce a fright response. It did. Feeling ready to begin the conditioning procedure, Grether now rang the bell, intending to follow it with the bright light. To his horror, however, the animal immediately jumped with fright at the sound of the bell alone, even before the onset of the light flash. This looked very much like conditioning, except that the CS (the bell) and the UCS (the light) had never in fact been presented together.

On further analysis it became apparent that this was no more a product of classical conditioning than when a tense person jumps at the sound of a telephone bell in a quiet room. In Grether's case, it is likely that the series of bright flashes of light preliminary to the main experiment had so trauma- tized the poor animal that any novel stimulus, in this case the bell, would have produced the fright response. Another way of saying this is that an ani- mal or person can become *sensitized* by a series of strong stimuli to the point where they will respond to almost any stimulus, whether or not it has been paired with the UCS. *Pseudoconditioning* applies to any case where a neutral stimulus produces a response similar to the CR without any pairing of that stimulus with the UCS (Bolles, 1975b, pp. 37–38). As the term im- plies, such instances may look like conditioning, but strictly speaking, they are not.

We mention this story for one important reason. The serious student of learning will have a natural inclination to look for instances of classical conditioning, or any other phenomenon, in everyday events. The examples are numerous, and the exercise is worthwhile. In the case of classical condi- tioning, a critical factor to verify is not only that events looking like a CS and a UCS have occurred in a person's past experience, but that they have occurred close together in time, usually on several occasions, and that this pairing was necessary to produce the CR.

ADDITIONAL FEATURES OF CONDITIONING

In addition to demonstrating the basic principles of classical condition- ing, Pavlov, and those who followed, began a detailed examination of addi- tional features of the conditioning process. These included a study of *extinction, spontaneous recovery, stimulus generalization*, and *higher-order conditioning*.

Extinction

Once a conditioned response has become stable, the animal (or human) can be expected to continue to produce the CR on each subsequent occur- rence of the CS for some time. Continual presentation of the CS without the accompanying reinforcement of the UCS, however, will eventually lead to a gradual reduction in the strength of the CR and, eventually, to its com- plete disappearance.

This apparent disappearance of the association is referred to as *extinc- tion*, and it occurs with the same gradualness as the initial acquisition of the conditioned response (see Figure 4.1). Few generalizations can be made about the expected number of unreinforced presentations of a CS before eventual extinction. It depends very much on the strength of the initial learning, the animal involved, and the nature of the response.

In human affairs, some irrational associations unfortunately do not extinguish because persons often avoid those conditions necessary for their extinction. In still other cases, other forms of learning can inadvertently reward many of these responses and thus keep the association alive. It might be parenthetically noted that one aspect of a particular type of psychotherapy (so-called behavior modification) addresses itself directly to the extinction of such long-lasting conditioned response (Kalish, 1965).

Spontaneous Recovery

Pavlov's very tight experimental control as he studied the conditioning process allowed him to observe a number of special characteristics that could easily go unnoticed in less controlled circumstances. One such observation was an interesting phenomenon that occasionally occurs after extinction of a CR. This is *spontaneous recovery:* the appearance of a CR some time after it has apparently been fully extinguished.

When spontaneous recovery is observed, it is usually under the following circumstances. An animal trained in the conditioning apparatus is presented with the CS without reinforcement until the response is fully extinguished. Presentation of the CS, for example the bell, no longer produces any measurable salivation. The animal is then returned to his home cage and is later brought back to the testing apparatus where the bell is again rung. Obviously, the extinguished response should not appear. It sometimes happens, however, that an animal will respond by again salivating when the bell is rung! To be sure, the effect is not always observed, and when it is, it is typically a small one which extinguishes rapidly if not again reinforced (see Figure 4.1).

The term *spontaneous recovery* is quite apt, as it appears as a recovery of an apparently extinguished response without any apparent cause. It would seem almost as if the animal has forgotten that he has forgotten!

However small the effect, the very existence of spontaneous recovery has suggested to many that extinction is not simply a passive weakening and eventual loss of an association. As Pavlov put it, there must still remain in the nervous system some "trace" or memory of the association even after a complete disappearance of the response. One suggestion is that extinction may actually involve a very active process of *learning not to respond*. In theoretical terms, the unreinforced extinction trials are thought to create a specific *inhibitory block* which prevents elicitation of the CR. The association itself, however, is not necessarily destroyed. The time away from the testing situation may result in a decay of this inhibition such that the response is again produced when the animal later encounters the CS.

What really happens during extinction? All we can really say for sure is that the organism no longer responds when presented with the CS. In Pavlov's case, the bell no longer caused the animal to salivate. As we have seen, Pavlov rejected the notion of extinction as simply the passive "forgetting" of an association through the passage of time. He used the term *internal inhibition* to explain extinction or the "blocking" of a response, as we referred to it above. Indeed, Pavlov further discovered that one can exert some control over both the "blocking" (*inhibition*) and "unblocking" (*disinhibition*) of responses. On the one hand, a conditioned animal will temporarily cease salivating to the bell if a very loud, startling sound is presented in the course of the conditioning trials. Pavlov referred to this as *external inhibition.* On the other hand, he found that the same startling loud sound presented to an animal during extinction trials will sometimes *produce* salivation. If the terms are not too confusing, the loud sound may be said to have "disinhibited" the "inhibition."

Although the theoretical implications of spontaneous recovery are complex, there is other evidence for the notion that observed extinction may still leave an existing trace of an association in the nervous system. One of these is the results obtained on *reconditioning* an extinguished response. Significantly fewer trials are typically needed to bring the CR up to full strength than are initially required for the original conditioning process (see Figure 4.1). This would only be the case if there was already some basis for the relearning in the animal, such as a slight but existing trace of the original connection.

Spontaneous recovery is not restricted to lower animals and can sometimes be observed in classical conditioning in humans as well. Indeed, something akin to spontaneous recovery is also seen in more complex forms of learning. Sometimes referred to as *reminiscence,* many of us are familiar with the experience of unexpectedly recalling the lines of a poem or a methematical formula which we thought had long been forgotten. As we will see later in Chapter 11, forgetting in complex human learning, like extinction, may well be far more an active process than is generally realized.

Stimulus Generalization

Earlier we saw the way in which little Albert *generalized* his conditioned fear response from a white rat to all white fluffy objects. Generalization seems to be a fundamental and important process in all forms of learning and explains in part the rapidity and flexibility of learning. The child or adult (or animal) will respond not only to the specific CS on which he or she was conditioned but to all stimuli similar to it.

As we observe stimulus generalization in everyday life this general statement is readily apparent. Very early studies of conditioning, however, were able to show that stimulus generalization can be related to a very precise function of similarity between stimuli. Hovland (1937) illustrated this for human subjects who had a GSR conditioned to a pure tone sound of 1000 Hz by initially pairing the CS tone with a mild electric shock. As sounds of lower and higher frequency were presented, the amplitude of the GSR (taken as the strength of the response) was found to be inversely related to the difference between these sounds and the CS tone.

Figure 4.2 shows a composite curve of the subjects' reactions to various tones as a function of their degree of difference from the original 1000 Hz tone. This smooth function is referred to as the *gradient of generalization*, and can be demonstrated in every case where the experimenter is astute enough to be able to specify the relevant or salient dimensions of similarity between stimuli (cf. Brown, B. L., 1970).

Hovland's study remains somewhat of a classic in Pavlovian psychology, even though later experiments have not always found such neat results as those he reported (e.g. Epstein & Burstein, 1966; Burstein, Epstein & Smith, 1967). The important point to remember is that the principle of generalization is as valid today as it was when Hovland first presented his data; the greater the similarity between a CS and other stimuli, the more likely we are to respond to those stimuli in place of the original CS.

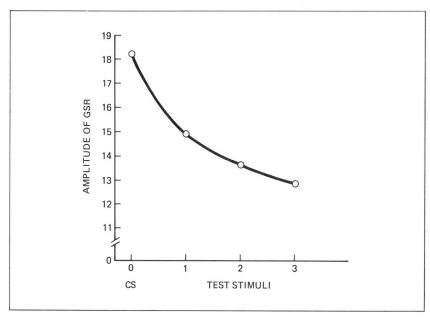

Figure 4.2 Gradient of generalization for a galvanic skin response conditioned to a 1000 Hz tone (CS), followed by the presentation of tones of increasingly different frequency. (*Source:* C. I. Hovland, The generalization of conditioned responses: I. The sensory generalization of conditioned responses with varying frequencies of tone. *Journal of General Psychology,* 1937, 17: fig. 2, pg. 136. Reprinted by permission of The Journal Press.)

The nature of a conditioned association, in other words, is more interesting than it may first appear on casual observation. The organism is in reality responding not so much to a single specific stimulus as to what we might refer to as a *category* of stimuli. We can, if we wish, increase the specificity of the response and reduce the size of the category by repeated presentation of the CS with reinforcement, along with presentation of the related stimuli without reinforcement. By this process of differential reinforcement, the response to related stimuli will gradually extinguish, beginning first with responses least similar to the CS. This process of refining the stimulus category is referred to as *stimulus discrimination.*

It is thus possible to view stimulus generalization in classical conditioning as a very primitive form of *categorization*: the treatment of similar events as identical, or nearly identical, because of shared common properties. Generalization in higher forms of learning, however, is far less passive and is often viewed as a learning process in itself (see Chapter 8). Stimulus generalization in classical conditioning may represent the genesis of this ability, in however rudimentary a form.

Higher-Order Conditioning

If stimulus generalization is part of the explanation of the rapidity and flexibility of learning, even in the simple process of classical conditioning, then *higher-order conditioning* is another. Once a CS→CR relationship has been established, new associations can be conditioned *using the CS itself as reinforcement.*

Consider, for example, a child's fear of fire. The initial association may have been formed through the child actually having been burned or by being frightened by a parent's strong fear response when the child went near the flame. Either of these stimuli could have served as the UCS to reinforce an involuntary fear response (CR) in the child at the *sight* of fire alone. How does the spoken word "fire" now come to produce an immediate fear response? It might be that the child was burned as the word "fire" was spoken. This, however, need not be the case. Once a conditioned fear response to fire has been formed, simply the sight of a fire when the word is spoken can now reinforce a new relation between the word "fire" and the fear response. Unlike stimulus generalization, higher-order conditioning involves a new association with a new stimulus which need not bear any physical similarity to the orginal CS. (Although we do not intend to complicate matters unduly, it should be pointed out that the *voluntary avoidance* of fire is usually seen as involving a distinct and different learning process than the diffuse emotional response of fear of fire. The distinction is important and will be pursued in the following chapter.)

If we return to Pavlov's laboratory, we can look at higher-order conditioning in a simplified form and hence with greater clarity. Recall the dog who had been conditioned to salivate at the sound of a bell. Pavlov demonstrated higher-order conditioning by later presenting an animal with a new stimulus; for example, a light followed only by the bell. After a number of presentations of the light and the bell together, the animal now salivated to the light alone. The original CS (the bell) had functioned to reinforce the new association, operating much in the same way as the original UCS of food. This is referred to as *second-order conditioning* and can be diagrammed along with the initial *first-order conditioning* which involved the UCS reinforcement of the taste of food.

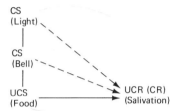

The process of higher-order conditioning has been demonstrated as far as third-order conditioning, such as now using the light to reinforce yet another new association. The process cannot go on indefinitely, however, as the initial associations on which they are based are no longer being reinforced by the UCS and are, therefore, in the process of extinguishing as the new learning is taking place.

THE SPEED OF CONDITIONING

It is difficult to generalize about the ease with which a conditioned response can be expected to become established. As noted earlier with regard to extinction, it depends on a variety of factors such as the nature of the response, the conditions of learning, and so forth. Ordinarily, a fairly large number of reinforced occurrences of the CS and UCS are necessary for the formation of a conditioned association. In some cases, such as the experience of little Albert or the conditioned fear of fire, only one or perhaps a few occurrences are necessary for the beginnings of an association.

That there are individual differences among people in their speed of conceptual learning should come as no surprise. It may be surprising, however, that this statement is also true to a lesser extent on the primitive level of classical conditioning. Figure 4.3 shows illustrative acquisition curves for three groups of adults who had their eye blink reflex conditioned to some signal using a puff of air in the eye as an UCS. This is not a very direct or "natural" association, and a fairly large number of trials were required. That there are very real differences in the speed of conditioning among subjects, however, is readily apparent (Spence, 1956). These differences not

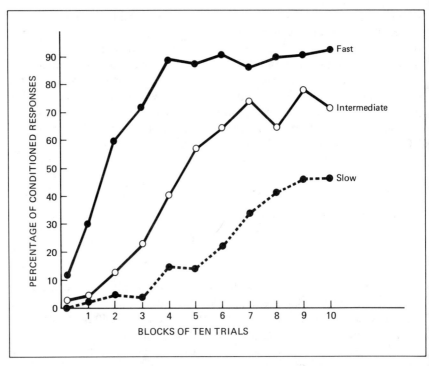

Figure 4.3   Acquisition curves for a classically conditioned eye blink for three groups of subjects showing high (fast), average (intermediate), and poor (slow) conditioning performance both early and late in training. (*Source:* K. W. Spence, *Behavior Theory and Conditioning*, fig. 9, pg. 66. New Haven: Yale University Press, 1956. By permission of the publisher.)

withstanding, it is equally apparent that the general shape of the acquisition curves are strikingly similar for all of the groups. Indeed, this similarity in shape of acquisition curves in classical conditioning holds equally true for retarded as well as for normal subjects (Lobb & Hardwick, 1976). The process is identical—it is only the relative speed that varies.

One factor affecting the speed of conditioning which the experimenter (or the environment) can control is the timing relationships between the occurrence of the CS and the reinforcing UCS. Generally speaking, the sooner the UCS occurs after the presentation of the CS, the faster will be the rate of learning.

Pavlov observed early in his work that the fastest conditioning by far occurs when the CS *precedes* the UCS by a short period of time. Although the optimal time interval will vary with the type of stimuli being conditioned, intervals in the order of $^1/_2$ second generally seem to produce the fastest results (Kimble, 1961). The reason this is so tells us something about the conditioning process. As we saw earlier, one can view the CS (e.g., the bell in Pavlov's experiments) as a *signal* to the organism that the UCS is soon to follow. Specifically, on hearing the bell the animal salivates in antic-ipation of the smell of food which usually follows it. Classical conditioning is sometimes referred to as *signal learning* for just that reason (cf. Gagné, 1970). On the other hand, if the CS precedes the UCS by too long an inter-val, especially if a number of intervening events occur before the UCS, the association may never be formed. For a stimulus to act as a signal, it must be both salient and uncluttered by intervening events. It must, in short, be un-ambiguously tied to the UCS which follows.

This reference to the CS leading the animal to *anticipate* the occurrence of the UCS, incidentally, adds a slight twist to the classical Pavlovian view of the conditioning process. That is, the process may not be as passive as it is usually thought to be. Rescorla and Solomon (1967), for example, have taken a more "cognitive" view of the CS-UCS association, stressing an ap-preciation on the part of the animal (or human) of the relationship between the CS as a *predictor* of the UCS. Perhaps what is learned in the Pavlovian paradigm is not so much a particular response to the occurrence of the CS as an expectancy, whether conscious or not, that the UCS will follow. Read-ers interested in this theoretical treatment of the conditioning process are referred to, for example, Rescorla and Solomon (1967), Rescorla and Wagner (1972), Rescorla (1972) and Bolles (1975b, pp. 159–164).

Timing Patterns and Speed of Conditioning

Three general timing relationships, each with predictable consequences on the rate of conditioning, are diagrammed in Figure 4.4. The first of these

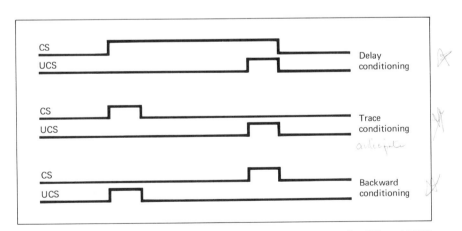

Figure 4.4   Three timing relationships between occurrence of a CS and UCS in classical conditioning. *Delay conditioning* typically produces the most rapid learning. *Trace conditioning* is possible but requires more trials to reach the same level. The timing relationship in *backward conditioning* is the poorest of the three, and conditioning ordinarily proves impossible.

is referred to as *delay conditioning*, and ordinarily produces the most rapid buildup of a conditioned association. The CS (e.g., a light or a buzzer) is presented first and remains on until the UCS (e.g., the smell of food) is presented. As we have seen, a half-second delay between the onset of the CS and the UCS is frequently found to be optimal.

The second configuration is referred to as *trace conditioning*, in which the presentation of the CS in terminated prior to the onset of the UCS. Conditioning in this case is still possible, although the number of trials may have to be increased to achieve the same level of conditioning produced by fewer trials of delay conditioning. Generally speaking, the longer the time interval separating the CS and the UCS, the more difficult it will be for the association to be formed. Although claims for some effectiveness after delays as long as several hours have been reported, these seem to be very special cases, such as learned aversion (Garcia, Ervin & Koelling, 1966). Pavlov referred to this as trace conditioning because the association must be based not on the physical presence of the CS itself but on a presumably fading trace of the CS in memory.

A final category, *backward conditioning*, refers to cases where the UCS preceeds the CS. It is by far the most difficult circumstance for conditioning and is ordinarily unsuccessful when attempted.

CLASSICAL CONDITIONING AND LEARNING

Classical conditioning is as surely a variety of learning as it is a limited one. We usually think of learning either as an acquisition of conscious knowledge or as a way of coping with the environment. As we have seen, classical conditioning does neither. For example, feeling uncomfortable at the sound of a dentist's drill, salivating in response to a realistic picture of food, or experiencing a feeling of dread when passing a place where a terrible car accident had once been witnessed, are all the result of classical conditioning. These reactions may supply the *motivation* for further learning. They may also *prepare* the organism for active coping. For example, the sight of food can initiate salivation preparatory to eating, or a conditioned reflex can warn of imminent danger. They are in themselves, however, neither under conscious control nor in a direct way instrumental in coping with, or influencing, the environment. We are more captives than masters of classical conditioning.

We also know that a well-conditioned response can last for a long time before extinguishing. For example, just think of sucking a cut lemon and tasting the tart juices produced. You may at this moment feel yourself salivating simply at the thought of the taste. Through experience, the *thought* of the lemon has gained the power to replace the physical object itself and to produce virtually the same reaction as when the lemon is actually presented. Once we realize that conditioned reactions can be elicited by simply the thought of a CS, it becomes obvious that the conditioning process has powerful implications which go beyond the limited framework of Pavlov's salivating dogs.

As we have already mentioned, classical conditioning is thought to be importantly involved in the acquisition of emotional responses to various stimuli and events. Emotions such as love, hate, fear, and joy may or may not be learned (there is still much controversy on this subject). What is learned, however, is the *attachment* of these emotional responses to one stimulus or another. Because of the involuntary, often accidental association of events, many of these reactions fall into the category of "irrational" responses, and they are often counterproductive. Inappropriate emotional outbursts, some allergic reactions, and other maladaptive behaviors have all been linked to a complex variation of Pavlov's conditioning model.

If classical conditioning can cause maladaptive behavior, can conditioning be used to eliminate it? The answer, in the form of one variety of behavior therapy, would appear to be a qualified "yes" (cf. Wolpe, 1974). The position, however, remains unchanged. Classical conditioning causes an immediate, involuntary, and often diffuse reaction to the environment. It does not, in itself, produce a way of coping with that environment. For that we must turn to another variety of learning which goes by many names, *instrumental learning, operant conditioning,* or, simply, learning through "trial and error."

SUMMARY

Pavlov's early study of the "conditioned reflex" led to the development of modern notions of classical conditioning in both animal and human learning. As we have seen, classical conditioning is a passive form of learning which begins with some preexisting unconditioned stimulus (UCS) which reflexively elicits an unconditioned response (UCR). If some new stimulus happens to occur whenever the UCS is present, the chances are very likely that this stimulus will begin to acquire the same properties as the UCS. That is, through the conditioning process, the new stimulus alone becomes capable of producing the UCR. At this point the new stimulus is referred to as the conditioned stimulus (CS), and the response as a conditioned response (CR).

As we shall see, classical conditioning has a number of features in common with other, more complex forms of learning. First, discontinuation of reinforcement (in this case, the occurrences of the UCS along with the CS) will lead to a disappearance, or extinction, of the response. Second, the conditioned response tends initially to generalize to other stimuli which are physically similar to the CS. Discrimination can be trained by repeatedly presenting these similar stimuli while only reinforcing the CS itself. This leads to extinction of the generalized response while simultaneously reinforcing the response to the specific CS. Finally, the CS itself can be used to reinforce a new association by repeatedly pairing a new stimulus with the CS. This is referred to as higher-order conditioning.

If human learning were limited only to responses acquired through classical conditioning, our ability to cope with the environment would be far from complete. We would salivate at the sight of food and feel fear in the presence of danger. Classical conditioning equips us to anticipate and to react emotionally in the presence of appropriate signs. What it does not do is to directly imply a means of coping with these signals. For this we must acquire the appropriate voluntary responses to obtain the food or to cope with the threat. For this form of learning, a whole new set of conditions are required; conditions associated with voluntary responses learned through "trial and error."

chapter 5

Learning
by Trial
and Error

The simplest way of learning to cope with the environment is learning through trial and error. There are occasional newspaper accounts of passengers in a small aircraft who have safely, if not elegantly, landed the plane after the pilot became ill and unable to fly. Put yourself in that position. It is not hard. You pull, push, twist, or turn every knob in sight until the radio comes on and contact is maintained with the nearest airport. An experienced pilot is called in to tell you step by step which controls cause the plane to climb, dive, turn, and change speed. The rest is learned by trial and error. Push too far forward on the control stick and you dive too fast; pull too far back and you climb. First too much, then too little, until the correct "feel" for the control is discovered. The delicate balance of each of the controls is practiced until, in someone's judgement, you are ready to land the aircraft. It has been done.

Learning to pilot an aircraft alone at the controls at 6000 feet is not exactly the recommended way to learn to fly. It is also not the best medium for a systematic study of trial and error learning. Nevertheless, it has all of the elements associated with this form of learning. Let us take a more pedestrian example which does allow a closer look at these elements.

ELEMENTS OF INSTRUMENTAL LEARNING

Trial-and-error learning is formally referred to as either *instrumental learning* (Kimble, 1961) or *operant conditioning* (Skinner, 1938). As distinct from classical conditioning, the individual is "instrumental" in making the correct response; he or she "operates" on the immediate environment to attain some goal.

Imagine a small room, totally devoid of any distractions, save for a single lever fixed to one of the walls. The "pilot" will be a hungry rat, and its task will be to discover that pressing the lever causes food to be delivered through a nearby chute. Here is the sequence of events.

1. MOTIVATION. The sequence begins with the organism in some drive-state which will be satisfied by the attainment of some goal. In this case it is a hungry rat seeking food.

2. EXPLORATION. Any goal-seeking creature, human or animal, is typically seen to increase its general activity. This is referred to as "exploratory behavior." It need not be purposeful and often takes the form of random activity.

3. RESPONSE AND REWARD. The effect of motivationally induced exploratory behavior is to increase the chances of the organism making a rewarding response; the rat accidentally bumps against the lever and the reward is delivered.

4. PRACTICE. Repeatedly pressing the lever and receiving a reward will gradually strengthen the association, increase the frequency with which the response if performed, and culminate in the response becoming a "habitual" way of reacting in these circumstances.

5. EXTINCTION. Other accidental responses which were not rewarded will gradually cease to be performed at the same time the rewarded response becomes strengthened. If we cease to deliver food when the lever is pressed the rat will eventually stop pressing the lever as well. The term *extinction* is borrowed from classical conditioning to describe the weakening of unrewarded responses.

Instrumental learning differs from classical conditioning in several ways. First, it involves the use of "reward" in learning, whereas classical conditioning does not. Second, it is up to the animal (or human) to initiate the correct response, with delivery of the reward *contingent* on the performance of that response.

Like classical conditioning, however, "learning curves" are typically gradual and may well be produced without any "understanding" on the part of the learner. To emphasize this similarity, the term *reinforcement* was also borrowed from classical conditioning. The reward is considered a "reinforcement" since, like the UCS in classical conditioning, it too first establishes, and then strengthens, a response.

Learning by Successive Approximations: "Shaping"

Both the novice pilot operating the controls and the rat pressing the lever are examples of instrumental learning. So too is the young child learning the first few words of his or her language. Consider the stimulus as a child's mother, and the response as the utterance of the word *mommy* in her presence.

From the previous outline we might infer that the infant must produce a variety of random sounds until the sound *mommy* is accidentally produced. This would be followed by the evident reward of affection and excitement from the mother. This in turn would increase the likelihood of *mommy* being uttered again, rewarded again, and thus becoming the habitual mode of response. It is hard to imagine how long it would take for *mommy* to be randomly produced, let alone produced in the presence of the potential reward-giver. Happily, there are a number of factors which make the acquisition possible.

First, the word *mommy* begins with a sound made primarily with the lips. To produce an *m* sound, the lips begin together, are held for a brief instant, and then opened slightly to release the buildup of air in the mouth. This is a very common "random" sound with infants. It is the same movement involved in blowing bubbles after a feeding.

While *mommy* has about as much chance of being "accidently" produced as a statement on Cartesian dualism, the *ma* sound is very likely indeed. (This is why words like *ma* or *mama* appear in so many different languages.)

The utterance of *ma*, or something like it, brings immediate reward. There is excitement, joy, and cuddling. Each time *ma* is produced in the mother's presence it is followed by reward. *Ma* without the presence of the mother remains unrewarded. All of the conditions of instrumental learning are present, and gradually the response *ma* in the presence of the mother becomes stable.

Ma is only an approximation to *mommy*. After some time, usually measurable in weeks, the baby's *ma* no longer excites the mother. Sometime later, however, the baby "playing" with the word *ma* might accidentally produce a closer approximation to *mommy*, perhaps *mama*. This leads to renewed excitement by the mother. *Mama* is rewarded, just as the simpler response *ma* had been earlier. Thus, through a series of successive approximations, each one rewarded in turn, the child acquires the appropriate response, *mommy.*

Skinner referred to such learning as learning by *successive approximations,* or *shaping.* A complex response is analyzed in terms of a sequence of simpler responses, each a closer approximation to the desired one. As each closer approximation is produced it is rewarded, while at the same time reward for the earlier ones is witheld. Shaping of the word *mommy* is no less effective simply because its use is intuitive rather than intentional.

Mommy Is Not Mother

Trial-and-error learning implies that the individual "tries." Our example of the accidental production of *ma* may be an apt one for illustrative purposes, but it is limited. Think only of the likelihood of the accidental production of *mother.* By the time the average child produces *mother,* she has been *mommy* for a long time. The name fits, and it works.

The final response, *mother,* is typically produced by conscious imitation. To be sure, the child's initial trials may be in error. After all, the *th* sound is often not established until the age of 6. But the point is, the child by this age is consciously trying to produce the correct response. There is *intention* to learn.

This is one reason why "pure" cases of instrumental learning are often difficult to observe in human behavior. Much of the trial and error is eliminated by conscious imitation which effectively short-cuts the preliminary stages. There are other reasons why "pure" instrumental learning can easily go unnoticed in casual observation.

1. Human instrumental learning is often accelerated by *transfer* of previous knowledge to the new task. Transfer of learning will be discussed in the next chapter, but it is a simple principle. Many tasks have shared components: learning to ride a motorcycle is easier if one already knows how to ride a bicycle; learning to use a computer teletype is faster if one can already type. In addition to specific skills, whole approaches to problems can be transferred from one learning situation to another. We hope that the child in the earlier grades will learn good "study habits," as well as the content of a particular exercise. Sometimes called *learning to learn,* or *learning sets,* such transfer of learning may partially account for the sudden solutions of problems associated with "insight" (Harlow, 1949).

2. Instrumental learning implies the acquisition of connections between stimuli (Ss) and responses (Rs). Most often in human learning we observe "chains" of many S-R connections. These are whole sequences of actions which appear as a single response. In the view of, for example, Gagné (1970), such complex chains must be preceded by initial learning of each of

the S-R links. In human learning, however, the process is often too rapid to be recognized.

3. Finally, the analysis of human learning is complicated by the presence of language mediation in the learning process. Through our language ability we do not always have to try and err. Language allows direct instruction by others. When used internally, it allows us to work out alternative possibilities without actually performing them. Human intellect, in other words, whether mediated by language or not, allows for a consideration of alternative possibilities without the need for physically manipulating objects in the environment for all the world—and especially psychologists—to see.

It was primarily for these reasons that learning in simple creatures like rats, pigeons, and cats became the focus for many early students of learning theory. By studying simpler organisms they might discover the principles of learning, and thus derive adequate theories to explain these principles. This done, they would use these studies as a model for human learning. Or at least it would guide their study. This was a crucial strategic decision in the history of learning theory, and one worth closer examination.

The Study of Instrumental Learning

THORNDIKE AND THE PROBLEM BOX

At about the same time Pavlov in the Soviet Union was conducting his pioneer studies of classical conditioning, E. L. Thorndike (1874–1949) in the United States began the study of what later would be known as instrumental, or operant, learning (Thorndike, 1911). Thorndike was a graduate student at Harvard when he began these studies, working first under William James, and later under Lloyd Morgan. Undoubtedly Thorndike's best known studies were those conducted with cats in a learning device he called a "problem box."

A cat is placed in a wooden, cagelike box with open slatted sides. The animal can see outside of the box but cannot escape unless the door is opened. Our vaunted human intellect would allow us to see that the cat could open the door by pulling a string loop which hangs from the ceiling of the cage and is connected to the door release mechanism. However, the cat cannot "see" this connection. It must discover the means of escape through trial and error.

Initially, the cat's activity is typical exploratory behavior. He runs around the cage, scratches and pokes the slats, tries unsuccessfully to squeeze his way out, and paws at the door. If he keeps this up long enough, and knowing the cat's penchant for pulling hanging strings, he will eventually claw the string and release the door mechanism. Once outside he is free to run and eat—the necessary reinforcement for the learning process.

We now come to the crucial step that lays the groundwork for the development of Thorndike's views. When the cat is returned to the box and the door latch mechanism reset, the cat does *not* immediately pull the string to gain release. Rather, he again runs around the cage, pawing, poking, and trying to squeeze out through the slats. As before, his eventual pulling of the release string seems as accidental as it did the first time. Thorndike replaced the cat in the cage for trial after trial, each time observing the initial random behavior, followed by the "accidental" pulling of the string.

We put "accidental" in quotes since Thorndike found the time interval between being put into the cage and pulling the release string to systematically decrease with each block of trials. While the correct response was always preceded by random activity, the time spent in such preliminary activity became less and less. As the trials were repeated, the escape time became shorter until, finally, the animal would go immediately to the string to effect his release. If we were to plot a graph of the response latencies as a function of the number of trials, we would see a progressive reduction in latency over the course of the trials. What Thorndike did *not* see was a sudden drop in latency, which would signify "understanding." Rather, the improvement was marked by a gradual reduction in the number of incorrect responses and the time devoted to their execution.

Common sense might suggest that, although the process was slow, the cat came to understand the connection between pulling the string and gaining release. It was the gradualness of the process, however, which suggested to Thorndike that this was *not* the case. He described what he saw as a gradual "stamping in" of an association between seeing the string (stimulus) and pulling it (response). The escape from the cage served to reinforce, or "strengthen," this S-R association. Contrary to the prevailing views of his day, Thorndike argued that animals solve problems neither by reasoning nor by instinct; they solve them by the gradual trial-and-error learning of the correct response.

Principles of Instrumental Learning

Thorndike's experiments led him to postulate three principles of instrumental learning.

1. THE LAW OF EFFECT.   Thorndike's view of the role of reward in learning has been called "behavioral hedonism." He argued in his *law of effect* that responses whose consequences are "pleasureable," or "satisfying," to an organism will tend to be repeatedly performed; those which are not, or are unpleasant, will diminish. His law of effect emphasized the consequences,

or "effect," of the response on the organism after it had been performed. He did not believe the cat performed the response in order to get the reward in any conscious or unconscious way. The learned association is between the stimulus (the string) and the response (pulling it). The reward only serves to make the consequences of that association satisfying and, hence, to encourage its repetition.

2. THE LAW OF EXERCISE. The *law of exercise* says that S-R connections will become strengthened through repetition. The more frequently the S-R association is used, or "exercised," the stronger the bond will become.

3. THE LAW OF READINESS. Thorndike's final principle, the *law of readiness*, was the precursor to the drive-reduction theory of reinforcement. An event will be "pleasurable" only if the animal is in a state of motivational "readiness" for it to be so. That is, in more current usage, a potential reinforcer will be effective only to the extent that it satisfies some preexisting drive in the animal.

THE DEVELOPMENT OF S-R THEORY

A notable feature of Thorndike's account of trial-and-error learning is the absence of such notions as "understanding," or "intentional planning," on the part of the animal. The reader may feel that, at least for him or her, learning is not the result of a gradual "stamping in" of associations. It is very much a cognitive operation, replete with conscious intent and understanding. However, could not associations be formed through Thorndike's S-R principles, and only later be explained introspectively by us in cognitive terms? After all, people are notoriously ineffective reporters of their own mental processes. Further, Thorndike might have countered, if we can account for instrumental learning without having to invoke abstract internal mental states, why invoke them at all?

These views were the driving force behind the behaviorist tradition in early learning theory, and came to be referred to simply as the *S-R theory* of learning (Spence, 1948, 1951, 1960). As later research moved away from simple learning tasks to the greater complexity of concept and rule learning, and of human memory, S-R theory and its behaviorist parent found fewer and fewer adherents. Some felt that the postulates of S-R theory were wrong; others simply found them too limited. It is certainly the case that the impatience of youth (psychology is still a young science) led us to attack problems the early S-R theorists felt ill-equipped to handle.

S-R theory, however, played a dominant role in early thinking, and many of its principles have stood the test of time. The major behaviorists, like Watson, Hull, Guthrie, and Skinner, made important contributions to learning theory. The last three played a very special role in S-R theory and deserve special attention.

Clark L. Hull (1884–1952)

Hull began with Thorndike's basic principles and developed them into a highly sophisticated system of postulates and theorems (Hull, 1943, 1951, 1952). Like other behaviorists, he saw human and animal learning in stimulus-response terms, arguing that a single set of principles could potentially explain the learning of both.

Most noteworthy was Hull's development of Thorndike's laws of effect and readiness into the drive-reduction theory of reinforcement (see Chapter 3). His overall goal was the eventual production of a systematic set of formulas, such that, given knowledge of a stimulus and surrounding events, one could accurately predict the resultant behavior.

Hull introduced the term "habit strength" to learning theory. He represented it symbolically as $_sH_R$, to denote the bond between a stimulus and a response after learning. Using algebraic notation, he developed tentative formulas relating $_sH_R$ to such variables as the number of reinforced trials, the delay of reinforcement, the strength of the drive state, and the amount of reinforcement. His hope was that a limited set of such formulas could be derived, such that given certain values, one could predict the theoretical values of others.

Much of the "raw data" for such a model is now available. As we shall see, however, the complexity of the interactions make it unlikely that Hull could have succeeded in the complete specification he argued so strongly for in principle.

One of Hull's notions, that of the *habit family hierarchy*, later appeared in the development of modern *behavior therapy*. In any instrumental learning situation, a particular stimulus may acquire a number of habitual responses, provided they all lead to the same goal. Hull's use of the term *hierarchy* implied that some responses will be stronger than others. This is usually due to the relative frequency of their being reinforced in past experience.

Desensitization, one technique in behavior therapy, is sometimes used in the treatment of irrational fears (phobias). The therapy begins with the client and therapist specifying the client's "fear hierarchy." For example, if the problem relates to an irrational fear of insects, it is likely that some insects are more upsetting to the client than others. Once the hierarchy is specified, the therapist and client start at the bottom of the list, "unlearning" the fear response to the least upsetting of insects (e.g., ants). This typically involves gradual exposure first to pictures, then to live ants, much in the manner of *shaping* as previously discussed. Once ants can be confronted without fear, the therapist and client systematically work up the hierarchy until they are ready to deal with the most upsetting creatures on the list (e.g., spiders).

Edwin Guthrie (1886-1959)

While Hull built his ideas on Thorndike's principles, Guthrie actively challenged them. While somewhat of a rebel, Guthrie rebelled not against S-R theory or the behaviorist viewpoint; he adopted both with enthusiasm. His disagreement centered on the roles of *reinforcement* and *practice* in S-R learning.

First, Guthrie denied the necessity of reinforcement for the establishment of a learned response. He argued that, as long as they occur close together in time, events will become associated. When a stimulus occurs contiguously with the performance of a response, a bond will form between them. This became known as the *contiguity S-R theory* (Guthrie, 1935, 1959). Reinforcement might be important only to the extent that it calls attention to the stimulus or makes it worthwhile for the animal to perform the learned response.

Guthrie's denial of the law of effect was accompanied by a questioning of the law of exercise. He argued that S-R bonds can be formed completely on their first pairing, and do not need to be strengthened by further practice. This notion of "one-trial" learning is an interesting one, especially as it reappeared later in connection with human verbal learning (Estes, 1960). (This will be discussed in Chapter 7.)

How would Guthrie handle the obvious importance of practice? Since no recurrence of a stimulus is ever exactly identical, what appears to be improvement with practice may in fact be a series of "one-shot" learning of each new S-R connection. In other words, what appears as a strengthening of a single S-R bond may actually represent the attachment of the response to a variety of slight variations in the stimulus.

One implication of Guthrie's contiguity theory is that associations, once formed, are never lost. All that happens over time is that new habits replace old ones. We know this view in the form of learning to reach for chewing gum instead of a cigarette. What others might call the "breaking" of a habit Guthrie would call, "substituting one habit for another."

B. F. Skinner (1904-   )

It is appropriate to end this brief discussion with Skinner, since, by doing so, we come full circle. Skinner is very much a learning theorist in the behaviorist tradition. Skinner stands out among other theorists precisely for the reason that his system of learning is largely "a-theoretical," in the sense that he has consciously devoted his energies to systematic description of the relevant variables and conditions that affect behavior change and has avoided the postulate of theoretical, causal explanations for what is observed.

Skinner termed responses in trial-and-error learning, *operants*, to stress that the organism operates on the environment. For this reason, he called instrumental learning *operant conditioning*. (He referred to responses in classical conditioning as *respondents*, because the animal merely responds to the environment. Classical conditioning he referred to as *respondent conditioning*.)

Skinner, like Hull and Thorndike, stressed the importance of reinforcement to behavioral change. Any response followed by reinforcement increases the probability of that response being produced again in the presence of the same stimulus. For any situation there exists a number of possible responses which might be performed. Recall, for example, Thorndike's cat poking the slats, trying to squeeze its way out, and pawing at the door of the cage. We might refer to pulling the release string as R_1, and the other responses as R_2, R_3, and R_4. Over the course of the training trials, only one response (R_1) is reinforced. That is the one which allows the animal to escape.

This reinforcement acts to strengthen the escape response, while other potential responses gradually weaken by remaining unreinforced. In this way, differential reinforcement of some responses rather than others thus establishes particular patterns of behavior.

Skinner, incidentally, distinguished between *extinction*, which he viewed as an active process, and *forgetting*, which he viewed as passive. Forgetting he saw as the weakening of a response through disuse; an act not repeated over the course of time becomes lost. Extinction involves the repeated performance of the response without reinforcement; thus, it represents a more active weakening of a response and occurs more rapidly than pure forgetting.

However a-theoretical Skinner may be, his impact on the general public has perhaps been greater than that of any other learning theorist. On the one hand, he developed a "technology" of learning which influenced the development of *programmed instruction* and the modern techniques of *behavior modification*. On the other hand, he has extended, in provocative ways, the idea of contingencies of reinforcement to the behavior not merely of individuals but of whole societies (Skinner, 1948a, 1953, 1971).

SUMMARY

It would be a very "satisfying effect," in Thorndike's terms, if we could treat these major theorists in a chronological sequence, showing how each improved upon the ideas of those who came before. As you can see, however, there was a considerable time overlap as each of these authors was writing. Thus, their theories of S-R learning tended to develop parallel to each other; each with its own message and its own goal.

Thorndike, Hull, Guthrie, and Skinner can all be classed as behaviorists, concentrating on acquisition of S-R bonds in instrumental learning and downplaying what to them was the hypothetical role of cognitive factors such as intention, understanding of relationships, and strategies of learning. These latter factors, which characterize so much of modern viewpoints of learning and memory, will be developed as our survey continues in subsequent chapters. However, let us return to the process of instrumental learning itself. We will want to look more closely at the comparison between instrumental learning and classical conditioning and at the factors which have been found to facilitate acquisition of learned associations.

Principles of Learning

CLASSICAL CONDITIONING AND INSTRUMENTAL LEARNING COMPARED

Importance of Contiguity

Classical conditioning and instrumental learning have a number of features in common. The first of these is the principle of *contiguity.* In classical conditioning, both the CS and the reinforcing UCS must occur fairly close together in time for a conditioned response to be acquired. The sense of "reinforcement" in instrumental learning is very different. In instrumental learning it takes on the connotation of "reward," in that it satisfies some need of the organism, and its availability is contingent on performance of the correct response. The principle of contiguity, however, still applies. To be most effective, the interval between response and reinforcement should be as short as possible, at least in the initial stages of training.

Acquisition and Extinction

A second similarity between classical conditioning and instrumental learning is in the shape of the *acquisition* and *extinction* curves. Figure 4.1 in the previous chapter shows the acquisition curve for classical conditioning. When repeated pairing of the CS and UCS occurs, the frequency with which the CR is elicited by the CS steadily increases until the curve reaches its asymptote. The learning curve then levels off as the association is fully formed. In instrumental learning, an animal might be required to turn in a particular direction in a maze to find food reinforcement. In this case, the strength of the learning would be represented by the relative frequency with which it turns in the correct direction in the maze. While the conditions of learning are very different, the learning curve itself shows the same gradual rise, and tapering off, of the negatively accelerating learning curve observed in classical conditioning.

Extinction in instrumental learning occurs when reinforcement is withheld following the correct response. Should we remove the food from the goal arm of the maze, the frequency with which the animal turns in the correct direction will gradually diminish until he begins to turn either right or left randomly. Indeed, extinction curves in instrumental learning very frequently look quite similar to those for extinction in classical conditioning (see Figure 4.1).

Spontaneous Recovery

A third similarity is the frequent appearance of *spontaneous recovery* (Figure 4.1). In both the case of classical conditioning and instrumental learning, responses sometimes reappear after apparent extinction. If an animal is removed from the maze for a few hours, or a day, and then returned to the maze, it will often turn immediately in the old, correct, direction. As in classical conditioning, the appearance of spontaneous recovery in instrumental learning implies that some trace of the old habit still remains in the nervous system after apparent extinction. In both cases, reextinction will rapidly occur unless the response is again reinforced. Similarly, relearning after extinction can be accomplished at a more rapid rate than was initially required.

Stimulus Generalization

A fourth similarity is the appearance of *generalization* early in the learning process. Figure 5.1 shows a typical gradient of generalization in an instrumental learning situation. The data are taken from Guttman & Kalish (1956), who reinforced a pigeon whenever it pecked at a square of a certain color (arrow). Once the response was established, they introduced a variety of different colors to the bird. The closer each of these colors was to the training stimulus, the greater the number of pecking responses the bird gave to each. As in classical conditioning, repeated reinforcement of the single training color will gradually reduce the spread of the gradient of generalization, until the animal responds only to the specific, reinforced, color. This is again referred to as *discrimination*.

Secondary Reinforcement

Finally, instrumental learning also shows something analogous to the *higher-order conditioning* of classical conditioning. In instrumental learning

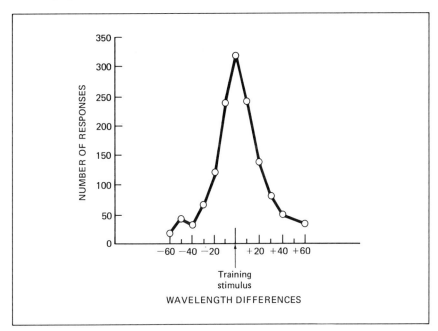

Figure 5.1 Gradient of generalization demonstrated for pigeons who were trained to respond to one color (training stimulus) and were then tested on other colors of varying degrees of similarity to the training stimulus. The generalization gradient was measured by the number of pecking responses to each of the test colors. (*Source:* N. Guttman and H. I. Kalish, Discriminability and stimulus generalization. *Journal of Experimental Psychology*, 1956, 51: fig. 3, pg. 83. Copyright 1956 by the American Psychological Association. Reprinted by permission.)

the same phenomenon is referred to as *secondary reinforcement*. Although briefly discussed in Chapter 3, secondary reinforcement is an important concept and warrants further attention.

SECONDARY REINFORCEMENT. The phenomenon of higher-order conditioning in classical conditioning referred to the way in which a CS may acquire reinforcing properties of its own through its association with the UCS. For example, Pavlov conditioned dogs to salivate at the sound of a bell. Once this was established, he then repeatedly paired the bell with a flashing light. Using the bell alone as reinforcement, he was able to condition the dog to salivate whenever the light was flashed.

Secondary reinforcement in instrumental learning (sometimes called *conditioned reinforcement*) follows the same principle. We referred earlier to the studies by Wolfe (1936), who rewarded chimpanzees with poker chips which could be inserted into a vending machine to receive the primary reinforcement of food. This association between the token reward and the food reward itself became so strong that the chimps began to value the poker chips almost as highly as the food itself. Indeed, both Wolfe and later workers have observed chimps to put the chips in their mouth as if they were actually the food they had come to represent (Kelleher, 1957).

Secondary reinforcement has a special place in instrumental learning for its broadening of the concept of reinforcement. As we saw in Chapter 3, the notion of secondary reinforcement has been used to bridge the gap between learning for primary reinforcement such as food or water, and the more complex human motivations such as drives for achievement, status, and, perhaps, for self-actualization.

CLASSICAL CONDITIONING AND INSTRUMENTAL LEARNING CONTRASTED

Having pointed to the similarities between classical conditioning and instrumental learning, we can now summarize the contrasts between the two.

1. In classical conditioning, reinforcement refers to the presentation of a CS in contiguity with a UCS, usually defined as a stimulus which reflexively produces a UCR prior to any learning. In instrumental learning, reinforcement refers to the presentation of a reward (or punishment) following the performance of some response.
2. In classical conditioning, the organism is passive, in the sense that the UCS occurs independent of the organism's behavior, and it elicits the response. In instrumental learning, the organism is active, in the sense that the reinforcement follows the response, the response must be initiated by the organism, and the reinforcement is contingent on the performance of the correct response.
3. Classical conditioning usually involves the reflexive, autonomic nervous system, while instrumental learning usually involves the voluntary, somatic nervous system.
4. In human learning, classical conditioning is involved in learning emotional responses, such as fears, attitudes, or feelings toward objects. Instrumental learning is involved in goal seeking behavior, where the person operates actively upon his or her environment.

Escape and Avoidance Learning

Although classical conditioning and instrumental learning are conceptually quite different, the two can interact within a single learning situation. Some very early animal experiments illustrate this point (cf. Solomon & Wynne, 1953). Rather than take a single experiment, a composite picture of several will best illustrate the point.

A rat is placed in a small box with an electric grid on the floor, an overhead light, and a lever connected to a shock apparatus. First, the light is presented. Ten seconds later, the rat receives an electric shock from the floor of the cage. The rat accidentally pushes against the lever, which automatically terminates the shock. It takes relatively few trials before the rat learns to press the lever as soon as the shock is felt. This is referred to as *escape learning;* the rat learns the means to escape the painful shock.

If the experiment continues long enough, the rat may learn to avoid the shock altogether. That is, as soon as the light comes on, and before the ten-second interval has elapsed, he rushes to press the lever to prevent the administration of the shock. This, appropriately, would be called *avoidance learning.*

Do we classify avoidance learning as classical conditioning or as instrumental learning? In fact, it contains elements of both. This view, expressed by Mowrer (1947), has been referred to as a *two-factor theory* of avoidance. His argument runs as follows. The first stage of learning involves classical conditioning. Over the first few trials, the animal's fear reaction (UCR) to the electric shock (UCS) becomes associated with the warning light (CS). This first stage of learning is complete when the onset of the warning light induces conditioned fear in the animal.

The second stage involves the animal's learning of the *instrumental response* of pressing the lever. This is discovered through trial and error in the usual instrumental fashion. The reinforcement, of course, is the "reward" of avoiding the shock or, more specifically, the fear reduction associated with pressing the lever.

PUNISHMENT VERSUS NEGATIVE REINFORCEMENT. This study of avoidance conditioning may strike the reader as a rather traumatic experience for the rat. And indeed it is. As we recall from Chapter 3 (if not from our own experience), the consequences of negative reinforcement as an incentive for learning can be disastrous, especially if the means of avoiding the punishment are not quickly discovered. Learning through fear, in experiments such as this one, can produce a complete breakdown in performance. If the shock is severe enough, no learning at all will take place (Moyer & Korn, 1964).

The avoidance experiment offers a good illustration of the earlier mentioned formal distinction between "punishment" and "negative reinforcement." *Negative reinforcement* refers to the removal of a noxious stimulus which has the effect of increasing the probability of a response being performed. The termination of the shock in this experiment can be called negative reinforcement. When the lever is pressed, the shock is turned off, and this increases the likelihood of the rat pressing the lever on later occasions.

Punishment refers to the presentation of any noxious stimulus which, when applied, decreases the probability of a response being performed. For example, if a rat were to receive a shock when it pressed the lever, this would be called punishment, since it would reduce the likelihood of his pressing the lever on subsequent occasions.

SUMMARY

Instrumental learning shares a number of features with classical conditioning. The principle of contiguity continues to apply. The more closely in time the reinforcement follows the instrumental response, the more rapidly learning will take place. Performance curves for acquisition, extinction, spontaneous recovery, and gradients of generalization follow the same form over learning trials as they do in classical conditioning. Finally, the higher-order conditioning of classical conditioning has its instrumental counterpart in secondary reinforcement. An originally neutral stimulus can acquire reinforcing properties through its association with a primary reinforcer, such as food.

The differences between classical conditioning and instrumental learning center largely on the use and meaning of reinforcement. In classical conditioning, reinforcement is represented by presentation of the UCS in contiguity with the CS which leads to the development of the conditioned response. In instrumental learning, reinforcement takes the connotation of "reward," is presented after the response has been performed, and is contingent on it being performed correctly.

Positive reinforcement in instrumental learning refers to the application of any pleasurable stimulus, following a response, which increases the likelihood of that response. Negative reinforcement refers to the removal of any noxious stimulus which has the effect of increasing the probability of that response. Punishment refers to the application of any noxious stimulus which inhibits or decreases the probability of a response which precedes it.

Reinforcement in Instrumental Learning

PARAMETERS OF REINFORCEMENT

We said earlier that one of Hull's goals was the eventual specification of a set of formulas such that, given the stimulus and the surrounding events, one could predict behavior without error. Although his dream has remained unfulfilled, it is not surprising that students of learning theory have devoted considerable effort toward this end. The "surrounding events" to receive the most attention have been the parameters of reinforcement and the way they interact with speed of learning.

The complexity of human behavior, and the important role of instrinsic motivation, again led theorists to the study of lower animals in simple learning tasks.

Amount of Reinforcement

We know from previous discussion that any organism, human or animal, will perform a learning task in order to satisfy a drive, and that this satisfaction supplies the reinforcement necessary for learning. It should thus follow that, the greater the drive, and/or magnitude of reinforcement, the faster will be the rate of learning.

The upper panel (A) of Figure 5.2 shows results obtained by Clayton (1964) for three groups of rats, each rewarded with a different amount of food on reaching the correct goal arm of a maze. Whether reinforced with one, two, or four food pellets, all three groups eventually attained the same level of performance, and all show learning curves of a similar shape. The difference lies in the rate of learning. The four-pellet group reaches this level an average of some six training sessions sooner than the other groups receiving smaller amounts of food.

Wolf, Giles, and Hall (1968) applied this principle to an analysis of reward and behavior with a remedial class for retarded children. Magnitude of reward was varied by allowing the children to earn various numbers of points for successful completion of assignments. Some assignments had their point value increased, while others did not. In all cases the points could later be exchanged for more tangible rewards such as candy or field trips. (This exchange principle is cometimes referred to as a "token economy.")

As might be expected, the more points given for a completed assignment, the greater was the amount of assigned work completed. What might not have been expected, however, was a disappointingly task-specific effect of magnitude of reward. Only those assignments which had their point values increased showed the increase in performance. Other assignments whose point values were left unchanged showed virtually no carry-over of the effect. Reinforcement magnitude is an important parameter for performance, but, as this study suggests, other factors must be introduced to insure generalization of good performance from one task to another. More on this will be said later.

There is another limit to the effectiveness of increasing reward. The learning organism will eventually satiate in the presence of too much food, candy, or other primary reinforcers. Studies have shown that secondary reinforcers such as praise and attention can also be subject to satiation if overused (Gewirtz & Baer, 1958; Winkler, 1971). One notable exception may be the reward value of money. The desire for money may be truly insatiable precisely because it is but a token which can be used to obtain an infinite variety of different reinforcers.

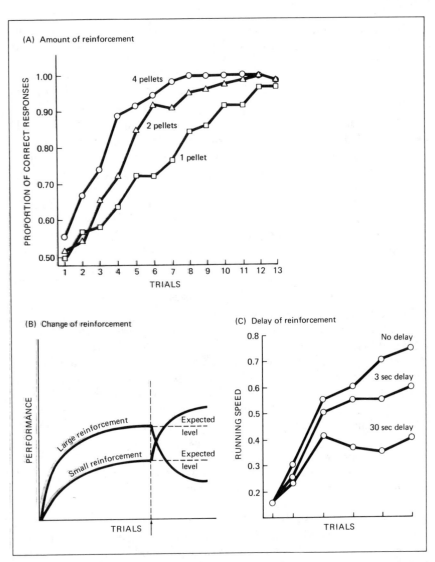

Figure 5.2 Effects of amount of reinforcement, reinforcement contrast, and delay of reinforcement on performance in animal learning. *A.* Effects of amount of reinforcement on speed of maze learning in the rat. (*Source:* K. N. Clayton, T-maze choice learning as a joint function of the reward magnitude for the alternatives. *Journal of Comparative and Physiological Psychology*, 1964, 58: fig. 1, pg. 335. Copyright 1964 by the American Psychological Association. Reprinted by permission.) *B.* Effects of changing amount of reinforcement in the course of learning: The Crespi Effect. (*Source:* Adapted from J. A. McGeogh and A. L. Irion, *The Psychology of Human Learning*, 2nd ed., New York: Longman, 1952. By permission of the publisher.) *C.* Effects of delay of food reinforcement on speed of rats running to correct arm of maze. *(Source:* Data from F. A. Logan, *Incentive*, New Haven: Yale University Press, 1960.)

Reinforcement Contrast

The principle of distributive justice was described in Chapter 3. The reward value of a stimulus often depends less on its absolute magnitude than on its magnitude relative to what the individual expected to receive, or what he or she thinks others may be receiving. This may be another seemingly unique human trait that is not so uniquely "human" after all. Studies with lower animals have shown an effect intriguingly similar to distributive justice.

Zeaman (1949) reinforced two groups of rats with different amounts of cheese when they ran to the end of a straight maze. As we would expect from the previous discussion, the rats receiving the larger amount of food reward ran down the maze significantly faster than the group with smaller reward. Halfway through the experiment, however, Zeaman switched the amount of reinforcement each group received. The rats who had been rewarded with the large amount of cheese now got the smaller amount, and vice versa.

The results were clear: those rats who had started on the smaller amount of cheese increased their running speed, while the group which had started on the larger amount decreased their speed. Can we describe the second group as "disappointed," or "depressed"?

This study is an example of the *Crespi Effect*, shown in idealized form, in the lower left panel (B) of Figure 5.2. In fact, Crespi (1942) used these very human terms to describe the effect of successive contrast from a large to small reward, or from a small to a large one. He called the better-than-expected performance following sudden increase in reward magnitude an "elation effect" and the dramatic drop in performance following reduced reward a "depression effect."

Figure 5.2 (B) is an idealized graph, and more recent studies have shown the depression effect to be a more reliable finding than the elation effect. That is, the negative contrast of a sudden reduction in reinforcement will reliably produce the depression effect. The positive contrast of increasing the magnitude of the reward, however, is not always found (Hulse, 1973). Nevertheless, the parallel between the Crespi Effect and distributive justice is interesting. If frustrated expectation is truly the genesis of distributive justice, it appears to be a parameter of reinforcement which generalizes across species.

Delay of Reinforcement

It is axiomatic in education that a reward has its greatest effect when it is received as soon as possible after the correct act has been performed. This is an important principle, recognized by any teacher who works late into the night to insure rapid return of graded examinations. This too is not unique to the human. The final panel (C) in Figure 5.2 is based on research by Logan (1960) who trained three groups of rats to run a maze for the same reinforcement. The only difference was that one group received reinforcement immediately after reaching the goal arm, one group had to wait 3 seconds for the reward, and the third group had a 30 second delay in reward. As Figure 5.2 (C) shows, the shorter the delay between the correct response and the reinforcement, the faster the animals ran to the correct arm of the maze.

The principle of effectiveness of immediate reinforcement has been well established in both the human and animal literature (Skinner, 1953; Kimble, 1961). While rats can show learning with surprisingly long delays in reinforcement, sometimes up to 60 minutes, its effectiveness is significantly reduced (Lett, 1975). Interestingly, however, it is possible in some cases to partially offset the detrimental effects of a delay in reward by increasing its magnitude (Logan, 1965; Shanab & Biller, 1972). Indeed, the interaction between magnitude and delay is so intricate that it is possible to contrive experiments where, for example, pigeons are given a choice of pecking one key for a small reward delivered after a short delay, or a larger reward delivered after a long delay. In such cases, pigeons will invariably choose the smaller reward with a short delay (cf. Ainslie, 1974).

In human learning, immediate reinforcement is especially important in the early stages of response acquisition. Once the response has become consistent, however, the delay between response and reinforcement can often be extended without serious performance decrement. Once performance has been stabilized, reinforcers can be delivered every other day, or at the end of several days, with good effectiveness (cf. Cotler, Applegate, King & Kristal, 1972). Indeed, as we shall see in the following section, intermittent reinforcement can have certain advantages.

PARTIAL REINFORCEMENT

It might be thought that, in some ideal world, reinforcement should follow each and every performance of a desired behavior. The parent should notice and praise the child each and every time he or she looks both ways before crossing the street. The teacher should reward a pupil each and every time he or she pays attention in class or completes an assigned project on time.

This ideal world does not exist. Good behavior often goes unnoticed and, hence, unrewarded. It is one of the fascinations of instrumental learning, however, that the natural inconsistencies of reward often have considerable advantage over the "ideal" world of constant reinforcement.

In learning theory, reinforcement following each and every response is referred to as *continuous reinforcement*. Reinforcing only occasionally is referred to as *partial reinforcement*. In controlled laboratory settings it can be reliably shown that while continuous reinforcement yields a more rapid rate of learning than partial reinforcement, partial reinforcement results in greater resistance to extinction. That is, once the response is learned, it will continue to be performed for a longer time after reinforcement has been terminated.

Figure 5.3 shows results from an experiment by Weinstock (1954) for three groups of rats who had learned the same maze. One group learned with continuous (100 percent) reinforcement: they were fed each and every time they reached the correct goal arm. The other two groups learned with partial reinforcement: one group was rewarded 80 percent of the time; the other group, 30 percent of the time they reached the correct goal arm.

From the first principle of partial versus continuous reinforcement, we know that the most rapid learning took place with the continuous (100 percent) group. The graph shows, however, the dramatic differences in *extinction rates* when the rats were allowed to run through the maze 20 times

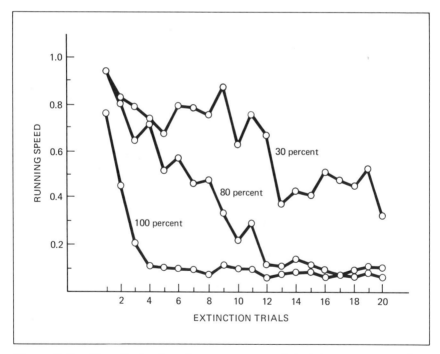

Figure 5.3   The effects of continuous versus partial reinforcement on extinction rates in maze learning. (*Source:* S. Weinstock, Resistance to extinction of a running response following partial reinforcement under widely spaced trials. *Journal of Comparative and Physiological Psychology*, 1954, 47: fig. 2, pg. 320. Copyright 1954 by the American Psychological Association. Reprinted by permission.)

without any reinforcement at the correct goal arm. The continuous (100 percent) reinforcement group shows a precipitous drop in running speed to the correct arm, almost as soon as the reward is discontinued. This is sharply contrasted with the partial reinforcement groups, especially the 30 percent group, both of which show greater resistance to extinction.

Schedules of Reinforcement

Partial reinforcement simply means that the correct response is not necessarily reinforced every time it occurs. Largely through the impetus of B. F. Skinner (1956), a variety of potential "schedules" of partial reinforcement have received systematic study. As we shall see, each produces its own characteristic form of behavior.

FIXED SCHEDULES. The most common way to explore these schedules in lower animals is through a free-responding situation in a *Skinner box.* The animal, say a pigeon, is placed in a specially constructed cage which has a mechanism for automatically supplying a food reward when the pigeon happens to press a small plastic key mounted in the wall. A recording apparatus registers the number of responses per unit time, which allows one to look at rate of responding of the animal under various schedules either in acquisition or extinction.

Fixed schedules of partial reinforcement are of two general types. The first is a *fixed ratio* (FR) schedule. In this case, the apparatus is set so that reinforcement is automatically delivered after a fixed number of responses. For example, we might put the bird on a 10 : 1 ratio schedule. That is, it receives food every tenth time it pecks the response key. The FR schedule is analogous to "piece work" in a factory. Payment depends on the "worker's" rate of output.

The second type of fixed schedule is a *fixed interval* (FI) schedule. Here reinforcement is automatically delivered for the first response the pigeon makes after some time interval, say, five minutes, has elapsed. This has been likened to a salaried employee, who receives a constant wage at the end of each week, provided the work exceeds some minimal level.

Although there are differences in the pattern of extinction between FR and FI schedules, they are both examples of partial reinforcement. As such, animals under both FR and FI schedules exhibit a higher resistance to extinction after reinforcement has been discontinued than do animals trained under continuous reinforcement. A singular feature of both schedules, however, is that the animal's rate of responding tends to increase just before reinforcement is due, and then slackens to a slower rate after the reinforcement has been delivered. One cannot help but be reminded of the "clock-watching" behavior of many humans!

VARIABLE SCHEDULES. Variable schedules of partial reinforcement can have the same ratio and interval variations as the fixed schedules. In the *variable ratio* (VR) schedule, we first decide on some total proportion of responses which will be reinforced. For example, we might again use a 10 : 1 ratio, as previously described. Unlike the FR schedule, however, in this case the reinforcement will come irregularly. The animal may receive reinforcement for 3 responses in a row, and then not receive reinforcement for another 13. The overall average ratio is kept at 10 : 1, but in this case, the animal never knows which peck of the key will be reinforced.

The *variable interval* (VI) schedule follows the same principle. Instead of being reinforced for the first response after every five minutes has elapsed, the animal is reinforced an average of every five minutes; sometimes sooner, sometimes later. Thus, over the course of the entire training session, animals on FR and VR schedules, and ones on FI and VI schedules, might receive the same number of reinforcements. What differs is the *predictability* of their arrival.

Experimental studies have shown variable schedules to completely eliminate the "clock-watching" behavior typical of fixed schedules. Rates of responding remain high and regular. Further, while all partial schedules are more resistant to extinction than continuous reinforcement, variable schedules are the most resistant (Skinner, 1956). A case in point is the habitual gambler who plays slot machines to a compulsive degree. This behavior can be maintained, even in the face of repeated losses, because the machine "pays off" on a VR schedule of reinforcement. That is, we have a high response rate, combined with extraordinary resistance to extinction.

Skinner (1956) has reported experimental switching from ratio to interval schedules to produce remarkably reliable and predictable changes in behavior patterns of rats and pigeons. No less striking than the control of the behavior itself has been his demonstration of the uniformity of the effects across different species. (Learning and extinction curves under these schedules are remarkably similar whether the results are obtained from pigeons, rats, or humans.)

The Application of Schedules

In summary, continuous reinforcement produces a high level of performance, but only as long as the behavior is reinforced. Partial reinforcement, although typically showing a slower acquisition of responses, has the advantage of greater resistance to extinction once reinforcement has been discontinued. The advantages of both can be combined by developing the response through continuous reinforcement and maintaining the reinforcement until the performance has reached a good level. At that point, the continuous schedule can gradually be changed to a partial schedule, with increasingly intermittant reinforcement. This will insure the maintenance of a high response level for longer periods after the reinforcement is eventually withdrawn (cf. Kazdin & Polster, 1973).

Bugelski (1971) applies these principles to the use of reinforcement in teaching children. (1) *In the early stages of training, reinforce the child at every occurrence of the desired response.* This quickly identifies the desired behavior for the child, and also produces enough occurrences of that behavior for the connection with the reinforcement to become established. (2) *Once learning is well under way, begin to omit reinforcement from time to time.* Although reinforcement is important, we have seen that a lack of consistent reinforcement does not have disastrous consequences. On the contrary, benefits of partial reinforcement to extinction are clearly established. Decreasing the frequency of reinforcement also prepares the child for experience outside the training situation where continuous reinforcement is rare.

The essence of instrumental training, in other words, ". . . involves the careful witholding and delaying of reinforcers; in short, manipulating the reinforcement schedules" (Bugelski, 1971, pg. 96).

REINFORCEMENT AND THE REINFORCER

The essential condition of instrumental learning, regardless of the reinforcement schedule used, is that reinforcement should be contingent on the performance of the desired response. If reinforcement arrives in an uncontrolled way, the results are hard to predict.

Superstition in the Pigeon

What would happen if the response key in a Skinner box were disconnected from the mechanism which ordinarily delivers food when the key is pressed, and reinforcement is automatically delivered every 10 seconds, regardless of what the pigeon happens to be doing at that moment? Skinner (1948b) did just this with pigeons. After a period of such reinforcement, the birds began to display bizarre, stereotyped behavior, such as flapping their wings or circling the cage. In short, they repeatedly performed whatever they happened to be doing when the reinforcement was delivered. Skinner referred to this as "superstitious" behavior—habitual behavior bearing no systematic relation to any conceivable gain to the environment.

Superstitious behavior in children (or adults) is not uncommon. A child might take a "lucky charm" to an examination and do unusually well. From that point on, the charm becomes imbued with "magical" properties and becomes a fixed item of examination equipment. Ironically, if the charm gives the child needed confidence, it could actually influence his or her behavior. Examination scores will go up, and the superstition continues to be reinforced. Similarly, the loss of the charm could so unnerve the child that he or she does poorly in the next examination. And so, the "magical" properties of the charm become further established.

Skinner's study of superstition in the pigeon makes an important point. Unless reinforcement is carefully geared to the desired behavior, almost any behavior could be inadvertently reinforced. For example, in Chapter 3 we cautioned against the use of reprimands for bad behavior which might inadvertently reinforce the child who desires the attention such a reprimand brings. The thoughtless administration of reprimands can indeed reinforce disruptive, "attention-getting" behavior. Numerous studies have shown how the frequency of bad behaviors followed by reprimands can increase, rather than decrease (Madsen, Becker, Thomas, Koser & Plager, 1970; O'Leary, Kaufman, Kass & Drabman, 1970).

Freedom Versus Control

If we understand the needs of the child (or adult), and know how to supply these needs, one can both control behavior and create a climate which promotes learning and other productive behavior. All that is needed, suggest these studies, is an environment where the parent, teacher, or society, can control the application of reward.

The demonstrated ability for controlled manipulation of behavior through schedules of reinforcement has culminated in the technology of *behavior modification*. As these techniques have seen increased use in both classroom and clinic, so too have concerns been voiced (cf. Kazdin, 1975, pg. 50).

First, care must be taken in the choice of reinforcement. For example, there is some evidence that the means of behavior control used by parents may be adopted by their children. Parents who use punitive methods in training their children may find themselves with children who are likewise aggressive in their interactions with playmates (Bandura & Walters, 1959).

Second, there is a danger that the desired behavior will only be performed when it is specifically rewarded. Kazdin cites a study of the use of monetary reward for good behavior in a classroom of institutionalized adolescents. These children were described as aggressive, manipulative, and uncontrollable. When money was paid for good behavior in afternoon classes, the frequence of inappropriate behavior diminished. However, in the morning sessions where the reward was not used, the bad behavior actually increased. As one of the girls in the study said, "If you don't pay us, we won't shape up" (Meichenbaum, Bowers & Ross, 1968, pg. 349). As Kazdin observes, it is hard to tell in this case who was manipulating whom.

The concern in the previous example is that when the reinforcement stops, so too will the desired behavior. Thus, the argument goes, why use reinforcement at all, if when we no longer reinforce the desired behavior, it will eventually extinguish? There are two counterarguments. First, we have already seen how the careful use of partial reinforcement can prolong the desired behavior before extinction. Second, and more important, instrumentally changing a person's behavior with extrinsic reinforcement often changes how other people respond to that person (Kazdin, 1975, pg. 53). Thus, the extrinsic reinforcement of tangible reward may later be replaced by the potentially more powerful and spontaneous reaction the child elicits from others when he or she behaves appropriately.

All of these concerns relate to the fear that control of behavior through contingencies of reinforcement may in some cases be ineffective. Interestingly, a much wider concern is expressed by those who fear that its effectiveness may be *too* great. One aspect of this fear is the societal question of how the control of behavior can itself be controlled.

There is a related fear that the increasing development of a technology of learning could produce an undesirable dependence on external control. This latter danger can arise from mistaking the *means* of control, for its desired *end*. As Howe (1972, pg. 37) points out, a teacher may use the means of rewarding a child to encourage activities which facilitate and stimulate learning. This *means* of behavior control, however, has as its ultimate goal the child's discovery that the learning activity itself is rewarding.

Thus, what begins as external control of behavior by others may end with the child initiating learning experiences for their own sake. As Howe argues, the issue of "freedom" versus "control" is, in truth, simply a contrast between the control of an individual by himself or herself and the control of the same person by someone else. The difference lies primarily in the "locus" of the controlling agent rather than in the basic principles of control (Howe, 1972, pg. 38).

SUMMARY

Reinforcement plays a central role in both animal and human learning, and the several principles of reinforcement can be summarized as follows. (1) Within limits, the greater the amount of reinforcement, the more rapid the rate of learning. (2) The shorter the delay between performance of a correct response and reinforcement, the more rapid the rate of learning. (3) Partial reinforcement produces slower initial learning than continuous reinforcement, but once reinforcement is discontinued, the learning is significantly more resistant to extinction. (4) Schedules of partial reinforcement can take the general form of either ratio or interval schedules which, in turn, can be either fixed or variable. Both VR and VI schedules yield high response rates which are less likely to fluctuate over time than performance under FR or FI schedules or reinforcement. (5) Because of the effectiveness of behavior control through contingencies of reinforcement, considerable care must be taken both in its application and in the broader implications of its use.

Some Final Questions

REINFORCEMENT: LEARNING OR PERFORMANCE?

We noted earlier that "pure" instrumental learning of single S-R associations is difficult to observe in human behavior. First, isolated response learning can be obscured by *transfer* from previous learning. Second, human learning is rapid, and *chains* of associations can appear without our noticing underlying, individual links. Third, the learning of *relations* through language meditation could obscure any S-R association learning which might be taking place.

As mentioned previously, it was for these reasons that early learning theorists opted for the study of simpler animals (rats, pigeons) in simple learning situations (mazes, Skinner boxes). From these studies, one could attempt to isolate the "pure" elements of instrumental learning. This, then, would be the solid foundation on which to build our knowedge of human learning; the base camp any explorer needs before he or she ventures to more dangerous regions.

One critic within the ranks of animal learning was E. C. Tolman (1886–1959). He publicly cautioned that current interpretations of S-R learning based on animals in simple learning situations could not only give us a limited account of animal (and human) learning, but it might also give us a misleading one (e.g., Tolman, 1938). A major problem is the distinction between acquiring *knowledge* (a capability) and exhibiting this capability in the form of an *action* (what the organism is observed to do). This distinction, which became a central one, is the distinction between *learning* and *performance.*

To understand Tolman's position, it is important to note that his criticism was a double-barreled one. One barrel was a caution in generalizing from rat learning to human learning. The other was a deep concern that S-R theory itself was too simple a model to account even for the behavior of a rat at the choice-point of a maze. Specifically, he asked two questions:

1. Is reinforcement really necessary for learning, as Hull and Thorndike had argued, or is reinforcement only necessary to give the animal an incentive to perform a learned response?
2. What does the rat really learn when it learns to run a maze? Is it truly a

series of left-right turns (i.e., S-R sequences), or could the animal be learning some rudimentary, but abstract, *relationship* between his starting point and the location of the food in the maze? Tolman metaphorically referred to this latter possibility as learning a "cognitive map."

Latent Learning

The question of whether reinforcement operates primarily on learning or on performance is a basic one. Recall the girl in the Meichenbaum et al. study, who said, "If you don't pay us, we won't shape up." In the realm of animal learning, we have seen the Crespi Effect, in which changing incentive in a learning task changes the level of performance.

Perhaps learning can take place without reinforcement. If a stimulus occurs at the same time as a response is performed, an association between the two will be formed (Guthrie, 1952). If this is true, the role of reinforcement in learning might be, first, to draw attention to the relevant stimulus so as to hasten the learned association and, second, to supply the incentive the animal (or human) needs to perform the learned response.

Tolman saw some evidence for this in the appearance of *latent learning* in lower animals. Latent learning, also known as *incidental learning*, refers to learning without any apparent intention to learn, or any apparent source of reinforcement. Examples in human learning are numerous. One can recall the clothes worn by a friend the previous day, or remember passing a restaurant on a particular street when on the way to somewhere else.

It may come as a surprise to discover that some learning theorists considered latent learning to be a "pseudophenomenon." They argued that reinforcement is always involved when learning occurs, but sometimes we are just not astute enough to recognize it. If latent learning does exist, however, it is obviously a direct contradiction to Thorndike's law of effect: learning occurs only as, and if, it is followed by satisfying consequences.

Blodgett (1929) claimed to have seen latent learning in a group of rats who were allowed to explore a maze without any reinforcement. When a particular goal arm was later reinforced with food, the rats given unreinforced experience with the maze quickly learned its location. They learned so quickly, that it seemed that some learning must have taken place prior to the introduction of food reinforcement. Encouraged by such reports, Tolman conducted a now classic experiment in latent learning in the rat (Tolman & Honzik, 1930).

Three groups of rats were run in the complex maze illustrated at the top of Figure 5.4. One group was trained over a two week period with food always found at the correct goal arm of the maze. The graph in Figure 5.4 shows the expected gradual reduction in errors as this group learned the most efficient route to the goal. The second group was allowed to run freely through the maze for the same period, but without any reinforcement. Not

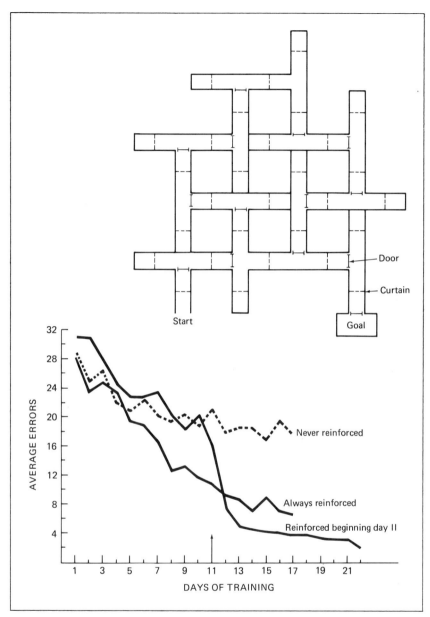

Figure 5.4 Latent learning in a complex maze. Three groups of rats were run through a maze similar to the one shown, containing both curtains and one-way doors. One group never had food at the goal box, and one group always did. The group of main interest was unreinforced until the eleventh day (arrow), when reinforcement was now always placed at the end of the goal arm. (*Source:* E. C. Tolman and C. H. Honzik, Introduction and removal of reward and maze performance in rats. *University of California Publications in Psychology,* vol. 4, fig. 4, pg. 267. Published in 1930 by The Regents of the University of California; reprinted by permission of The University of California Press.)

surprisingly, they show no particular preference for the unreinforced goal arm.

To answer the question of whether the reinforcement was actually necessary for learning, Tolman and Honzik took a third group of rats and, for the first ten days, allowed them to run through the maze without reinforcement. Up to this point their performance matched that of the second group (see Figure 5.4). That is, no special learning is evident. On the eleventh day, however, they began to reinforce the correct goal arm with food. The results are dramatic. By the next training session the rats' performance matched—even slightly exceeded—that of the group reinforced from the very start of the experiment. Clearly, the third group must have learned a great deal about the maze in those ten days without reinforcement.

To Tolman, this experiment suggested that learning can, and does, occur without reinforcement. It is only when reinforcement is introduced that we are able to see the effects of what has been learned. Reinforcement provides the incentive for performance. It is not, as Thorndike considered it, the adhesive for creating an S-R bond (Tolman, 1948).

The argument about latent learning was not closed by this experiment. Nevertheless, the results were challenging enough that by 1951 over 70 relevant studies on the subject had appeared in the research literature (Thistlethwaite, 1951).

Cognitive Learning in the Rat?

As Tolman's studies of latent learning questioned the law of effect, he also questioned exactly what it is the rat learns when we say it has learned a maze. As we have seen, the earliest view was that each choice-point acts as a stimulus to which the rat learns to associate a particular response (i.e., "turn right" "turn left," etc.). The maze was thus seen as an ideal model for S-R learning theory (Spence, 1951). Could it not be, however, that it only looks as if the rat learns a sequence of S-R turns? Perhaps the rat in fact learns relationships between stimuli; as Tolman called it, a "cognitive map" of the maze (Tolman, 1948).

Suppose we teach a group of rats to run the simple maze as illustrated in the left-hand panel of Figure 5.5. Sometimes they are made to begin from position S_1, and sometimes from position S_2. Each time, however, we shift the position of the food reinforcement (indicated by + in the diagram), so that reward is always obtained by turning to the right. We can call this group the "response learners," since it is assumed that they are learning the S-R association: "choice point (stimulus)→turn right (response)." Compare this with a second group of rats who learn the same maze with the arrangement shown in the right-hand panel of Figure 5.5. They also start from either S_1 or S_2, but in this case goal arm G_2 is always reinforced. Thus, sometimes food is obtained by turning right, and sometimes by turning left. We

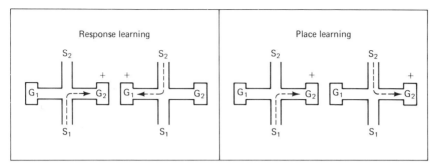

Figure 5.5 The response learner is started alternately from S_1 or S_2, with food placed either at G_1 or G_2, respectively. The animal is always reinforced for turning right. The place learner has the food always at G_2, such that sometimes he is reinforced for turning left, and sometimes for turning right. This group must learn spatial position, rather than a single turn sequence.

can call this *place learning,* since the only way the animals can obtain reinforcement is to learn its spatial location, independent of their own orientation in the maze.

Common sense, or at least the common sense of S-R theory, would predict faster learning for the response learners. After all, they simply have to learn a single association: "choice point→turn right." The fact is, place learners typically learn the task significantly faster (Tolman, Ritchie & Kalish, 1946). From this, Tolman and his colleagues inferred that *both* groups learned the spatial location of the food. The response learners took longer because shifting the location of the goal from trial to trial simply complicated their task.

These studies were followed by others, called "blocked-response" experiments. First, the animal is trained to follow a particular pathway to find food in a complex maze. At this point, the usual route is blocked, thus forcing the animal to find an entirely new route to the same goal. Blocked-response experiments typically show very quick adaptation to the new pathway, again suggesting that rats really do acquire some "understanding" of relationships within the maze (cf. Gleitman, 1955, 1963). Such evidence has led many to conclude that rats can indeed develop a cognitive map which only looks as if they had learned a simple sequence of left-right turns. Indeed, more detailed analyses have suggested that rats have the capacity for either place *or* response learning, depending on the situation and task requirements (Restle, 1957).

We need not belabor the point that studies of lower animals can give only limited help to the understanding of human learning. Indeed, Spence (1954), a strong supporter of S-R theory, recommended caution in applying it to real-life situations and also recognized that it was not yet, ". . . sufficiently abstract or complete to account for all the laboratory findings."

Tolman, credited with pioneering cognitive learning theory, based his position on two kinds of experiments. The first were studies of latent learning, which suggested that reinforcement is not necessary for the acquisition of associations, but supplies the incentive for the animal (or person) to demonstrate its knowledge. The second were studies of place learning, which suggested that the learning of relationships between stimuli is as characteristic of some lower animal learning as it appears to be of human learning. Ironically, while a critic of premature generalization from animal to human studies, Tolman in fact went some way in "reinforcing" a continued link between the two: S-R theory could not be the sole explanation of learning for either.

AUTONOMIC CONDITIONING: "BIOFEEDBACK"

Part of Skinner's (1938) distinction between classical conditioning and instrumental learning was an emphasis on the different character of the response in the two situations. Classical conditioning has its influence on the physiological responses of the involuntary, autonomic nervous system. These include such responses as salivation, pupil dilation, heart rate, and visceral, emotional responses. Responses in instrumental learning, on the other hand, are typically voluntary motor responses, such as taking the correct turn in a maze, pressing a lever, or sitting quietly in a classroom.

The possibility that autonomic behavior (the traditional province of classical conditioning) might be controllable through instrumental procedures has only recently received wide attention (cf. Kimmel, 1974).

Practitioners of yoga have long claimed voluntary control of many so-called involuntary autonomic responses, such as heart and respiration rate (Wenger & Bagchi, 1961; Wenger, Bagchi & Anand, 1961). How this could be possible seemed to defy logic until it was realized that such processes remain involuntary largely because we ordinarily have minimal feedback concerning their activity (Miller & DiCara, 1967; Miller, 1969). In other words, one cannot instrumentally condition a response unless one is aware of precisely when, and if, such a response is occurring. That is, the distinction may not be so much one of autonomic versus voluntary motor responses, as one of whether or not effective feedback is ordinarily available to the person.

Once this information is made available, the argument goes, there is no reason why control of these processes through instrumental procedures should not be possible. It is for this reason that research into this area is popularly referred to as *biofeedback;* the technology of signalling a person's biological state as a preliminary to learning its voluntary control.

A popular example is the control of a particular brain wave pattern known as the *alpha rhythm.* The alpha rhythm is commonly associated with a mental state paradoxically referred to as "passive alertness." It often occurs when a person is sitting quietly with his or her eyes closed. The regular alpha pattern abruptly changes to a more irregular brain wave pattern if the eyes are suddenly opened, or the person actively concentrates on some task such as mental arithmetic.

Ordinarily we have no direct control of this alpha activity, nor are we even aware of its existence. The first step in alpha conditioning is to make this information available by monitoring the brain wave patterns on an electroencephalograph (EEG). The volunteer subject is given a signal tone when the alpha rhythm appears, and it is turned off when the alpha stops. The subject's task is to voluntarily produce and terminate the alpha rhythm by regulating his or her mental activity.

The procedure itself takes the form of standard trial-and-error learning, reinforced by the feedback of the tone which signals moment-to-moment success or failure. Surprisingly little practice is needed for quite successful control of alpha rhythm (Nowlis & Kamiya, 1970).[1]

Studies of instrumental control of autonomic responses have covered wide ground, including the possibility of voluntary control of such medically critical responses as diastolic blood pressure (Shapiro, Schwartz & Tursky, 1972). It should be recognized, however, that this area of research is not without its disagreements and controversy (cf. Blanchard & Young, 1973; Engel, 1974). One central area of controversy is whether such biofeedback procedures *directly* control autonomic responses, or whether they do so only indirectly through somatic muscle involvement (Miller & Dworkin, 1974).

SUMMARY

The present chapter has attempted to trace the development of S-R learning theory, beginning with the pioneer work of E. L. Thorndike. To Thorndike, instrumental learning represented the gradual "stamping in" of associations through reinforcement of correct responses. These early studies led to his postulate of three laws of learning: the laws of effect, exercise, and readiness.

Reinforcement has always played a key role in learning theory, although its exact function has been a matter of some dispute. Thus, Hull was to develop Thorndike's most fundamental law, the law of effect, into the drive-reduction theory of reinforcement. Others showed how the secondary reinforcement qualities of learned drives could be derived from these basic principles. Finally, and largely through the impetus of B. F. Skinner, many years of research on contingencies and schedules of reinforcement led to the

---

[1] This particular research has some popular appeal because high alpha levels are thought to be associated with states of meditation—itself an increasingly popular subject.

beginnings of a systematic technology of learning. With it came the potential for very precise control and modification of behavior through careful control of contingencies of reinforcement.

While all learning theorists recognize that reinforcement is a key factor in learning, both Guthrie and Tolman were to question whether reinforcement is necessary for learning itself. Making the distinction between learning and performance, many were later to argue that learning can occur without the necessity of "satisfying consequences." Reinforcement may be critical in learning tasks both because it calls attention to the stimulus, and because it gives the organism the necessary incentive to perform the learned response.

We ended our discussion with Tolman's questioning of the applicability of simple S-R learning theory, not only to human learning, but to learning in lower animals as well. He argued that what often appears as a learned association between a stimulus and response may in reality reflect the learning of relationships between stimuli. In the context of maze learning, Tolman was to use the expression, "cognitive maps." In human learning, others were to adopt his term and refer more generally to "cognitive learning."

One distinction we made between learning in lower animals and learning in humans, is that, even when simple association learning is involved, one rarely sees the building up of isolated connections between single sets of stimuli and responses. Such connections do occur, but in human learning we tend to notice their appearance only as they form chains of associations. The types of association learning common to humans, and the relative rapidity of the learning process, tends to obscure the observation of the learning of the links themselves. It is to this subject that we now turn.

chapter 6

The Chaining
of Multiple
Associations:
SENSORIMOTOR
LEARNING

Limited associations between sets of simple stimuli and responses are hardly characteristic of human learning. When we think of human learning, we tend to think of two particular abilities which seem more representative. The first of these is a consequence of a highly developed sensory ability and manual dexterity, combined with a cognitive function which enables us to learn the use of tools. Variously referred to as *sensorimotor learning, motor learning, or skill learning,* this includes all related abilities from manipulating a pencil, learning to operate a complex machine, to playing a musical instrument with perhaps virtuoso ability.

A second class of human learning results from an equally happy coincidence of physical and mental endowment: the ability to learn and to use *verbal* materials.

Our own experience tells us that learning a motor skill, such as riding a bicycle or playing a musical instrument, requires considerable practice. Correct movements must be learned in their proper sequence, incorrect ones must be eliminated, and the entire set of movements must then be practiced until they become habitual. The elements of motor skill, in other words, are just those associated with instrumental learning, as described in the previous chapter.

Skill learning is accomplished through instrumental (operant) learning often facilitated by conscious imitation or direct verbal instruction. In this regard it includes, but is not limited to, the principles of learning discussed in the previous chapter. Because human motor learning includes such an enormous range of skills, it is easy to lose sight of the similarity in these underlying principles.

There is certainly a quantitative if not a qualitative leap from a child practicing the scales on the family piano to the expert pianist perhaps composing as he or she plays. In a similar way, the product of verbal learning includes both the student memorizing lines from a poem (perhaps with minimal understanding), and the poet in the act of creating the words which later come to haunt the memorizing student. In this latter regard, we might consider the thoughts of that controversial but brilliant master of extemporaneous speech, the British parliamentarian, Aneurin Bevan.

Bevan had a message as important to psychology as to the aspiring political orator, to whom these thoughts were primarily addressed.

At the heart of genius is mystery. If this were not so, then the secret of genius could be uncovered and made accessible to all. Thus genius is beyond science, for science is concerned with behavior that repeats itself with sufficient frequency to establish a pattern which we call laws. A scientific law is therefore nothing more or less than a description of events that can be predicted beforehand. The essence of genius consists in the fact that it contains a plus factor not amenable to prediction.

. . . The genuine orator, like his peers in other arts, cannot be predicted. He produces his results unexpectedly—quite often as much to himself as to his audience (Foot, 1973, pg. 244).

And Bevan, who considered himself less a politician than "a projectile discharged from the Welsh valleys," produced many such a devastating surprise.

Let us turn now to those aspects of motor and verbal learning which, in Bevan's words, repeat themselves "with sufficient frequency to establish a pattern which we call laws."

CHAINING OF ASSOCIATIONS. A concept often used to take the step from simple S-R learning to complex human sensorimotor and verbal learning, has been the notion of chaining. Chaining can be defined as connecting together, through practice, a sequence of two or more previously learned S-R associations (Gagné, 1970, pg. 42). Chaining can be described as an "association of associations," the learning of *sequences* of associations, or "links," which together form a chain of multiple associations.

In this chapter and the next, we will look first at sensorimotor learning, and then at one class of verbal behavior; that of rote verbal learning. As we do so, remember that while the notion of chaining may simplify our analysis, chaining itself is not simple. The person who says, "as simple as tying your own shoelaces," has obviously never tried to list in detail the sequence of motor responses actually required. More on this will be said later.

Elements of Skill Learning

Motor skill learning is a fascinating subject of study for a variety of reasons. One of these is the extraordinary resistance of forgetting shown by many motor skills. So-called continuous motor tasks, such as riding a bicycle, swimming, or skating, can be readily revived even after years of disuse (Bilodeau & Bilodeau, 1961). Second, really well-practiced, skilled performance can reach a state of "automaticity," in the sense that conscious attention seems no longer necessary for its execution (Fitts, 1964). Yet, paradoxically, we can often destroy the fluidity of skilled movements simply by trying to think consciously of how we are performing them! Finally, one can see an ability to learn motor sequences even when damage to the brain has made ordinary verbal memory virtually impossible (Starr & Phillips, 1970). You will recall the patient, "H. M.," whose operation to the brain left him almost totally debilitated when it came to the learning of new information. Although he could still not remember his current home address after several years since moving, examination showed that he could learn simple motor skills. We should add, of course, that while he showed consistent improvement over several days of training at a motor task, he had no conscious recollection of having ever practiced the task before (Milner, 1965).

This seeming separation between skilled performance and mental awareness is captured in the following example provided by Posner (1973, pg. 25). While a skilled typist can type the alphabet rapidly and accurately, this same typist may show considerable difficulty if asked simply to recite the keyboard positions of the letters from memory. Indeed, our typist might have to imagine the actual act of typing the letters in order to do this at all.

In spite of its intriguing character, and the fact that serious study of skill learning had already begun before the end of the last century, its study has had a surprisingly uneven history in the development of psychology. It is only fairly recently that the study of motor learning has achieved a renewed spurt of interest. In the course of this study, it has become apparent not only that skill learning is extraordinarily complex, but that it is often far more cognitive than our previous observations might have suggested. The present chapter will examine some major features of motor learning and look briefly at the changing theoretical trends in its study. We will begin first with the traditional view of motor learning as a form of chaining of individual S-R associations.

CHARACTERISTICS OF SKILL LEARNING

When you think of chaining, think first of a set of learned S-R associations, and second, of the formation of many of these sets into a particular sequence through practice. Finally, think of this sequence being further practiced until the entire chain becomes so habitual that it can be performed without conscious effort or awareness. Think, in other words, of something "as simple as tying your shoelaces."

The sequence of actions involved in learning to drive a car is fairly easy to specify, at least if we are willing to list as "responses" acts which themselves consist of a chain of many subresponses less easy to identify.

S (properly seated behind wheel)→R (insert ignition key); S (key positioned)→R (turn clockwise); S (engine starts)→R (release key); S (engine running)→R (check rearview mirror); S (road clear)→R (put car in gear); S (engine engaged)→R (release brake). . . .

Several major points emerge from this illustration of motor performance as a chaining of associations. (1) Each component S-R association must be learned before the entire sequence can be put into operation and practiced. (2) The correct order of the sequence is important to the final goal. (3) Some elements in the sequence follow each other more naturally, or more easily, than others. (4) The response to each stimulus serves both as the stimulus for the next response and as a source of information that the response has been correctly performed. For example, the sound of the engine starting both signals that the key was turned correctly and acts as a stimulus for the next response of releasing the key.

Having watched a Russian bear at the Moscow Circus driving a motorcycle with more consummate skill than many human drivers, one is confronted with a reality. Understanding the operations being performed may well facilitate learning, but conscious understanding of their implications is by no means a requisite to skilled performance.

Stages of Skill Learning

Earlier we remarked on the wide range of ability characteristic of the different stages in skill learning: the 8-year-old child practicing on the family piano, versus the concert pianist; the child in the early school years learning each letter of the alphabet on a stroke-by-stroke basis, versus the adult dashing off a quick note to a friend. At the same time, there are no distinct "stages" of skill learning. The learning, in Fitts's (1964) words, seems more an "evolving" process in which different strategies and tactics come into play as part of the learning process. As we shall see later, part of this evolution is the organization of motor sequences into larger and larger units.

However gradual the evolution of a motor skill, one can describe at least three phases of its development. The descriptions below are attributed to Fitts (1964, pp. 261–268), who stresses a continuity from phase to phase, rather than any clearly defined points of separation.

1. THE EARLY PHASE. The first phase of skill learning in the adult is a relatively brief period required for the understanding of instructions, completing a few preliminary trials, and establishing the proper cognitive set for the task. Fitts's reference to "set" has several aspects. The student of the skill must first decide on the level of ability that will constitute his or her goal, whether to aim first for speed or for accuracy, and to determine how to pace the practice sessions.

When verbal instruction is involved, the student and teacher must develop a common language to facilitate instruction. A novice aircraft pilot might receive the words "right wing down." But what the student pilot does will depend on whether he or she interprets this as a command or as a report of error.

This first phase of skill learning may have to be repeated if the particular skill involves the simultaneous use of two or more separate motor responses. Examples of this include a typist learning to use a foot pedal to control playback of a dictating machine, a student pianist learning to produce different rhythms with the two hands, or a novice swimmer first learning to coordinate breathing and arm stroke in a single motion.

2. THE INTERMEDIATE PHASE. The intermediate phase is characterized by the process of chaining, as previously described. Fitts refers to this as the "hook up" or "association" phase of motor learning, in which each individually practiced element of the sequence is practiced in its correct serial order. It is also during this second phase that a reorganization of the motor behavior often occurs as individual motor sequences become subsumed as a part of a larger motor response. For example, the individually practiced motor acts required to operate a car's gear shift lever and clutch pedal evolve into a single cognitive operation, such as "shift gears."

3. THE LATE PHASE. The late phase of motor learning is characterized as the continued practice of the task once its basic elements have been mastered. As we shall see, even quite simple sensorimotor skills such as typing and industrial assembly work can be expected to continue to improve even

after literally millions of cycles of practice, provided there is continued motivation for speed (Crossman, 1959).

Practice is the key to motor learning, and it will receive considerable attention in subsequent pages. While most of this discussion will concentrate on relatively short-term practice, we are nevertheless aware that championship caliber performance in athletics, and artistic performance such as singing or playing a musical instrument, often does not reach its peak before several years of intensive, almost daily practice. "And the fact that performance levels off at all, appears to be as much due to the effects of physiological aging and/or loss of motivation, as to reaching a true learning asymptote or limit in the capacity for further improvement" (Fitts, 1964, pg. 268).

As Fitts has recognized, "talking to oneself" is often characteristic of the early phase of motor learning. Subjects frequently repeat verbal instructions to themselves, contemplate alternative movement strategies, and so forth. One thinks, for example, of the novice golfer telling himself or herself to keep an eye on the ball, or to watch the backswing, as he or she prepares for a shot. That this covert verbalization is far more characteristic of the earlier stages of motor learning than the later ones has been nicely demonstrated by Boucher (1974). The motor task in this case was simply learning to move the arm exactly ten centimeters in distance. Over the course of 50 training trials subjects were required to engage in a verbal task between each trial (reading word lists aloud). This extra verbal task was intended to interfere with any covert verbal activity which might be occurring between trials. Boucher's findings were consistent with these earlier observations: the verbal distractor was found to interfere far more with performance during the first 25 trials than it did with the last 25.

Most skill learning eventually becomes so automatic with practice that there are typically only two occasions when we realize how complex a sequence of actions we are performing. The first occasion is the initial learning of the sequence. The second occasion occurs when a well-practiced sequence becomes inadvertently interrupted. For this driver, the termination of a car trip follows something like this: (1) stop car→(2) put gear in "park"→(3) set brake→(4) turn off ignition→(5) remove key→(6) leave car→(7) press door lock button→(8) slam car door. Several times a year this sequence is interrupted by, for example, looking for something dropped behind the car seat between operations 4 and 5. It is often only after the terminal response, 8, that it is realized that step 5 was omitted, and we are locked out of the car with the key still in the ignition. And it is usually raining.

Elements of Learning

To aid our analysis of sensorimotor learning, recall several important elements of instrumental learning. These elements included practice, extinction, reinforcement, shaping, and generalization. Each has its counter-part in sensorimotor learning.

As in the case of single S-Rs, practice in sensorimotor learning both strengthens associations and makes them more resistant to extinction. In motor learning, however, there is an expansion of the role of practice. Con-tinual practice not only leads to smoother and more rapid performance of the motor sequence, but it can also lead to the development of understand-ing of patterns of responses, and to the discovery of alternative ways of per-forming the same motor task. This will be referred to later as *qualitative change with practice.*

Reinforcement in human motor learning takes a different form from the externally controlled contingencies of reward previously studied. In motor learning, *knowledge of results* plays this critical role. Immediate knowledge of results not only supplies information for adjusting responses to overcome error ("corrective feedback"), but knowledge of success can also act as a source of encouragement for completion of the entire chain.

Human motor learning allows the use of verbal instructions to select subgoals in order to divide a total complex task into logically coherent com-ponents. Usually discussed in terms of the contrast between *part* versus *whole* learning, the process, like shaping, allows for the intermediate re-ward of partial success.

Finally, the notion of generalization is also important to sensorimotor learning. In this case, it refers not only to treating similar stimuli in a similar fashion, but also introduces the importance of *transfer* of training. Prior learning of similar tasks may either facilitate or retard the acquisition of a new skill.

Before we turn to an examination of these features in greater detail, we should insert an important qualification. These similarities between motor skill learning and the elements of instrumental learning in general are im-portant, especially if we wish to look for evidence of continuity across all of the varieties of learning. At the same time, there has been a recent trend to look more closely, and somewhat more skeptically, at many of these paral-lels. Adams (1971, 1976), for example, has taken exception to an early ten-dency to equate the role of knowledge of results in motor learning too directly with the traditional, Thorndikian, view of reinforcement.

There certainly are elements of reward in verbal or other feedback, and this feedback typically does follow the performance of the response. On the other hand, Adams stresses three additional factors which must be added to any equation. First, a limited reinforcement interpretation of knowledge of results would hold that feedback about the correctness of a response would tend to increase the probability of that response being repeated. In motor learning, knowledge of results is also used to correct errors. That is, rather than attempting to repeat a response on the trial following feedback, the subject more often attempts to vary it. Second, the motor activity of the response is not the only behavior occurring during the learning of a skill. As we noted earlier, subjects tend to talk to themselves during the early stages of skill learning, formulating ideas and hypotheses as to how to best perform the movement. In short, Adams suggests, skill learning is far more cognitive than many early analysts were willing to admit. Third, a subject "knows" the correctness or incorrectness of a response as it is made, and continues to adjust the movement until he or she "knows" that it is correct. Self-knowledge of competence, and responding on the basis of that knowledge, Adams suggests, is not part of the traditional view of reinforcement.

Thus, while we may build on our knowledge of instrumental learning as we seek to understand the acquisition of motor skills, and to note important parallels as and when they arise, we must do so with caution. It is certainly the case that we will have to pay very close attention to the role of knowledge of results in subsequent discussion.

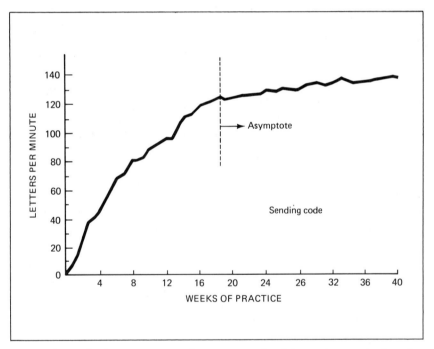

Figure 6.1   Performance curve for an apprentice telegraph operator learning to send Morse code. Sending speed begins to asymptote at about the sixteenth week of practice. The rate of improvement beyond this point begins to decrease, showing a curve of "diminishing returns." (*Source:* W. L. Bryan and N. Harter, Studies on the telegraphic language. The acquisition of a hierarchy of habits. *Psychological Review,* 1899, 6: fig. 10, pg. 350. Copyright 1899 by the American Psychological Association. Reprinted by permission.)

Learning Curves for Sensorimotor Skill

The study of sensorimotor learning has a long history in psychology, beginning with a publication in the last century of "learning curves" for apprentice telegraph operators developing their skill (Bryan & Harter, 1899). Figure 6.1 shows the performance curve for one such operator learning to transmit the Morse code. The graph shows the gradual increase in average sending speed for this operator over some 40 weeks of practice. The incremental gains from one practice session to the next produce a curve of generally the same shape as acquisition curves for classical conditioning and instrumental learning. At first there is a high rate of improvement with practice, which eventually reaches an asymptote of performance as the curve begins to level out. It is a curve of *diminishing returns;* the additional practice brings about improvement, but each gain from one trial to the next is always smaller than the change which occurred on the previous trial.

The principle of diminishing returns should not imply that practice beyond a certain point is worthless. As we shall see in a moment, additional practice beyond the asymptote can produce desirable qualitative changes in performance and influence the retention of the skill following a long period without practice. In addition, there are many tasks which continue to show significant gains even after years of practice. Crossman (1959), for example, has analyzed learning curves for skilled machine operators over periods as long as seven years. In many cases the asymptote of performance does not even begin to appear until well after four years of practice, and literally countless thousands of responses.

PRACTICE IN SENSORIMOTOR SKILL

As in other forms of learning, there is considerable truth to the notion that "practice makes perfect." Three issues related to practice have special importance in the context of sensorimotor learning. These three issues are the frequent appearance of qualitative change in the manner of performance of a skill with practice, the effects of different distributions of practice on performance, and the effects of overlearning on retention of a motor skill.

Qualitative Change with Practice

Figure 6.2 shows data also taken from Bryan and Harter's apprentice telegrapher, this time showing his learning curve for receiving code. Like the "sending" curve, it also shows an overall gradual increase in operating speed over the many weeks of practice. If we look closely, however, this particular curve shows an interesting feature: an *intermediate plateau* in the

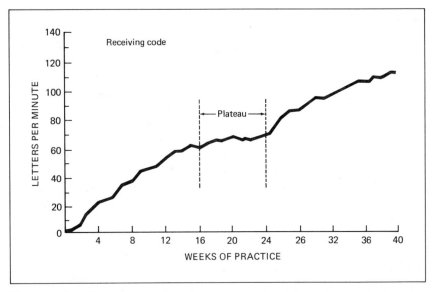

Figure 6.2   Performance curve for an apprentice telegraph operator learning to receive Morse code. The curve shows an intermediate plateau between the sixteenth and twenty-fourth weeks of practice, followed by a further increase in gains with still more practice. (*Source:* Bryan & Harter, Studies on the telegraphic language, fig. 10, pg. 350.)

performance curve. Somewhere between the sixteenth and twenty-fourth weeks of practice, performance begins to asymptote until, after additional practice, the curve again begins to rise, showing further improvement.

Bryan and Harter attributed this intermediate plateau to their operator learning to progress from subjectively hearing short sequences of dots and dashes as individual letters (and showing an asymptote for this approach), to organizing what he heard into longer sequences such as whole words or phrases. The learning of this "new" skill effectively builds a second learning curve on the asymptote of the first one.

Such plateaus are not always found in motor learning (Keller, 1958). When they do occur, they usually reflect a qualitative change in performance as a result of practice. Practice contributes not only to speed and accuracy, but can also lead to new approaches, either by eliminating redundant steps or by allowing the discovery of alternative routes to the same goal. There is many a "hunt-and-peck," two-finger typist, whose performance has asymptoted at a surprisingly high speed/accuracy level. This is equally true of many "bad" tennis players, and "bad" golfers. In such cases, however, the qualitative change of shifting to ultimately more promising approaches may mean not merely a plateau prior to renewed improvement. It can mean an initial decrement as new techniques (touch-typing, a correct backhand, etc.) are mastered. While the end result will be an overall improvement beyond the limits possible with the earlier technique, the frustration of the temporary setback can be defeating. It is here that moral support and encouragement on the part of a teacher can be the difference between ultimate success or failure.

Distribution of Practice

Generally speaking, skills are learned more rapidly if practice sessions are spread out over time (*distributed practice*), than if practice is massed into a single marathon session (*massed practice*). This can be shown under a wide variety of conditions, such as the two illustrated in Figure 6.3.

The upper panel (A) of Figure 6.3 shows results obtained by Lorge (1930) in a study of mirror writing. The task involves learning to trace a simple form with a pencil while both the hand and the form are obscured by a screen. The volunteer can see what he or she is doing only through the reflected image of an appropriately placed mirror (with right-left relationships reversed). Learning curves for two groups of volunteers are shown. Both learned the identical task, and both had the same number of practice trials. The difference was in the distribution of practice. The massed practice group had all 21 practice trials in a single session, while the distributed practice group had them spread out with one trial per day. Both groups show improvement, but the superior rate of improvement for distributed practice is clearly evident.

The lower panel (B) of Figure 6.3 shows results obtained by Bourne and Archer (1956) for a very different kind of motor task, and with very different practice/rest intervals. Here the task is to keep the tip of a hand-held stylus in continuous contact with a small metal plate ("target") fixed to one side of a revolving turntable. Contact between the stylus and the target completes an electrical circuit which operates an automatic timer accumulating the total time on target. The massed practice group worked continuously, while the distributed practice group had the task divided into a series of 30-second practice trials, separated by 30-second rest intervals. As in the case of mirror writing, the advantage of distributed practice is dramatic.

There are cases where the usual superiority of distributed practice may not appear. Typically these are tasks which require one to keep track of a variety of variables, or to try out and remember a number of alternative strategies. In such cases, frequent interruptions can be both inefficient and frustrating. This is especially true if returning after a period away requires some time to "get back into" the problem.

With this proviso, however, numerous studies have shown an advantage to practice for relatively short periods, separated by frequent rest intervals, as opposed to continuous practice for extended periods. This is usually true, even when rest periods result in less time at the task than in massed prac-

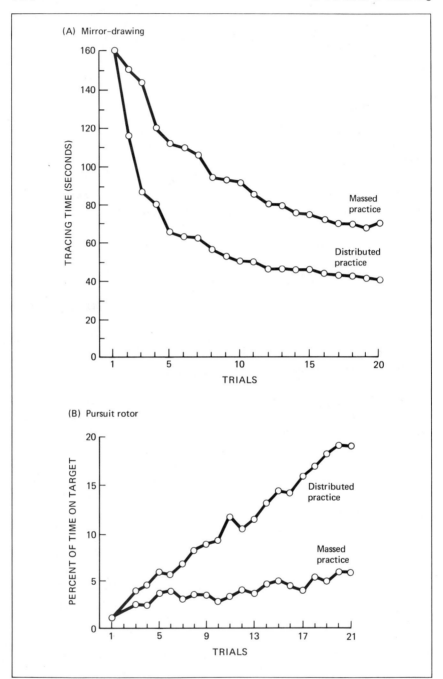

(A) Mirror-drawing

(B) Pursuit rotor

tice. Further, a rest interval simply means engaging in some activity different from the task at hand. In other words, the effectiveness of the rest interval in distributed practice is not diminished if the interval is occupied not by rest but by other work.

Several reasons might account for the general superiority of distributed practice. The most obvious ones are the limiting factors of fatigue and boredom which can be reduced by frequent rest intervals. In addition, rest intervals can allow for "consolidation" of gains from the previous work periods. Massed practice may interfere with this consolidation time, counteracting the positive effects of practice. For example, whether due to recovery from fatigue, or opportunity for consolidation, studies have shown that the level of performance at the start of a new practice session can actually be higher than the level at the end of the previous one (Digman, 1959).

In general, short periods of practice and shorter periods of rest (perhaps 30 minutes/10 minutes) work best, although the ideal durations must vary from task to task and individual to individual, and be discovered empirically. The primary factors affecting the choice of intervals are such considerations as fatigue (which argues for frequent rest intervals) and time taken to reorient oneself to the task (which favors less frequent rests).

Overlearning and Retention

In principle, one should expect the conditions which led to a loss of singe S-R associations outlined in the previous chapter to also hold for sensorimotor chains. To a degree they do, and we see similar "forgetting curves" for disused motor skills. On the other hand, motor learning is uniquely resistant to loss. Even after many years without practice, once an early component of a motor sequence is recalled, the entire chain usually returns with surprising spontaneity. The greatest loss in motor learning seems to be less from disuse than from the interference of similar, but better learned, competing motor responses.

Retention of motor skills is also interesting because of the differences in rates of loss observed for different types of skills. London (1975, pg. 264), for

◀**Figure 6.3**   Effects of massed versus distributed practice on performance in two sensorimotor learning tasks. Panel *A* shows time to trace a form visually reversed by a mirror for massed (all trials in one day) and for distributed practice (one trial per day). (*Source:* Data from I. Lorge, Influence of regularly interpolated time intervals on subsequent learning. *Teachers College Contributions to Education,* 1930, no. 438.) Panel *B* shows percentage time-on-target in a pursuit rotor task for massed (continual practice) and for distributed practice (30-second practice trials separated by 30-second rest intervals). (*Source:* L. E. Bourne and E. J. Archer, Time continuously on target as a function of distribution of practice. *Journal of Experimental Psychology,* 1956, 51: fig. 1, pg. 27. Copyright 1956 by the American Psychological Association. Reprinted by permission.)

example, suggests that "continuous" motor tasks, such as the pursuit rotor task previously mentioned, riding a bicycle, or driving a car, can be retained almost indefinitely, even after years of disuse. By contrast, "discrete" motor skills, such as pulling switches, or pushing buttons in response to signal lights, show much more rapid rates of loss, closely resembling the rate of loss of verbal memory.

Numerous studies have supported this contention that rates of loss for continuous skills are very low (Fleishman & Parker, 1962), while those for discrete tasks are lost much more rapidly without practice (Adams, 1954). Why continuous skills show such little forgetting is unclear. One possibility is that continuous tasks, in general, are highly practiced ones.

One feature all motor skill learning has in common is the effect of *overlearning* on retention. By overlearning, we mean practicing a motor skill beyond what is necessary to perform it correctly the first time. For example, overlearning a particular piece on the piano would mean going over the piece again and again, past the point where it could be played through once without error.

The extent to which overlearning a particular task is worthwhile depends entirely on the importance of perfect retention to the individual. The greater the amount of practice on a motor task, the greater will be the degree of retention after a period of disuse. But the effects of overlearning on retention show a principle of diminishing returns. Krueger (1930) demonstrated this principle with college students given various amounts of practice with complex pencil mazes.

Krueger defined 100 percent learning as the amount of practice necessary to complete the maze once without error. He defined 150 percent learning as an additional 50 percent more trials. For example, if 10 practice trials were needed for 100 percent learning, subjects were now given an additional 5 trials beyond that point. In 200 percent learning, subjects receive 100 percent more trials (i.e., another 10 trials), while in 300 percent learning, subjects receive twice as many trials (i.e., a total of 20 overlearning trials).

Testing retention after 1 to 28 days without practice, Krueger found that each additional degree of overlearning yielded a significant additional savings in retention. However, the percentage of savings for each degree of overlearning increased retention by smaller and smaller proportions. In the case of maze learning, the point of diminishing returns, where further practice became uneconomical, fell somewhere between 200 and 300 percent learning.

The degree to which one is willing to invest additional practice in the face of such diminishing returns must be an individual decision. As Crafts et al. observe:

> If it is essential that . . . memory for some particular material be as accurate and reliable as . . . possible . . . for example, when a pianist practices for a

forthcoming concert—then, in spite of the principle of diminishing returns, very large amounts of overlearning will still be profitable to him. For there is no reason to suppose that even the last 100 trials of 10,000 would not add something, however small, to the excellence of his subsequent performance (Crafts, Schneirla, Robinson & Gilbert, 1950, pg. 295).

What would be the added "something" of further practice? We can highlight three variables already mentioned. (1) Overlearning will increase resistance to loss when the skill is no longer practiced. (2) Overlearning can lead to finer precision in motor control—that element we call "style" in performance. In practical terms, style often translates into an economy of motion that reduces fatigue. (3) Overlearning can lead to a qualitative change in which either the perceptual or response aspects of the task are reorganized into larger units. Bryan and Harter recognized this in the telegraph operator learning to organize the dots and dashes of Morse code into "units" of letters and words. This notion was developed by Lashley (1951) who argued that very rapid performance *must* involve a reorganization of individual motor responses into a program, or plan, of execution.

More on the subject of the programming of motor sequences will be said later. At this point, however, it may be said that there is no evidence that sensorimotor performance ever ceases to improve with practice, however subtle and unnoticed the changes. This is a strong statement. But it may be, as Fitts (1964) suggested, that performance ceases to improve only when the effects of physiological aging or loss of motivation intrude.

SUMMARY

We can define sensorimotor skill as a sequence (or chain) of motor actions, which remain under sensory control. Examples of sensorimotor skills include riding a bicycle, driving a car, playing a musical instrument, or operating any set of mechanical controls.

Learning and retention curves for sensorimotor skills are of the same general shape as those for learning single S-R connections, whether acquired through classical conditioning or instrumental learning. Among the special features of motor learning is the frequent appearance of a qualitative change in the actions of a skilled performance with practice. That is, learning curves often show an intermediate plateau, or even a decrement in performance, as alternative strategies are attempted to accomplish the same goal.

A second special feature is an emphasis on the distribution of practice in sensorimotor learning. As a rule, practice for short periods, separated by frequent rest intervals (distributed practice), yields more effective learning than continual practice within a single session (massed practice).

A final feature of sensorimotor learning relates to retention of skills both as a function of the type of motor skill involved, and the degree of learning or "overlearning" employed. "Discrete" motor tasks show more rapid rates of loss than "continuous" motor tasks, the latter being retained almost indefinitely.

Regardless of the type of motor task, the greater the degree of overlearning (practice beyond the point of the first perfect performance of the task), the greater will be the resistance to loss. Overlearning, however, follows the principle of diminishing returns. Each additional degree of overlearning yields progressively smaller increments of improvement.

Feedback, Strategies, and Transfer in Skill Learning

KNOWLEDGE OF RESULTS

As a response must be reinforced for its repeated performance, so sensorimotor learning will be ineffective without the immediate *feedback* of knowledge of results (Ammons, 1956; Bilodeau & Bilodeau, 1961). Typical of the effects of feedback in sensorimotor performance is the case of the motorcycle rider who "leans into" a high speed curve at just the correct angle. It truly exemplifies the fluid and seemingly automatic monitoring of results, and compensation for error, characteristic of motor skill performance.

In this case the feedback is *intrinsic* to the task; information from visual and bodily senses are continuous with the performance, and are a natural consequence of it. In a similar way, a child attempting to copy letters in learning the written alphabet has the constant feedback of seeing his or her own results. At first the comparison will be with sample letters supplied by the teacher. Later, the comparison will be with the "mental" image of the letter he or she is trying to produce.

Although our earlier discussion stressed the differences between knowledge of results and the traditional view of reinforcement, such knowledge does contain an important element of reinforcement as it supplies the satisfaction, or feelings of accomplishment, necessary to encourage continued performance. It is certainly the case that the principle of contiguity holds for knowledge of results as it does for the application of reward. The sooner knowledge of results is available after a correct response, the more rapid and effective will be the learning.

In the case of intrinsic feedback, knowledge of results is a naturally available consequence of the response, in the sense that no external agent is needed to indicate to the person that his or her response was, or was not, correct. The child can see that the letter he or she has made, or the word he or she has written, "looks right," or that the knot tied in the shoelace has not fallen apart.

In formal teaching, however, we often look for additional forms of feedback, over and above those intrinsic to the task. This can be referred to as *extrinsic* or *augmented* feedback; information which is supplied beyond that ordinarily obtained as a consequence of the performance itself. Such extrinsic feedback is embodied in the teacher who tells the child that the letter or word he or she has written does indeed "look right." So too is praise and encouragement accompanying correct performance, or the ubiquitous examination and prompt return of the test scores.

Augmented Feedback

If adequate feedback is good, is more than adequate feedback better? The answer would appear to be a limited "yes," and sometimes in unexpected ways. Smode (1958), for example, studied the performance of students learning to operate a control knob which kept a randomly fluctuating needle centered on a dial. The task is not unlike a novice driver regulating accelerator pressure in order to keep a car's speedometer needle centered at the desired speed. The task is also common to a variety of skilled industrial and technical operations.

Smode's task offers immediate intrinsic feedback; the operator is able to continually see the positioning of the needle as he or she moves the control knob. With some practice, Smode's subjects quickly learned to keep the needle "on target" more than off.

A second group learned the same task, but with this natural feedback augmented by being able to see the cumulative time-on-target continuously displayed on an electric timer. They also received a buzzer signal whenever the needle was correctly centered. This additional feedback, although logically redundant, in fact had a dramatic and positive effect on rate of learning.

Figure 6.4 shows Smode's results, and also suggests an answer to this apparent paradox. Not only is the augmented feedback group superior throughout the training, but this superiority is evident from the very first session. It seems likely that the augmented feedback—which supplied no more real information than the intrinsic visual feedback—had its main effect in keeping the task interesting. The auditory signal of moment to moment success and failure kept the volunteers at a higher level of motivation. But then the manufacturers of pinball machines, with their bells and clicks and flashing lights, have known this for a long time.

The Importance of Feedback

Intrinsic feedback is so much a part of sensorimotor learning that it is easy to overlook its importance or even to conclude that "no feedback" is

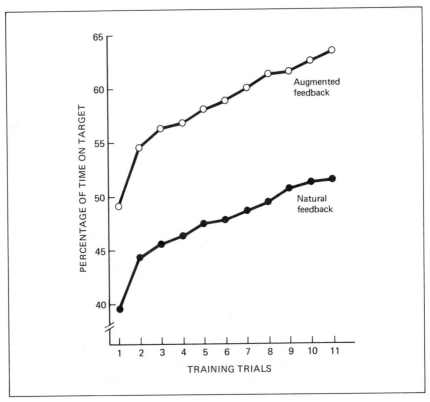

Figure 6.4   Performance on a visual tracking task over eleven 1½-minute training trials, for two conditions of feedback. In "natural feedback," subjects could observe their own performance, as well as receiving their total time-on-target after each trial. In "augmented feedback," subjects had in addition their cumulative time-on-target on continual display, plus hearing a loud buzzer signal whenever they were on target. (*Source:* A. F. Smode, Learning and performance in a tracking task under two levels of achievement information feedback. *Journal of Experimental Psychology*, 1958, 56: fig. 1, pg. 300. Copyright 1958 by the American Psychological Association. Reprinted by permission.)

necessary for the performance of motor skills. Part of the answer lies in the fact that most motor skills contain many sources of potential feedback. Typing, for example, contains at least three: visual feedback as the typist sees whether or not the key pressed was the correct one, kinesthetic or touch sensation from the fingers, and muscle feedback from finger, wrist, and arm movements which can yield important information to detect whether the movement sequence was or was not the one intended.

West (1967) examined error detection rates for typists of varying degrees of skill when visual feedback was prevented by a large screen which totally obscured the typewriter keyboard. Deprived of visual feedback, and relying on "feel" alone, good typists (100 words per minute) nevertheless detected and corrected about 50 percent of their errors, while novice typists (11 words per minute) detected and corrected about 20 percent of their errors. With the screen removed, the addition of visual feedback raised the detection and correction rates to as high as 76 percent.

The results without visual feedback are nevertheless impressive, and similar results have been found in choice reaction time studies, where subjects must decide which of several keys to press in response to particular stimuli. Because they are put under time pressure, errors are occasionally made. In such cases, however, subjects may spontaneously detect and correct as many as 70 to 80 percent of their error responses, even though no one specifically told them when their responses were wrong. They had pressed the wrong key, and they knew it (Rabbitt, 1967, 1968).

Part of the feedback process in motor skill must involve the subject's own analysis of a movement, using as a reference some internal "motor program" of the movement as it was intended. While the neural basis of such a motor program remains speculative, we can envisage it as a *plan* representing coordinated muscle movements and sequencing instructions prepared in advance of the actual movements. (A very readable introductory account of the requisites for such motor programs can be found in Lenneberg, 1967, pp. 12–15.) It is the case that visual or verbal feedback can be withdrawn for well-practiced responses without serious effects on performance (cf. Newell, 1974). These same studies, however, show that such feedback is quite important in the early stages of learning.

One of the most dramatic ways to see the importance of feedback to motor performance is when special steps are taken not merely to deprive the subject of some source of feedback, but to actively *distort* a primary form of feedback ordinarily available in the task.

The study of mirror writing previously cited is just one example. When normal visual feedback is distorted by the reversed image of the mirror, the immediate effects are devastating. As we have seen, however, one can accommodate to this right-left distortion fairly quickly with practice. The same cannot be said of *time-distorted* visual feedback.

A closed-circuit television has been used in studies where subjects' hands and arms are not directly in sight, but are viewed instead on a tv monitor. The televised image can now be reversed, inverted, or—through a delay loop on the video tape—delayed in time. In the latter case, disruption is very severe, and even the most extended practice seems to bring little improvement (Smith & Smith, 1962). Human adaptability apparently does have its limits.

A very simple modification of an ordinary tape recorder can allow a person to monitor his or her own speech through earphones, but with a delay introduced between the spoken utterance and the time it is heard. This is referred to as delayed auditory feedback, or DAF. At a critical period of delay (about 0.18 seconds), speech becomes halting, imprecise, and often totally inarticulate (Black, 1951; Huggins, 1968). The advent of the radio talk show has necessitated the routine use of recorded voice delay. This allows the alert MC to monitor the caller's speech before it goes out on the air and to make that continuing and fateful decision as to when to press the "cut" button and thus preserve the delicacy and decorum of the program. You can often hear the effects on callers who fail to turn down the volume on their radio while talking on the telephone. They inadvertently become "subjects" in a delayed speech experiment.

PART VERSUS WHOLE LEARNING

Since motor tasks consist of a chain of practiced responses, it is often possible to approach the task in a step-by-step way, first learning components of the total act to some degree before practicing their final integration. Swimming coaches, for example, sometimes employ this *part method* by working separately with the swimmer's breathing, leg movements, and arm stroke.

With some tasks, a separation into meaningful subcomponents is virtually impossible, and they must, by default, be practiced in their entirety (the *whole method*). To the extent that it is desirable, one of the challenges in teaching motor skills is to determine, and find appropriate verbal instructions for, the isolation of coherent and intelligent subcomponents.

The question of whether the part or the whole method is generally preferable is a hard one to answer. It was long ago suggested, for example, that older and more intelligent people do better with the whole method (Peckstein, 1918). It is difficult to make such a generality. The answer depends almost entirely on the nature of the learning task.

One advantage of learning through the part method is its positive effects on morale. As in the case of shaping, the use of intermediate goals allows for frequent goal attainment, and hence more frequent satisfaction and reward. Also similar to shaping, the part method may be the only way to guide the learner successfully through a series of subgoals to what might ordinarily be a skill of such complexity that the whole method would be impossible. A final advantage of the part method is its amenity to distributed practice. This avoids the negative effects of massed practice which would be a consequence of using the whole method for extended tasks. The singular disadvantage of the part method is that it requires the extra learning step of putting the component parts together.

The variable factors of size and availability of subgoals, fatigue, intelligence, and interest of the learner, and the relative ease of final integration of the sequence, leave the question of preferred method an open one.

TRANSFER OF TRAINING

In sensorimotor learning it is not uncommon to find new tasks which contain components of previously learned ones. The more experience one has with the world, the greater this likelihood, since there are only so many different motor sequences one can reasonably expect to encounter. Learning to handle a motorcycle is easier if you already ride a bicycle, and the novice computer programmer who already knows typing approaches the computer Teletype terminal as an old friend. Particular skills learned in one context, then, can frequently be generalized to other tasks. In sensorimotor learning the influence of prior learning on new tasks is referred to as *transfer of training*.

The term *positive transfer* refers to those cases where responses learned in one task facilitate the performance of a new task. This typically occurs in cases where responses learned in the old task are the same as, or similar to, responses required in a new one. Under these conditions, significant benefits of prior learning can be expected. In spite of their legendary competitive zeal, car manufacturers have standardized the positioning of critical controls such as brakes, gas pedal, and gear shift operations. This encourages positive transfer and reduces confusion when drivers change from one make of car to another.

The term *negative transfer* refers to cases where responses learned in one task actively interfere with performance in another task. Modern cars again serve as a prime example. Standardization in the past has typically not included positioning of such controls as lights and windshield wipers, or their mode of operation (push, pull, or turn). If anything, one is struck by the remarkable, if misplaced ingenuity exhibited by car manufacturers in this regard. In extreme cases, negative transfer can be so great that more time is required for relearning in the new situation than was originally required.

The primary factor affecting transfer, whether positive or negative, is the degree of similarity in the two situations and their response requirements. Airline pilots, for example, feel less confusion in operating counterpart controls when changing from an airplane to a car, where the layout of instruments and controls are completely different, than they do when changing from one car to another.

A FINAL NOTE ON "CHAINING" AND "MOTOR PROGRAMS"

We began this chapter with the notion of chaining, as a way of introducing our analysis of motor skill learning, while recognizing that chaining itself is not simple. We have already touched upon the difficulty of actually determining the specific links in any given motor task. In illustrating the chain of events in operating a car, for example, we accepted a series of S-R chains which, themselves, were really a consequence of many subresponses less easy to identify.

If the notion of chaining has helped the reader take the step from simple association learning to an understanding of complex motor skill, then its job has been done. As a theoretical construct, however, chaining has suffered some very severe blows. Is chaining a passive process akin to Hull's "habit strength" or Thorndike's "stamping in" of associations? Indeed, does the notion of chaining itself adequately describe motor performance?

We had a hint of the problem when discussing qualitative change with practice. If we characterize motor skill as chains of responses, each "hooked" to the next, how can we account for people's proven ability to easily substitute one motor pattern for another as they search for more efficient means of performance? On logical grounds, it seems more likely that any particular motor pattern we observe is the consequence of a *plan* or *strategy* of action, rather than merely the execution of a practiced sequence of specific motor associations (cf. Miller, Galanter & Pribram, 1960, pg. 84). That is, if Tolman could question the passive model of association learning in favor of a cognitive "understanding" of relationships on the part of rats (see Chapter 5), can we argue less for the human?

The most severe attack on the principle of chaining came from Lashley (1951) who, in a classic paper, questioned whether the order of the overt sequence of motor acts we see is actually the order in which they are planned mentally. To Lashley, the sorts of motor sequences we have been discussing (e.g., tying one's shoelaces or playing a piano) occur too rapidly for each response to be initiated only after the previous one has been completed. Available evidence suggests that there is literally not enough time for nerve impulses to travel from muscle receptors to the brain, and back to the muscles, in order to accomplish the movements at the rates we commonly observe. (See Lenneberg, 1967, pp. 93–106 for a summary of this evidence.)

While chaining may be a convenient device for describing the unpracticed beginnings of a motor skill, there is thus a basic incompatibility between known rates of neural transmission, and the sequential feedback model of chaining implicit in much of our discussion. More direct evidence pointing to the necessity of positing some form of motor program has come from cases of persons temporarily deprived of kinesthetic feedback from the hands who, nevertheless, can continue to perform controlled finger movements (Lazlo, 1967).

Because there are typically many potential sources of feedback intrinsic to most motor skills, we have seen that it is certainly possible to deprive a subject of major sources of feedback without necessarily producing a total disruption of performance. In this case the feedback eliminated was kinesthetic feedback; earlier we cited studies of skilled performance continuing in the absence of visual or verbal feedback. On the one hand, such studies have raised the question of how important feedback really is to skilled performance (cf. MacNeilage, 1970; Adams, 1971; Keele, 1973; Newell, 1974). On the other hand, these studies also provide evidence for the existence of internal motor programs which are sufficiently abstract that they may operate in the absence of any one specific source of feedback, even when this source was critical in the original development of the skill. As we noted earlier, the exact nature of such motor programs, and the way in which the planning of motor movements occurs in advance of their actual performance, remains unknown. The interested reader, however, can find no shortage of interesting speculation (e.g., Miller, Galanter & Pribram, 1960; Keele, 1975).

SUMMARY

Many of the essential features of human sensorimotor learning follow directly from the principles of instrumental learning as discussed in Chapter 5. Sensorimotor learning can be seen as an example of learning through trial and error. The individual must voluntarily or accidentally make the correct response, with reinforcement (in the form of corrective feedback) contingent on the performance of the response.

In addition to supplying incentive for performance, knowledge of results in motor learning gives the subject critical feedback regarding the accuracy of his or her approximation to the desired response. Rather than repeating a previous response, subjects use knowledge of results to vary and adjust their performance to bring it closer to the target movement. Extrinsic feedback is characterized by verbal instruction and correction, while intrinsic feedback is represented by information which arrives as a natural consequence of the task. In both cases, feedback seems to be more critical in the early stages of learning than in the later stages when the skill has become well practiced and automatic.

As in the formation of single S-R associations, human sensorimotor learning requires practice. Practice can be viewed as an extension of Thorndike's law of exercise. A developing motor skill typically shows a learning curve of the same form as simple S-R learning, as does the shape of the retention curve following a period without practice. Practice in motor learning, however, has several effects which have received special attention.

Repeated practice at a task beyond the point of a single correct performance is called overlearning. Practice increases resistance to loss, and also allows for qualitative change in the person's performance of the motor response. One may discover more efficient ways of performing the response, eliminate redundant steps, or reorganize the motor sequence in a major way.

Studies of the distribution of practice have shown marked advantage to practice for limited periods, separated by frequent rest intervals (distributed practice), as opposed to continued, uninterrupted practice for long periods (massed practice).

The notion of shaping has its counterpart in sensorimotor learning with the advantages of the part method of motor learning. This involves a step-by-step approach to the task in which the full motor task is divided into logical components for individual mastery before the full sequence is integrated. The part method offers the advantage of frequent goal attainment and attendant reward and is more amenable to the use of distributed practice. Like shaping, the part method can guide the individual through a series of easily obtainable subgoals to performance of a complex motor response which might otherwise be difficult to learn.

The counterpart of generalization in sensorimotor learning is referred to as positive transfer. This occurs when skills from previously learned tasks facilitate the acquisition of a new one. Negative transfer occurs when previous motor learning interferes with the acquisition of a new skill. The similarity of the situation and response requirements in the related tasks is the primary determinant of the likelihood of transfer, whether positive or negative.

While sensorimotor learning has traditionally been described in terms of the chaining, or "hooking up," of individually learned response sequences, many writers have stressed the importance of organization in sensorimotor learning. This latter view sees skilled performance in terms of the development of organized patterns of responses, where the order of responses as observed may, or may not, reflect the actual order in which they were internally programmed. This question, although raised quite early in the study of motor skills, remains one of considerable complexity which must await the results of future research.

chapter 7

The Study
of Verbal
Learning

As sensorimotor learning can be understood by building on the principles of instrumental learning, so too can one class of verbal behavior. In the literature of learning theory, this class of behavior is referred to as *verbal learning*. In everyday language we would refer to it as *rote learning;* that activity we engage in when called upon to memorize foreign language vocabulary, word-for-word formulas and definitions, and those helpful homilies such as "Thirty days hath September. . . ." While conceptual understanding may follow, the memorization process itself can often be described as the chaining of verbal associations.

Methods of Research

Before looking closely at this form of human learning, we should address an important issue. It relates to some erroneous views which have appeared from time to time in the history of learning theory.

VERBAL BEHAVIOR: CLIMBING OUT OF THE MAZE

The development of learning theory sometimes shows what might be described as the theory's search for its own fountain of youth. Here is what we mean. To some, the early studies of animal learning by Pavlov, Thorndike, and others, belong to the history of psychology; rudimentary approaches to the study of learning which have little bearing on human behavior. The cruelest of these critics might say: "Rat psychology (they mean S-R association theories based on the study of lower animals) is an idea whose time has passed. It should be allowed to die." Other critics might be only relatively more compassionate. "Let the students of simple S-R theory carry on with their experiments, so long as they don't try to apply their ideas to human learning." In other words, relegate S-R learning to a sort of intellectual nursing home, where the senior citizens of learning theory can remain out of sight, so as not to impede or embarrass the younger generation of workers.

At the same time, others tried to breathe new life and vigor into the "old" theories. They did this by stressing a continuity in learning that builds progressively from classical conditioning, to S-R learning and drive-reduction theory, to notions of secondary reinforcement and instrinsic reward, and to the chaining of multiple associations.

These two views clashed head-on with the study of verbal learning. From the two camps emerged champions to represent the extreme ranges of both opinions. From the "older" group came the view that verbal learning (rote learning) not only represented a direct extension of simple S-R principles, but that it could serve as a model for both human memory and for language acquisition by children. They tried to view linguistic behavior as nothing more or less than "verbal habits" acquired through simple S-R principles.

From the other side, the "younger" group, came an expression of horror at the thought of extending associationist principles to the study of language. Like Bevan, they saw a creativity in language that defied any simple analysis in S-R terms. If children learn language by a process analogous to the way we memorize a string of words such as "thirdy days hath September," how could one account for children's ability to produce novel utterances, "new" sentences, they have never heard before? Whatever children learn when we say they learn language, it must be something considerably more abstract than a chain of verbal associations. As one writer summarized the position, "However successful [learning theory] might be in accounting for the way in which certain networks of 'habits' and 'associations' are built up in the 'behavior patterns' of animals and human beings, it is totally incapable of explaining [the] 'creativity' . . . manifest so clearly . . . in language" (Lyons, 1970, pg. 93).

We would like to argue for a course somewhere between these two extremes. On the one hand, there is some life yet left in the continuity viewpoint. On the other hand, we must recognize the limitations of S-R theory along with its applications. We should, by all means, climb out of the maze of animal studies. But we should do so carefully, taking with us what is good, and leaving behind the rest. This is a dangerous course to steer. The reward of compromise in psychological theory is more often enmity from both sides, than praise from either.

Verbal learning, by which we mean nothing more or less than the study of rote learning, should interest us for two reasons. The first reason is a theoretical one. Learning a list of words in the form of foreign language vocabulary, or memorizing a set of lines verbatim, can illustrate chaining of multiple associations, and serve as a vehicle for the further development of the principles of learning. The second reason is a practical one. Whether desirable or not, rote learning represents a large bulk of formal learning in the early school years and later. We should be able to specify those parameters known to facilitate or retard the process. The goal of this chapter is to do just this.

At the same time, we must reject the notion that such studies will tell us a great deal about how language is learned, or about the normal processes of human memory. As we will see later, language is better described in terms of the acquisition of rules, than as the learning of associations. Similarly, while rote learning describes a process which is reproductive in nature, human memory is ordinarily more reconstructive than reproductive.

Reconstructive Memory

Word-for-word literal recall of verbal materials is not terribly representative of most learning and memory. As we shall see in Chapter 10, human recall is seldom exact. More often, we *reconstruct* recall from a few remembered details, fleshed out by a general impression of what we have learned, and by related knowledge. This reconstructive view of memory is attributed largely to the early work of Sir Frederik Bartlett (1932), and has been supported by a variety of more recent research (e.g., Bransford, Barclay & Franks, 1972; Johnson, Bransford & Solomon, 1973; Sulin & Dooling, 1974).

Kintsch (1975) describes a typical experiment in which students read familiar themes, such as the biblical story of Joseph and his brothers. Immediately after reading the stories, recall was generally accurate except for some omission of small detail. After 24 hours, however, the students' recall showed "an almost complete lack of differentiation . . . between the contents of the paragraph read a day ago, and the subjects' general knowledge of the story" (Kintsch, 1975, pg. 99). To put it simply, many subjects wrote down everything they knew about Joseph and his brothers, whether it had been mentioned in the "memorized" passage or not.

Numerous other studies have shown that when memory for meaningful material is involved, it is often hard to tell whether correct recall is in fact a reproduction or a reconstruction (Cofer, Chmielewski & Brockway, 1975; Bransford & Franks, 1971; Cofer, 1973; Griggs, 1974). In other words, from the experimenter's point of view, the only difference between apparent verbatim recall and reconstructions based simply on remembered outlines may be only that the experimenter knows which ones were presented, and which were not. The so-called verbatim response may have been no less a product of reconstruction.

The dynamics of human memory obviously create a problem for the study of "pure" learning and retention of verbal materials. The earliest solution to the problem of apparently accurate recall based on reconstruction from meaning was to study people's recall of essentially meaningless material. It was an attempt, in Bevan's words, to get behind the "genius" of linguistic creativity to an understanding of behavior which could be predicted on the level of scientific laws.

EBBINGHAUS AND THE NONSENSE SYLLABLE

Experimental studies of rote learning were pioneered in the nineteenth century by the German psychologist Hermann Ebbinghaus (1850–1909). Like many workers in that first golden age of psychology, his research set the pattern of technique and approach for decades to come. It is ironic that his ideas, like many of his contemporaries in other fields, were perhaps too promising, and kept research pinned to these early approaches long after it should have moved on with changing times and needs. It was Ebbinghaus who gave us the *nonsense syllable:* sets of three-letter, consonant-vowel-consonant (CVC) combinations which served as the preferred stimuli for studies in human learning for far longer than he himself would probably have anticipated.

The use of CVCs (e.g., *POV, RIN, NIF*) were intended to serve as pronounceable verbal materials which could be learned, remembered, and recalled, in a "pure" fashion, uncontaminated by such variable factors as meaning, prior associations, and so forth. In a typical study, Ebbinghaus

(1885) set to work memorizing lists of about 12 or 13 nonsense syllables, recording not only the number of practice trials required to learn them, but also retesting himself and relearning the lists at various later intervals. In this way, he could plot learning curves for verbal learning (they are similar in appearance to the other learning curves we have already seen) and trace their decay in memory after various periods without practice.

The Measurement of Recall

Three measures of retention have seen wide use in studies of verbal learning. (1) *Free recall:* the most direct measure of retention, free recall, simply involves reproducing, in correct order, as much of a learned list as possible from memory. (2) *Savings:* even after one is no longer able to recall a list under free-recall conditions, there may still be some residue of the initial learning. The savings method can discover the level of this trace by having the subject relearn the "forgotten" material. The measure of retention is the difference between the number of trials originally required and the number required to relearn the material to the same level. This, incidentally, was the method favored by Ebbinghaus. (3) *Recognition:* if free recall is the most demanding, recognition is the least. This requires only that the person be able to select from a larger ensemble those items previously learned from those which had not been. While one may need to correct for guessing, this is usually the most sensitive measure of recall and may show evidence of retention missed by the other two methods.

Figure 7.1 summarizes typical results using these three measures. The data, taken from Luh (1922), show retention curves over a two-day period for lists of CVC nonsense syllables of the sort used by Ebbinghaus. Recognition memory, incidentally, can show some startling results, often missed with less sensitive measures of recall. In one well-known study, Shepard (1967) had college students learn lists of over 500 words and sentences. Recall was later tested by showing the students pairs of words (or sentences) and asking them simply to indicate which member of each pair had been seen before, and which had not. Scores as high as 89 percent correct out of the 500 were not unusual. The trick, of course, is to make sure the incorrect alternatives are very different from the test stimuli. If the distractors are close enough to the originals, one can actually reverse the usual superiority of recognition over other methods of recall (Bahrick & Bahrick, 1964; Bruce & Cofer, 1967).

The development of sensitive measures of retention had to be paralleled by equally sensitive techniques for the analysis of learning. The goal was to make the learning task possible but sufficiently difficult so that its gradual acquisition could be carefully followed. This can be accomplished by using lists of 12 or 13 CVCs; few enough for the average person to learn them in a

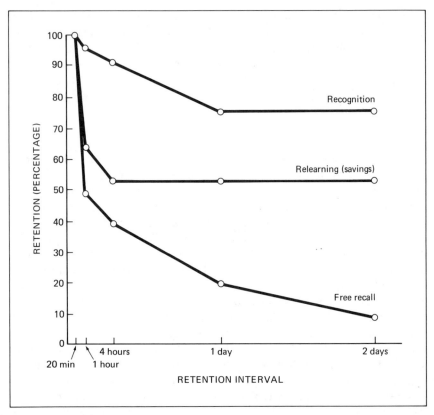

Figure 7.1   Retention curves for lists of CVC nonsense syllables over a two-day period using three measures of retention. (*Source:* C. W. Luh, The conditions of retention. *Psychological Monographs*, 1922, 31 (no. 3) (whole no. 142): fig. 1, pg. 22.)

short period of time, but more than can possibly be learned on a single glance. In addition to the materials, two methods of presentation were developed toward this same end.

Serial Anticipation

This method requires the volunteer to learn a list of CVCs in a set serial order. It is analogous to a child's learning of the alphabet, or perhaps the first ten presidents of the United States. One such list might be: *BIC, TEP, REK, FOM, GID, POV, SAR, TUL.* . . . One must take special care as some CVCs are more or less emotive of real words than others and consequently show differences in ease of learning (Glaze, 1928; Noble & McNeely, 1957).

The term *anticipation* comes from the unusual way in which the stimuli are presented and the subject responds. The CVC lists are typed vertically on a paper roll which is inserted into a device known as a *memory drum*. The memory drum is simply an electrically operated drive which moves the paper roll at a controlled speed such that each CVC in the list appears in a small window for a set duration. As each stimulus appears, the subject's response is to try to recall, or "anticipate," the next one on the list. When the next CVC appears, it gives him or her immediate knowledge of results and also serves as the stimulus for the next response—the next item in the list. The list is repeated in this manner until each and every CVC can be correctly anticipated, or some other criterion (e.g., 80 percent correct) is reached.

The end result can be described as a chain of associations, with each CVC serving as a response for the prior item and as a stimulus for the subsequent one. The fruits of serial learning can sometimes be seen by asking a child (or adult) what letter follows *n* in the alphabet. They may find it necessary to go through all or part of the alphabet before coming up with the correct answer.

Paired-Associate Learning

This technique requires the association of pairs of items, rather than a serial list. Again using the anticipation method, the memory drum would now be set to expose the first member of the pair (the stimulus) and after a controlled interval, the second member (the response). The list might consist of pairs of CVCs, or perhaps sets of real word- CVC associations: *hat-JIN, car-RET, pin-GAN*. . . . The list is repeated until the subject can anticipate the correct response for each stimulus word. In this case, the order of the pairs would be changed from trial to trial, since the sequence of the pairs is not crucial to the task. Paired-associate learning is analogous to the study of foreign language vocabulary, such as learning English-French equivalents, such as *hot-chaud, cold-froid*.

As in serial learning, rate of acquisition is measured by the number of trials necessary for perfect mastery, or some less demanding criterion of success.

SUMMARY

The study of verbal learning examines the processes involved in rote, verbatim memorization of verbal materials. To overcome the problems inherent in the study of verbal memory, which is ordinarily a creative, reconstructive process, early students of verbal learning followed Ebbinghaus's lead by concentrating on meaningless materials such as nonsense syllables.

Three measures of retention were devised: free recall (the most demanding), savings, and recognition (the least demanding). In addition, they devised two standard methods of teaching such materials, serial and paired-associate anticipation, so as to allow the careful analysis of the acquisition process.

Let us now turn to the fruits of their labor and examine those parameters which facilitate, and are thought to underly, verbal learning.

Elements of Verbal Learning

ACQUISITION, OVERLEARNING, AND RETENTION

The results of verbal-learning studies show the sort of continuity with other forms of learning that delighted many of the early theorists. That is, a graph of the number of verbal items learned over a series of practice trials shows the same gradually rising learning curve as all of the other forms of learning discussed to this point; those observed for classical conditioning, instrumental learning of a single response, and chained responses in sensorimotor learning. In a similar way, retention curves after a period of disuse (see Figure 7.1) show the same gradual loss in recall accuracy as all other retention curves.

Verbal learning also shows the same effects of overlearning on retention as we observed earlier for sensorimotor skills. For this, we again turn to a study by Krueger (1929). In this case, a group of volunteers learned lists of nouns through the anticipation method. On the first few trials the words were unfamiliar, and the subjects could only read each word aloud as it appeared. On each subsequent trial as the words became increasingly familiar, anticipation could begin. The subjects attempted to give the second word in the list when the first one appeared, the third word when the second one appeared, and so on. The subject tried, in other words, to make each word a stimulus for producing the response of the subsequent word.

Krueger again defined "100 percent learning" as the first complete trial in which all the words in a list were correctly anticipated. Analyzing the effects on retention of further practice beyond this point showed strong benefits to 150 percent learning (50 percent overlearning). That is, the additional 50 percent practice produced at least 50 percent better retention. Further, the longer the retention interval, the more valuable this additional practice was. Additional practice to 200 percent learning (100 percent overlearning), however, again showed the law of diminishing returns. While the additional practice did improve retention, the extra 50 percent overlearning produced far less than 50 percent improvement in retention.

As in the case of sensorimotor learning, there is a clear trade-off between the time invested in overlearning and the decreasing benefits of this additional practice on retention. The decision can only rest on the individual need for perfect, error-free recall in a particular situation. When such cases exist, however, continued overlearning can be justified.

EFFECTS OF SERIAL POSITION AND RELATED PHENOMENA

Unlike the learning of structured material (such as sentences), the learning of unrelated items (such as CVCs or lists of nouns) shows differential speed of learning depending on the item's relative position in a list. Specifically, items at the beginning and end of a list are more rapidly learned, with progressively greater difficulty encountered for items toward the middle of the list. This *serial position effect* is a robust phenomenon and occurs at all stages of learning and under conditions of both massed and distributed practice.

Figure 7.2 shows typical results for serial learning of 12 CVCs presented either with six seconds (massed practice) or two minutes (distributed prac-

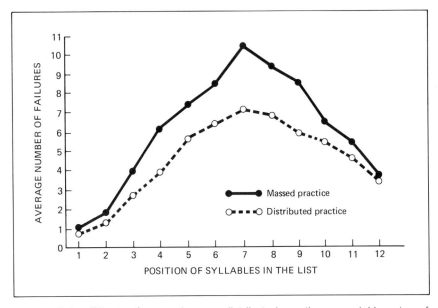

Figure 7.2   Effects of massed versus distributed practice on serial learning of 12 nonsense syllables. List presentations were separated by six-second (massed practice) or by two-minute intervals (distributed practice). Average number of failures to reach criterion for each of the 12 stimuli shows the characteristic serial position effect in serial learning. (*Source:* C. I. Hovland, Experimental studies in rote-learning theory. III. Distribution of practice with varying speeds of syllable presentation. *Journal of Experimental Psychology*, 1938, 23: fig. 2, pg. 178.)

tice) between practice trials. The results show both the systematic nature of the serial position effect and the same relative superiority of distributed over massed practice for verbal learning as was true for sensorimotor learning (Hovland, 1938).

One of the earliest attempts to account for the serial position effect was the so-called Lepley-Hull hypothesis. It illustrates the view of serial learning as a sequential chaining of individual S-R associations (Woodworth & Schlosberg, 1954, pp. 711–712). This hypothesis begins with several assumptions. In the early stages of practice, the associations between each of the items in the chain are weak, and few, if any, of the responses can be anticipated correctly. A weak bond is nevertheless beginning to form, even though it is still "subthreshold." With repeated practice, the association strength increases until gradually all associations exceed the threshold of report and all of the items can be overtly produced by the subject. This is a direct application to verbal learning of Thorndike's law of exercise, and Hull's notions of the growth of habit-strength. It is, if one needs one, the theoretical underpinning of "practice makes perfect."

Why are items at the beginning and end of the list easier to learn than those in the middle? While the associations are being strengthened through practice, there is also a counteracting effect of *interference* between the items in the list. The early items interfere with the learning of the later ones, and inhibit their retention, with remote items receiving progressively less inhibition. At the same time, interfering effects of later items on the earlier ones operate backwards toward the beginning of the list. The combined effects of this forward and backward interference would thus tend to build up from both ends of the list toward the middle where the total amount of interference would be greatest. Hence, the inverted U shape of the serial position curve. The fact that the serial position effect is usually less marked with distributed than with massed practice lends some credence to the hypothesis with the argument that the delay between trials in distributed practice allows time for some of the inhibition to decay.

The Von Restorff Effect

A qualification to the effects of serial position on learning is that items which are in some way perceptually isolated from the rest will be learned before the others. One could, for example, print one syllable in red among a list of black ones, a single letter in a list of digits, and so forth. The fact that distinctive items tend to be most readily learned and retained has been called the *Von Restorff Effect* (1933) after one of its early students. The Von Restorff Effect underlies the advantages of italic and boldface type in textbooks and the underscoring of major points on a blackboard.

As it happens, similar disruption of the serial position curve can also be brought about through the use of verbal instruction. Glanzer and Dolinsky (1965), for example, were able to eliminate the usual serial position curve by verbally redefining the subjective starting point of the list. Subjects were told, for example, to consider the fifth syllable in a ten-syllable list as the "beginning" of the series. Following these instructions, the fifth item showed the most rapid learning (even though its position should make it the slowest). Further, items one through four and six through ten began to show two separate, traditional serial position curves. The subjects seem to have been treating the initial ten-item list, whether consciously or not, as two separate, smaller lists for learning.

Breaking a long list, whether by perceptually or verbally isolating items, is just one of many ways of organizing material for more rapid learning. Reciting a long list of numbers in groups of three or four, with a pause between each group, seems almost intuitive for most people. According to traditional views, this would facilitate learning by reducing interference across the groups. As we will see in the following section, however, grouping may also aid learning by supplying anchors for the learning task.

REPETITION AND LEARNING

There is an alternative explanation for the shape of the serial position curve which, like the Lepley-Hull hypothesis, is more interesting for its broader implications than for its account of the curve per se. Feigenbaum and Simon (1962) related the effect not to forward and backward acting interference between items, but to the consequences of *strategies* in learning. Although the complete theory is complex, the character of their explanation is easy to understand. It is diametrically opposed to the spirit of the Lepley-Hull hypothesis. That hypothesis saw a gradual buildup of learning for all items in the list on each trial, with repeated trials increasing the strength of all of the associations equally. The observed inequality arises from the secondary effects of interference.

Feigenbaum and Simon imply that the first and last items in a list serve as anchors for learning the neighboring items. On some trials, subjects will attempt to learn the association between the first and second items, and on others they might attend to the last few items. In so doing, they work their way gradually toward the middle of the list, adding an additional item or two on each successive trial. It might be that limits of attention allow only one or two items to be learned on any one trial.

Repeated practice, then, serves not to give added strength to the entire list uniformly, but to give the opportunity for additional complete items to be learned on each trial. This view, although relatively simple in its assumptions, nicely accounts for the shape of the curve. It could also account for the Von Restorff Effect and the results of Glanzer and Donlinsky. Isolating items in the list would supply additional anchors for the learning of adjacent items.

The traditional view of practice as illustrated by the Lepley-Hull hypothesis is an *incremental theory* of learning. Each additional bit of practice strengthens associations in regular increments until the links are fully formed and correct responses are available without hesitation. If one can question the Lepley-Hull explanation for the serial position curve, perhaps one can also question the very notion of incremental theory upon which it is implicitly based. That would be a very courageous thing to do, since, from the earliest days of Pavlov and Thorndike, the incremental view has been an implicit assumption underlying all learning theory. Indeed, incremental theory had been so taken for granted that it was not really labeled and recognized as such until it was challenged.

The Theory of One-Trial Learning

Suppose a subject intends learning a list of eight paired-associate CVCs. With repetition, the number of associates produced will increase until eventually all eight can be given correctly. A learning curve showing the percentage of items correct as a function of the number of practice trials will show the usual smooth S-shaped learning curve. Suppose further, that a particular response is given correctly for the first time on the fifth practice trial. Incremental theory assumes that the previous four trials were necessary to build up that item's strength until some threshold was reached and the response could be correctly produced. What direct evidence do we have, however, that any such subthreshold learning was in fact taking place prior to the trial which allowed for the production of the correct response? Can we assume, in other words, that the smooth progressive learning curve for an entire list is reproduced in microcosm for each individual item in the list?

Perhaps the learning of a single item is an all-or-none process; that the association is completely formed on the single trial preceding the one on which it is correctly reported. To look at this question, Rock (1957) designed an ingenious experiment specifically intended to see the effects when subjects are systematically deprived of the benefits (if any) of subthreshold learning.

Two groups of subjects learned lists of eight paired-associate CVCs. One group received the usual procedures of repeated presentations until the eight sets were correctly learned. A second group followed similar procedures with one main difference. As the trials proceeded, each S-R pair correctly reported was retained in the list. Whenever an item was missed, however, it was replaced with an entirely new S-R pair on the next trial. If correctly reported on the following trial it was retained, and if not, it was again replaced by a new pair. This procedure was continued until eight complete paired-associates were all correctly reported on a given trial.

Rock's findings showed, surprisingly, that both groups learned the eight paired-associates at approximately the same rate. This was true even though the second group had to learn any given response with only a single practice presentation. From this, one might conclude that practice is not required for incremental strengthening of the associations. Rather, in a manner similar in character to Feigenbaum and Simon's position, the practice trials are necessary only to give added opportunity for additional items to be learned in an all-or-none fashion.

Appropriately called the theory of *one-trial learning*, Rock's challenge to the accepted notions of incremental learning excited a flurry of activity, both pro (Estes, 1960) and con (Underwood & Keppel, 1962; Postman, 1962). Questions, both methodological and theoretical, were raised. Could it be that the initially missed items were especially difficult and were on average replaced by easier ones? The end result of such an accidental event might be that the subject, while deprived of the benefits of subthreshold learning, would be exactly compensated by ending up with a relatively easy list. What about overlearning on retention? We know that continued practice beyond the point where an item can first be correctly reported will result in its being retained longer than an item which has not been further practiced. Could one argue that learning per se takes place on a single trial, but that the bond can be further strengthened with additional practice? This is hardly a logical proposition from the one-trial learning point of view.

The argument, which we will not attempt to resolve here, is a subtle one. First of all, it is not dealing with a situation such as a person's ability to read a novel or see a film once and remember the plot. This is not one-trial learning in the sense of this theory. The controversy addresses itself specifically to the more microscopic levels of learning of the sort described here, with brief exposures of nonmeaningful, unstructured materials. Second, both incremental and one-trial views accept practice as essential for learning. One's everyday experience could not argue otherwise. They differ not in its necessity but in the question of *why* it is necessary.

Whether this argument will continue to a final resolution, or whether it will ever be generalized beyond the limited ground on which it has so far been fought, remains to be seen. It is certainly the case that this very spirited controversy has served to bring into sharper focus many critical parameters of associative learning which otherwise might have been taken for granted or overlooked.

SUMMARY

In order to study the principles of "pure" verbal learning, Ebbinghaus and his followers created the consonant-vowel-consonant (CVC) nonsense syllable and special methods for its study: serial anticipation and paired-association learning.

Using these methodologies, the early students of verbal learning showed the benefits of distributed versus massed practice, investigated the serial position curve, and explored the Von Restorff Effect.

The tight control allowed by these methods also led to a closer theoretical analysis of the learning process itself. This culminated in the controversy of one-trial learning. It was with this theory that explanations of learning in terms of passive associations began to be replaced by notions of strategies of learning—the recognition that well motivated subjects are very active participants in the learning situation.

Meaningfulness and Transfer in Verbal Learning

LEARNING OF MEANINGFUL MATERIALS

Meaningful material is far easier to learn than nonmeaningful material. Like many facets of human learning, this general truth in fact hides a statement of extreme complexity. For example, how should one even define "meaningful"? Consider the following "sentence": "Cruel tables sang falling circles to empty bitter pencils." This sentence—if we can call it that— did not come from the pen of a modern poet. It comes from an experiment in verbal learning. While the sentence itself is obviously meaningless, on another level it contains a good deal of meaning. It says that human learning rarely takes place in isolation from other knowledge.

This alternative meaning becomes clear if you look at Figure 7.3 which contains a selection of additional examples from the experiment in question (Epstein, 1961).

College students were shown passages of each of these types in a series of seven-second presentations until they were correctly learned. The right hand margin shows the average number of trials necessary for learning passages from each of the four categories. Category I is composed of nonsense words with occasional real words (A, the, in). Category II consists of exactly the same passages, but with English sentence structure simulated by the addition of "grammatical" endings, such as ed for the past tense, a plural s, an adverbial ly, and so forth. Although this latter category contains more elements necessary for learning, the results summarized in the last column show that in fact it was easier to memorize. Categories III and IV are composed of real words, although these too make no sense as sentences. Adding "appropriate" grammatical endings in Category IV, however, makes them easier to learn than their "unstructured" counterparts in Category III. It is also interesting to see that while there is an overall advantage to memoriz-

Category	Sentences	Mean number of trials for learning
I	(a) A vap koob desak the citar molent um glox nerf. (b) The yig wur vum rix hum in jeg miv.	7.56
II	(a) A vapy koobs desaked the citar molently um glox nerfs. (b) The yigs wur vumly rixing hum in jegest miv.	5.77
III	(a) Sang tables bitter empty cruel to circles pencils falling. (b) Loudly trees paper from days lazy shallow to stumbled.	5.94
IV	(a) Cruel tables sang falling circles to empty bitter pencils. (b) Lazy paper stumbled to shallow trees loudly from days.	3.50

Figure 7.3   Examples of four categories of "sentences" presented in a series of seven-second trials until correctly learned. Mean number of practice trials required shown to the right of each category. (*Source:* Based on W. Epstein, The influence of syntactic structure on learning. *American Journal of Psychology, 74:* 80–85. Copyright © 1961 by Karl M. Dallenbach. Reprinted by permission of the University of Illinois Press.)

ing real words, a comparison of results for Categories II and III shows that nonsense words with grammatical endings are as easy to learn as real words without them.

As we said before, material which is meaningful, which contains structure or any possibility of organization, is far easier to learn than material without such structure. In everyday learning, as opposed to an experiment like Epstein's, it is the task of the teacher and/or student to bring understanding and meaning to the learning materials. Both know that a formula or definition understood can be retained and used for a lifetime. Mechanical rote learning of the same information may at best survive in memory until the next examination. However, in spite of superficial appearances to the contrary, organization and meaningfulness of material comes from within the individual, and is not an inherent property of the material per se. When we commonly say that the *material* is organized or meaningful, we really mean only that it is relatively amenable to organization by the individual because of past learning and experience with the language.

This much should be obvious and it stands, in Bevan's earlier words, as "nothing more *or less* than a description of events that can be predicted beforehand" (italics added). That learning is facilitated by meaning is nevertheless an important statement, and one at the very heart of intelligent learning.

Very good descriptions of the advantage to learning and memory of meaningful materials have been given by Bartlett (1932), who emphasized the role of cognitive structure in memory, and by Ausubel (1968), who stresses its role in learning. Acquired information is not stored in memory in isolation as so many files in a filing cabinet. It is stored in organized conceptual categories, with these categories expanded and reorganized as new information is acquired. It is into this existing cognitive structure that meaningful information is assimilated. It is this assimilation that gives the material its meaning. The existence of these structures gives anchoring points in learning, just as the elements of some of those nonsense passages could be anchored on their simulated English syntax. Learning becomes facilitated to the degree that (1) such anchoring points preexist from prior learning, and (2) sufficient meaning is given to the new materials to recognize their correspondence.

If one were to use a filing cabinet analogy, it would have to propose not only that new information finds its way to the appropriate file(s), with a constant updating of an unbelievably complex system of cross-referencing, but also *that the existing documents already on file are themselves rewritten in the light of the new information.* It should be noted that some experimental computer programs that "learn" now have such a goal in sight, and to that extent are indeed approaching a pale model of human learning. It has been a long time since psychologists viewed learning and memory as simply the accurate reproduction of practiced materials.

While a study of rote verbal learning can tell us about only a small proportion of what goes on in human learning, it does begin at a level simple enough to serve as an "anchor" for progressing to the more central issue of cognitive learning. It gives us an opportunity to extend one more step some of those fundamental principles of learning outlined in the previous chapters. This additional step is the role of transfer and mediation in human learning.

TRANSFER OF LEARNING

The advantages of structure and meaning in Epstein's experiment could be viewed as an example of *transfer* of learning. The topic of transfer of learning from one situation to another was already discussed in the context of sensorimotor learning in Chapter 6. A similar principle also applies in verbal learning.

As long as two learning tasks, or elements of two learning tasks, share formal similarity, there is a good chance that some transfer of learning will occur. As in the case of sensorimotor learning, such transfer may in some cases facilitate, and in other cases interfere with, the new learning.

Consider, for example, the following list of Danish words and their English equivalents as one might encounter them in a language text.

POSITIVE TRANSFER

Danish	English	Danish	English
adresse	address	falsk	false
bager	baker	hus	house
balkon	balcony	klar	clear
bluse	blouse	op	up
dame	lady	stof	stuff
derefter	afterwards	turist	tourist

Before you conclude that you are ready to tackle the sights of Copenhagen without so much as a phrase book to help you, consider the following additional vocabulary.

NEGATIVE TRANSFER

Danish	English	Danish	English
dog	however	grim	ugly
fart	journey	handel	trade
ham	him	marmelade	jam
mad	food	sky	cloud

Things are not always what they seem, and your advantage in learning Danish from a knowledge of English may be at best highly problematical. The confusion in this case is between new learning and very old, well-practiced learning (your knowledge of English). You may get confused in your Danish, but it is highly unlikely—one hopes—that you will get confused about your English. In education, we are more usually concerned about confusion between learning materials which have been acquired fairly close together in time. Will learning French in junior high school later cause negative or positive transfer in learning Spanish in high school? Will a "generally true" statement learned in the early grades help or hinder the pupil when a fuller and slightly different statement on the same principle is encountered in later years? The areas of practical concern in transfer of learning are innumerable and would seemingly defy anticipation. Studies of verbal learning, however, showed themselves quite adept at outlining schematic models of the various contingencies one might conceivably expect to encounter.

Conditions of Positive Transfer

One of three general circumstances which can be expected to produce some degree of positive transfer occurs when a new learning task retains the same responses as the old task, requiring only that they be attached to new stimuli. Returning to CVCs, suppose the first list had the paired-associate items *BEC-LIM*. If a new list contains the item *DAX-LIM*, positive transfer would be expected. Such a paradigm is usually noted as *A-B, C-B*, to indicate a sequence of any two tasks or items where the stimuli are different but the responses are the same.

Although the *A-B, C-B*, paradigm can yield some positive transfer, the more similar the new stimuli are to the original ones, the greater will be the positive transfer. For example, a list with *BEC-LIM* followed by a list with *BES-LIM* would show even stronger positive transfer. We might refer to this paradigm as *A-B, a-B*.

A final case where some positive transfer might be expected would be a reverse of the above; the stimuli remain the same while the responses are different but highly similar to those on the first list. This can be referred to as *A-B, A-b*, and would be encountered if, for example, *BEC-LIM* were followed by *BEC-LIN*.

Conditions of Negative Transfer

Negative transfer can be expected when a previously learned set of associations is followed by an attempt to learn a new set where different responses are now attached to the same, previously learned stimuli. Unlike the previous case, the new responses bear no similarity to the old. An example of this paradigm, conventionally indicated as *A-B, A-D*, might be first learning a list with *BEC-LIM*, followed by a list with *BEC-MOT*.

The most severe case of negative transfer comes when both old and new lists have the same sets of stimuli and responses, but the particular combinations of stimuli and responses are rearranged. This would be an *A-B, A-B$_r$* paradigm (the *r* subscript means "rearranged"), and would be typified by first learning a paired-associate list containing *BEC-LIM, CUZ-RAD*, and then attempting to learn a new list containing *BEC-RAD, CUZ-LIM*. It is like trying to learn to stop in response to a green traffic light, and to go when it turns red.

Similarity and Interference

As we shall see in more detail later (Chapter 11), negative transfer in learning and memory is usually seen in terms of *interference*, and numerous studies have supported our own experience of the confusion brought about when trying to learn two sets of slightly different materials close together in time.

This is true whether the effects are seen most strongly on new learning interfering with the retention of older learning, or prior learning causing confusion in the learning of new materials. As we will see later, these are referred to respectively as *retroactive inhibition* (RI) and *proactive inhibition* (PI).

Obviously, interference, whether RI or PI, is not total. If all learning interferred with all other learning, retention of any information would be logically impossible. The answer to this paradox lies in the similarity principle of transfer, and in the way human memory is organized. Materials tend to be categorized as they are learned, and there is relatively little interference from one category to another.

This may strike the reader as reasonable and consistent with his or her own experience. An ingenious experiment by Wickens (1973) supports our intuitive notions. Wickens had four groups of college students memorize lists of words in the usual rote learning fashion. Each list consisted of different items and was presented for a single trial. In this case, however, the words learned by each of the four groups belonged to a particular category. One group learned lists of professions; another group learned names of meats; another, names of flowers; and a final group, names of vegetables. We would expect interference to increase as more and more lists from a particular category are learned. That is, when we test for recall after each trial, it would become progressively harder for the students to recall which particular names had been presented in the preceding list.

Figure 7.4 shows the percentage of words recalled by each of the four groups. Retention scores show a systematic decrease over three successive learning trials. The interference, in this case PI, builds up, as more and more items from the same category have been learned. This much is to be expected. Look carefully, however, at the results for the fourth trial. On this trial all four groups were given another new list to learn, but in all cases the list contained only names of fruit: a different category from those they had previously been learning. The group which had been learning names of professions showed excellent recall for this final list. Since fruits and professions are very different categories of items, there is virtually no interference from one to the other.

Recall for meats and flowers both show less improvement. They are of a different category than fruits, but not so different as fruits and professions. Vegetables, although formally in a different category, are for most of us rather similar, and this is borne out by Wickens's results. The group which had been learning names of vegetables continues to show evidence of proactive inhibition when they shifted to names of fruits on the fourth trial. The final curve shows a control group who did not have the category of items changed on the final list. This group shows the poorest recall of all. Wickens (1973) referred to this phenomenon as a "release" from proactive interference.

MEDIATED TRANSFER

The study of negative transfer, or interference, has played a central role in psychologists' attempts to explain forgetting under ordinary circumstances. As we shall see in chapter 11, the common sense notion that we forget things simply with the passage of time has been increasingly ques-

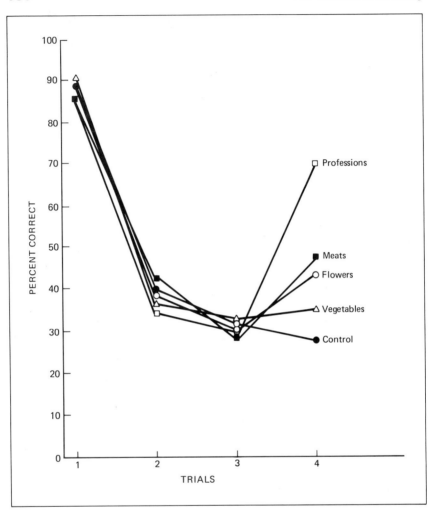

Figure 7.4 Effects on proactive inhibition (PI) of changing response category on final trial. After learning three successive lists of words from one category, learning a fourth list of words drawn from a different category (names of fruits) shows a "release" from PI proportional to the dissimilarity between the new category and the old ones. The control group continued to learn names from the same category on the fourth trial. (*Source:* D. D. Wickens, Some characteristics of word encoding. *Memory & Cognition,* 1973, 1: fig. 4, pg. 490. Reprinted by permission of The Psychonomic Society.)

tioned by modern theorists. The emphasis has been more and more on the conclusion that it is interference of new experience that occurs during the passage of time which is the actual cause of forgetting. But that is getting ahead of our story. Let us return for a moment for a closer look at the conditions of positive transfer, and *why* meaningful material is more easily learned and remembered.

The concept of *mediation* in learning, or *mediated transfer*, recognizes that while an S-R association may contain two overt elements, the learning process may in actuality include three (or more) associations. A mediator is a linking association which forms an intermediate connection between a stimulus and response to facilitate learning. A paired-associate set such as *SKY-LOUD*, for example, might be mediated by making use of prior associations between *SKY-thunder*, and *thunder-LOUD*. Hence, what appears as a two-element association may be learned as three: *SKY→ (thunder)→LOUD*.

Foreign language vocabulary learning is well stocked with useful possibilities for mediated transfer. Here are a few examples from French. Notice, incidentally, how the mediators reproduce one of the earlier mentioned conditions for positive transfer; that of the *A-B, A-b* paradigm. The first example, for instance, involves forming a first association, *door(A)→portal(B)*, followed by the association, *door(A)→port(b)*. The rapidity of the learning, of course, is explained by the *door→portal* association already existing in the student's linguistic knowledge. In each case listed, however, the *A-B, A-b* structure is diagrammatically rewritten in the notation of mediated transfer, which underlies the *A-B, A-b* paradigm.

English	*French*	*Mediated Association*		
door	port	door⟶	(portal)⟶	port
end	fin	end⟶	(finish)⟶	fin
engaged	occupée	engaged⟶	(occupied)→	occupée

The topic of mediated transfer returns us almost full circle to our opening comments regarding the facilitating effects of meaningfulness and structure in verbal learning. As we noted earlier, even the ubiquitous nonsense syllable is not always devoid of meaning because of its frequent evocation of real words. *BAL* may be reminiscent of "balance," "ball," "Baltimore" . . . *WIS* of "whisk," "whistle," "wisdom," and, for the psychologist, WISC (Wechsler Intelligence Scale for Children).

Although it may be a rather peculiar use of the word, Noble and his colleagues (Noble & McNeely, 1957; Noble, 1961) referred to the degree to which nonsense syllables are associated with real words as their "meaningfulness." One might quibble with the use of this term, but they were able to show reliably high correlations between ease of learning lists of nonsense syllables and their rated meaningfulness. These studies are usually seen in terms of mediation: the recall of CVCs can be mediated or "linked" through real word associations already known to the individual.

Natural Language Mediation

Adams (1967) referred to cases such as those above as *natural language mediation* (NLM). Numerous studies have shown how NLMs can go beyond a single link, to whole chains of associations.

Jenkins (1963) had college students learn lists of paired-associate sets of CVCs and word combinations. Such a list, for example, might contain the pairs, *DAX-hammer, WUG-king,* etc. Once these sets were learned, the same group of people were given a second list to learn, containing CVC word pairs such as *DAX-nail, WUG-queen.* Jenkins found that the second list was learned extremely rapidly. He interpreted this in terms of the use of NLMs. Thus, there already exists a strong association between *king* and *queen,* and between *hammer* and *nail.* Once the first list is learned, the new response can be attached through the mediation of the associated words:

DAX→hammer→nail
WUG→king→queen

Earlier we said that whole chains of associations could be exploited in verbal learning. Consider learning a paired-associate list with a CVC word pair such as *ZUG-soldie*r, followed by a second list containing *ZUG-navy.* Since most people already associate *soldier* and *sailor,* and *sailor* and *navy,* the second list can be learned through the chain: *ZUG→soldier→ sailor→navy.* All that we actually observe is a student very rapidly learning *ZUG-navy.* We can infer from the rapidity of the learning that such a chain of NLMs was most probably underlying this very rapid acquisition (Russell & Storms, 1955.)

Other Forms of Mediation

The examples of mediation in verbal learning are numerous and should hardly be surprising. That is, most of us discovered early in life that giving meaning to learning materials—even if contrived—aids the learning process. Epstein's (1961) example of learning the "sentence," "Cruel tables sang falling circles to empty bitter pencils," is an example of using grammatical structure as a form of mediation. Other experiments have shown the use of sentences for mediated learning in a slightly different way. Bobrow and Bower (1969), for example, have shown how isolated words can be easily learned if we are astute enough to incorporate them into a meaningful sentence. A paired-associate set such as *boy-pencil* is easy to remember if we remember the sentence, "the *boy* is writing with a *pencil.*"

The use of mediation does not necessarily imply the learner's conscious awareness of the intermediate association. Often one can only infer its use from the outward evidence that learning has taken place more rapidly than would be expected without it. (Presumably some related explanation would have to account for the accidental appearance of the item GYM in a published list of alleged nonsense syllables actually used in a verbal learning study.)

The role of prior associations in verbal learning need not be logical or direct. In one study, a group of volunteers had to recall bed, rest, awake, tired, dream, wake, night, eat, comfort, sound, slumber, snore. About half erroneously "remembered" sleep from the list, a word independently associated with each of the memorized items (Deese, 1964). One now has to ask how many of the *correctly* recalled items from the list were truly remembered, and how many were in fact not learned, but were analogous recall "errors" which happened to be correct.

If associations are sometimes direct and conscious, they need not necessarily be logical. Some individuals are ingenious in the number of devices they can employ to facilitate learning. Some find, for example, that an item such as *JEG* is much easier to remember if it is thought of as a person's initials, J. E. G., rather than as a nonsense syllable. The conscious use of such associations can be highly developed as a skill to aid memory. Associations, visual imagery, rhyming connectors, and other techniques commonly known as *mnemonic devices*, are merely another example, albeit a dramatic one, of anchoring effects in learning and memory. We will discuss the use of mnemonics in more detail in Chapter 11.

SUMMARY

It is axiomatic that meaningful material is more readily learned and retained than material which is not. Learning theorists have explained this in terms of transfer from prior learning.

We can expect transfer of learning from one task to another whenever the learning of similar materials is involved. In some cases the transfer will be negative. That is, the sets of learning materials may interfere with each other and retard the learning process. When this occurs we refer either to proactive interference, where old learning interferes with newer learning, or retroactive interference, where new learning interferes with the retention of the old.

Positive transfer refers to the facilitation of new learning as a result of prior knowledge. Most cases of positive transfer are the result of mediation in learning. Mediation is defined as the use of a linking association which forms an intermediate connection between some stimulus and response.

The introduction of mediation begins to lead us beyond an analysis of learning in terms of single S-R associations. Mediated learning can be viewed as a logical extension of S-R learning, through the acquisition of chains of multiple S-R associations. The break with the traditional S-R analysis, however, comes with the dual notions of meaningfulness and strategies in learning. While the use of meaningfulness in mediated learning is amenable to an S-R analysis, the acquisition of meaning itself seems to go beyond these simpler notions. It is to this question that we now turn.

chapter 8

Concept Learning I:

DISCRIMINATION AND CATEGORIZATION

This chapter is about concept learning. To set the stage, here are a few observations for a moment's contemplation: "Hospitals could be managed more efficiently if it were not for all the patients" or, "Schools would be far more pleasant if one did not have to contend with all those teachers and students." In the same spirit, here is one more: "Concept attainment would be far easier all around if the environment were not so complex."

We may be permitted to wonder whether hospital or school administrators have ever spent long winter evenings before the fire meditating on such "ideal worlds." In a manner of speaking, students of learning and concept attainment have in fact done such meditating, and one can conjure up what would be an irrational vision of a totally rational world. Here are some of its characteristics: (1) All concepts to be formed are simple and consistent, with defining attributes always present and in the same form. (2) Reinforcement or feedback always follows each encounter with an example of the concept. (3) Category names are consistent and invariant. (4) Children and adults approach concept learning with logic and consistency.

Happily, such an "ideal world" of an orderly experiential universe, appreciated by an equally orderly mind, does not exist. If it did, life and learning would be a nightmare world with all the excitement and creativity of a cash register. In fact, if this were the case, the human ability of concept learning would fall into the same category as hospitals without patients or schools without students; it would have no need to exist at all.

Before we go any farther, let us say exactly what we mean by concepts and concept attainment. In brief, concept attainment begins with the experience of a wide variety of different stimuli, centers on the recognition that some of them share important common features, and ends with the tendency to group these stimuli conceptually by treating them in some sense as if they were equivalent. The process of recognizing that certain objects or events seem to "go together" by virtue of their shared features is sometimes referred to as abstraction, and the ability to recognize newly encountered instances of such classes is referred to as generalization.

In no sense does this definition of concept attainment imply that persons can specify these shared properties of the stimuli, or that they can systematically list all those stimuli which belong to one conceptual category or another. This is in fact rarely the case. As often as not, we can only infer that concepts have been learned when we see newly encountered instances named correctly or used appropriately. We know that a child has the concept of a *ball*, not when he or she can specify properties such as roundness, bounciness, and so forth, but when he or she sees a new instance of the class and correctly calls it a ball or simply picks it up to throw it.

CAN CONCEPTS BE TAUGHT?

Concepts, like examples of good art, or for that matter pornography, are far easier to recognize than to define. Concepts involve abstractions; the appreciation of relationships between stimuli which give rise to generalizations free of the specific stimuli from which they were derived. Some concepts can be formally presented and defined, such as the commonality of the sets $1 + 2 + 3$, $4 + 2$, and $5 + 1$, or the familiar, "square of the hypotenuse of a right triangle is equal to the sum of the squares of the two sides." Other concepts are simpler to learn, but paradoxically harder to define, such as "bigger than," "smaller than," or "equal to." Still other concepts, such as "truth," or "honesty," or "love," often seem as hard to learn as they are to define.

It is partly this elusive quality of concepts that underlies the belief on the part of many people that while one can teach facts, one cannot "teach" concepts. Concept learning is uniquely internal. We can supply the necessary examples of a concept and create the external conditions conducive to its attainment. The actual process of abstraction and generalization, however, comes almost entirely from within the individual; and, as often as not, without his or her conscious awareness that it is taking place. To put it another way, renaming a second grade addition and subtraction class as "teaching number concepts," surely implies more about the goals of the program than about any aspect of the process over which the teacher has direct control.

Response-Learning: The Visible Tip of the Iceberg

If learning to correctly name new instances of a concept signals that the concept has been acquired, so the learning of the verbal response can often be confused with the more important learning of the concept itself. An easy way to keep this distinction clear is to ask in any response-learning situation exactly what the stimulus is to which the response is being attached.

Let us take the case of the child in the early school years learning to identify and name the letters of the alphabet. The observable process is largely one of association learning as discussed in the previous chapter. This is true whether the child is learning to name letters $(S_s \rightarrow R_{``es"})$ or to give the sounds they typically make $(S_s \rightarrow R_{``sss"})$.

From the principles of the previous chapter, this might often be described as association chaining because of the frequent use of *mediating links* in the initial stages of learning. Common examples are $a \rightarrow$ apple $\rightarrow$ "ah," or $s \rightarrow$ snake $\rightarrow$ "sss". As we have seen, the role of such mediators is important for they can serve as concrete, visualizable links between the abstract symbols and the relevant responses. An imaginative child's dictionary might have a stand for the concrete "aardvark," but never for the abstract "anarchy." Good mediators, incidentally, can be deceptively hard to find. We could suggest to the child that o is round like an *o*range, but it is also round like an *a*pple. The letter o might be associated with the rounded mouth used when saying it. Will the child wonder whether Q is articulated with a rounded mouth with the tongue hanging out?

All of this, however, relates only to the attachment of verbal responses to the letter stimuli; that visible tip of the iceberg that is relatively easy to see and to work with. But what of the part of the process which lies below the observable surface; the one which emerges only when we stop to ask what is the *stimulus* to which the response is being attached?

What is the stimulus for the "ah" response? Is it A, a, A, $\mathcal{A}$, a or a ? The answer obviously is that it must be all of them. The child may begin with the single invariant a of the reading book. Eventually, however, he or she must learn to recognize and abstract those common visual features of that class of stimuli we would all call a. These features, furthermore, must be generalized to include new and unique examples of a as potentially varied as the endless varieties of human handwriting. In short, what the child must learn is not so much the correct response to the stimulus a but the response to the concept of a. It is this ability of concept attainment, which sometimes precedes and sometimes accompanies response learning, that is the crucial and hidden key to the learning process.

Ideal Worlds and Quasi-Ideal Worlds of Concept Attainment

THE HEIDBREDER EXPERIMENT

Whether or not it is possible to "teach" concepts directly, it is certainly possible to examine those conditions necessary for their acquisition. To do this, we might best begin with what we shall call a *quasi-ideal world* of concept attainment. This would be a specially structured learning situation having some of the simplifying properties of our previously described ideal world but also sharing some important elements of real-world concept learning.

Of the many experimental studies of concept attainment one might choose, the one which probably best meets these criteria is in fact one of the earliest of such studies. Although Edna Heidbreder used adults in her work, her general conditions were not unlike the experiences of children in the early years of discovering the meanings of named concepts.

At first glance, Heidbreder's experiment looked very much like a typical study in paired-associate learning (Heidbreder, 1946). Her volunteer subjects would view a series of nine pictures shown one at a time in the window of a rotating memory drum. As each picture appeared she would give it a nonsense name, repeating the set of nine pictures until all of their names were correctly learned. To further the similarity with paired-associate studies, she used the familiar *anticipation method*: as each picture appeared, subjects would try to recall its name before Heidbreder could give the correct response. Like the child, Heidbreder's subjects were not told to learn concepts. On the contrary, she specifically implied that this was a study of rote memorization of the pictures and their names.

Once the first series of nine pictures and their names were learned, a second series of nine different pictures were introduced. This was followed by a third series, then a fourth series, and so on, until a total of 16 different series of nine pictures each had been presented. The important point is that

Figure 8.1   Five of the 16 series of pictures and names used in Heidbreder's study of concept attainment. Stimuli representing *pran* (two verticals crossed by a horizontal) are circled for illustration. (*Source:* E. Heidbreder, The attainment of Concepts: I. Terminology and methodology. *Journal of General Psychology,* 1946, 35: fig. 1, pg. 182. Reprinted by permission of The Journal Press.)

while the nine pictures of each new series were different, the *names* they were given were not. The first five picture sets are shown in Figure 8.1, along with the names of the first three. A few minutes' study of these stimuli and their names shows the thrust of the Heidbreder experiment. The pictures of each set sharing the same name also share similar properties. *Ling* represents two objects, *fard* is always a round object, *relk* is a human face, *pran* is a configuration of two verticals crossed by a horizontal, and so forth. (We have circled the *pran* concept to emphasize the point.)

It is important to remember that the pictures were presented one at a time, such that the "plot" was not quite as transparent as when we see them all together as they are shown in Figure 8.1. Nevertheless, somewhere along the line her subjects must have become aware that the names were being repeated from series to series. They would be unusual individuals indeed if they did not suspect that, as in real life, objects sharing the same name may well have something in common. It is of course the discovery and the utilization of common properties between stimuli that represents the essence of concept learning.

Heidbreder's results were clear. Although her subjects were not necessarily able to state the underlying principles used, the time required to learn the names of each "new" set of pictures systematically decreased from series to series. Further, her subjects soon began to anticipate the correct names for new objects on the very first trial in which they were presented, even before Heidbreder had a chance to name them.

The Concept of a Concept

The Heidbreder experiment became something of a classic in the field of concept attainment for its early emphasis on the critical importance of stimulus variation in concept learning. Her study not only captured the essence of the process but showed that it could be modeled, to some extent, under laboratory conditions. Heidbreder's concepts, however, were still far removed from the real world. As Pollio (1974, pg. 98) has emphasized: "Right at the beginning it is important to emphasize how difficult a concept is the concept of a concept."

Pollio's position becomes clear if we take a specific example, such as a child learning to recognize that class of stimuli we call "a dog." The very young child, of course, may apply the term to any number of four-footed creatures including horses, cows, and sheep. We have all seen children do this. Older children and adults, however, have a finely developed concept of a dog. What defines this concept? The dog has four legs and a tail. However, cows, horses, and sheep also have four legs and a tail. We could add that dogs are of a certain size, and that they are friendly. But a large dog can exceed the size of a small sheep, and "friendly" is unfortunately not universally descriptive of all dogs. We cannot seem to define our concept of a dog, and yet we certainly do know one when we see one. We must agree with Pollio; the concept of a concept is, without doubt, an exceedingly difficult concept.

A Concept Is More than a Composite Picture

Hull (1920), a S-R theorist we encountered in Chapter 5, made a brave attempt to understand concept learning within the S-R paradigm whose cause he did so much to champion. Here is how he saw it work. The child sees a particular dog (S_1), and at the same time hears someone say the word "dog" (R_d). On subsequent occasions he or she sees other dogs $(S_2, S_3 \ldots)$ and again hears the same word "dog" (R_d). Initially, the child may treat each of these cases as separate S-R associations; $S_1 \to R_d$, $S_2 \to R_d$, $S_3 \to R_d$, and so on. After sufficient experiences with a variety of dogs, however, the child comes to abstract the concept of a dog, based on attributes which were common to all of the examples encountered. If the abstraction, based on common elements, is a good one (i.e., if the concept is valid), the child can now correctly recognize new instances of the dog concept whenever they are encountered. The child's first meeting with, for example, a Labrador retriever or a borzoi (Russian wolfhound) immediately evokes the notion "dog." The process of discrimination, as described in Chapter 5, would also be important to the developing concept. That is, the ability to generalize from previously encountered examples to new ones would be accompanied by the ability to utilize the absence of critical elements to exclude nonmembers. Just as all varieties of dogs should evoke the concept "dog," so cats and horses, for example, should not.

Heidbreder's experiment presents just such a picture and appears, at least at first glance, to be a perfect illustration of Hull's notion of concept learning. Perhaps, after all, the concept of a concept is not such a difficult concept.

Unfortunately, the physical similarities between real-world stimuli belonging to the same class only rarely approach the neatness envisaged by Hull or exemplified by Heidbreder's experiment. It is not so much that Hull's explanation was wrong as that it failed to address the most difficult part of the problem; *how* these relevant attributes are "abstracted" and "generalized." No simple solution to this problem lies within S-R theory.

One attempt to find the solution in S-R terms can be described as the formation of a "composite picture," one derived from all encounters with examples of a category (cf. Vinacke, 1974, pp. 153–154). We can visualize this metaphorical composite picture by imagining laying down, one on top of the other, a series of photographic negatives of particular dogs encountered in past experience and viewing the entire set held up before a strong light. What we would see, according to this argument, is a composite picture of a generic, or "average," dog. In reality, such a composite picture would be nothing more or less than a vaguely recognizable blur (see Figure 8.2).

The flaw in the theory of the composite picture lies in its assumption that the entire visual pattern of the conceptual example serves as the stimulus for the response of the concept's name. As we have seen, the degree of variation from stimulus to stimulus within a category eliminates this possibility. Further, as research by Rosch (1973) has shown, when subjects were

Figure 8.2 Schematic representation of the "composite picture" notion of conceptual identification, derived from specific encounters with examples of a conceptual category. The top row shows the specific exemplars, and the bottom row shows the developing composite. In reality, such a "composite picture" would be nothing more or less than a vaguely recognizable blur.

asked to rank category members as to their *degree* of membership, her adult subjects showed high agreement in deciding that some examples were subjectively more typical of a given conceptual category than others. For example, to most subjects, robins and eagles are very central to the concept "bird," chickens and ducks are less so, while penguins are definitely marginal. The child must clearly be detecting some general principle, or "ideal type," from his or her specific encounters with examples of a concept, which, in turn, can be applied to the identification of new examples as they are encountered. We may wish to call this process "generalization." We are safe in doing so, however, only if we recognize that generalization merely describes a process we have yet to explain.

TYPES OF CONCEPTS

Before leaving the quasi-ideal world of concept attainment, let us take another well-known example from the experimental literature. Like the Heidbreder experiment, this series of studies also utilized the learning of artificially well-structured concepts and employed adult volunteers as subjects. It differed from Heidbreder in that it moved away from simply setting up the external conditions necessary for concepts to be acquired. The goal was to specify the nature of different types of concepts and some of the ways in which they are learned.

This series of studies, reported by Bruner, Goodnow, and Austin (1956), centered primarily on the set of stimuli shown in Figure 8.3. This set of raw materials from which the concepts would be formed consisted of some 81 cards which differed from each other in terms of four clear *attributes*, with each attribute having three *dimensions*. The attributes are the *shape* of the central figure (square, circle, or cross), the *number* of figures (one, two, or three), the *color* of the figures (red, black, or green), and the number of *borders* (one, two, or three).

Bruner, Goodnow, and Austin's stimuli are in some ways less natural than Heidbreder's and in other ways more so. However artificial Heidbreder's experiment, one could contemplate a language system in which human faces are called *relk*, round objects are classed together as *fard*, and pairs of objects are called *ling*. Undoubtedly she took great care in selecting

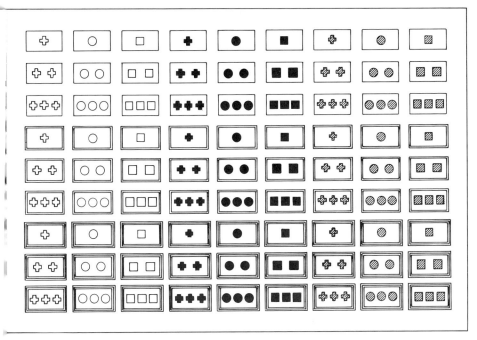

Figure 8.3 Stimulus cards used for the study of concept identification. The cards were designed to display four *attributes* (each with three dimensions): shape of the central figures (square, circle, or cross), number of figures (one, two, or three), color of figures (red, black, or green), and number of borders (one, two, or three). The plain figures were in green, the striped figures were in red, and the solid figures were in black. (*Source:* J. S. Bruner, J. J. Goodnow, and G. A. Austin, *A Study of Thinking,* fig. 1, pg. 42. New York: Wiley, 1956. Reprinted by permission of the publisher.)

stimuli that would seem as natural to her subjects as possible. This is not the case with the 81 cards used by Bruner, Goodnow, and Austin. These are far from anything which would naturally arise in the world as we know it. The advantage of their stimuli is that the same cards can be recombined in a number of different ways so as to allow for an endless variety of concepts based on the same stimuli. This is roughly analogous to a man classed in different contexts, as a "neighbor" by the people on his street, "Daddy" by his children, "Grandfather" by his children's children, and "policeman" when he puts on his uniform and is seen by the general public. As his category membership changes, so too does his role, and the way in which he is perceived and reacted to by others. He is, however, the same man.

To define a concept with Bruner, Goodnow, and Austin's materials, one could, for example, specify the concept, "all cards with one red figure." Another concept might be "all cards with two figures and/or with circles." Still a third might be defined as "all cards possessing the same number of figures as borders." Although superficially similar, these three examples represent three very different types of concepts, each with its own implications for learning. The types of concepts they represent are, respectively, *conjunctive, disjunctive,* and *relational* categories.

1. Conjunctive Categories

A *conjunctive category* is a concept defined by the joint presence of two or more attributes, with the presence of *all* of the attributes required for class membership. Using the cards in Figure 8.3, we could define such a category as the "conjunction" of three figures, redness, and circles. Put more simply, this means that all cards containing three red circles belong to the category, and all others do not. The number of borders is irrelevant. Figure 8.3 shows three examples of the concept, all in the second-to-last column.

The concepts used in the Heidbreder experiment were generally of this simple conjunctive form, and it represents the basis of many of the simpler concepts encountered in everyday life.

2. Disjunctive Categories

A *disjunctive category* is intuitively more complex than a conjunctive one. Although no less clearly defined, in this case the criteria for category membership are on an "either/or" basis, such that no two members of a class need necessarily possess the same attributes. A disjunctive category in Figure 8.3 might consist of all cards with *either* three figures (of any color or shape), *or* red figures (of any shape or number), *or* round figures (of any color or number). While there are only three cards which possess all of the attributes (three red circles), full category membership in fact totals 57 cards which acceptably fulfill this either/or definition.

To an observer not "in" on the definition, disjunctive categories may seem quite arbitrary and unfathomable. It may be hard to see any clear relationship between the attributes which must somehow exemplify the class. A local library which extends borrowing privileges to "any person living in *or* paying taxes to the town" is such a disjunctive category. So too is a "strike" in baseball. A strike is *either* a pitch that crosses the plate between the batter's knees and shoulders, *or* it is any pitch at which the batter swings but fails to hit into the boundaries of the field. Diagnostic categories of mental illness are also sometimes of this disjunctive form, and may in part underlie the impression that such diagnoses often seem "private, quasi-rational, and non-repeatable" (Hammond, 1955, pg. 255).

3. Relational Categories

A final type of concept is a *relational category*, in which category membership is defined not by the mere presence or absence of defining attributes but by a *relationship* between them. In Figure 8.3, for example, one could define a relational category as "all cards with the same number of figures as borders" or "all cards with fewer figures than borders."

Federal income tax brackets in the United States are relational categories, as they are defined in terms of a relationship between the number of dependents a person has and his or her level of income after deductions. A less esoteric example has already been mentioned. Written letters of the alphabet are in fact relational concepts. The characteristics of the A concept are not merely the presence of three straight lines but a particular spatial relationship between them.

STRATEGIES IN CONCEPT ATTAINMENT

The way in which Bruner, Goodnow, and Austin used their card stimuli was different from Heidbreder's approach in two other main respects. First, their subjects were allowed to see the entire array of cards and were always told the type of concept under study (i.e., conjunctive, disjunctive, or relational). The second difference was the way in which the concepts were "taught."

Naming, as used by Heidbreder, is one way that the child learns to conceptually group objects in the environment. The child hears some animals called "cat," others "dog," and still others "horse." The child's task is to discover what nonoverlapping attributes distinguish one category from another. An equally common approach, which often accompanies categorization through naming, is to isolate a category by directly indicating those stimuli which do and do not belong to it. This is exemplified by the parent who answers a child's overgeneralization of a category with, "No, that (a horse) is not a dog. That (a dog) is a dog." It is this latter approach which Bruner, Goodnow, and Austin attempted to model in their studies.

Let us say, for example, that the concept to be learned is the simple conjunctive one of all cards containing two crosses of any color and two borders. The subject begins by selecting a card, perhaps at random. The experimenter simply says "yes" or "no" depending on whether the chosen card is an example of the concept. The subject continues to select cards, and the experimenter continues to answer "yes" or "no," until sufficient positive and negative instances have been encountered for the subject to correctly infer the concept.

We can use the cards in Figure 8.3 to study both the ease of learning different types of concepts and alternative strategies which may be used in the course of the learning. The term *strategy* refers to the kinds of information the subjects seek in order to discover the concept and the kinds of hypotheses they seem to be testing as they do so. It is important to stress that a strategy is a plan but not necessarily a conscious one. On the contrary, numerous studies have shown that intricate concepts can be acquired and used without the subject having the foggiest notion of exactly what they are. One can still infer the principles they must be using, just as one can when a young child is heard to pluralize the word *foot* as *foots*.

1. Scanning Strategies

Imagine yourself in the position of a subject about to learn the previously mentioned conjunctive category of two crosses and two borders. Your first random selection might be a card with two green crosses and two borders. You would be told that this is an example of the concept. From this you know that the concept must therefore be either two figures, two crosses, the color green, two borders, or perhaps some combination of these attributes. The field is narrowed, but not by much.

The simplest of the scanning strategies which might now be employed is known as *successive scanning*. The principle is simple. The subject begins by forming an initial hypothesis, such as the possibility that the concept is "two green figures and two borders." A good scanning strategy would then be to pick a card which would be a positve instance of the concept if the hypothesis is correct. Such a card might be the fifth one in the second row which contains two green circles with two borders. If the experimenter announces that this is *not* an instance of the concept, the initial hypothesis is automatically invalidated, and a new one must be considered. The subject might now try the hypothesis "green objects" and test it by again picking a card which should be a positive instance. This general process is repeated again and again until the correct hypothesis has been found and verified. Note that in successive scanning, a hypothesis as to the *entire concept* is tested with each card selection.

2. Focusing Strategies

An alternative strategy to the all-or-none approach of successive scanning is to begin without an overall hypothesis but instead to focus on one attribute at a time, testing each in turn until the complete concept is discovered. This approach, the simplest of the possible focusing strategies, is known as *conservative focusing*. Here is how it works.

Suppose the same concept of two crosses and two borders is the correct one, and the first positive instance selected is again the card with two green crosses and two borders. In this case the subject begins with a single attribute, such as "green," and selects the next card concentrating only on its color. This could be the fifth card in row seven with its two crosses and two borders, but with red figures. The subject would be told that this is also an exemplar of the concept. Color must therefore be irrelevant. The next step might be to test the number of borders, with the second card in row two chosen because of its single border. This would not be an exemplar, thus telling the subject that two borders must be important to the concept. The subject would then test in turn the shape and the number of the central figures in a similar way until the correct concept of two crosses and two borders becomes apparent.

Such a focusing strategy always demands a certain minimum number of selections for discovering the correct concept. For this reason it can be unnecessarily slow and cumbersome with simple tasks. The virtue of focusing lies with more complex concepts, where its systematic step-by-step approach guarantees success with a minimum strain on memory and reduced risk.

The limitations of memory represent a critical factor in concept learning, and we can expect the memory loss to be greater when the task involves complex rules rather than simpler ones. To put it bluntly, it is possible to eliminate a hypothesis early in the task but later to simply forget that we have done so. Any strategy which reduces the memory load is bound to facilitate the task (cf. Denny, 1969). Once a concept has been correctly identified, subjects generally show better memory for the hypotheses tested than they do for the specific stimuli used to test these hypotheses (Coltheart, 1971).

SOME PARAMETERS OF CONCEPT ATTAINMENT

The sort of experimental studies we have been discussing are of course highly artificial and one can generalize from them to the "real world" only with some element of risk. The findings of such studies, however, seem plausible enough that the risk may be minimal. Thus, for example, they have shown that the ease or difficulty of learning concepts is a combined function of the complexity of the stimuli, the nature of the strategies employed, and the conditions present during the course of learning. These conditions include such factors as the availability of feedback and the subject's own motivation or "set" as he or she approaches the problem.

1. Number of Defining Attributes

In the above examples, subjects discovered the nature of the concepts by determining which *attributes* were the relevant ones for their definition. We can define an attribute as "any discriminable feature of an event that is susceptible of some discriminable variation from event to event" (Bruner, Goodnow & Austin, 1956, pg. 26). As a general rule, the greater the number of such defining attributes, the greater will be the difficulty in acquiring the concept. This will be the case because additional time will be required for testing each of these attributes and their dimensions in all of their possible combinations (Vinacke, 1974, pg. 194).

The number of dimensions necessary to define a concept is thus one measure of the general complexity of that concept. A category rule based on a single dimension (*A* must be present) will be easier to learn than rules based on two (*A* and *B* must be present), or three dimensions (*A*, *B*, and *C* must be present). This finding has been well confirmed (Neisser & Weene, 1962; Bourne & Guy, 1968; Laughlin, 1968).

2. Strategy Preference

All things being equal, conjunctive concepts are typically the easiest to learn. These are followed in difficulty by relational concepts, with disjunctive categories being the hardest of the three to acquire (Bruner, Goodnow & Austin, 1956; Schwartz, 1966). Furthermore, when the nature of the concept is left unspecified, subjects show a strong tendency, or "set," to assume that the category is conjunctive and to search first for conjunctive rules. For example, when stimuli are specially constructed to allow for their legitimate classification according to any of the three types of category rules, disjunctive categories are far less frequently discovered than either conjunctive or relational ones (Hunt & Hovland, 1960).

Part of the advantage of conjunctive categories is that, on average, they contain fewer attribute dimensions than disjunctive ones and hence require less time for their systematic discovery. However, disjunctive concepts typically remain the most difficult even when special steps are taken to insure that the number of salient dimensions are held constant. Bruner, Goodnow, and Austin (1956) offer a possible explanation.

Once we know the defining attributes of a concept, we can recognize new category members when they are encountered. This is true of disjunctive as well as of conjunctive or relational categories. Disjunctive categories seem to be unique in that encountering a category member does not immediately supply unambiguous information about all of the possible attributes. In other words, it is difficult to test the relevance of a particular attribute present in an exemplar, since all members of the same category need not necessarily have the same attributes. This difficulty does not hold to the same degree for conjunctive or relational categories.

3. Positive Versus Negative Instances

Regardless of the type of category or the number of attribute dimensions, encountering positive instances is generally more useful for concept identification than encountering negative instances (cf. Smoke, 1933). This is consistent with our everyday experience. For example, children clearly get more information from being shown a horse and being told that it *is* a horse, than being shown some other animal and being told that it is *not* a horse. The salience of positive instances for concept identification, however, seems to go beyond the fact that they typically contain more information. Studies have shown a preference for positive over negative instances even when they are equated for the amount of information they theoretically contribute for the concept's identification (Hovland & Weiss, 1953).

We can learn to use negative instances as effectively as positive ones, but special training and considerable practice is ordinarily necessary for this (Friebergs & Tulving, 1961). There are, for example, many professional skills which rely heavily on negative instances for classification, such as those of the trained botanist or the medical diagnostician. Such abilities, however, can be acquired only after extensive training, and deliberate instruction is usually necessary for people to learn to attend as carefully to negative information as to positive information (Hulse, Deese & Egeth, 1975, pg. 269).

4. Number of Nondefining Attributes

Not all "discriminable variations" between stimuli are necessarily relevant to a concept, even in a conjunctive category. Trying to learn to identify different makes of cars by their color would be an example of an attribute dimension which may vary from instance to instance, but which is hardly defining. Such variable, but nondefining features, are referred to as "noisy" attributes. Like truly defining ones, the greater their number, the more difficulty there will be in learning the concept. Since they do vary from instance to instance, they must be tested as possible relevant attributes before being discarded.

"Noisy" nondefining attributes can be contrasted with "quiet" nondefining ones. All cars have metal parts. This too is nondefining, but it is "quiet" in the sense that it does not vary from instance to instance. As such,

this sort of nondefining attribute is effectively neutral, neither helping nor hindering the attainment of the concept.

5. Attribute Redundancy

The earlier statement that task difficulty increases with the number of defining attributes does not always hold true when some of the attributes are redundant ones. For example, if a conjunctive category is defined by the joint presence of attributes A, B and C, there may be cases where, whenever A is present, B and C will also be present. That is, A is never, or almost never, present without B and C. The attributes may be described as redundant; recognizing the presence of only one or a few attributes eliminates the need to invest additional time searching for the presence of others. Airplanes fly, they have fixed wings, they are made of metal, and they have engines. Seeing a flying object with fixed wings and a glint of metal is sufficient for its identification as an airplane without waiting to hear the sound of the engine. Relevant redundancy generally facilitates concept identification, and the more redundant information present the better will be the level of performance in recognizing category members (Bourne & Haygood, 1959, 1961; Keele & Archer, 1967).

We can conveniently contrast the independent effects of relevant redundant attributes, which facilitate performance, and the effects of irrelevant "noisy" attributes, which retard it. Figure 8.4 shows the results of an experiment by Bourne and Haygood (1961) in which they examined the number of errors in a concept attainment task as these two factors were independently varied. The overall heights of the four curves on the graph show how task difficulty increases as the number of irrelevant ("noisy") dimensions were increased from zero to five. When we look at each curve separately, however, we can see that, independent of overall task difficulty as determined by the number of irrelevant dimensions, there is a relative *reduction* in errors as more and more relevant *redundant* dimensions are added. The different slopes of the four curves tell us that the more complex the task, the more helpful this redundancy is.

6. Attribute Variation

We have previously emphasized the real-world likelihood of considerable variation in attributes from instance to instance of a single category. Some of these variations will take the form of noisy nondefining attributes. Commonly, however, especially in the case of disjunctive categories, we have to deal with defining attributes that need not always be present whenever a specific instance of a concept is encountered. An important attribute of clocks is their round face, but this does not mean that a square clock will go totally unrecognized.

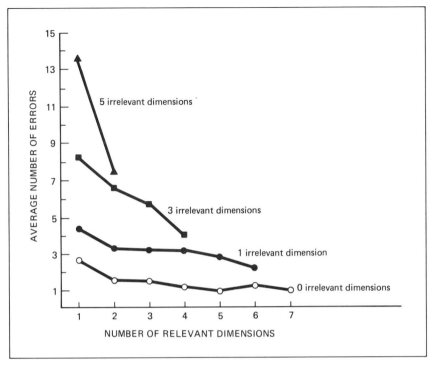

Figure 8.4   Average number of errors in a concept identification task as a joint function of the number of redundant relevant and nonredundant irrelevant stimulus dimensions. (*Source:* L. E. Bourne and R. C. Haygood, Supplementary report: Effect of redundant relevant information upon the identification of concepts. *Journal of Experimental Psychology,* 1961, 61: fig. 1, pg. 259. Copyright 1961 by the American Psychological Association. Reprinted by permission.)

As one might expect, encountering major variations in attributes during the course of the learning of a concept will significantly delay its acquisition. On the other hand, once such concepts are finally mastered, a greater variety of exemplars will be readily recognized as member of the category (cf. Luborsky, 1945). Thus in "teaching" concepts, whether letters of the alphabet or scientific principles, there is an advantage to beginning with ideal, invariant examples, and later, supplementing them with guided experience with a wide range of allowable variations. This combines rapid initial learning with the eventual certainty that a valid concept has in fact been formed.

7. Delay of Validation

As in other forms of learning, the sooner knowledge of results is given in a concept attainment task, the more effective this feedback will be. From our earlier studies, it would be surprising if this were otherwise. In classical conditioning we saw the importance of following the CS with the reinforcing UCS as soon as possible, and reinforcement in the form of a reward in instrumental learning is most effective when it closely follows performance of the correct response in time. Similarly, corrective feedback in both motor and verbal learning is most effective when it is made available immediately following the subject's response.

The situation is no different in concept learning. Concept attainment is generally most rapid when there is only a minimal delay in the subject's ability to validate (or invalidate) his or her working hypothesis. Numerous studies have shown that learning is most rapid when the instances of a concept, which serve this validating function, are experienced in rapid succession and are interrupted by few if any intervening events (cf. Dominowski, 1965; Kurtz & Hovland, 1956; Haygood, Sandlin, Yoder & Dodd, 1969).

Surprisingly, some early studies of concept attainment appeared to show some advantage to a delay of validation. The reason for these apparently contradictory results became clear when the experimenters looked more closely at the sequence of events in a typical concept attainment task. First, the subject is shown a number of instances defining the concept. Second, he or she begins to form a tentative hypothesis about what this concept might be (e.g., "a red cross inside a double border"). Finally, the subject begins a systematic selection of cards which seem to exemplify this concept. As each card is selected, the experimenter announces whether that selection is, or is not, an instance of the concept.

As we can see, there are in fact two possible occasions for a delay to be introduced. The first delay can occur between the subject's selection of a card and the experimenter's validating call of "right" or "wrong" for that selection. This is the true feedback interval, and it is here that the delay should ideally be minimal. Those cases where a delay seemed to offer an advantage turned out not to involve the feedback interval at all, but a second possible occasion for delay, the interval between the subject being given the feedback and being able to make the next selection.

When the two intervals are experimentally manipulated, results show that while the first interval (between selection and feedback) should be as short as possible for best performance, the second interval (between feedback and the next selection) can often be longer for best performance (Bourne & Bunderson, 1963). This is undoubtedly because longer postfeedback intervals allow the subject more time to consider alternative hypotheses and to decide which cards to select for the most efficient test of these hypotheses (Bourne, 1971, pp. 70–72).

Delayed validation in real-world situations, especially when long-held hypotheses are disconfirmed, often result in individuals searching "backwards" in an attempt to find defining attributes which may have been present, but which went unnoticed. A star performer in this theater of the absurd is a person who was always assumed to be a pillar of the community until it was discovered that he or she had been systematically pilfering the church funds for years.

Hearing the news people will often react by searching backwards to "recall" signs that must surely have predicted it. They may "recall" that the person sometimes gambled, that he or she often had "too much" money, or if all else fails, that he or she always did have a rather "shifty demeanor." As often as not, these recollections may rely as much on imagination as on fact.

SOME PARAMETERS OF THE CONCEPT ATTAINER

Our discussion to this point has dealt with the external conditions necessary for concept attainment and those task variables which will directly affect the ease of learning. Let us now turn from the tasks themselves and briefly consider several important factors within the learner that influence concept learning.

There is an intriguing but probably untestable feeling on the part of many that the tendency of children and adults to try to categorize stimuli as they are encountered in the environment is virtually spontaneous. We cannot say, in the absence of evidence, that this drive toward categorization is "instinctive" as the word is ordinarily used. All we can say is that the naturalness of this tendency has long fascinated psychologists, especially when the issue of instinct or innate propensities is raised in the context of human behavior. Whatever its source, numerous psychologists have tended to characterize it as either a natural "effort after meaning" (Bartlett, 1932) or an individual's need to bring order and stability to his or her perceptual world (Hilgard, 1951).

Motivation and Set in Concept Attainment

While the drive to categorize may or may not be spontaneous, differences in motivation and set remain important factors in studies of concept attainment. In a study similar to Heidbreder's, Reed (1946) gave subjects either instructions that stressed simply learning the names for the stimuli or specific instructions to try to discover the basis for the stimulus groupings. While the first group showed a 67 percent success rate when they were later tested on their knowledge of the underlying concept, the success rate for the second group jumped to 86 percent.

All of this is to say that the naturalness of ordinary concept attainment is exceedingly difficult to reproduce in the laboratory—a major source of the previously mentioned risk in trying to generalize from such studies. This is especially true when university students serve as the subjects, as they may well see the task as a game or an opportunity to demonstrate their mental agility. A case in point is cited by Simmel (1953) who confronted one subject in a problem-solving task who pleaded desperately for more time, even though he had already found an acceptable solution. He wanted more time, he said, because his solution, though adequate, was nevertheless "inelegant."

Inhibiting Factors in Concept Formation

Any observations on the alleged "naturalness" of concept learning are bound to cause no little gnashing of teeth, especially for the teacher who has seen pupils stubbornly fail to grasp classroom concepts with an almost religious zeal, or for the student who has encountered example after example and has waited in vain for the underlying concept to spontaneously burst forth like a wounded whale from the depths of the consciousness. As any student who has failed freshman chemistry can tell you, it sometimes just doesn't happen.

There are numerous factors which can inhibit the acquisition of concepts, independent of the person's intelligence or the complexity of the task. The source of these factors lies in the simplifying assumptions we made earlier in this chapter in building our "ideal world" of concept attainment. Our assumptions, you will recall, were that (1) all concepts to be formed are simple and consistent, with defining attributes always present and in the same form, (2) reinforcement or feedback always follows each encounter with an example of the concept, (3) category names are consistent and invariant, and (4) children and adults approach concept learning with logic and consistency. In the real world of concept learning, such simplifying assumptions rarely survive.

Leeper (1951, pg. 748) cities several notorious conceptual failures which exemplify human limitations in the face of a complex world. We can mention three of the more famous ones, and their presumed causes.

1. TIME DELAY BETWEEN CAUSE AND EFFECT. Because of the long time delay between cause and effect, the connection between mosquito bites and malaria resisted discovery for years after it should have been possible.

2. PERCEPTUAL INCONGRUITIES. The dramatic difference in physical appearance betwen maggots and flies led early scientists to take refuge in the conceptual dead end of "spontaneous generation" rather than recognize that one was derived from the other.

3. MENTAL SETS. Existing habits of thought, or *mental sets*, are notorious as a bar to conceptual problem solving, often because they lead to perceived connections where none in fact exist. The earlier discovery of bacteria and

of communicable diseases, for instance, ironically prevented the solution of the riddle of beriberi. Now known to be a dietary deficiency in Vitamin B_1, early medical scientists devoted years to a dogged pursuit of a nonexistent bacteria hypothetically transmitting the disease from one person to another.

Of the various forms of debilitating mental sets, one of the best known is that of an all too common phenomenon known as *functional fixedness*. In the course of early studies of formal problem solving (Duncker, 1945; Maier, 1970), the term came to be applied to those cases where an object had been so associated with a particular function in the past that persons became "fixed" on that function and could not recognize any of its alternative potential uses. Here is a typical example taken from an experiment by Adamson (1952).

A volunteer subject is brought into a room containing only a table upon which are a small empty box, several thumbtacks, a candle, and some matches. The subject is then told that his or her task is to find a way of fixing the candle in a vertical position without using either the table or the floor. This is a fairly easy problem, and 24 out of 28 subjects quickly found the solution. They attached the empty box to the wall with the thumbtacks and then used the matches to melt the bottom of the candle onto the top edge of the box (see Figure 8.5).

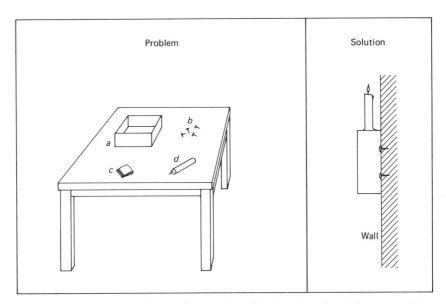

Figure 8.5   The candle problem used to illustrate functional fixedness. The correct solution is to attach the box (a) to the wall with the thumbtacks (b) and then use the matches (c) to melt the bottom of the candle (d) onto the top edge of the box. This solution will occur less readily if the box is used to hold the tacks, candles, and matches when the problem is first presented.

Another group of subjects received exactly the same problem and the same instructions. The only difference was that all of the objects—the candles, tacks, and matches—were inside the box when the problem was presented. In this case, the number of subjects arriving at the correct solution dropped by one-half.

The reason for this dramatic difference may be obvious, but it is no less intriguing. When the box is presented as a holder of the materials, that is seen as its sole function. "Fixed" on this function, the subjects seemed totally incapable of seeing its potential use as part of the solution.

The degree of fixedness in such problems becomes even more extreme when subjects are induced to name the objects aloud. Verbally labeling the box as "a box" apparently even further limits its perceived function to a "container" at the expense of its potential use as a "candle supporter" (Glucksberg & Weisberg, 1966).

Problem Solving by Children

The ways in which perceptual incongruities are handled, together with differences in mental set, can give rise to major variations in cognitive approach from one individual to another, and there are a number of good discussions of such differences in "cognitive style" available in the literature (Kagan, 1966; Kagan & Kagan, 1970).

The most obvious differences in conceptual attack, however, are those associated with children of different ages as they pass through the successive stages of *sensorimotor, preoperational, concretely operational,* and *formally operational intelligence* (see Chapter 13). Some of these differences are so major and consistent that what the adult might call a conceptual failure might be a perfectly valid and correct solution from the child's point of view. Brown (1965, pg. 322) brings together several related examples which make just this point.

DIFFERENCES IN CONCEPTUAL GROUPING.   Let us begin with a very simple experiment in which subjects are given jumbled sets of cutouts consisting of pictures of animals, flowers, people, foods, furniture, and geometric shapes. Their task is simply to sort the stimuli into several groups which, in some sense, seem to "go together."

Adults and older children typically approach the task the same way, sorting the stimuli into neatly defined generic categories (shapes, animals, flowers, etc.) just as we listed them above. Below the age of 6, however, children's sorting categories can be quite different. A child might, for example, select a picture of a stove, a sink, and an item of food, put these together, and call the result "a kitchen" (Piaget & Inhelder, 1959). It is better to say that this grouping is *different* from the adult's than to say it is necessarily "incorrect."

SHORT-RUN SIMILARITIES.　We can get close to one source of this difference by looking at the performance of young children in studies more analogous to those of Bruner, Goodnow, and Austin. While we would have to use simpler stimuli (such as wooden blocks of various shapes, colors, and sizes), we could nevertheless follow their traditional procedures. For example, the subject's task would be to discover a particular conjunctive category by selecting a series of blocks with the experimenter announcing after each selection whether or not it had exemplified the concept.

A young child might well begin the task in a very "adult" manner, choosing perhaps a large triangle, followed by a small one, and a third triangle of a different size, as each in turn is confirmed as an instance of the concept. Just as the correct concept, "triangle," seems to be emerging as a stable hypothesis, however, the situation may abruptly change. This may come about if the child is suddenly distracted by an irrelevant but prominent feature of the last stimulus chosen.

For example, if the last triangle selected in the above sequence happened to be a brightly colored red one, the child might next select not another triangle (of a different color) but a square of the same bright red color. This might then be followed by the child selecting a second square, a third square, and so on, as both the concept of triangles and of the color red seem to give way to this new grouping strategy (Vigotsky, 1934).

Studies such as these have illustrated a common tendency in young children to be drawn by short-run similarities that lead them to sudden and inappropriate shifts in conceptual hypotheses in the middle of a task (Vigotsky, 1934).

HYPOTHESIS SHIFTING.　This reliance on short-run similarities can paradoxically discourage a hypothesis shift even when it is appropriate, as the following example, taken from a study by Bruner and Olver (1963), illustrates.

Given the two words *banana* and *peach* and asked in what way they are similar, children, like adults, might well say that both are yellow. However, if we now add to the list the words *potato, meat,* and *milk,* a reasonable adult reaction will be to shift the basis of similarity away from the fact that bananas and peaches are yellow, and to say that all five objects are items of food, or "things to eat." A young child, on the other hand, may tell you with equal certainty: "bananas and peaches are yellow, peaches and potatoes are round, potatoes and meat are served together" (Bruner & Olver, 1963).

THE LOGIC OF THE CHILD.　To suggest that the child has failed to categorize the stimuli correctly is surely to miss the point. The child has categorized them as logically and as naturally as the adult, but he or she has done so in terms of single dimensions and short-run similarities which simply give rise to a different grouping strategy.

Part of this difference can be attributed to a lack of experience with the full range of a concept, as when a 4-year-old boy says to his father, "When I grow up, I won't be your son anymore." This may surprise the parent, who has heard the child using the word "son" appropriately for some time. That this child's concept of "son" was specifically limited to "a young child living at home with the parents" may until then not have been appreciated. In addition, the child's concepts may also be limited by a span of apprehension which is not up to the demands of some long-range solutions. We will have more to say on this topic in Chapter 13.

It would be misleading to leave this discussion with the implication that most adults are models of coherence and logic in concept attainment tasks. Hanfmann (1941) reports a not atypical incident in which an adult was sorting "Vigotsky blocks" in search of a particular category grouping.

> The subject noticed two small blocks that happened to lie close to each other, started adding other small blocks to them, all the while saying in an astonished tone of voice: "I really do not know why, but I just feel like putting this one with them, and this one, and this one." Only after she had grouped all the blocks correctly, she said, as if discovering something: "Oh, I see. Of course it is size!" This sequence of events—grouping first and formulating the principle after, or at least during, the process—is typical of the approach that is guided by perception (Hanfmann, 1941, pg. 318).[1]

SUMMARY

Concept learning was described as the process of experiencing a wide variety of different stimuli, recognizing that some of them share important common features, and then conceptually grouping these stimuli and reacting to them in a similar way. The process of recognizing that certain stimuli "go together" by virtue of their shared features is called abstraction. The term generalization refers to the ability to recognize new instances of a category when they are encountered.

Three types of concepts were discussed: conjunctive categories, in which a concept is defined by the joint presence of two or more attributes; disjunctive categories, in which category membership is based on either the presence of one or another attribute; and relational categories, in which category membership is defined not merely by the presence or absence of attributes, but by a specified relationship between them. In general, disjunctive concepts are the most difficult to acquire, while conjunctive concepts are the easiest. An attribute is any discriminable feature of a stimulus which may vary from event to event, such as color, shape, or size, while a

---

[1] From E. Hanfmann, "A Study of Personal Patterns in an Intellectual Performance," *Character and Personality* (1941), 9:315-325. Copyright 1941 by Duke University Press. Reprinted by permission.

dimension refers to the possible variations within that attribute, such as "red," "triangle," or "small."

Both the nature of the stimuli and the task will affect the speed of concept learning. The greater the number of defining attributes possessed by a concept, the more difficult that concept will be to acquire, and positive instances are generally more useful in conveying information about these attributes than negative instances. Nondefining, "noisy" attributes, which vary from instance to instance but do not define category membership, will retard concept learning; redundant attributes will facilitate acquisition. Redundant attributes are those which invariably occur together, such that when one attribute is encountered, the others will also be present. All things being equal, validating feedback is most effective when given immediately after a response selection.

Differences in motivation and set have a strong influence on concept attainment, the most noticeable inhibiting factor being functional fixedness: an inability to see alternative potential applications of a stimulus because of an overconcentration on its most familiar use.

Real-World Concept Attainment

PERCEPTUAL LEARNING

The basis of concept learning in the studies both of Heidbreder and of Bruner and his colleagues, centered on a process of *perceptual discrimination*, reinforced by a repetition of names in the former case, and by a more direct signaling of category membership in the latter. Perceptual discrimination in this context implies a deductive operation, whether conscious or not, based on similarities in potentially discriminable attributes. In those studies, the similarities were in terms of visual features of the stimuli. The same principles would apply when distinctions are based on recurring attributes involving shared function, similarity of context in which the stimuli are encountered, or potential similarities in emotional response induced by the category members. Thus broadly defined, it can be argued that perceptual discrimination, or *perceptual learning*, is at the heart of most concept learning in both the child and adult.

At this point, we must leave our "ideal worlds" of concept attainment, and look again at the process in the full range of real-world complexity.

Attribute Redundancy Revisited

The early stages of concept acquisition are marked by a perceptual scanning of stimulus attributes for categorical similarity. In the course of

determining which attributes are relevant to category membership, however, a second stage emerges in which some defining attributes begin to appear more important or salient to the concept than others. It is at this point
in perceptual learning that the process takes a qualitative leap.

As the individual discovers that some attributes are more salient than
others, so too does he or she make use of the fact that many attributes are
redundant; to observe the presence of a few salient ones eliminates any
need for further exhaustive scanning of the stimulus. A bird, for example,
has wings, feathers, a bill, and legs of a particular type. The whole set of
attributes need not be observed for a correct identification. Were this not
the case, speed of identification would be unacceptably long, and it would
be logically impossible to recognize a poorly drawn picture or a briefly
glimpsed object. Redundancy, as previously defined, implies that once some
of the salient features are identified, the others are highly predictable and
need not necessarily be present for a positive identification.

Experiencing more and more exemplars of a category can lead to the development of a series of expectancy distributions relating to the likely presence of each of the defining attributes and to the presence of groups of them
in concert. The culmination of this gradual process gives rise to what we
commonly refer to as a sense of the unity or the *gestalt* of a concept (as, for
example, "birdness").

Once this occurs, a stimulus can be readily identified in terms of its general configuration. It no longer requires a selective scanning of individual
features. Missing attributes, whether actually absent from the stimulus, or
simply not scanned, are cognitively "filled in" and cause no problem to accurate and rapid identification. Studies of mature readers, for example,
show how words are identified by length, general configuration, and context, as much as by analysis of the individual letters themselves (see Massaro, 1975, pp. 376–403). Inevitably, the reader makes some mistakes. Such
errors, however, are a relatively small price to pay for rapid and efficient
reading in the face of such potential distractors are misspellings, unclearly
written letters, or even missing words.

The Role of Distinctive Features

The term *distinctive features* refers to perceptual characteristics which
individuals are found to actually use in distinguishing one stimulus from another (as opposed to what they may think they are using). As such, distinctive features serve as the basis for what we have been calling defining
attributes for conceptual identification. Distinctive features in the visual
mode can be such factors as size, shape, color, and so forth. In the case of
alphabetic letters, such distinctive features are lines, curves, angles, free
ends, and spatial relations between them.

Auditory distinctive features in speech perception are no less intricate, especially as we realize that the recognizable sound units or *phonemes* of a language are in reality psychological categories rather than discrete physical stimuli (Brown, 1956). Place the tongue in various positions behind the upper teeth, behind the upper gum, or against the palate, and produce a series of *d* sounds. The result will be discriminably different sounds, but all of them clearly acceptable as members of the phoneme category *d*. While all of the physical correlates of the English speech sounds have by no means been fully specified, the features which distinguish different phonemes relate to such factors as their duration, stress, and whether the sounds are voiced or voiceless (the difference between a *p* and *b*, or *t* and *d*) (cf. Jakobson, Fant & Halle, 1963).

Perceptual Reorganization

Much of the "practice" time in both concept identification and in response learning is now known to be occupied by this initial stage of perceptual discrimination of the relevant visual features of the stimuli. For example, when subjects are given intentionally confusable paired-associate CVC lists, such as, *LIM-dax, LIF-zer, LIN-pov, RIN-wug*, etc., a careful analysis of the learning process shows that two distinct operations are involved. First, the subjects learn to discriminate between the stimuli, and second, they learn to attach the appropriate responses. While ordinarily the two processes go hand-in-hand, giving initial practice with stimulus discrimination alone can yield considerable savings when the response terms are later introduced (Saltz, 1961). So adept are we at discrimination learning that methods as indirect as the Heidbreder procedure can be used to "teach" untrained subjects to discriminate between as unidentifiable a set of stimuli as finger-print patterns (DeRivera, 1959).

An important consequence of perceptual learning is the previously mentioned perceptual reorganization of a stimulus which occurs when important features gradually begin to "stand out" as perceptually more salient than others. A familiar example in early education is represented by practice at naming examples of equivalent and nonequivalent sets in modern mathematics instruction. Examples of the sort shown in Figure 8.6 are common in children's mathematics training, and are intended to emphasize that *number* is the salient feature, while color, shape, and size are, in our terms, "noisy" nondefining attributes for the equivalence concept. Perceptual reorganization in a deeper sense also underlies practice at, for example, renaming the number 26 as "two tens and six ones." It is this approach of the so-called new math which gives rise to the expression, "teaching number concepts."

The importance of naming as a way of directing attention to certain perceptual features of a stimulus implies that the choice of a category name is by no means trivial.

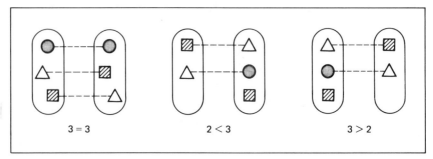

Figure 8.6   The use of the symbols < , > , and = to name equivalent and nonequivalent sets in learning mathematical concepts.

NAMES AND CATEGORIES

When Heidbreder presented her pictures of *dilts, mulps* and *relks,* she was attempting to model an essential feature of concept attainment. Concept learning, as we have seen, involves the understanding that certain stimuli or events can be, and *should be,* classed together on the basis of some common property or properties. The different methods of concept learning primarily represent different ways of signaling these similarities to the individual. In Heidbreder's case, she concentrated on what is probably the most important of all forms of signaling: the use of category *names.*

Names as Signals

Naming is important to concept learning for two reasons. First, the repeated use of a name in the presence of different stimuli signals to the individual that there is some underlying connection between them and, hence, some concept to be formed. In Heidbreder's experiment the repeated use of the name *dilt* gave rise to the concept "five objects." You see a dramatic example of this signaling function simply by turning to the person next to you and casually saying, "Hand me a *corplum.*" The new word acts as a starting gun for a frantic search for the meaning.

The second function of naming was also seen in the Heidbreder experiment. That is, once a concept is learned, we can signal this to others by an appropriate use of the correct name whenever a new example of the concept is encountered. The feedback obtained by using the name can represent a further source of concept validation. Indeed, to the young child, names are so important that they seem at times to the child to be an inherent property of the named objects or concepts.

Names as Properties

The well-known Soviet psychologist L. S. Vigotsky tells what happened on one occasion when he asked a child whether one could, if one wished, call a *cow* "ink," and *ink* a "cow." The child replied that this would be quite impossible since, Vigotsky was informed, "ink is used for writing, and a cow gives milk." As Vigotsky went on to argue, "the exchange of a name means for them also the exchange of the qualities of the objects, so close and inseparable is the connection between the two" (Vigotsky, 1939, pg. 36).

These considerations force a return to another of our simplifying assumptions of that hypothetical "ideal world" of concept attainment: an orderly universe where category names are always consistent and invariant. This, like the other features of our ideal world, rarely exists in human experience.

Variability of Names

As almost any object can belong to more than one category, so too can an object be called by more than one appropriate name. One way to see this is to ask someone to name several different objects. Two things become clear. One is that while many different names can be used for the same stimulus, some names seem intuitively more appropriate and certainly more available than others. Asked to name one object, the superordinate category name "musical instrument" might be more readily available than "xylophone," but asked to name another, the subordinate name "chair" might be a more natural response than the superordinate "furniture." There is a systematic hierarchy in response selection that is sometimes easier to predict than to define (Wingfield, 1967).

Another way to see this variability is to observe parents as they name everyday objects for their young children. Take, for example, the common *dime* as it might be potentially named for the child. It could be called a *dime*, a *coin, money,* or, in some unlikely circumstance, a *metal object* (Brown, 1958). All of these are "correct" names, but each implies a subtle difference in conceptual meaning. In naming objects for the child, parents implicitly recognize this by placing themselves in the position of the child and trying to determine what aspect of the stimulus is most relevant to the child at that time. For the young child who does not yet make purchases, the chosen name for a dime might be *money.* The distinction between this coin and a nickel or a quarter is not yet crucial, nor is the distinction between a dime as a *coin* versus larger denominations such as a dollar as *paper money.* At this stage they are all "money"; a functional category implying a thing with value, not to be lost, and not to be thrown away.

In general, the parents' choice of a name, and hence the specificity of category placement, will change as the level of functional utility changes for the child's own needs. What is *the* name for an object? As Brown puts it: *"The* name of a thing, the one that tells what it 'really is,' is the name that constitutes the referent as it needs to be constituted for most purposes. The other names represent possible recategorizations useful for one or another purpose" (Brown, 1958, pg. 17).

OTHER METHODS OF TEACHING CONCEPTS

In addition to the methods of concept learning already cited, two others should be mentioned: *formal definition* and *linguistic context.*

Formal Definition

Giving the formal definition of a concept is the most direct method of "teaching," and it represents a mainstay of instruction in the later school years. Its limitations lie in the requisite that the subconcepts underlying its definition must already have been mastered, and that it works well only with concepts amenable to formal definition. The latter point may appear as a non sequitur of lofty proportions. Yet ironically, the more basic the concept the less likely this situation is to obtain. We must also recognize, in light of our previous discussion, that to "know" a concept does not always imply that one can verbally formalize the principles one is in fact using. The belief that one can is often rudely shattered when put to the test. This test, of course, is one of the challenges of teaching, and the derivation of workable definitions is an important goal.

In later education, the use of formal definitions works well, as these "study questions" that could be found in a junior high school science text show:

What is meant by an element? Give at least five examples.

What is one way to discover whether a material is an element or a compound? Explain your answer.

How are electrical charges or particles alike? How are they different?

How is reproduction in animals like reproduction in plants? Give as many ways as you can.

Linguistic Context

As the human is a "verbal animal," so concepts can be acquired through linguistic context without either direct observation of physical attributes or the use of formal definitions. A well-known illustration is that of Werner and Kaplan (1950), who decided to teach a group of university students the meaning of the word *corplum*. The students were shown each of the statements listed below and asked after each statement exactly what they thought a *corplum* was—and why.

1. A *corplum* may be used for support.
2. *Corplums* may be used to close off an open space.
3. A *corplum* may be long or short, thick or thin, strong or weak.
4. A wet *corplum* does not burn.
5. You can make a *corplum* smooth with sandpaper.
6. The painter used a *corplum* to mix his paints.

As a model of concept learning, the *corplum* paradigm is appropriate if oversimplified. Far more realistic is the problem faced by the child attempting to learn the referents of such words as *you* or *me*. These words will be heard used in reference to a number of people, including the child himself or herself, and often in the course of a single conversation. If one needed convincing that concept learning is a highly developed human ability which occurs in the face of almost all odds, few examples would supply more dramatic evidence.

VERBAL MEDIATION IN CONCEPT LEARNING

Names, verbal definitions, and linguistic context can all be involved in concept learning as they signal critical similarities and differences between stimuli and so set the stage for concept attainment. When Heidbreder later questioned her subjects about the way in which they learned her concepts, it became apparent that *verbal mediation* is as potentially useful to concept learning as it is to associative chaining (see Chapter 7). From her subjects' reports, it was clear that mnemonic devices were both frequent and imaginative. Several people used the same mediator for *ling* (first seen as two stockings). The word was remembered as the sound of Christmas bells ringing, and from that, associated with two Christmas stockings hanging by the fireplace. When the object itself was an abstraction, there was a strong tendency to use verbal descriptions to make it more concrete. The seventh picture in Series I of her experiment (*stod*) was, for one subject, "like a thickly salted pretzel, broken at the end" (Heidbreder, 1947, pg. 112).

In recent years considerable attention has been paid to a wide range of considerations about the potential role of speech in the regulation of behavior, the learning of concepts, and in the stabilization of concepts once they are learned (Luria & Yudovich, 1959; Luria, 1961).

One illustration of this is in studies of *reversal learning* by adults and children of various ages. In essence, reversal learning refers to cases where one first learns to make one sort of response to a stimulus and then must "unlearn" this response and make quite another one to the same stimulus. One aspect of *negative transfer,* as previously discussed, reversal learning can meaningfully illustrate the role of verbal mediation in concept learning.

Take the problem facing a child in the task diagrammed in Figure 8.7 (Kendler & Kendler, 1962). First the child sees a succession of four squares like those on the left of the diagram. In the first part of the experiment, the child is consistently rewarded whenever he or she selects the larger square, regardless of its color. Once this initial discrimination is learned, the reward is suddenly shifted (mirroring the horrible inconsistencies of life). One group of children is now rewarded for selecting the small square (color is still irrelevant). Illustrated by the upper set of four squares on the right, this is referred to as a *reversal shift.* The same attribute of *size* is still important, but the rewarded dimension is now shifted from *large* to *small.*

A second group of children has the first discrimination followed by a second one as depicted by the lower set of four squares on the right. For this group, the big square is apparently sometimes rewarded, and sometimes not. The reason for this seeming inconsistency is simply that size is no longer the relevant attribute. Referred to as a *nonreversal shift,* selecting a black square is now always rewarded, regardless of its size.

Now we come to the crucial question. Which is the easier of the two

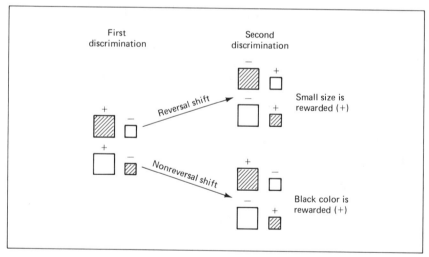

Figure 8.7 Example of reversal and nonreversal shift. After being rewarded for selecting a large square in the initial discrimination, the reward is shifted either to the small square (reversal shift) or to the previously irrelevant dimension of color (nonreversal shift). (*Source:* H. H. Kendler and T. S. Kendler, Vertical and horizontal processes in problem solving. *Psychological Review,* 1962, 69: fig. 2, pg. 5. Copyright 1962 by the American Psychological Association. Reprinted by permission.)

tasks, the reversal or the nonreversal shift? As it happens, the answer depends primarily on the age of the child involved. For children under the age of 6 or 7 (and for rats and monkeys), the nonreversal shift is much easier. For children above the age of 7 (and for adults), the reversal shift is the easier of the two (Kendler & Kendler, 1959, 1962; Kendler, Kendler & Wells, 1960; Kelleher, 1956; Tighe, 1964). (Children at about the age of 7 learn both types of shift with approximately equal facility.)

This difference is certainly provocative, and it has been attributed to the way in which the two groups may have learned the initial discrimination in the first place. One assumption is that older children and adults make heavy use of verbal mediation in the initial discrimination, by saying to themselves something like, "Size is important." When entering a reversal shift, the critical attribute of the verbalized concept remains unchanged. "Size is (still) important." The principle still holds, even though the rewarded dimension has shifted from "big" to "little." Thus, for them, the reversal shift, which would ordinarily be the more difficult task, becomes the easier one.

This explanation began only as speculation, since whatever verbalization may have been taking place, it was certainly not overt. Support for the idea came when Kendler (1964) repeated the task with 4- to 6-year-olds, but this time encouraging them to "use words" to describe the stimuli in the initial discrimination. When this was done, their ability to handle the reversal shift relative to the nonreversal shift was greatly improved.

The implications of such studies of verbal mediation are far reaching, not only for their theoretical interest, but for their potential application to a variety of very real learning problems. Training severely retarded children in the use of verbalization of principles, something they are ordinarily disinclined to do, may well hold considerable promise for special education with these children (cf. O'Connor & Hermelin, 1963).

CATEGORIZING WITH PROBABILISTIC CUES

The basic elements of concept attainment have now been built to the point of considerable complexity, and we need consider only one final variable for the picture to be complete. That variable relates to the last of our simplifying ideal-world assumptions; all concepts are consistent, with defining attributes always present, and in the same form.

In most real-world cases, concepts are based on attributes which are probabilistic in nature; they are frequently important to category membership, but need not always be present in all exemplars. Take for example, the symbol p as an exemplar of the letter p of the alphabet. Whatever the defining attributes of a p are, this symbol most surely has them. But what about the symbol þ ? It is probably also the letter p, although perhaps poorly written. But it might also be a b. It has some attributes of each category. Categorical judgments in such ambiguous cases can often be helped by context. The likelihood that it is one or the other becomes more of a certainty when it is seen in the context of þottle, versus the context of þaint. But context is not always the solution, as in the case of "The doctor gave me a þill—which was hard to swallow."

How do people go about categorizing with probabilistic cues, and how good are they at it? Bruner et al. (1956, pp. 196–199) cite a study by Goodnow (1954) which answers this question. The task in this case was to learn to identify a series of aircraft silhouettes by categorizing each new example seen into either one of two specified types: *type X* or *type not-X*. The subjects were told, however, that type X airplanes often have some variations in appearance as they were still experimental and undergoing continual modification. (This cover story was necessary to give the individuals a feeling for the task, without giving away its primary purpose.)

Before the experiment began, the relevant attributes were pointed out to the subjects. In the silhouettes they would see, the wings might be either swept back or delta-shaped, the tails might be either rounded or straight, and the air scoops might be either single and under the fuselage or double and at the sides. The illustration in Figure 8.8 shows examples of the two types of hypothetical aircraft, along with an illustration of how the silhouettes could be presented so as to vary the number of cues visible and thus complicate the subjects' task in a very realistic way.

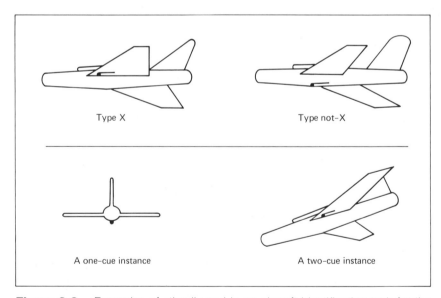

Type X   Type not-X

A one-cue instance   A two-cue instance

Figure 8.8   Examples of stimuli used in an aircraft identification task for the study of categorization with probabilistic cues. (*Source:* Bruner, Goodnow, and Austin, *A Study in Thinking,* fig. 6, pg. 197.)

As each instance was presented, and the subjects were told whether it was or was not a type X, some attributes were made to be criterial 100 percent of the time. That is, whenever a swept-wing airplane appeared, it was always type X. The other two attributes were made to be probabilistic only. A straight tail would be found on type X aircraft 67 percent of the time, but it would also be found on type not-X 33 percent of the time. Similarly, the air scoops were not absolute cues for type X identification, but were valid only on a 67 : 33 ratio.

The relevant question is how subjects will handle cues which are usually but not always defining. For example, will the subjects ignore them completely, always use them, or use them with a frequency which matches their objective usefulness? The situation is reminiscent of a gambler who discovers that a particular number comes up on a roulette wheel 70 percent of the time. Should the gambler maximize his or her chances by betting on it 100 percent of the time, thus assuring more wins than losses? Or should the gambler really gamble, and bet on it 70 percent of the time, and the others 30 percent, in the hope of reducing those 30 percent losses?

The Goodnow study showed clearly that subjects do utilize all of the cues available, even when they are probabilistic in nature. Further, the way in which they are used can best be described as attempts at *probability matching:* the weight given each attribute approached the relative frequency with which experience had shown it to define the category. Although the probability matching was close, incidentally, it was never perfect. Subjects tended to underuse high frequency attributes, and to overestimate the importance of low frequency ones. For example, 100 percent cues were used to categorize the airplane only about 90 percent of the time, while a cue with 67 percent validity was used as if it had an 80 percent probability of being a criterion. (The gambling example cited, incidentally, is interesting in that persons under stress behave in a different way. When the penalties for failure are high, people tend to "maximize," consistently choosing the single response with the highest frequency.)

The finding that 100 percent cues are treated with less certainty than they should be was explained by Goodnow in terms of what she called a "spread of doubt." Finding that some of the attributes are uncertain, subjects begin to question the validity of all of them (Bruner, Goodnow & Austin, 1956, pg. 200). This point relates to our earlier discussion of the advantages of using conventionalized, "nonnoisy" examples in the early stages of teaching concepts. It may, in part, account for the more rapid learning of concepts when initial experience with their examplars has minimal variation.

The use of conventionalized examples in teaching concepts does not require that there be no variation of any attributes from example to example. Rather, it implies that their *salient* features should be kept relatively invariant, or emphasized. Here again, the Goodnow experiment is illuminating. Even when attributes were made to be equally predictive for identification, it turned out that some attributes (e.g., tails) tended to be overvalued, while others (e.g., air scoops) tended to be undervalued. This finding adds a further wrinkle to real-world concept learning: the relative importance of attributes is determined only in part by the objective frequency with which they have defined the category in past experience. Their importance is weighted also by what one might call "cue preferences." That is, some features seem inherently more salient than others to categorical judgments, even when logically they should be no more or less predictive than others.

IS CONCEPT LEARNING UNIQUELY HUMAN?

When first we discussed the principles of stimulus generalization and discrimination in Chapter 4, we pondered aloud whether one might see in them the genesis, however rudimentary, of the stimulus classification which would later form the basis of concept learning. As we saw at that time, most animals, at least from the level of the rat, do respond to more than the single conditioned stimulus. To what extent, however, is the ability to learn concepts unique to human behavior?

In a classic study, Harlow (1949) taught monkeys a simple discrimination task using operant procedures. Two cutout shapes, such as a circle and a square, were shown to animals who were selectively rewarded with food for always picking the square. Once this discrimination was learned, Harlow then shifted the animal to another problem, such as now being rewarded for selecting a tall block versus a short one. After this second discrimination was learned, Harlow then gave the animals a third task, a fourth task, and so on, each involving further discriminations between pairs of stimuli varying in size, shape, color, and height.

On the first 32 problems, Harlow's monkeys were given 50 practice trials for each discrimination. On subsequent problems, the number of trials was reduced to between 6 and 11. How could Harlow afford to reduce the amount of practice on subsequent discriminations? Figure 8.9 shows a sample of the learning curves for the animals' discriminations as they were given over 300 different discrimination problems to learn. Although only the first six trials of each new learning task are shown in the graph, we can see that after some 200 problems, a new discrimination could be mastered in a single practice trial. That is, if on the first trial the monkey was rewarded for selecting a triangle versus a star, it would consistently choose the triangle from that point on. There was no apparent need for any further trial and error.

In Harlow's (1949) words, the animals were "learning how to learn," or developing a *learning set* for discrimination problems. We might say that the animals had developed the concept underlying the discriminations.

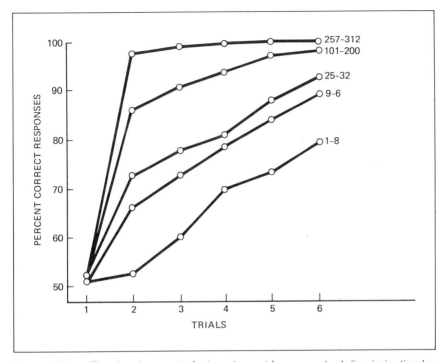

Figure 8.9   The development of a learning set for perceptual discrimination by monkeys. (*Source:* H. F. Harlow, The formation of learning sets. *Psychological Review*, 1949, 56: fig. 2, pg. 53.)

A circle and a square have little meaning to a monkey in its natural environment. You can see this from the slow, gradual learning curves for the average of the first eight problems in Figure 8.9. Obviously, such shape discriminations did not come easily to the animals. Not merely did they have to learn that only one of any two shapes would be rewarded, but they had to learn to detect the salient attributes which would allow for the discriminations.

While this particular study involved only simple, physical attribute discriminations, Harlow (1950) went on to show similar results with monkeys for even more complex problems. Others were later able to demonstrate the development of analogous learning sets not only for monkeys (and humans) but for species as disparate as rats, racoons, and dolphins (Herman, Beach, Pepper & Stalling, 1969; Kintz, Foster, Hart, O'Malley, Palmer & Sullivan 1969).

To be sure, the discrimination between a circle and a square is far simpler than learning to discriminate A (a, *a*, **a**) from B (b, *b*, **b**), not to mention discriminations related to word meaning. Whether the monkey, armed with the appropriate sensory apparatus, could handle such discriminations is not as important as the impression one would get if one were to have accidentally walked into Harlow's laboratory just as a monkey was about to receive problem set number 257. We would be told that this monkey, while familiar with both of the shapes to be presented, had never before had to discriminate between them. We would see the monkey pick up one of the blocks and either receive, or not receive, a reward. From that point on, the animal would consistently choose the correct shape, without ever reverting to the wrong one. Observing this performance without any knowledge of the antecedent events, we might be tempted to erroneously conclude that "no learning was involved," or that the monkey was showing "insight."

In fact, some early attempts were made to account for human insight in terms of the transfer of prior learning, as was the case with the monkey (cf. Pechstein & Brown, 1939). Like the monkey, human concept learning seems to improve with practice with different but related problems. In the case of human learning, we simply need to use concepts with more complex rules to demonstrate this. For example, training in formal logic shows strong positive transfer for concept learning tasks such as those used by Bruner and his colleagues (Dodd, Kinsman, Klipp & Bourne, 1971).

Without further research, it is difficult to say whether such comparisons between concept learning by humans and by lower animals merely show superficial similarities, or whether the relationship is a more meaningful one. The most striking difference, of course, and one which clearly separates us from lower animals, is the extent of involvement of language in human concept attainment. Human language acquisition is, appropriately, the subject of the next chapter.

SUMMARY AND CONCLUSIONS

The study of perceptual learning concentrates on how subjects learn to recognize stimulus attributes for concept identification, and how they use this experience to further refine their concepts. Distinctive features refer to the perceptual characteristics subjects actually use in complex perceptual discriminations, for example, between individually written letters of the alphabet or between sounds of speech.

An important role of practice in concept learning is the perceptual reorganization of stimuli, in which some attribute dimensions are given more importance, or salience, than others. The most common methods of teaching concepts are the use of names to signal category membership, the use of formal definitions, and the use of linguistic context.

Subjects show good ability to categorize with probabilistic cues, although their effectiveness is hampered by the subjects' tendency to undervalue high frequency cues and to overvalue low frequency ones, as well as by the tendency of some attributes to assume a subjective importance which exceeds their actual usefulness.

In the real world of concept attainment, a benign regularity of attributes and categories is the exception, rather than the rule. A dime is not always called a dime (as opposed to "money" or a "coin"): it *usually* is. A clock *usually* has a round face. *Most* birds fly. The rule "*i* before *e*, except after *c*" *usually* works. In short, the defining attributes and rules relating to many concepts are those which are usually, rather than invariably, associated with the category.

To this extent, early education has its share of delusions. In order to speed the learning of concepts, we present them in idealized forms, often conventionalized by the use of artificially regularized attributes. We try, if we can, to illustrate them in their essential form, free of "noisy" attributes. The letter *A* in the reading book or on the blackboard is kept the same, and is printed with as little individual style as possible. The right triangle is invariably shown with two equal sides, however questionable it may be that this is true of most right triangles.

The reason for this is the belief that the use of generic instances with minimal variation in attributes will increase the speed of initial learning. This is true. But we are also aware that this may raise problems when the person later encounters new and slightly atypical instances of the learned concept. We have all seen children's dismay when they encounter such things as their first real anchor, or their first real pig, after learning these concepts from the highly conventionalized illustrations of the children's picture book.

Somehow, however, children do manage to survive our well-meaning attempts to bring order to a conceptually "noisy" world. They survive, one suspects, because they know more than they let on. Their reading skills when they enter school may be rudimentary or nonexistent. They may nevertheless really suspect that all *A*'s are not as neat and regular as presented on the classroom blackboard. They have, after all, already been learning concepts for a long time.

chapter 9

Concept Learning II:

RULES AND
LANGUAGE
ACQUISITION

Our analysis of learning to this point has shown how learning takes very different descriptive forms as it appears in classical conditioning, operant conditioning, association chaining, and concept attainment. Past attempts to bring order and clarifying unity to this variety of human ability have led to either one of two general propositions.

The first argument was that all human and animal learning can be accounted for, at least in principle, solely in terms of simple associations acquired through classical or operant conditioning. Facing the manifest difficulty of extending this position to the complexities of human learning (creative problem solving, language acquisition, and so forth) some suggested simply the need for further research. Others found relief by defining these problems as outside the field of "learning."

The second major view was to recognize the various forms of learning as being to a very real degree distinct but not necessarily unrelated. This view implied that learning is hierarchical. Increasingly complex and abstract forms of learning each introduce new elements, although they may be ultimately dependent on, and developed from, the simpler forms on the hierarchy.

Both views have had some currency in learning theory over the decades, and they were able to coexist as two sides of the same coin. They were considered perhaps not so much in opposition, as different in emphasis. There does come a time, however, when differences in emphasis become so great that even the most conciliatory among us must recognize that an opposition exists. In learning theory, the end of the détente came with the study of human language. It was here that the logical consequences of the two views met head-on. Only one view survived.

Early Language Acquisition

The most striking feature of language acquisition is that so much is learned so fast by one so little. From the humble beginnings of differential cries for hunger and discomfort, single words soon appear and before too long, sentences. The normative ages for language development are, for our present interests, less important than their sequence. One reason for this is that age norms tend to be notoriously unreliable. Some time between the ninth and eleventh months most children have acquired their first word. Some counts allow "mama" or "dada" as a word; others demand some word other than these two. In a similar vein, many a proud parent will argue (with extraordinary emotion) that their child's peculiar grunts, which sound nothing like English as you or I know it, are nevertheless words. And many experts will go along with the proud parent; any sound used for an object, and used for no other, is a "word." Whether the sound approximates the appropriate English word or not is irrelevant. Others' criteria are more demanding.

Using most norms, however, it is the case that by the first birthday the child has an average of three words. By 3½ he or she has a speaking vocabulary of 1200 words and a comprehension vocabulary of very much more. And the child can combine these words into sentences or phrases with an average length of 4.4 words per sentence. By the end of the fifth year the child has approximately 2000 words, with an average sentence length of 4.6 words. Although the child's vocabulary seems to be increasing many times faster than the average length of his or her sentences, this is only half the picture. Average sentence length may increase slowly with age, but—as we shall see—it is accompanied by an impressive increase in grammatical sophistication which is belied by the simple statistic of sentence length.

One thing is certain. However it is taking place, language development is extraordinarily rapid and complex. Indeed, its very rapidity has suggested to many that language learning may represent a very "natural" function for the child. It seems natural in the sense that both the structure of the child's vocal mechanism and, more important, the structure of his or her mental organization seem to predispose him or her to the ready acquisition of language. This may sound like an argument that language is not "learned" at all, but that it is in some sense an innate capacity of the human child. That is an extreme position.

To get closer to the concept of predisposition in this context, consider the following analogy. Learning to write—as any teacher knows—is anything but natural. It is a slow, painful process, complete with letter reversals, inversions, and some attempts at letters that simply defy description. This is surely sensorimotor learning, with the accent on learning. At the same time, the structure of the hand, with its opposing thumb, is already there, and ready and able to grasp a pencil when (1) society puts it there, and (2) it teaches the child how to use it. In a similar way, it might well be that the child's mental structure is analogously ready to "grasp" language, provided that (1) we make it available in the form of early stimulation, and (2) we guide him or her in its use.

IS LANGUAGE SPECIES SPECIFIC?

There is a view that only man can acquire language. It was proposed (in this century) by Chomsky (1965, 1968), supported by, among others, Lenneberg (1967), and denied by "Washoe." Washoe is a female, wild-born chimpanzee who some years ago was taught to communicate using the American Sign Language (ASL), which is a sign system developed for the deaf in the United States.

We are not alone in the animal kingdom to communicate, as witness the intricate symbolic dance of bees that can indicate by its pattern not merely the direction of a food source but also its distance and quantity (von Frisch, 1962, 1967). Many animals also have "words," if we extend the definition of a word to include any sign (including body posture) that has a specific meaning.

When we speak of *language*, however, we speak of the ability to take our individual discrete symbols (words) and combine them in various orders to convey different meanings. It is safe to say that no lower animal even approaches the level of sophistication of this human ability. Indeed, until the late 1960s, it was assumed that the human child was uniquely alone in having the cognitive capacity to acquire true language of any sort. Certainly, all attempts to teach animals to speak had been totally unsuccessful (cf.

Kellogg & Kellogg, 1933; Hayes, 1950). Psychology questioned only the source of this apparent biological uniqueness. The following were the two most common views.

The Human as a "Smart" Ape

As learning theory developed in the United States through the efforts of Thorndike, Hull, and others, so developed the view that all learning, human learning and animal learning, maze learning and language learning, could potentially be understood merely by the principles embodied in classical and operant conditioning (and their extension into the study of rote verbal learning). This unifying view of learning was an act of courage (and of faith), since the mechanisms of language acquisition were still something of a mystery. In principle, however, the leading theorists saw no need to treat language as anything more than a special, although uniquely human, form of S-R learning.

Why, then, was language thought to be unique to human behavior? To some, it meant only that apes and other infrahuman animals were less "intelligent," or, in the view of Mowrer (1960, pg. 111), that they had insufficient neural connections between the speech centers of the brain and the speech organs (see Chapter 12). That is, the difference between response learning in lower animals and language learning in the human child rested only on the level of neural hardware each could bring to the task; the principles of learning, however, were the same.

Language as an Innate Property

A contrary, and philosophically fascinating, position was taken by a number of writers such as Chomsky (1965, 1968) and Lenneberg (1967). To them, the potential task of learning so many verbal "habits" through experiencing such an enormous range of adult language seemed just too immense. Surely, they argued, the speed with which language is learned, and the uniformity of ages at which it develops from culture to culture, could only be understood if the human child had a head start on the process; certain innate, "built-in" mental structures upon which language experience need only be mapped (Chomsky, 1968). This view explicitly postulated the evolution of a human brain with unique mental structures for the development of linguistic ability. It also implied that such abilities could never be mastered by any creature without these structures, or solely through S-R learning derived from experience and reinforcement.

Enter Washoe

Both views were rudely shaken by reports that a chimpanzee had indeed been taught to understand and to use a surprisingly sophisticated form of language (Gardner & Gardner, 1969).

The Gardners knew of the earlier failures to teach apes to "talk," but felt that perhaps these failures said more about the apes' limited vocal apparatus than about their true potential for language. For that reason, they adopted the use of ASL. Through a combination of extraordinary patience, imitation, reward, and love, their chimpanzee, Washoe, soon developed an impressive repertoire of signs which could be used in meaningful communication (see Figure 9.1). To Gardner and Gardner, Washoe's sign language showed all the properties of true language; she could combine her signs ("words") in different orders to convey different meanings, and she could use these signs to express semantic relations. Indeed, Washoe used ASL to communicate not only with her human trainers but also with a slightly less sophisticated student chimpanzee named Lucy.

Premack (1971) later took advantage of chimpanzees' proven abilities in shape discrimination (see Chapter 8) by teaching a chimpanzee, Sarah, to use various visual forms to represent "words." These were plastic shapes with magnetic backs which Sarah could move about on a metal slate so as to reorder them in different ways and thus produce primitive "sentences." Although Sarah's language is far less impressive than Washoe's (she does not yet use her skills to communicate spontaneously as Washoe does), she can nevertheless handle some 60 nouns, 20 verbs, and 30 other words, including adjectives and adverbs.

Neither Washoe's nor Sarah's communicative skills come close to the sophistication of human language, and not everyone is ready to consider it "language" in the sense that it is acquired by human children (cf. Foder,

Figure 9.1 Washoe signing "book," "baby," and "listen." She can also combine these and other signs in various orders to form rudimentary "sentences." (*Source: Eugene Linden, Apes, Men, and Language.* Illustrations by Madelaine Gill Linden. Copyright © 1974 by Eugene Linden. Reprinted by permission of E. P. Dutton, Publishers).

Bever & Garrett, 1974, pp. 449–452). On the other hand, many are. As Brown (1973) has said, to the extent that we can state that an 18- to 24-month-old human child has language (and we can), so too does Washoe.

The reader is at liberty to make up his or her own mind on the subject, but it is certainly the case that the early 1960s battle cry, "Only man can acquire language," would be uttered with considerably more caution today. For the reader interested in pursuing this question, Schrier and Stollnitz (1971) offer a good background to the study of animal communication, while a very readable account of Washoe's development of language and its implications can be found in Linden (1974).

BIOLOGICAL READINESS FOR LANGUAGE

Whether unique or not, the human infant's sensitivity to language is certainly impressive. This can be seen in children's receptive capacity as well as in their early use of oral language. Some years ago, a technique was developed to study infants' ability to discriminate speech sounds at far younger ages than ever before tested. An infant is connected to an electro-cardiograph (EKG) which records the child's heart rate. The experimenter suddenly says "ga" and observes the EKG as it shows a dramatic change in heart rate in response to the mild startle of the sudden sound. If the sounds, "ga, ga, ga, ga . . ." are repeated at a regular rate, the child ceases to respond to the novelty of the sound, and the heart rate settles back to its normal level. The startle response of the change in heart rate has *habituated* to the novelty of the sound.

We can now exploit this simple phenomenon to determine whether the infant can distinguish between, for example, "ga" and "ba." As we rhythmically repeat "ga, ga, ga . . ." we suddenly introduce a "ba" sound along with the stream of "ga's": "ga, ga, ga, ga, ba, ba, ba . . ." If the heart rate remains stable, the child has not noticed the change in sounds. If we do see a change in the EKG, the "ba" must have been a "novel" stimulus in the background of the "ga's," such that the child must have detected that "ga" and "ba" are, in some sense, different. The speech sounds, in other words, are not to the infant just so much "noise."

The process of pairing and presenting each sound of the language with each other sound is slow and exhausting (for the experimenter, not for the infant). The use of this technique, however, has produced the startling discovery that infants can perceive distinctions between many speech sounds *as early as the first two weeks of life.* Using a similar technique, infants as young as 4 weeks old can be shown to distinguish between synthetic, computer-produced speech sounds, reacting to differences as subtle as "ba" versus "ga" (Eimas, Siqueland, Jusczyk & Vigorito, 1971). The advantage of using computer-produced speech, incidentally, is its guarantee that perceived differences are not due just to changes in loudness or stress which an experimenter might accidentally introduce but to the actual differences in the acoustic pattern of the different speech sounds themselves. The way these sounds are discriminated, moreover, seems to be very much along the lines of phoneme categories as we discussed them in the previous chapter. That is, much like the adult, infants tend to discriminate between phonemes while failing to discriminate between nonphoneme contrasts (Eimas, 1974).

These results do not imply that infants can "identify" these sounds, in the sense that they have any meaning to the child. Rather, they demonstrate that the human infant's sensory system is already "tuned in," even at this young age, and is ready when the time comes for sound identification.

Between the fifth and seventh months, the child ordinarily enters a "babbling" stage, which is specifically defined as the child making repetitive sounds to himself or herself when alone ("ba, ba, ga, ga, pa, pa," and so forth). Many parents are unaware that their children have gone through this stage, since children invariably stop this babbling when the parent enters the room, and they begin again only when the parent leaves. It is rather like the light in the refrigerator, only in reverse.

This latter fact, incidentally, led to a suggestion many years ago that while babbling may begin as a reflexive maturational phenomenon, it is maintained through these several months because the sounds the infant makes remind him or her of the "babbling" of the parents, and thus give the infant the pleasant feelings associated with those loved objects. For that reason, so the theory goes, there is no need to babble when the parents are present (Mowrer, 1950).

In the beginning stages of babbling, the child produces all of the sounds spoken by all people on the face of the earth; from the French nasalized *n* and the Germanic *ch* to the Swahili tongue click. As the babbling continues over the months, however, the sounds which are not in the child's native language begin to drop out of the babbling repertoire. At the same time, the babbling sounds the child tends to make begin more and more to correspond to those of the parents' native tongue (DiVesta, 1974). Clearly, we are seeing a very real influence of environmental experience at this point.

Somewhere along the line, the child further develops a primitive sense of the communicative value of speech. His or her cries—at first reflexive—are reinforced by the appearance of the parents in "answer" to his or her call. According to traditional learning theory, a combination of this reward of the vocal activity, plus identification with the speaking parents, sets the stage for language learning.

From this point on, the acquisition of language is extraordinarily rapid. From the "start" of the single-word utterance, to the "finish" of five-word sentences, little more than two years has elapsed. It may be, as Pollio has observed, that the period of 12 to 36 months represents the most critical time for the development of language (Pollio, 1974, pg. 442).

During this time, it would be entirely wrong to see the child in a passive role, simply imitating what he or she has heard (and being reinforced for doing so). This may be partly true, as the sequence in which words are acquired tend to reflect the naming practices of the parents (Brown, 1958). In another sense, however, this is not true. An analysis of the first 50 words learned by a sample of children through the age of 2 shows that they prefer to talk about some things and not others, regardless of what their parents talk about in their presence (Nelson, 1973). Most of their chitchat seemed to center on animals, food, and toys. While the parents are spending much of their time with the child talking about clothes (diapers, pants, etc.), the children's first 50 words only rarely include these terms. When the children do use clothing words, they tend to name items which they, themselves, can manipulate, such as shoes and socks (Glucksberg & Danks, 1975, pg. 129).

The acquisition of language in the early years thus represents an active partnership between the parent, or other linguistic model, and the child. It is a partnership in which both seem intuitively to do the right things for rapid learning. Before turning to the question of how this learning occurs, however, we should cite several factors which are known to delay or interfere with the process.

Requisites for Normal Language Development

HEARING. Moderate to severe hearing loss can be a very real cause of slow development in oral language. This may be obvious, but there are a number of related issues which may be less so. The first of these is that very few children have profound losses to the point where they could be called deaf. The great majority of hearing problems are moderate or slight and frequently affect only the upper pitch ranges of hearing. As such, they may go undetected until difficulties with speech are first noticed. In fact, early audiometric testing and special educational help for hearing-impaired children are both possible and beneficial at the preschool level, counter to the unfortunately frequent practice of waiting until school age before making such special help available.

One can also encounter children who have experienced temporary hearing loss due to middle-ear infection during the critical years of language development. By the time the child's delayed language is observed, the medical problem may have resolved itself, and we are left with a child with normal hearing whose speech difficulties appear as a mystery.

EMOTIONAL INTEGRITY. Children are amazingly resilient, and only the most severe of emotional disorders can be expected to have a major impact on language acquisition. One of the better known, but really very rare, examples would be that of the *autistic* child, whose withdrawal of contact from others may manifest itself in delayed language, virtually nonverbal behavior, or a reluctance to develop or use what language he or she has (cf. Berry, 1969, pp. 335–369).

STIMULATION. The bedtime story and parental chitchat with the infant are more than fun, they are also necessary language stimulation. Since surprisingly little stimulation is minimally needed for the acquisition of language, it is easy to overlook its importance. One tends to notice only extreme cases, such as children from "nonverbal" homes, where the necessary stimulation and speech model can be almost totally lacking. By way of example, the author once came into contact with a set of 5-year-old twins whose parents worked different shifts. One parent would come home and go to sleep as the other parent would leave for work, and even this minor interaction invariably occurred when the children were asleep.

While the twins' elementary needs were supplied by a teenage babysitter, their social contacts were limited almost entirely to each other. The twins, as we later discovered, could understand adult language, but they had in fact developed their own private language, and it was in this language only that they would communicate. It was incomprehensible enough to the adult world, however, that the parents brought their children to a speech clinic in an attempt to find out why they made "peculiar noises" but had no speech. (The fact that they had a highly developed private language was only accidentally discovered when one of the children produced a series of clicks, hisses, and grunts, which the other child responded to by bringing the first child an attractive toy from across the room. When the twins were later put in separate rooms and allowed to communicate only by sending tape-recorded messages to each other, it became clear not only that they could communicate, but that they could do so with a surprisingly high degree of sophistication.)

INTELLECTUAL LEVEL. Some speech and simple language can be learned by even quite severely retarded children, although in extreme cases of profound retardation this may be limited to simple naming (cf. Lenneberg, 1967). Such severe cases are unlikely to be found in ordinary school classrooms, but cases of borderline and mild retardation may occasionally be encountered. Their communicative skills will be quite functional, but they will show a noticeable lack of richness in language.

Within the range of normal intelligence, IQ has more of an effect on the richness of vocabulary than on the child's day-to-day linguistic ability. More on the subject of mental retardation will be said in Chapter 13.

BRAIN FUNCTION. Brain damage, whether due to accident or disease, can cause mild or severe difficulties with language or other cognitive function. Although we will look at this problem more closely in Chapters 12 and 13, we should emphasize at this point that the diagnosis of mild brain damage is by no means easy, and educational authorities are only now becoming equipped to recognize and to deal with these problems. The problems associated with brain damage can include difficulties in reading (dyslexia), writing (dysgraphia), or language in general (aphasia).

A more detailed discussion of these requisites for language acquisition, and the clinical problems one can encounter, can be found in relevant sections of Travis (1957).

SUMMARY

Beginning with the first word at about the age of 1 year, to the development of four-word sentences at the age of 3 or 4, the speed and apparent ease of language acquisition is extraordinary. Indeed, the process seems so "natural" as to have caused some to speculate whether there may be a unique human predisposition for language acquisition. This question has too long a history in psychology and philosophy for us to expect it to be easily laid to rest. Recent developments in teaching chimpanzees to communicate through sign language have certainly called the human uniqueness of language ability into question.[1]

The requisites for normal language acquisition are surprisingly minimal. Provided the child has adequate hearing, intelligence, emotional integrity, and language stimulation, we can expect language acquisition to be rapid and deceptively easy. Indeed, even some difficulty in any of these areas often has only slight effect on language acquisition, and it must be quite severe for major problems to be encountered.

What Is It the Child Learns When the Child Learns Language?

In simple learning where the stimuli and responses can be readily identified, the question generally asked is *how* learning takes place. We wish, in those cases, to determine the necessary antecedent conditions, the factors regulating speed of learning, and so forth. When we turn to language learning, on the other hand, the first question we must ask is *what* it is the child learns when we say that the child learns language. In fact, this ques-

[1] The question of the uniqueness or the innateness of language to the human is a problem second only in complexity to its origin in the species. By 1866 this latter question had become so confounded with speculation that the Société de Linguistique in Paris passed a resolution forbidding any further discussion of the subject (Simon, 1957, pg. 8). In the interests of space, we are willing to abide by that resolution.

tion is not as straightforward as it may seem, and it has been the cause of some spirited disagreement in recent years.

The traditional view of American learning theorists has been to see language learning as an extension of the chaining of associations as it was discussed in Chapter 7. As the child learned individual words, and experienced fluent discourse, he or she was thought to learn *associations* between frequently encountered words, strings of words, and sentences. Today, an opposing view sees sentence production as far less passive, even in the youngest children. As soon as children begin to string even two words together they begin to reflect the utilization of *rules* governing word combinations, and they use these rules in the generation of even these simple phrases.

ASSOCIATIONIST VIEWS OF LANGUAGE

The traditional view of language not only saw it as an extension of chaining of verbal associations, but much of the verbal learning research described in Chapter 7 was initiated precisely with a view to understanding early language acquisition by children. Consider, for example, a serial CVC learning list repeatedly presented until the sequence becomes so well learned that it can be produced without effort: *jeg dax tum vil.* Now compare: *The boy threw the ball.* Each word *could* be learned as one item in a left-to-right sequence. Certain stimulus sets, *the boy*, might occur together more frequently in experience, and hence be more strongly associated than others. We are all too familiar with a variety of habitual word-sequences, where the first word seems to trigger the entire phrase: *how's it going, pair of shoes,* or, for some in public life, *winds of change* or *law and order.*

The associationist views of language took two major forms. The first was represented by S-R learning theories of language, and the second was the extension of these ideas into a view of language as a process governed by sequential probabilities between linguistic events.

S-R Theories of Language

It is necessary to speak of S-R theories of language in the plural, since this was a general approach which had many advocates, each with a noticeably different view or emphasis (cf. Mowrer, 1954; Skinner, 1957; Osgood, 1963, 1968; Staats, 1958). Their common goal, however, was to take the basic laws of learning as derived from studies of animals and humans in simple learning situations and to apply these laws—with as little change as possible—to the explanation of human language behavior. The approach would be to view speech as a *response,* and to determine how the processes of imitation, trial and error, and reinforcement, might result in the formation of "verbal habits" (words) and "verbal chains" (sentences).

Our discussion of classical and operant conditioning in Chapters 4 and 5 included some examples of how shaping in operant conditioning could be used to describe the attachment of verbal responses to stimuli, and how classical conditioning might give such responses their emotional connotation. (We have already seen in Chapter 8 how these views became complicated by the cognitive theorists' emphasis on word meaning as concept attainment rather than as simply response learning). By far the most interesting application of S-R theory to language, however, came with the attempt to explain children's learning of sentences; the combination of individual words in different orders to produce a variety of different meanings.

The most provocative contemporary spokesman for the S-R view has been B. F. Skinner (1957), whose book *Verbal Behavior* provoked Noam Chomsky (1959) into a heated attack. In his review of the book, Chomsky charged that the extension of laws derived from simple learning to the complexities of human language is doomed before it begins. There is in language, he said, no clear identification of "the stimulus" and "the response," or reinforcement, upon which such laws must be based. Further, he argued, laws based on imitation and reinforcement cannot account for children's ability to produce a theoretically infinite variety of different sentences they have never before heard spoken. (In fairness to the full picture of this decidedly fascinating controversy, see MacCorquodale's, 1970, subsequent rebuttal.)

One definition of a good theory in psychology is one which stimulates research. Whether or not this research ends in supporting the theory, it is said, is perhaps secondary to the accumulation of factual data which might not otherwise have been obtained. In this sense, some of the S-R approaches can be said to have had their share of success. We can learn a great deal about language (and by implication, about S-R theory), if we look briefly at some of the implications of these views and at some of the logical and empirical points later raised in opposition.

Language as a Stochastic Process

The basic elements of an S-R theory of language can be illustrated with the following scenario. The process begins with the child hearing sequences of words (sentences or phrases) spoken by the parents or older siblings. Although not essential to the theory, in practice these would ordinarily be "child-size" phrases, conforming to the parents' notion of what the child can handle (e.g., "daddy go bye-bye," "baby hungry," "nice doggy," and so forth).

With repetition, the stimulus sequence becomes familiar to the child, and he or she begins a faltering attempt to reproduce the phrase. Each successful attempt strengthens the interword associations until the entire sequence becomes stable, and the probability that each word in the chain can elicit the next one approaches 100 percent. At this point, we say that the child "knows" the sentence: he or she can produce all of the words in the correct order whenever he or she chooses.

This picture of language learning is familiar to anyone who has attempted to learn a little of some foreign language through a conversational phrase book. We learn, for example, to say "Undskyld, jeg forstar ikke" which, we are assured, is Danish for, "I'm sorry, I don't understand." We can accomplish this feat without the slightest notion of the independent meanings of each of the words, much less the grammatical rules which underlie the utterance. The relation to serial learning is clear, except that, in this case, meaningless CVC nonsense syllables are replaced by responses which, at least to Danes, do have meaning.

At some stage the child, or the novice speaker of Danish, will acquire an understanding of the individual words and of the grammar. But is understanding of the grammar necessary for the correct production of language, or is it merely a later formalization of already learned sequential associations? In other words, can language be adequately described as a linear process, in which linguistic events (words) are governed by statistical probabilities determined by their degree of learned association?

This view of language, as the acquisition of strings of practiced associations, has been likened to a mathematical form known as a *stochastic*, or *Markov process* (Shannon, 1948; Miller & Frick, 1949; Miller, 1952).[2] Essentially, a stochastic (Markov) process is any nonrandom series of events whose occurrence is governed by contextual probabilities. In other words, if an event *a* occurs, there is a certain probability or likelihood that it will be followed by event *b*. If events *a* and *b* both occur, there is an additional probability that they will be followed by event *c*, and so on. As we have seen, in the case of language, these "events" would be words, the sequence of events would be sentences, and the *contextual* or *transitional probabilities* between the words would be a measure of their frequency of prior association in past experience.

One way to visualize the production of sentences based on the association strengths between words is shown in Figure 9.2. The principle is based on a formulation by Miller (1958), although simplified here for our purposes. For reasons which will soon become apparent, it is sometimes called a *finite-state grammar*, or *finite-state sentence generator*.

Begin by imagining a hypothetical creature with a seven-word vocabulary as shown in the upper-right corner of Figure 9.2 (*the, big, ran, old, boy, race, fast*). Each word has stored with it the words which have most frequently followed it in past experience. Our hypothetical creature will

---

[2] A stochastic process is formally defined as any system which produces a sequence of symbols (letters, words, musical notes) according to certain probabilities. A Markov process is a special case of a stochastic process, in which the probabilities are dependent on prior events (Shannon & Weaver, 1949; Attneave, 1959).

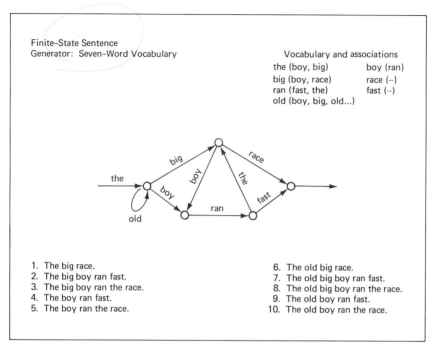

Figure 9.2   A finite-state sentence generator with a hypothetical seven-word vocabulary, and the sentences it would produce.

now begin to produce meaningful, grammatical sentences based solely on these transitional probabilities.

The process begins by selecting the first word of the sentence, the word *the*. Once *the* has been selected, we are in a state where we have the option of selecting either the word *big* or the word *boy*, based on past experience. If *big* is selected, we have moved to the state where we can select either *race* or *boy*. By following each arrow through the "maze" in the directions shown, we can move from state to state and produce the variety of acceptable English sentences shown at the bottom of the figure. (The small circular arrow marked by the word *old* is referred to as a *recursive rule*. It allows the option of inserting the word *old* between *the* and *big* or *the* and *boy*. It can also be repeated indefinitely, as, "The old, old, old boy ran the race," or "The old, old, old big race.")

While this illustration with its seven-word vocabulary should not be taken too seriously as a model of human language, it does illustrate the basic principles of the associationist approach to sentence production: (1) Sentences are derived solely from associations between individual words as encountered in past experience through a S-R mode. Neither meaning nor grammatical rules need be postulated. (2) The direction of the arrows tell us that while *big→race* has occurred in past experience, *race→big* has not. Therefore, this sequence will not be produced. (3) If the word *big* were not followed equally often by *race* and by *boy* in the past, this would be represented by different associative probabilities that each of these two words would be produced. We could, in other words, increase the sophistication of the model by adding "association strength" values to each of the association arrows. (4) The model is capable of producing the variety of grammatical sentences shown, but it will not produce anomalous sentences like, "The boy boy the fast," or "The big the ran boy race."

We have to admire the elegant simplicity of the finite-state grammar, and it would be intriguing to build a device with vocabularies of 10, 20, 80, or 1000 words which would produce an enormous variety of acceptable English sentences without any recourse to meaning, or syntax, as it is usually conceived. Such an exercise would be one way to model a S-R association theory of the growth of a child's language as he or she adds new vocabulary words and new word associations.

The half-life of most psychological theories is something less than infinite, and this approach to the study of language proved to be no exception. Throughout a 15-year period, beginning in the 1950s and ending in the middle 1960s, however, studies of the statistical properties of language became an all-consuming passion. And with each study came implicit support for the S-R, or associationist, view of language. Under the umbrella term, *information theory*, psychologists became mathematicians and began to systematically explore the statistical redundancy inherent in human language and the way in which these mathematical regularities could be used to describe, and (it was hoped) to understand, language and language acquisition. A superb contemporary account of this approach can be found in Cherry (1957), and a good introduction to the mathematics of information theory can be found in Attneave (1959).

Some Language Statistics

One estimate gives the college-educated adult a speaking vocabulary of some 75,000–100,000 words (Oldfield, 1963). The thought of "searching" memory and "finding" each word as and when it is needed in rapid conversation truly stretches the bounds of imagination. Clearly something must be added to this random storage of words to facilitate their rapid selection and production. It is very tempting to see this aid in the form of well-practiced associations which facilitate word selection. Finding the first few words of a sequence leads to the rapid availability of words frequently associated with them in the past.

As we study the statistical characteristics of language, we discover that word usage is in fact hardly random. While we may have a vocabulary of impressive size, the majority of our known words are only very rarely used. As it happens, on the average, we can get along for only about 10 to 15 words before repeating a word. Some words tend to reoccur much more frequently than others. (In writing, for example, the most frequently used word is *the*, while in spoken telephone conversations it is *I*.) In fact, the 50 most commonly used words in the English language make up about 60 percent of all the words we speak, and about 45 percent of those we write (Miller, 1951). Our actual speaking vocabulary during the course of everyday conversation can be as little as 5000 different words and, sometimes, only several hundred. Were it not for the alleged greater profundity of what we say, college-educated adults would compare very favorably (or unfavorably) with the speaking vocabulary of the bright 5-year-old!

Thus, both as speakers and as listeners, the words we use show considerable regularity, and it is actually possible on a statistical level to *predict* what words will be chosen by a person in a particular context, simply on the basis of the relative frequency with which they have occurred in the past. When it comes to fluent discourse, for example, estimates have suggested that English is ordinarily as much as 30 to 50 percent redundant (Shannon, 1951; Chapanis, 1954). In other words, if you were shown the page of a book, or listened to a tape recording of a speaker, we could randomly erase from 30 to 50 percent of the words and still expect you to be able to infer or "guess" the missing words and thus follow the meaning with little difficulty. In language, then, there is *redundancy*—predictability limited by context.

Probably the most familiar example of this principle is "telegraph speech." We have no trouble, for example, sending or receiving a wire which says, "Flight delayed stop arriving 10:00 stop wait stop," rather than "My airplane flight was delayed in taking off. I will be arriving at 10:00. Please wait for me." When words cost money, we soon find ourselves serious students of linguistic redundancy in the English language.

It is this redundancy which allows us to piece together a conversation heard over a bad telephone connection where much of the speech is indistinct. It is also this redundancy that formed the basis of code breaking in the years before sophisticated coding and decoding computers became available. Knowing the relative frequency of occurrence of sequences of letters and of words in a language gave critical clues for deciphering code symbols which recurred with equivalent rates and patterns. This redundancy also accounts for the annoying habit of some people who, in conversation, repeatedly finish our sentences for us even before we have had a chance to say more than the first few words.

Statistical Approximations to English

One can get a good feeling for the nature of this redundancy by examining so-called statistical approximations to the English language. These were materials which were constructed for experiments and were intended to mirror the statistical properties, or "association frequencies," of the language.

Tables had long been available which gave the relative frequency of occurrence of letters of the alphabet in English print (e.g., the frequency with which the letter *e* appears versus the letter *x*). There were also letter counts available which gave both digram and trigram frequencies; the frequencies with which all two-letter and three-letter combinations occur in English print. (For the code breaker, of course, these were also available for other languages of the world.)

Unfortunately, while researchers did have available frequency counts for individual words in the language (Thorndike & Lorge, 1944), there was no comparable data for frequencies of word *sequences*—the likelihood that any particular word would follow any other in English.

To overcome this problem, Miller and Selfridge (1950) devised a technique which assumed that, whatever these sequential probabilities between words might be, they must certainly be reproducible by speakers of the language. Here is how such samples were generated.

The process begins by showing a person a list of, for example, three words such as: *the boy and.* The person is asked to give what he or she thinks would be a likely fourth word to follow them in an ordinary English sentence. The subject might write the word *girl.* A second person is now shown the list except that the first word (the) is covered, and the selection must be based on the last three words only: *boy and girl.* A third subject is again shown only the last three words (this time it is *and girl went*) and asked for a fourth word. This process continues with enough different people to produce a passage of the desired length. This would be called a *fourth-order* approximation to English. Note that while such a passage might be 50 words long, each word is actually based on the three prior words of context only.

The examples given below are taken from Moray and Taylor (1960) and show samples of second-order, sixth-order, and eighth-order approximations to English, where word selections were based on one, five, and seven prior words of context respectively.[3]

Second order: The camera shop and boyhood friend from fish and screamed loudly men only when seen again and then it was jumping in the tree.

[3] The variations on this theme of producing statistical approximations to English can be endless and amusing. Attneave (1959) cites two examples. The first is a sample of Shannon's efforts to produce fourth-order approximations to *words*, based on a sampling of letter transitions in printed speech. The result would do justice to Lewis Carroll: *Grocid pondenome of demonstures of the raptagin is regoactiona of cre* (Shannon & Weaver, 1949, pg. 14).

His second example is a fourth-order approximation to a mystery story, in which the subjects were told of this context as they contributed their words to the sequence: "When I killed her I stabbed Paul between his powerful jaws clamped tightly together. Screaming loudly despite fatal consequences in the struggle for life began ebbing as he coughed hollowly spitting blood from his ears" (Atteneave, 1959, pg. 19).

Sixth order: I have a few little facts here to test lots of time for studying and praying for guidance in living according to common ideas as illustrated by the painting.

Eighth order: In the early days following my first enquiry I thought of asking if he could hope to win everlasting renown by writing a complete set of confused accounts.

As the number of words of context on which each word is based increases, the passages begin to look more and more like normal prose, but there is always something wrong. Our "speaker" seems continually on the verge of saying something meaningful, but never quite does.

In one of the first of many experiments employing statistical approximations, Miller and Selfridge (1950) tested the ability of subjects to memorize various orders of approximation as each was read aloud just once for immediate recall. Figure 9.3 shows the percentage of words correctly recalled for passages of various approximations and lengths. Independent of the length of the passage, ease of handling the materials increased systemat-

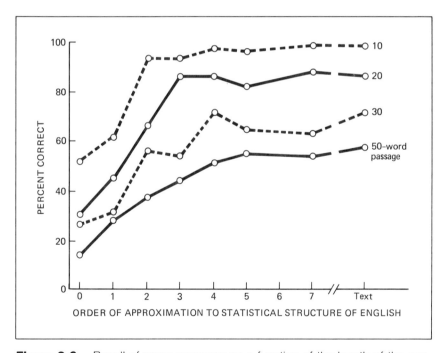

Figure 9.3   Recall of prose passages as a function of the length of the passages and their order of approximation to the statistical structure of English. (*Source:* G. A. Miller and J. A. Selfridge, Verbal context and the recall of meaningful material. *American Journal of Psychology,* 1950, 63: fig. 1, pg. 181. Copyright © 1950 by Karl M. Dallenbach. Reprinted by permission of The University of Illinois Press.)

ically with their order of approximation to English. Especially interesting are the final points on the right-hand side of the graph, which show recall performance for a sample of normal English prose. Beyond fourth- or fifth-order approximations, the "nonsense" seems to be handled just about as easily as normal text. To Miller and Selfridge, the key to memorizing the passages was not their degree of "meaning" versus "nonsense," but the degree to which they preserved "the short-range associations of the English language."

These general results would have come as no surprise to Ebbinghaus (1885), who had himself compared the ease of learning strings of CVC nonsense syllables with that of normal prose. In one instance, he found that lines from Byron's *Don Juan* required only a tenth of the effort as nonsense syllables, concluding that the difference lay in "rhyme, rhythm, meaning, and the natural language" (Crowder, 1976, pg. 464). What might have come as a surprise, however, is the systematic nature of the results as one merely models the statistical structure of the "natural language."

The contextual constraints introduced by sentences, and statistical approximations to sentences, can also be shown to predict auditory intelligibility of passages heard under poor listening conditions (Rubenstein & Pollack, 1963), visual recognition thresholds (Tulving & Gold, 1963; Morton, 1964), and latencies to guessing words which have been deleted from a passage (Treisman, 1965).

Treisman (1965) used a very simple technique to demonstrate the effect of message redundancy on the time it takes to guess a word deleted from a passage. The experiment had to be conducted in two stages. First, one group of subjects saw printed passages with deleted words and were simply asked to say what they thought the missing words might be. The proportion of people guessing the correct word was taken as that word's *probability* in the context. In the second step, she now showed the passages to another group of subjects whose responses were timed with a stopwatch as they guessed the missing words. These latencies were found to be systematically shorter when the missing words had high contextual probability; response latency was inversely correlated with response probability (on a logarithmic scale).

The stochastic view of language was given even further support when Goldman-Eisler (1964, 1968) measured the places where people tend to pause in fluent discourse. Interestingly, she found that as much as 40 to 50 percent of spontaneous speaking time is in fact occupied by pauses, rather than by "speech." Even more interesting, she found that these pauses were related not to our breathing patterns but to the linguistic content of what we are saying. That is, counter to intuition, we do not pause in fluent speech in order to breathe; we take the opportunity to breathe during pauses which are determined by the linguistic content of what we are saying (Goldman-Eisler, 1961). Generally speaking, we tend to pause before words of low transitional probability: words unlikely to be said in that specific context.

Language viewed as a stochastic process is a linear explanation, which holds that speech is a result of learned associative links in a left-to-right sequence of word selection. It sees the production of fluent discourse as parallel to the way we try to teach children to read: left-to-right, word-by-word. A slight wrinkle in this simple scheme, therefore, appeared when Goldman-Eisler found that pauses were often correlated not merely with a word's probability based on the preceding context, but that pauses could also be correlated to some extent with the probability of the word based on the context which followed it. The pauses, in other words, seemed to have been determined not only by what had been said, which is consistent with the stochastic model, but they seemed also to have been influenced by what had yet to be said, which is not.

It soon became apparent that the planning of our sentences is much more complex than a direct left-to-right sequential selection of words. There are many logical, and some psychological, problems which arise in this connection. (1) The variety of different sentences produced by children, even before the age of 3, are far too numerous to have been learned by simple imitation of heard utterances. (2) Imitation also fails to account for children's ability to produce novel utterances which they have never before heard spoken. (3) Finally, there are numerous linquistic forms that demand an overall planning of sentence structure which would be impossible on a left-to-right, word-by-word basis. Embedded sentences such as, "There are no no smoking signs," are just one example. That is, the phrase, "no smoking," is embedded in the larger sentence frame of, "There are no signs." The general outline of the full sentence must be planned in order to retroactively insert the phrase, and these operations must be contemplated before the full sentence is uttered. An extreme case of embedding is the sentence, "The race that the car that the people that the man sold, won, was held last summer."

The above sentence is not easy to follow, and it is doubtful that we would even ever expect to hear such a linguistic abomination in the course of a normal lifetime. This, however, is the point: we have the *competence* to both produce and to understand sentences which have never before been experienced or practiced (Chomsky, 1957; Miller, Galanter & Pribram, 1960).

Summary: Associationist Views of Language

The essence of S-R theories of language is to view speech as a response which is learned through the direct application of the principles of reinforced association. Imitation, trial and error and reinforcement are seen as leading to the formation of "verbal habits" (words) and "verbal chains" (sentences).

Statistical studies of language have demonstrated that certain words and sequences of words occur with sufficient regularity for them to be highly predictable in a linguistic context. This finding led to the view of language as a stochastic process, in which selection of words in context are determined by their relative probability based on their frequency of association in past experience.

The so-called finite-state model of sentence production is one way to conceptualize this process. It has the simplifying virtue of producing a variety of acceptable English sentences based solely on associationist principles.

The weakness of finite-state models is their inability to explain children's ability to produce sentences never before heard or sentences with complex embedded structures. These concerns led to an alternative view to the S-R approach. This alternative is the possibility that children learning language may not be learning associations between words but, instead, *rules* for word combinations—a rudimentary "grammar" of their language.

LANGUAGE AS RULE ACQUISITION

Considerations such as those in the previous section led to the conclusion that even young children must be learning and utilizing rules to govern their sentence production.

At this point a firm caution is in order. The term for linguistic rules is, of course, a *grammar*. To suggest that a 3-year-old child, for example, "knows" the grammar of his or her language is bound to cause some confusion. Before we say what we mean by grammar in this context, it is important to say what we do *not* mean.

The proposition that a child (or adult) is using a grammar to generate his or her sentences should neither imply that the child is necessarily aware of these rules, nor that they necessarily correspond to "good grammar" as it is defined in high school grammar books. It is quite evident that neither is the case.

When we refer to grammar in language research, we mean only that the person's utterances follow consistent rules which are rarely violated. Thus, a young child who says, "Me go shopping," or an adult who uses double negatives, would be said to have "good grammar," to the extent that the usage is consistent.

We must also distinguish between linguistic *competence* and *performance*. The fact is, even adult speech is rarely typified by fluent transitions from one perfectly formed sentence to another. Our speech tumbles out in jerky phrases, often no more than three words in length, with "um's," "ah's," and silences being predominant features of our discourse (cf. Goldman-Eisler, 1968). The important point is that we have the competence to produce fully grammatical sentences and to recognize them when we hear them. Rules are no less rules simply because they are frequently violated. Indeed, as we shall soon see, the rules we are concerned with are so basic that they are in fact violated not all that often.

Rules, of course, come in many forms. There are rules for meaning (semantic rules), rules for sentence structure (syntactic rules), and rules which are purely pragmatic in nature. For example, we were unlikely to say "The train is late today" when the train is always late, or to say "it's raining" if we live in a tropical rain forest during the rainy season.

With the wisdom of hindsight, we now recognize that these rules in fact underlie the statistical regularity and redundancy that earlier workers so painstakingly observed in language behavior. The stochastic, or finite-state model of language seemed for a time to be an adequate description of language, not because transitional probabilities actually govern speech production, but precisely because such probabilities can quite accurately reflect the combined effect of these various rules which do.

The Cognitive Alternative

The turning point in the study of language came with Noam Chomsky's publication in 1957 of a short monograph, simply entitled, *Syntactic Structures*. In this monograph and later writing, Chomsky (1957, 1965), a linguist at M.I.T., outlined the elements of a new way to view human language. In point of fact, while the S-R approaches to language can be admired for their elegant simplicity, Chomsky's theory must, conversely, be admired for its elegant complexity.

Chomsky's theory represented a formal linquistic treatment, rather than a psychological model of how language is used by a speaker or a listener. His theory was one of language competence, not performance. Nevertheless, the translation of his ideas into such psychological models came to have an immense influence on the way psychologists began to view language.

To understand how psychologists of language (psycholinguists) began to view language, we can begin with the position that any sentence we hear (or read) actually has two components. The first, which is referred to as the *deep* structure, is the essence of the meaning we hope to convey. The second, which is called the *surface structure,* is merely the specific words we have chosen to convey this meaning. In essence, some argued that the speaker begins with an internal formulation of the deep structure of a sentence and then generates the specific words we actually hear. The task of the listener is to analyze, or "decode," this surface structure in order to detect its presumed deep structure. Two well-known examples may help to illustrate this point.

First, consider the following sentences: *The boy threw the ball, The ball was thrown by the boy,* and *Was the ball not thrown by the boy?* The surface structures of these sentences are obviously different, both in the specific words used and in their grammatical form (simple declarative, passive voice, and a passive negative question). In spite of these superficial differences, all three sentences obviously convey the same essential meaning: some boy threw a ball. Such examples make clear that different surface structures can represent what is, in effect, the same deep structure.

The opposite side of the coin is a case where the same surface structure can represent different deep structures. Ambiguous sentences are of this sort. Consider, for example, the sentence: *Flying planes can be dangerous.* This single surface structure can have two distinct meanings: first, that it is dangerous to be a pilot and, second, that it is dangerous to live near an airport. Thus, a single deep structure can be represented by a variety of surface structures, while a single surface structure can reflect more than one deep structure.

The thrust of Chomsky's argument, incidentally, has much in common with Lashley (1951) who, you may recall, cautioned the S-R chaining theorists for what he believed was their confusion between the order of events as they are seen and what might be a very different organization of events as they are internally programmed. In a similar way, Chomsky saw the error of traditional S-R theories of language as a mistaken concentration on the surface structure of sentences which, in an analogous way, tell us little about their internal organization. The surface structure we see, in other words, is merely a consequence of mental activity relating to the sentence's deep structure, which we cannot see.

As Chomsky's theory of grammar developed over the years since its first presentation, the question of the relationship between the surface and the deep structure of sentences, and how they might be internally represented, grew in complexity (cf. Chomsky, 1965; Lyons, 1970; Greene, 1972). Although our primary concern is with children's language acquisition, it is important to take a brief look at psychologists' development of Chomsky's notions, as they form the basis of these studies. We can only hope to give a flavor of these ideas, and the interested reader is referred to, for example, Fodor, Bever, and Garrett (1974) for a more detailed coverage of this development.

Another "Generative" Grammar

We have seen how a finite-state system can generate a variety of grammatical sentences on a left-to-right basis. Chomsky's alternative was a grammar which also generates meaningful sentences, but which does so in a very different way. It begins with the assumption that the speaker and the listener share a common set of rules which govern word relationships.

We can define a rule simply as a formalized statement of a concept or a principle such as, "Cars entering from the left have the right of way," "There is no smoking allowed in this supermarket," or "a *ling* consists of two objects." The form such rules might take in sentence production are il-

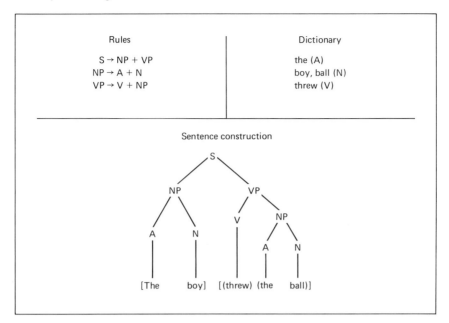

Figure 9.4   A phrase-structure grammar, showing types of rules and "dictionary" which would be involved in producing the sentence, "The boy threw the ball."

lustrated in Figure 9.4, which shows a *phrase-structure grammar* for a simple declarative sentence. A phrase-structure grammar is a convenient way of describing the structure of such a sentence.

The upper left-hand panel of the figure shows three such rules. The first says that "a sentence consists of a noun phrase plus a verb phrase." This is abbreviated as S→NP + VP. The second rule tells us that "a noun phrase consists of an article (such as *the* or *a*) plus a noun," or NP→A + N. The final rule says that "a verb phrase consists of a verb plus a noun phrase," or VP→V + NP.

The second element of the grammar is a "dictionary," as illustrated in the upper right-hand panel of Figure 9.4. Unlike the vocabulary of the finite-state grammar (Figure 9.2), the words in this case are tagged not with their frequent associates but with their *form classes*, or "parts of speech" (article, noun, verb, and so forth). As the tree diagram at the bottom of the figure shows, these elements are all that are needed to produce the simple sentence, *The boy threw the ball.* First we generate the noun phrase (*the boy*), then we expand the verb phrase to produce the verb (*threw*) and its complementary noun phrase (*the ball*).

This phrase-structure grammar makes two points. First, it shows that the noun phrase (*the boy*) and the verb phrase (*threw the ball*) can be seen as separate *units* of the sentence in that they derive from different sets of rules.

In a similar way, the verb phrase consists of two separate *subunits,* the verb *(threw),* and the noun phrase *(the ball).* Although the product of this internal schema may appear as a linear sequence of five words, the theory proposes that they actually derive from separate rules and, hence, may be organized in this grouped manner as people produce and process heard speech.

There is some evidence for this. For example, when subjects are required to memorize sentences, the majority of their recall errors tend to occur at the transition points between major phrases, such as between a noun phrase and a verb phrase (Johnson, 1965). Accuracy within a phrase is generally high, which suggests that subjects learn sentences in terms of these phrase groups. That is, when one element of a phrase is learned, we can expect good recall for the entire unit. Other studies using related techniques have added support to the notion that phrase-structure rules roughly approximate the way in which people organize and remember linguistic material (cf. Suci, Ammon & Gamlin, 1967; Kennedy & Wilkes, 1968).

The second point the phrase-structure grammar makes is that a limited set of rules can be used to generate an infinite number of different sentences simply as one acquires new words for the dictionary. For example, learning the new noun, *airplane,* allows us to say *The boy threw the ball, The boy threw the airplane.* Adding the verb *lost* now allows, *The boy lost the ball, The boy lost the airplane.* Thus, adding just two new words allows us to increase the number of potential sentences we can generate from one sentence to four.

In this way, a child's language repertoire could grow exponentially as he or she adds new word elements within the limited framework of a relatively simple grammar. More important, the child could incorporate a new word into the grammar to produce a fully grammatical sentence which he or she has never before heard spoken.

Transformational Rules

You will recall our earlier postulate that the sentences, *The boy threw the ball, The ball was thrown by the boy,* and *Was the ball not thrown by the boy?* are three ways of representing the same deep structure: a boy threw a ball. The question we now face is how a speaker might generate these alternative forms, and how the listener may detect the single deep structure underling them.

It is certainly possible to express some very complex syntactic forms in terms of increasingly complex phrase-structure grammars. While this may be possible, it is not very economical, especially if we are looking for principles which one might want to propose may actually be learned by human beings. A possible solution was seen with Chomsky's postulate of an addition to the phrase-structure grammar. This addition consists of sets of *transformational rules* which allow for the ability to derive a variety of syntactic forms from a single base structure, or what he originally called a *kernel sen-*

tence. For this reason, Chomsky's full grammar is sometimes referred to as a *transformational grammar.*

Since the first presentation of Chomsky's 1957 grammar, the transformational systems subsequently described have grown in number and complexity. We will make reference to this again later. At this point, however, it is worthwhile to attempt to briefly outline the general notion of linguistic transformations, if only in a very simplified way. More complete accounts can be found in Chomsky (1957, 1965) and in, for example, Fodor, Bever, and Garrett (1974) and in Glucksberg and Danks (1975).

To get a feeling for how transformational rules might work, consider the earlier sentence, *The boy threw the ball.* In this active declarative form, it could be said to represent the kernel sentence, which would be derived from phrase-structure rules, and which corresponds most closely to the deep structure. From this kernel sentence we could produce, for example, its passive form, through the following operations: (1) the second noun phrase *(the ball)* is moved as a unit to the beginning of the sentence, (2) *threw* is changed to its passive form and an auxiliary is added, (3) the initial noun phrase *(the boy)* is moved as a unit to the rear of the sentence, and (4) *by* is inserted before the final noun phrase. We can symbolize these operations in the abstract, such that they could apply to any kernel sentence of a similar form.

ACTIVE FORM (KERNEL)   PASSIVE FORM

(The boy) (threw) (the ball.)   *(The ball) (was thrown) (by) (the boy.)*

$$NP_1 + V + NP_2 \longrightarrow NP_2 + aux + V_{(pass)} + prep + NP_1$$

Although several operations were required in this derivation, we could still speak of the expansion of a kernel sentence to a passive sentence as involving a single transformation, since these operations work on the structure of the kernel sentence as a whole.

Listed below are examples of a succession of transformations from our kernel sentence (K) to increasingly more complex surface structures: passive (P), negative (N), question (Q), passive question (PQ), negative question (NQ), and a passive negative question (PNQ). Also shown are the number of transformations hypothetically required to get from the kernel to each of these forms.

Sentences	Form	Number of Transformations
The boy threw the ball.	(K)	0
The ball was thrown by the boy.	(P)	1
The boy did not throw the ball.	(N)	1
Did the boy throw the ball?	(Q)	1
Was the ball thrown by the boy?	(PQ)	2
Did the boy not throw the ball?	(NQ)	2
Was the ball not thrown by the boy?	(PNQ)	3

Some Psychological Studies of Grammar

The appearance of Chomsky's transformational grammar caused a flurry of activity in the ranks of psychologists studying language. The search began for experimental evidence that *rule acquisition,* in general, is a better description of linguistic behavior than association learning, and that Chomsky's transformational grammar in particular, was the best way to describe such rules.

Ironically, some of the earliest of this new breed of experiments bore more than a faint resemblance to their S-R ancestors. In 1950, Miller and Selfridge had compared recall ability for sentences and nonsentences to demonstrate the importance of association probabilities as a way of supporting a stochastic model of language (see Figure 9.3). Fourteen years later Marks and Miller (1964) again compared recall of sentences versus nonsentences. In this case, however, their aim was to show the importance of syntax and meaning as the critical variables for any model of language.

Marks and Miller began by selecting a number of sentences such as, *Fatal accidents deter careful drivers, Rapid flashes auger violent storms, Pink bouquets emit fragrant odors,* and *Noisy parties awake sleeping neighbors.* From these, they first constructed *anomalous sentences* by interchanging words between the original sentences to produce passages which seemed to follow the rules of syntax, but which were totally meaningless (e.g., *Rapid bouquets deter sudden neighbors*). Next they produced *anagram strings,* which consisted of the words of a single sentence presented in a scrambled order (e.g., *Rapid auger violent flashes storms*). Their idea was that anagram strings would be ungrammatical but might still preserve some of the original meaning. Finally, they both interchanged and scrambled words, to produce *word lists,* which were both meaningless and ungrammatical (e.g., *Rapid deter sudden bouquets neighbors*).

When examples of each of these forms were presented to subjects for memory over a series of five trials, recall performance exactly followed Marks and Miller's expectations. The results are shown in Figure 9.5. First, the normal sentences, which were both syntactically and semantically correct, produced the best performance. Second, as compared with performance for the word lists, syntax alone (anomalous sentences) and meaning alone (anagram strings) both facilitated recall to about the same degree. Further, the effects of syntax and of meaning seem to be additive; the combination of both, as represented by the normal sentences, yields better scores than either of them alone.

To be sure, Marks and Miller's experiment did not show *how* syntax and meaning facilitated recall, they merely showed that they did. The study was nevertheless important in its explicit recognition of meaning and syntax as psychological variables, as opposed to associative probability (cf. Fodor, Bever & Garrett, 1974, pg. 225).

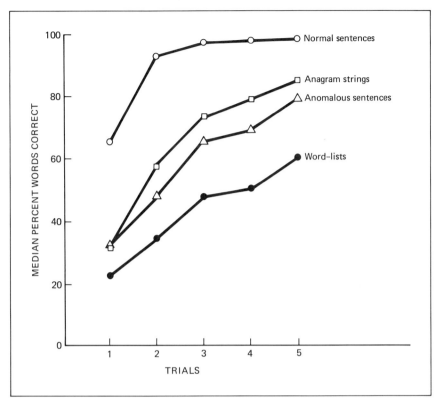

Figure 9.5   Median percent of total words correct for each of the four types of strings over five trials. A word was counted as correct regardless of its position in the string. (*Source:* L. E. Marks and G. A. Miller, The role of semantic and syntactic constraints in the memorization of English sentences. *Journal of Verbal Learning and Verbal Behavior,* 1964, 3: fig. 2, pg. 93. Reprinted by permission of Academic Press.)

Among the more interesting of the early experiments was one conducted by Savin and Perchonock (1965), who specifically set out to study the possible role of *transformational complexity* on sentence recall. In essence, their goal was to determine whether passive negative sentences (two transformations) would be harder to remember than either passive or negative sentences (one transformation), and whether these in turn would be more difficult than active declarative kernel sentences (zero transformations). However, since any fairly short, meaningful sentence will be recalled quite accurately, they had to take recourse to an indirect measure of retention difficulty.

The subjects heard a sentence spoken once, followed immediately by a string of eight unrelated nouns. For example, the subject might hear: *Did the boy throw the ball?—bush, horse, car, day, bed, rain, hat, green.* The assumption was that the more "space" the sentence occupied in memory, the less "space" would be available for storing the word list. The number of nouns remembered in addition to the sentence would thus serve as their estimate of the relative memory load required for different syntactic forms, even though the sentences themselves were recalled without error.

Savin and Perchonock's main findings fit very neatly into the standard transformational theory. For any sentence, recall difficulty was found to be a direct function of the number of transformations hypothetically required for its derivation from the kernel sentence. This and other experiments were generally interpreted as showing that the act of memorizing a sentence is a very active process indeed. Specifically, they suggested the following sequence of events: (1) the subject analyzes the presented sentence to determine its deep structure, as represented by its kernel form; (2) the subject stores in memory, not the surface structure, but the kernel sentence, plus the fact that it was, for example, a passive question; (3) on recall, the subject now goes through the reverse procedure, using the stored transformational rules to regenerate the original surface structure of the sentence as it was initially heard (cf. Miller, 1962; Mehler, 1963).

It was later realized that there were many problems with this particular experiment, not the least of which is the fact that, on average, complex sentences will be longer than simpler ones, simply in terms of the number of words one would have to remember. For this, and other reasons, the generality of their findings were called into question (cf. Mathews, 1968; Glucksberg & Danks, 1969; Wearing, 1970; Boakes & Lodwick, 1971).

No small difficulty with many of these experiments was the previously mentioned fact that descriptions of transformational systems seemed to have a life of their own. They grew in complexity, sophistication, and nuances at such a rate as to make many an otherwise interesting experiment frankly obsolete. That these experiments tended to concentrate on only very limited sets of transformations (passives, negations, etc.) was only one of the problems. More important, psychologists' attempts to simplify the linguistic formulations in order to fit them into workable experiments often found them offering "proof" for a position not in fact taken by the full theory (cf. Fodor, Bever & Garrett, 1974). The notion that sentence comprehension rests on a process of literally running through a set of transformations in reverse order (the so-called derivational theory of complexity) also seemed to become more and more untenable (see Fodor, Bever & Garrett, 1974, for a review of the literature on these and related questions).

We mention these criticisms to make clear that psycholinguistics research is still very much in a state of flux. It is certainly the case that syntactic structure is an important variable in sentence memory (cf. Miller, 1962; Mehler, 1963; Epstein, 1962; O'Connell, Turner & Onuska, 1968) and in the perceptual processing of heard speech (cf. Fodor & Bever, 1965; Garrett, Bever & Fodor, 1966; Wingfield & Klein, 1971; Wingfield, 1975).

On the other hand, some theoretical work as reviewed by, for example, Greene (1972), has called into question some of psycholinguistics' stronger claims for transformational grammar as a description of speakers' linguistic performance. Greene shares the views of others that, for example, the general concepts of deep and surface structure seem to rest on firmer ground than earlier notions of how transformational rules were used to get from one level to the other (Greene, 1972, pg. 173).

We must also recognize that the realities of everyday language experience will confound the simple interpretation of many of our experimental studies of language. A case in point is a study published by Goldman-Eisler and Cohen (1970) who conducted an analysis of the types of sentences people actually use in everyday fluent discourse.[4] In fact, simple declarative sentences were by far the most commonly used grammatical forms, accounting for some 70 to 80 percent of the sentences in their sample. The next most common were negatives (4 to 10 percent) and passives (0.7 to 11 percent). Passive negatives, they report, almost never occurred in their speech samples.

The point they wished to make was that any experiment which shows sentences of more complex syntactic forms to be harder to deal with by subjects than simpler ones, could simply be the result of different degrees of practice with these forms: ". . . the fact that declarative sentences belong to the class of learned and overlearned behavior, while N, P and NP were shown to be relatively infrequent, less practiced, indeed, rare forms of verbal behavior" (Goldman-Eisler & Cohen, 1970, pg. 193). On the other hand, it could equally be argued that simpler syntactic forms find more widespread everyday use precisely because they are easier to handle in terms of their transformational complexity!

Summary: Language as Rule Acquisition

The reader can now share the dilemma of a whole generation of psychologists, and others, who simply wanted to know how language was learned or, more properly, what it is children learn when we say they learn language. From the S-R tradition came the view that sentences represent chains of verbal associations, strengthened through their frequency of occurrence in past experience.

From the "new grammarians" came the view that we in fact learn rules of grammar which, in turn, can be used to generate the variety of possible sentences of our language.

---

[4] For a welcomed change from most studies, Goldman-Eisler and Cohen did not restrict their analysis to that standard experimental animal, the college undergraduate. The subjects used in their sample ranged from British members of Parliament (who used more passives and a greater variety of syntactic forms than the average speaker), to hospitalized schizophrenics (who used a narrower range of sentence structures and more negative constructions than the average speaker).

While this latter view was to predominate, the exact nature of these rules, and how they operate in linguistic behavior, remains a matter of continuing investigation.

Chomsky's theory of transformational grammar offered psychologists both a general view of the structure of language and a set of specific postulates regarding how this structure might be conceptualized. The theory makes an important distinction between the surface structure of a sentence, represented by the specific words of the sentence, and the deep structure, which corresponds to its underlying meaning.

As initially proposed, the transformational grammar was seen as composed of two elements. First, phrase-structure rules would be used to generate the basic, or kernel, sentence, which corresponds to the deep structure. The second element was seen as a series of transformational rules which could be used to expand on the kernel sentence to produce a variety of different surface structure syntactic forms corresponding to the same deep structure.

The earliest applications of the model to psychological performance postulated a neat symmetry in the use of transformational rules for both the production and the comprehension of sentences. Speech production would progress from the kernel sentence through a series of transformations to the surface structure, while sentence comprehension would reverse the transformational process to detect the underlying kernel sentence and deep structure.

The validity of the initial distinction between deep and surface structure still has strong support in the literature. The question of how one detects the deep structure from the surface structure, on the other hand, is still open to some debate.

The impact of Chomsky's generative grammar on the psychology of language, however, cannot be underestimated. As Greene (1972, pg. 189) has observed: (1) it called psychology's attention to the crucial importance of *linguistic creativity:* no theory of language can be considered adequate unless it at least attempts to account for language users' ability to produce an infinite number of sentences which have never before been heard or uttered; (2) it called psychology's attention to the true *complexity of language:* if Chomsky's generative grammar failed to provide all of the answers, it did convince psychology that it could no longer rely on the oversimple solutions of the past, however attractive they may have once appeared.

The rejection of linear, S-R models of language learning should not be taken to mean that learning, more broadly conceived, is not involved in early language acquisition. As we shall see in the final section of this chapter, learning is very much involved. The emphasis, however, has been shifted from postulated processes analogous to classical and operant conditioning in the S-R mode, to a concentration on the learning of *rules* and *ab-*

straction of principles, more analogous to the processes involved in studies of concept attainment.

The Grammar of Children

When a very young child produces a perfect utterance it tells us surprisingly little about his or her linguistic processes. This is because it may not be immediately apparent whether the correct response was produced through imitation, rule usage, or sheer luck. In fact, we generally learn more about children's language from the errors they make than from their correct responses. As we shall see, this fact has inspired the strategy behind a great deal of children's language research.

Some of the earliest indications that children are using rules come from the "errors" that children are prone to make. A typical 3-year-old, for example, may attempt to regularize our rather irregular language by producing an expression like "Take it to part," presumably by analogy to "Put it together." There would be no argument that this form was learned through imitation, any more than the child's use of *doed* for *did, goed* for *went,* or *foots (feets)* for *feet.* These very common errors are clearly a reflection of rudimentary attempts to apply learned rules. Interestingly, and perhaps significantly, we find that parents ordinarily do not devote much time to routinely correcting their children's grammatical errors. In fact, this is rarely the case. When a child asks a question or makes an observation, parents in real life more often than not either ignore the child or only answer the question. The following interactions, taken from a study by Brown and Hanlon (1970, pg. 49), show a mixed bag of correct and incorrect grammatical forms uttered by several different children, and their parents' reaction to them.

Child	*Parent*
Draw a boot paper.	That's right. Draw a boot on paper.
Mama isn't boy, he girl.	That's right.
Her curl my hair.	Um hmm.
And Walt Disney comes on Tuesday.	No, he does not.
There's the animal farmhouse.	No, that's a lighthouse.

In these examples, we can see that the parents tended to respond primarily to the content, or "truth value," of the child's utterances, rather than to their grammatical form. As a consequence, some utterances with grammatical errors can bring parental approval, while those spoken in correct form may not.

As we shall see, parents are nevertheless very much involved in their children's development of language. Their role in the process, however, is a very subtle one.

Our analysis of rule acquisition by children will first consider rules of word formation (morphology) and then rules for the formation of sentences (syntax). In the final section we will examine current thinking on the role of the parents' language as a model for their children's language development.

RULES OF ENGLISH MORPHOLOGY

A *morpheme* is defined as the smallest linguistic unit which conveys meaning. As often as not, morphemes thus correspond to words; *dog, cat,* and *man* are all morphemes. Compound words, however, may be composed of several morphemes, such as *scarecrow* and *baseball,* which each consist of two morphemes (*scare + crow; base + ball*). Finally, we also have word elements such as plural endings (*s, es*) which, although not "words," certainly do convey meaning. These are referred to as *bound morphemes* since, while they qualify as morphemes in the sense of having meaning, they must always be "bound" to other morphemes and cannot stand alone. Thus, the word *dogs* is composed of two morphemes: the free morpheme, *dog,* and the bound morpheme, *s*.

We can formalize morphological rules with notations such as: "Words ending in voiced consonants are pluralized by adding a /z/ sound (as in *dog/z/*), and words ending in a voiceless consonant are pluralized by adding an /s/ sound (as in *cat/s/*)."

When a given child correctly says "one dog, two dog/z/," however, it may not be apparent whether the child is utilizing the plural rule for the *dog* morpheme, or whether he or she has simply learned two separate items of vocabulary: *dog* and *dog/z/*. It must be remembered that this operation is performed on sound pattern alone, long before the child has learned to read. This is a limited example of the larger question we asked earlier: what is it the child learns when we say the child learns language?

A simple, but ingenious solution to this problem was found some years ago by Jean Berko (1958). Berko devised a series of pictures of cartoonlike imaginary animals whose names or activities were labeled with nonsense words. For example, children were shown a picture of an imaginary animal and were told: "This is a *wug.*" They were then shown a picture of two of them side by side and were told: "Now there are two of them. There are two . . ." (see Figure 9.6). The great majority of the children, who ranged in age from 4 to 7, responded without hesitation with *wugs,* using the voiced

This is a WUG.

Now there is another one.
There are two of them.
There are two _____ .

Figure 9.6   The use of imaginary creatures and artificial language to study acquisition of linguistic rules by children. (*Source:* Based on J. Berko, The child's learning of English morphology. *Word,* 1958, 14: 150–177.)

/z/ ending as appropriate. We can be sure in this case that they were demonstrating rule utilization and not repeating a form previously learned through imitation, since this name was made up especially for the experiment.

Berko studied a variety of word forms. A picture of a man with a pitcher on his head was accompanied by: "This man knows how to *spow.* He is *spowing.* He did it yesterday. Yesterday he . . ." (answer: *spowed*). Children were shown a picture of another man balancing a ball on his nose. "This is a man who knows how to *zib.* What is he doing? He is . . ." (answer: *zibbing*). "What would you call a man whose job it is to *zib?*" The distribution of the actual responses given for this last item are most instructive. All the adults questioned and 11 percent of the children gave *zibber.* Eleven percent gave *zibbingman,* 5 percent said *zibman,* 35 percent had no answer, and the remainder, demonstrating pitfalls of working with children, simply answered *clown.*

The use of such artificial languages, which insure that the children cannot respond with previously learned word forms, has shown that children as young as 4 or 5 years have largely mastered an impressive amount of the rules relating to English words. Not only are children invariably consistent in their "errors," but children of a given age group often show more consistency in rule application than do adults similarly tested.

A possible sequence in acquiring these rules may well involve initially the learning of some morpheme compounds as separate items of vocabulary before the endings can be extended by analogy to new words. Studying children between the ages of 2 to 3 years, Miller and Ervin (1964) contrasted the ages by which children could reliably pluralize real words (*blocks, blocks; boy, boys*), and nonsense words (*bik, biks; kie, kies*). While the size of the age gap varied, pluralization of real words in all cases preceded that of nonsense words.

Implicit in these investigations is the suggestion that children of certain ages are utilizing the fact that sound patterns of words are divisible into smaller units, and that these units are common to the sound patterns of other words. This ability, immediately relevant when children learn to read and write, has been examined by Bruce (1964). In his studies, children were required to make a simple phonic analysis of spoken words. His results paradoxically appeared to suggest that children tend to treat words as holistic units rather than as the sum of individual components.

Using words well within the speaking vocabulary of the 5- to 9-year-old English school children he studied, a word such as *start* would be presented orally, with the instructions to say what word would remain if the *t* were removed. In a similar manner Bruce also presented words with elisions from the beginning, such as (*n*)*ice*, and in the most difficult case, from the middle of words, such as *s*(*t*)*and*.

Among Bruce's specific findings was that such a phonic analysis is difficult in the extreme below the age of 7, an observation consistent with other suggestions that this mental age level may well be a qualification for the best use of phonics instruction. As is so common in educational practice, although children from classes where phonic instruction was stressed did better at the task than those from classes where it was specifically avoided, by the age of 9 they were all roughly showing the same level of performance.

The generally holistic nature of words for all the children is exemplified by the response of one 8½-year-old who was given the word *nest* and asked what would be left if the *s* were removed. The child replied: "I can't actually do it. You see, I can't say the last letter without the middle."

The apparent paradox between these findings and those of Berko, which showed good sound analysis by the children, is that Bruce's experiment required within-morpheme segmentation. While children of these ages—like most of their elders—could not be expected to formally define a morpheme, the psychological reality of the morpheme for them is nevertheless clear.

THE ACQUISITION OF SYNTAX

To the extent that children utilize certain grammatical rules to produce their phrases and sentences, our next step must be to specify the nature of these rules. The most fruitful approach to the study of children's grammar, however, has not been to analyze its departures from correct adult usage, as one might do to trace its progress toward the development of "good grammar." The approach more frequently taken in language research has been to analyze a child's speech so as to determine the linguistic rules he or she actually is using (rather than should be using) to generate his or her sentences. In this context grammar retains the earlier definition of rules for word combinations which are used consistently by the child. Such rules, a child's *generative grammar*, can serve as a productive hypothesis of exactly what it is the child learns when we say he or she learns language. In doing so, we must reject the usual form class labels of "noun," "verb," and so forth. On the one hand, a sentence like "Daddy go bye-bye" may for a particular child represent one "word" which defies categorization in any adult grammar. On the other hand, a child who approaches you with a box of toys and says "ball?" may not be using a "common count noun." The single word *ball* may for this child represent virtually the full sentence, "Will you play ball with me?"

A Grammar of Telegraphic Speech

If we were to characterize the two-word utterances of a typical child in the second year, we might well refer to it as *telegraphic speech*, as we described it earlier. That is, their utterances tend to be abbreviated forms which leave out function words and use only *content* words. Somehow, these children seem to recognize which words convey the greatest amount of information, and the order in which they should be delivered (Brown & Fraser, 1963). Telegraphic speech, whether used by the adult in sending a wire or by a 2-year-old child in daily conversation, represents an economy of style with a maximum of content.

What are the rules that children of this age may be using to produce this level of discourse? A typical example of an attempt to write such a grammar is that of Martin Braine (1963a, 1963b), who analyzed the spontaneous utterances of a particular 23-month-old child who at the time was producing a fund of two-word sentences. Braine's first step was to transcribe a good body of the child's speech and then to classify the child's utterances into what appeared to be similar sentence types. Here are some examples:

want ball	that ball
want baby	that baby
want train	that train
want chair	that chair

Braine proposed that this child's grammar might be represented by two major form classes or "parts of speech." He referred to one class as *pivot words* (also called *operators* or *modifiers*). These are few in number, occur in many word combinations, and are associated with particular positions in the utterances. In the above example, *that* and *want* are pivot words. The second form class, which has a greater number of different members occurring with the limited number of pivot words, Braine simply called "x-words". They are also called *open words*. In this example they are the common nouns *ball, baby, train,* and *chair.*

Thus, rather than learning all *want* plus noun combinations as separate associations, it can be argued that the child at this stage of development learns that *want* is, as it were, a pivot word with a given position, and that the remainder are x-words. With this simple grammar the child has a powerful tool for the generation of numerous novel, but "grammatical," sentences.

Using such a formulation, we can now characterize the early stages of the child's language learning as increasing the language structurally by classifying new pivot words, and verbally by adding new x-words. The pivot words, furthermore, are relatively slow to take on new members as compared with the open words.

The way in which children begin to grasp the concept that words "go together" in a grammatical class can be seen in the extensive analysis of a 2½-year-old's bedtime monologues as reported by Weir (1963). In these monologues one can find numerous instances of the child studiously substituting words for each other in common frames, such as "what color blanket? what color light? what color glass?" or "there is the light; where is the light? here is the light." The child almost seems to be practicing with the same dedication as an experimental subject learning a serial list of nonsense syllables, but with one large exception. The child is not so much practicing a chain of verbal associations as exploring, testing, and verifying tentative rules for word combinations.

The Child's Model in Language Acquisition

While it seems evident that even the youngest children have acquired a rudimentary grammar, it is equally evident that it is not the grammar of the adult world. Most parents, of course, do simplify their constructions when talking to their young children. Systematic analyses of parent-child interchanges show that simple, fairly redundant, declarative sentences predominate in parents' speech to their children (Snow, 1972). Indeed, even young children seem intuitively to tailor their syntactic forms when talking to still younger children. In one study, for example, it was found that 4-year-olds tend to use simpler constructions when talking to a younger brother or sister than they use when talking to their parents (Shatz & Gelman, 1973).

No matter how much parents may studiously attempt to use only "child-size" language around their children, it is primarily the normal adult speech with its pauses, clauses, and involuted syntax that the child most frequently hears. While simple imitation of heard utterances is not the answer, the child must at the same time be using some model for his or her language acquisition. One intriguing possibility was suggested some time ago by Roger Brown (Brown & Bellugi, 1964; Brown, 1965). It sees three important stages in the child's acquisition of syntax: a stage of *reduction*, a stage of *expansion*, and a stage of *induction*.

IMITATION AND REDUCTION. As the child hears the rather complex adult speech, the child tries to retain what has been heard and to map it on to his or her simpler linguistic forms. It is only in this way that understanding can take place.

According to Brown and Bellugi, the child's attempts to accomplish this are marked by a systematic reduction of the adult speech, bringing it within the child's limited span. This is accomplished primarily by omitting function words that convey little information, while still maintaining word order.

This systematic reduction was illustrated by the attempts of a 25-month-old to repeat the sentences of an adult. "I showed you the book" became "I show book." "I can see a cow" was repeated as "see cow," "Where does it go?" became "Where go?", and so forth. Not only was the uniformity of this reduction to telegraphic speech immediately apparent, but the average number of words correctly reported increased systematically with age. As this increase occurred, it took the form of now including the less critical words omitted by younger children. Their speech, in other words, became "less telegraphic" as, if we may say, each word came to "cost" less for the child to retain and to produce.

IMITATION AND EXPANSION. A later stage is marked by the parents now taking a more active part in the child's language development by imitating the phrases that their children say and expanding them to fully grammatical sentences. Thus, when the child says "Katie lunch," the parent may repeat, "Katie *is having* lunch." One of the examples of a parental response in the Brown and Hanlon study cited earlier shows a typical case of this. The child's utterance "Draw boot paper" brought "That's right. Draw a boot on paper" (see page 261). This stage, an exact reversal of the reduction process, seems extremely common in parent-child interactions.

The process of imitation and expansion, however, is only one strategy parents can be observed to use. A variation on this theme occurs when parents, instead of directly imitating their child's speech in expanded form, react to it as if it were correct adult usage. When the child says, "Katie lunch," the parent simply carries on the conversation with something like, "I'm having lunch too." The end effect of supplying an expanded model, however, is essentially the same.

Both expansion strategies seem to be commonly used by parents, and studies suggest that both have a positive effect on children's syntactic development (cf. Nelson, Carskaddon & Bonvillian, 1973).

INDUCTION OF LATENT STRUCTURE. The final stage is marked by the child's production of utterances which could not possibly be imitations in any direct form of the parents' speech. It is at this stage that the child can be found trying out the generative rules he or she has extracted from the model speaker, with the child's often limited success reflected in the type of logical errors previously discussed.

THE SEARCH FOR DEEP STRUCTURE

The so-called pivot grammar, and the studies which followed, were pioneer experiments in the cognitive approach to children's language. On the other hand, they are only a beginning. Brown (1970, 1973), for example, emphasizes that describing the two-word phrases of young children in terms of a pivot word plus an open word ("that book"), or an open word plus an open word ("mommy lunch"), could, at best, be only a surface description of the utterance. The underlying meaning, or deep structure, would be more complex than such pivot grammars could imply.

We hinted at this problem earlier when we noted that the words used by young children may have different meanings to them than their formal structure might indicate. Our example was a child's use of the word *ball*, which might sometimes represent adult noun usage, as "this is a ball," or sometimes a verb, as "Will you play with me?" These single-word utterances (often called *holophrases*) are thus susceptible to a variety of meanings, depending on the context in which they are spoken. As later writers were to note, even the two-word phrases of the sort analyzed by Braine can have more than one meaning. In a single day, for example, Bloom (1970) heard a youthful subject use the phrase, "Mommy sock," first with *mommy* as a possessive (the child was indicating her mother's sock), and later as an agent (the child's mother was helping her put on her own sock). In both cases, the phrase "Mommy sock" was, for this child, used appropriately.

These types of problems led writers such as Brown to argue that one should approach childrens' early language in terms of the functional significance of their words, rather than in terms of word classes. Specifically, Brown reinforced the notion that similar surface structures of even two-word utterances can represent a number of different semantic operations. They can, for example, reflect a *reference operation*, in which the single pivot plus open word surface form can be used to *name* ("that doggy"), to refer to an *action* ("all gone doggy"), or simply to signal something of *special interest* ("hi doggy"). Similarly, open word plus open word forms can express what Brown calls *relational operations*. These might include identifying *possession* ("Adam doggy"), specifying an *attribute* ("big doggy"), and so forth.

The major point, of course, is that the early pivot grammars, although an important step, share the weakness of any linguistic description, either for the child *or* the adult, which relies solely on surface structure. The pivot grammars have been important, however, in showing that children's language, although simpler than adult language, is no less governed by systematic rule usage. It must be these rules that the child learns when the child learns language.

Readers interested in treatments of child grammar which have made an attempt to take into account both surface structure and deep structure can find good examples in Bloom (1970, 1971) and a more complete discussion of the issues involved in Brown (1973).

SUMMARY

The study of children's language acquisition has followed closely behind research on adult language, with its emphasis on rule usage, and a major distinction between deep structure and surface structure.

One of the earliest systematic studies of rule acquisition by children dealt with the rules of English morphology, the grammar of word formation. Studies have shown that by the age of 4 or 5, children have mastered an impressive amount of the rules relating to pluralization, verb endings, noun compounding, and so forth. The process seems to parallel concept learning as previously described, with specific instances exemplifying the principle, being learned before the rule is abstracted and generalized to new instances. At this point, the child can use correct word endings even in the presence of artificial words never before heard.

A well-known attempt to write a generative grammar of children's language was a pivot grammar for the description of children's telegraphic speech.

The way in which the child models his or her language on the more complex structure of adult grammar was seen in terms of three stages: reduction, where the child imitates the adult sentence with a loss of low-information words which convey little meaning; expansion, in which the adult repeats the child's utterance in a more full syntactic form; and induction, where the child now attempts to apply his or her rule hypotheses to new linguistic situations. It is at this point that one hears "errors" in the form of *doed* for *did, goed* for *went,* or *foots* for *feet.*

Although pivot grammars represented a good beginning to the formal specification of the structure of children's language, they have more recently been criticized for concentrating on the surface structure of the child's language, at the expense of analyzing the deep structure.

The goal of the attempts to write children's grammars, however, remains unchanged. Rather than to describe children's language as an "inferior," or "incorrect," version of adult usage, current goals are to determine the rules actually being used by the child to guide his or her utterances.

part four
Human
Memory

chapter 10

In Search
of the
Mind's Eye:
MEMORY AND
EXPERIENCE

How good is human memory? How accurately can we expect a person to recall events which occurred hours, days, or years before? In this abstract form, this is probably a question without answer. It surely depends on the individual and the type of material involved. It is, as they say, as pointless as asking how many swallows are necessary to herald the arrival of spring. Perhaps we can put the question better in a more specific context.

Imagine the problem of a juror trying to assess the accuracy of a witness' testimony concerning some past event. Assume further, that we have complete confidence in the witness' basic honesty. There will be no attempt at deception. Our only question is the accuracy of recollection, and the guidelines one might use in making this judgment. We would not want the testimony to be either too vague or suspiciously too rich in detail. It should be reasonable and consistent with what we already know from other sources.

And finally, it might help if the testimony were delivered with spontaneity and confidence.

Unfortunately, confidence and reasonableness are no guarantee of accuracy. Nor is consistency with the testimony of other witnesses. Errors of recall are seldom random, and even a majority of witnesses can misinterpret or misremember factual details in exactly the same way. Numerous studies of prearranged incidents, which allow a check on accuracy, show just these results. First, errors can be, and very frequently are, shared by more than one witness. Second, witnesses often show a striking readiness to give confident and detailed reports of events which were only casually observed at the time. Finally, leading a witness with specific questions may not only be of little help to accurate recollection, but it can tend to yield more misinformation than is typically associated with free recall. This latter tendency is especially true for adolescents and young children. In a cross-examination setting, children may give false positive answers to as many as one out of four "catch" questions (Stern, 1938; Talland, 1968).

Why will many otherwise honest witnesses commit themselves to details of which they are unsure? Why is there this readiness to "recall" information which was, in a real sense, never learned in the first place? The answer to this question is surprisingly straightforward. In everyday situations, people do not passively absorb information like a sponge soaking up water. We give meaning to our experience, impose a pattern, and relate it to things already familiar. This offers not only an anchor for retention, but allows for rich and vivid detail in recall by bringing to bear other knowledge and experience. Recollecting the color of a schoolhouse attended during early childhood may be nothing more or less than a recollection that it was brick, combined with a knowledge that brick is generally red. In short, there is a creative quality to normal memory behavior which ordinarily works to our advantage. When successful, we receive praise for a good memory. When inference fails, we are accused of confabulation or worse.

Reconstruction Versus Reproduction

To his credit, Ebbinghaus (1885) recognized these problems when he decided to undertake the study of human memory and learning (see Chapter 7). The way he solved the problem was to avoid it: he deliberately concentrated his efforts on the rote learning of materials as devoid as possible of meaning and the influence of past experience. His hope was to avoid the seemingly unmanageable complexity of ordinary memory behavior, while at the same time bringing to its study the sort of uncontaminated purity and tight experimental control then gaining wide use in the physical sciences. The result was not only the introduction of the ubiquitous nonsense syllable but a turning point in the study of memory. His concentration on rote verbal learning contributed in no small part to the limited view of memory as nothing but the *reproduction* of learned associations. Consistent with later behaviorist learning theory, it was to pervade psychological thought on memory for years to come.

BARTLETT: A STRATEGY OF RESEARCH

As Ebbinghaus chose one strategy of research, the British psychologist Sir Frederick Bartlett (1932) chose another. To take Ebbinghaus's course would be to eliminate the very aspects of memory Bartlett wanted to study. But a study of "real" memory in a natural setting might result in nothing more than a collection of anecdotes whose true accuracy and validity could be as dubious as that of our wayward witness. His solution was also a compromise; yet it differed from those earlier studies in two important respects. First, he made extensive use of memory for very meaningful material such as pictures and short stories. Second, he concentrated most of his efforts not on various conditions of learning but on the nature of the errors which seemed to be the most common in the recall. While the approach of Ebbinghaus and his followers in verbal learning might model a student memorizing multiplication tables or a foreign language vocabulary, Bartlett's goal was conceptual memory, based on meaning and understanding of the learned materials.

In some cases, Bartlett had people read through a short story for understanding, and then tested their recall as they retold the story later at various time intervals. He referred to these conditions as *repeated reproduction.* In other cases, people would read a similar story, but this time recite it from memory to a second person who would then retell it to a third, and so on. This was called *serial reproduction.* It mirrors the sorts of losses in detail, embellishments, and shifts of emphasis which are common to ordinary gossip or the spread of rumor.

Bartlett was intrigued to discover that the character of the distortions in both repeated and in serial reproduction are almost identical. It seemed clear to him that memory is ordinarily more *reconstructive* than reproductive. He saw memory not simply as the reproduction of learned material but as a dynamic process in which reception, categorization, and reconstruction are all heavily influenced by past experience and the individual's understanding of what he or she has learned.

Schemata in Memory

From these early studies, Bartlett developed an elaborate theory whose central theme was the reconstructive nature of ordinary memory. Newly acquired information is mapped onto a preexisting organization of concepts and beliefs he called mental schemata. (The dictionary tells us that *schemata*, the plural of *schema*, are "plans," or "frameworks.") These schemata are not static. They change and develop as they are modified and made more complete by the acquisition of new information. His studies emphasized that they may also be individually unique: two persons experiencing the same event will later reproduce similar recall only to the extent that their schemata are similar or at least allow for equivalent mapping. In other words, when a person reproduces meaningful material exactly as it was first experienced, this is more a happy coincidence of a valid transformation than evidence that no transformations of the input have occurred.

One can illustrate the distinction between reproductive and reconstructive memory by giving two groups of volunteers the same list of ten unrelated words to memorize. One group studies the list as an exercise in rote learning. By contrast, the second group is instructed to invent some simple story which will include all of the words on the list. Both groups are given the same amount of time: the rote learning group to rehearse the list; the story group to integrate the words into a meaningful narrative. These procedures are followed for a total of twelve 10-word lists. The difference is dramatic. While a rote learning group might recall 17 of the original words, the members of a story group can average correct recall of over 100 of the original 120 words (Bower & Clark, 1969).

The way the story group apparently handled the task was first to recall the general theme of the story and then to use this theme to reconstruct the original word list. In Bartlett's terms, the story themes, or schemata, might vary widely from individual to individual. The end product of faithful reconstruction is nevertheless the same.

Once we begin to look for it, evidence in support of the reconstructive view of memory is easy to obtain. Bransford and Franks (1971) have shown that errors in recognition memory for sentences typically result from subjects falsely recognizing new sentences that carry the same theme as the ones actually presented. In a similar way, Sulin and Dooling (1974) had subjects read short biographical passages about famous (or infamous) people (e.g., Helen Keller and Adolf Hitler). Their subjects showed a common tendency to report having read information which, although not appearing in the studied passages, were items of common knowledge about the people in question. The longer the recall interval, the greater was this tendency.

These experiments may seem somewhat artificial, in the sense that they involve memory for verbal materials by college students who were fully aware that they were taking part in an experiment. However, the implications of these studies readily generalize to more natural settings. Memory schemata are ordinarily preexisting, and their use is no more obvious to the user than to an observer. Figure 10.1 comes closer to the point. It shows the sorts of drawings children of three different age groups give when they observe a tilted jar of water and are later asked to draw it from memory (Piaget & Inhelder, 1956). The mental operations these children are performing

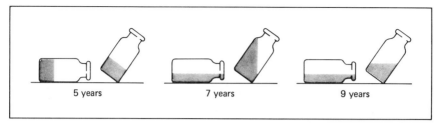

| 5 years | 7 years | 9 years |

Figure 10.1   The ability of children of various ages to draw the level of water in a tilted jar from memory. (*Source:* From *Psychological Theories and Human Learning: Kongor's Report,* by G. R. Lefrancois, fig. 3, pg. 39. Copyright © 1972 by Wadsworth Publishing Company, Inc. Reprinted by permission of the publisher, Brooks/Cole Publishing Company, Monterey, California.)

can of course only be inferred. We do know from other studies by Piaget and his associates, however, that the age of 9 typically marks acquisition of the concept of *horizontal.* Thus, when the 9-year-olds in this study remembered how the water level looked, they also knew the way it *should* look. The argument we wish to make here is not whether we should call this performance a test of memory, on the one hand, versus a test of knowledge, on the other. Rather, our point is that the interaction between memory and experience is an inherent one, and at the very heart of human memory.

Memory and the Sequence of Learning

Past experience and prior knowledge do exert a profound influence on the way things are remembered; memories will also be modified by such personal factors as attitude, belief, and our own sense of internal logic. Following the flow of information through the sequence of learning as outlined in Chapter 2 should show how this works. The three stages were *input, storage,* and *retrieval.*

1. INPUT.   In Chapter 2 we looked closely at the characteristics of the input stage in the sequence, and the way it operates to prevent the nervous system from being overloaded by the simultaneous arrival of too much information. The first limitation was imposed by a selective filter which directs focal attention to only one stimulus source at a time. Second, that information which does pass the filter is held initially in a temporary, limited-capacity "buffer" memory, commonly referred to as short-term memory. The limited capacity of this short-term memory puts an upper limit on both the quantity and the speed with which incoming information can be understood and, hence, assimilated into more permanent memory. There is a consequence of these ecologically necessary input limitations. The specific sequence of events in most ongoing activity, or even the individual words of a running conversation, arrive too rapidly for effective analysis and storage in anything like a verbatim form.

To cope with this inability to retain all details of an ongoing event, the observer must rely on another ability, that of rapidly summarizing or interpreting major themes and patterns as they develop. Individual elements of an event are retained only long enough to abstract essential features. It is ordinarily these abstractions from the specifics, rather than the specifics themselves, which are stored and retained in long-term memory. The exception will be only the most salient of specific details, or those which could not easily be reconstructed from the context. These might be proper names, unusual verbal expressions, or unusual or unexpected events.

It follows that when a person later attempts to translate abstracted features and themes back into a word-by-word narrative, the narrative will not only be necessarily in the person's own words but can, at very best, be only a faithful reproduction of the events as initially perceived and interpreted by the individual. This will be true no matter how deceptively literal the report may appear to be ("I said to him . . . then he said to me . . .") The effects of such transformations are bound to be subtle and easily overlooked in day-to-day recollections, especially when the report is a reasonable one, and the changes are inconsequential.

In extreme cases, the consequences of initial misinterpretation can be both noticeable and serious. Our own experience, not to mention courtroom testimony of the type discussed, bears adequate witness to this. One is reminded of the early study by Carmichael, Hogan, and Walter (1932) who showed unsuspecting subjects a set of ambiguous figures, each given a name to suggest one or another likely interpretation. Figure 10.2 shows four examples of the figures they used, and the influence of the alternative names on later attempts to draw the figures from memory.

2. STORAGE. The second stage of the sequence is the more permanent storage of information for future reference. Here there is a second opportunity for distortion and qualitative change. This occurs as the newly acquired information is mapped onto the schemata of existing knowledge and belief. Bartlett saw this interaction as a dynamic one, where inconsistencies may be reconciled by a selective forgetting of incongruities or by a major restructuring of the input to conform with what is already familiar or expected. Memories tend to become simplified (*normalization*) or transformed to fit existing knowledge (*assimilation*); however, this interaction works both ways. As existing schemata can influence the way in which new experience is retained in memory, so too can these experiences modify the structure of the schemata themselves. The point to keep in mind is that such transformations are normal memory functions. They allow not only for efficiency in memory storage but for the building up of *systems* of knowledge. Distortions in memory are by no means limited to emotional or ego-threatening experience.

A case in point is an early study by Davis and Sinha (1950). As part of a

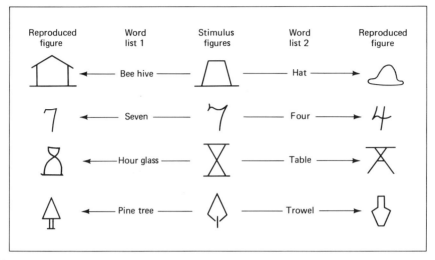

Reproduced figure	Word list 1	Stimulus figures	Word list 2	Reproduced figure
	←— Bee hive ——		—— Hat ——→	
	←—— Seven ——		—— Four ——→	
	←——Hour glass——		—— Table ——→	
	←—— Pine tree ——		—— Trowel ——→	

Figure 10.2   Subjects were shown ambiguous stimulus figures which were given either the names shown in Word List 1 or Word List 2. When later redrawn from memory the reproduced figures suggested systematic distortions heavily influenced by the verbal labels. (*Source:* L. Carmichael, H. P. Hogan, and A. A. Walter, An experimental study of the effect of language on the reproduction of visually perceived form. *Journal of Experimental Psychology,* 1932, 15: 80.)

larger experiment, they had volunteers read a series of short stories, one of which described a Dutch wedding that brought together two long feuding families for the first time in years. While the meeting did not result in open warfare, it certainly was an uneasy truce against a background of smoldering enmity just short of violence. Three days after reading this story, the same group of people were shown a number of paintings. One of them was Pieter Brueghel's *The Village Wedding,* which also depicts a Dutch wedding feast. By contrast with the story, the painting shows a scene of boisterous celebration and camaraderie.

As in any good confidence trick, Davis and Sinha (obviously keeping their motivation to themselves) had "set up" their subjects. Of interest, of course, was the degree and manner in which the memory of the short story might interact with recall of the painting when the subjects were later asked to describe it from memory. While recall accuracy was generally good, a group of harmless musicians in the painting were vividly remembered as servants with weapons. A gathering of guests at the back of the hall was somehow recalled as an "unruly throng."

Not every feature of an ongoing event can be apprehended and retained. What will be is also determined by the simple pragmatic question of what the person believes may later be demanded in recall. If you vaguely notice a person leaving a bank and getting into a car, your memory for detail will not be the same as if you know you are witnessing a crime and will later have to give evidence in court.

One is reminded of that tragic character in Peter Ustinov's *Add a Dash of Pity* who was an eyewitness to a crime without recognizing it for what it was. Devastated by the police's annoyance, and his own sense of failure, the man spent the rest of his life recording all daily events in a small note-book—just on the chance that one of them might later turn out to have been important. The thought of trying to retain everything is sufficiently absurd to have supplied Ustinov with an entertaining theme. It is also the raison d'être of simplification and reduction in memory.

The greater likelihood of storage for material of potential future useful-ness can be seen in terms of so-called open and closed learning tasks. Marked retention differences are found when students are led to believe they are involved in a one-time task (closed learning), versus a belief that the same material will be essential to some related future task (open learn-ing) (cf. Nuttin & Greenwald, 1968; Longstreth, 1970).

3. RETRIEVAL.   The transformations of encoding and storage yield the fragments and themes from which later recollections will be constructed. Recall thus involves the task of translating these fragments back into a co-herent and reasonable account of the experienced event. It is now these fragments which are the stimuli, subject to the same potential for misinter-pretation as the original inputs. Indeed, just as Carmichael, Hogan, and Walter induced systematic distortions by naming ambiguous figures when they were presented, the very same distortions can be obtained by giving the names at the time of the requested recall (Hanawalt & Demarest, 1939; Prentice, 1954).

The forgetting of some features, combined with undue attention to others of special personal significance, can lead to a drastic shift in the en-tire emphasis of a recollection. Accounts can include the interpolation of events which did occur but perhaps not when or as recalled. We can, for example, vividly recall a person's argument at a particular meeting which he or she in fact never attended, or recall a casual remark embellished with fine points and detail absent from the original. The more knowledge we have of the person, the more likely this is to happen. The analogy between this phenomenon and a 9-year-old's "recollection" of the water level in a tilted jar is close and relevant.

We can now return to the issue of leading, or "catch," questions, as we referred to them in the context of a witness' testimony. The principle to bear in mind is that the "memory" we wish to interrogate is, more often than not, fragmentary. Further, the more fragmentary the memory, the more susceptible it will be to transformation during retrieval.

A good place to begin is with a witness' testimony regarding the speed of an automobile involved in a traffic accident. First, the unfortunate frequency of such incidents makes the problem important. Second, people are not very good judges of speed. For a car traveling at 12 mph, for example, speed estimates of observers can easily range from as little as 10 to as much as 50 mph (Marshall, 1969, pg. 39).

With the cooperation of the Seattle Police Department, Loftus and Palmer (1974) obtained realistic films of staged and actual car accidents which were shown to a large group of volunteers. After each film, the subjects were asked to give an account of the accident as they remembered it and to answer a series of specific questions. Among these questions was the one Loftus and Palmer considered most crucial: "About how fast were the cars going when they hit each other?"

All of the subjects saw the same films, and all were asked the same question. The difference was in how the question was framed. For different groups of subjects, the word *hit* was replaced by the words *contacted, bumped, collided,* or *smashed.* Listed below are the average speed estimates for each of the groups. (The true speed of the filmed cars ranged from 20 to 40 mph.)

"About how fast were the two cars going when they_____?"	Mean speed Estimate
contacted	31.8
hit	34.0
bumped	38.1
collided	39.3
smashed	40.8

It would appear that cars which "smashed" were, on average, traveling nine mph faster than cars which simply "contacted."

Is speed the only recall we can shift with appropriate (or inappropriate) wording? In a follow-up study, Loftus and Palmer tested memory one week after subjects saw a filmed crash in which the cars were described as having either "hit" or "smashed." In this case, the crucial question was whether the subjects remembered seeing any broken glass in the accident. The cars described as having "hit" each other produced an average of 14 percent "yes" responses; those described as having "smashed" yielded 32 percent "yes's." (You may have already correctly guessed that there was in fact *no* broken glass in the film seen by these subjects.)

As you read these results, be aware that the subjects in this study were university students—presumably healthy young adults of above average intelligence. Remember also that they had no motive to deceive, no personal stake in the filmed accidents they observed. This, they would assure you, is exactly what they "remembered."

SUMMARY

The early research of Bartlett (1932) stressed that normal memory is ordinarily more reconstructive than reproductive. His typical studies involved a comparison between the changes in a story passed on from one person to another (serial reproduction) and a story repeatedly told from memory by the same person on subsequent occasions (repeated reproduction).

In both cases he found a tendency for narratives to become simplified (normalization) or transformed to fit preexisting knowledge or beliefs (assimilation). Bartlett used the term schemata to describe this preexisting framework onto which new experience is mapped.

Systematic changes in memory can occur at all three stages in the sequence of learning. At input, limitations of selective attention and short-term memory prevent the intake of all but a sampling of ongoing experience. In the process of storage, this information must be translated into a general theme plus outstanding detail for organization within existing knowledge, or schemata. Finally, retrieval allows for further transformation of recollection as the stored experience is reconstructed into a reasonable and coherent account.

Organization in Memory

One of the major reasons why the studies of Bartlett give such a different picture of memory than those of Ebbinghaus and other students of rote verbal learning is that organization in memory depends heavily on the kinds of materials involved and on the way in which they are initially learned. The discussion of organization in Chapter 7, for example, was limited largely to association chaining, where items learned as sequential associations are recalled in the same way. Each item in the chain serves to cue the next one in an essentially linear, left-to-right fashion. Ask someone how many days there are in April, and wait for the telltale lip movements as they spell out, "Thirty days hath September . . ."

Although important to rote learning, chaining is a relatively unique form of organization. Ordinarily, recall is cued by associations which are conceptual rather than sequential in character. The left-to-right chaining of verbal learning is replaced by associations based on meaningful, and often abstract, relationships determined by similarities of context, essential properties, or importance to the individual. One example of this is seen in the effects of contextual cues in recall.

CONTEXTUAL CUES IN RECALL

Contextual effects in recall can both facilitate and inhibit response availability. Talland (1968), for example, cites the common occurrence of a person who has seemingly forgotten a first language but soon recovers fluency when he or she hears it spoken. It is also the case that higher test scores can be expected if students are examined in the same room in which the material was originally taught. Indeed, even nonsense syllables show better recall if each is originally learned on a different colored background and then tested on the same color. Significantly poorer performance is obtained if the colors are switched (see related experiments by Dallett & Wilcox, 1968, and by Strand, 1970).

For the true flavor of the effect, however, an incident from the autobiography of the novelist Nabokov (1966) stands out better than any published experiment. Nabokov recounts a surprise visit he paid to his former college tutor at Cambridge, a man he had not seen for many years. Predictably, his old tutor had absolutely no recollection of him. That is, until Nabokov accidentally knocked over a tea tray, just as he had done when they first met. The tutor's memory of Nabokov, and everything about him, returned in a flash (Talland, 1968).

ASSOCIATIONS IN MEMORY

To say that memory is guided by associations sets the question, rather than supplies the answer, as to how these associations work. The reason this has been difficult to discover is because associations, like Bartlett's personal schemata, can be as unique as the persons having them. Spilling a tea tray may trigger recollection for Nabokov and his tutor, but surely for no other two people in the world.

Weston Bousfield set out to study how associations work in memory by focusing on categorical organizations which most people would be expected to share (Bousfield, 1953; Bousfield, Cohen & Whitmarsh, 1958). His hope was that one could use his simple paradigm as a model for the more complex associations of everyday memory.

In a typical study, students heard a list of perhaps 60 words read aloud at a steady rate. The words themselves were carefully chosen so that they could easily be classified into various categories: people's names, names of animals and vegetables, and so forth. Essential for the demonstration, the words were presented in a scrambled order, and any hint of these potential relationships was carefully avoided.

When asked to recall as much of the list as possible, two general findings usually appear. First, regardless of the order in which they are presented,

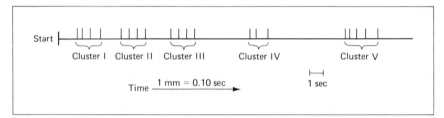

Figure 10.3   Schematic illustration of a typical time pattern in the free recall of categorized word lists. (*Source:* H. R. Pollio, *The Psychology of Symbolic Activity*, fig. 11.1, pg. 253. Reading, Mass.: Addison-Wesley, 1974. Reprinted by permission of the publisher.)

the words from each association category tend to cluster together in the report. Second, if one times the responses as they are made, a clear temporal pattern typically emerges. The members of each category cluster are produced in rapid succession, separated by a measurable time delay as the person shifts from one response category to another. Figure 10.3 is an idealized time record obtained in this sort of clustering experiment. The data are based on an experiment by Pollio, Richards, and Lucas (1969). The first four lines represent the "blips" of a rapid burst of responses for the four members of one category cluster (e.g., animals). This is followed by a noticeable time delay, and then four words of another category, produced in rapid succession (e.g., vegetables). This pattern continues throughout the recall: rapid production of category clusters, followed by a pause as the person shifts from one category to another (Pollio, Richards & Lucas, 1969; Pollio, 1974, pg. 253). Almost identical results are found in less artificial free-recall situations as, for example, simply asking a person to name all the birds or all the animals they know. Category clustering (e.g., birds of prey as one group, domestic fowl as another, etc.) also occurs, as does the same reliable pattern of temporal responses (Bousfield, Cohen & Whitmarsh, 1958).

The clarity of these results makes it apparent why Bousfield chose this paradigm as a vehicle for the study of associative clustering in memory. The results of these and other studies seem to translate into a highly organized, content addressable memory store, accessible through a refined form of search process. In the act of recall, the person scans memory until he or she encounters a relevant response category which is then rapidly produced. Once completed, a delay is introduced while the person resumes scanning to find and organize the next cluster of responses. This process continues until the entire set of categories has been exhausted. (Taken to its logical conclusion, the clusters themselves may well be tagged in terms of an even larger category: "words Bousfield gave me to remember.")

The question of whether organization of the lists occurs at input, retrieval, or perhaps both, has been the subject of some controversy (Cofer, 1966; Thomson & Tulving, 1970). Whatever the locus of the effect, however, in recall, individual items appear to be retrieved through their category membership. Thus, if an entire category is forgotten, a single reminder of the category identification may be all that is required to prompt recall of all the items in that cluster (Tulving & Pearlstone, 1966). This is exactly what underlies the facilitation effect of contextual cues as discussed earlier.

These observations, however simplified, seem to represent fairly the dynamics of memory organization. The principles, moreover, seem to apply equally well when conventional category hierarchies are unavailable, and people take recourse to unusual and uniquely personal associations (cf. Pollio & Foote, 1970). There should be one final caution. Even when conceptual associations are widely shared, they need not be logical, in any strict sense of the word. By way of example, here is what happened when Wells, Goi, and Seader (1958) asked 100 people to give the adjectives that first came to mind as they thought about various makes of cars and their owners. That the task is inherently illogical makes the fact of exceedingly high intersubject agreement even more provocative. Here are some samples from the list, and some of the responses given (Wells, Goi & Seader, 1958, pg. 121).

Cadillac owners:	Rich, high class, famous, fancy, important, proud, superior.
Buick owners:	Middle class, brave, masculine, strong, modern, pleasant.
Chevrolet owners:	Poor, ordinary, low class, simple, practical, cheap, thin, friendly.
Ford owners:	Masculine, young, powerful, good-looking, rough, dangerous, single, loud, merry, active.
Plymouth owners:	Quiet, careful, slow, moral, fat, gentle, calm, sad, thinking, patient, honest.

Before rushing off to sell your Plymouth (quiet, careful, slow, moral, fat . . .) to buy a Ford (masculine, young, powerful . . .) remember that these data were published in 1958. The lesson of these associations was not lost on the image makers of Detroit, and we know too well the fruits of their subsequent labor.

RECALL AS A SEARCH PROCESS

The picture that emerges from studies such as Bousfield's is of retrieval from long-term memory as an active process of *search* through a categorically organized memory store. If these terms—"retrieval," "search," "memory store"—are reminiscent of modern computer terminology, it is no accident. The analogy between human memory and information retrieval by computer is a surprisingly good one, and a borrowing of terminology is almost inevitable. The difference is that human memory is more flexible, less predictable, and, therefore, more interesting.

One way to get a feeling for memory as a search process is to observe its breakdown in certain cases of brain pathology. One of these, *aphasia*, can result in extreme difficulties in word finding due to damage to specific areas of the brain (see Chapter 12). Some time ago, we were involved in extensive studies of such patients and the special difficulties they can encounter (Newcombe, Oldfield & Wingfield, 1965; Newcombe, Oldfield, Ratcliff & Wingfield, 1971). One of these patients was a 54-year-old man of good education who had suffered injury to the left hemisphere of the brain as a result of war service. Although his general health and intellectual function remained intact, naming a simple object was for him a singularly difficult task.

Figure 10.4 shows what happened when he was given a picture of an anchor and simply asked to name it. The picture was a good one, and he had no difficulty in recognizing the object immediately. He looked briefly at the picture, nodded his head confidently, and put it down. He then devoted the next several minutes to what can only be called a systematic search for the correct name. His actual responses are given numerically in the figure, along with an attempt to classify them in terms of the alternate *strategies* he seems to have been using to guide his search. He first tried the use of the object, or where it is usually found (". . . belongs to a boat"). He then shifted to a phonetic approach by producing a word of similar sound ("hanger"). Then back to its use again (". . . throw it on the boat"), and so on. What we seem to be seeing is a process of search in which first one pathway and then another is tried until the goal is finally reached and the target word found. (Like any frustrating search, it was punctured with those annoyed, "It's got to be here somewhere!" comments, classified here as "noninformational utterances.")

If the difficulties described were encountered exclusively by aphasic patients, the argument for recall as a search process would be a weak one. All of us, however, have shared the experience of trying to recall some name or incident which seems to hover just on the threshold of memory. If it is a word, we may be able to produce one of similar meaning or sound, or know that it is short or long. If it is a fact, we might remember a part of it, and even when and where we first learned it. The complete fact, however, remains momentarily elusive. It is, as we say, "on the tip of the tongue."

The "Tip of the Tongue" Phenomenon and Response Availability

The "tip of the tongue" phenomenon, nicknamed the *TOT state* (Brown & McNeill, 1966), offers a striking example of the character of search and of

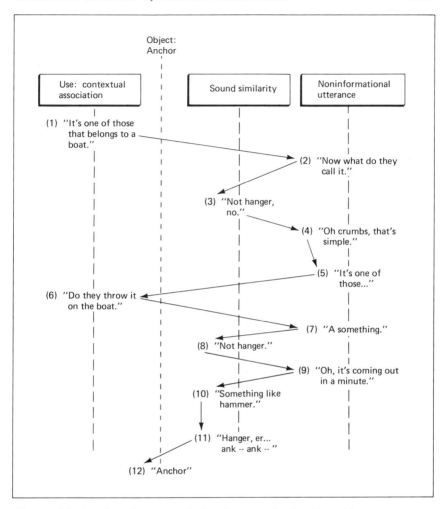

Figure 10.4   Complete record of aphasic patient's attempt to name an anchor. Responses are categorized by search strategies employed.

search strategies in recall. As Brown and McNeill have indicated, the signs of it are unmistakable. When a person is on the verge of an elusive recollection and "seized" by a TOT state, it is very much like being on the brink of a sneeze. There appears to be mild torment, followed by considerable relief when the task is finally accomplished.

A convenient way to precipitate a TOT state is to define some uncommon object, and then ask a person for its name. Here is an example, straight from the dictionary. Give the name of this object: "A navigational instrument used in measuring angular distances, especially the altitude of the sun, moon, and stars at sea." Brown and McNeill found this example to produce a TOT state in a fair number of people. Like the aphasic patient, normal adult subjects produced words of similar sound (*secant, sextet, sexton*), and of similar contextual association (*astrolabe, compass, dividers, protractor*). Further, and also like the aphasic, they fully realized in most cases that their answers were close to the target, but nevertheless incorrect.

While the search systems one might postulate are bound to be complex, one point emerges with clarity. One must distinguish between *knowledge* of items in memory and their *availability* to conscious recall. Inability in recall may not be due to the permanent loss of forgotten information. The problem may be one of an ineffective memory search. This distinction becomes apparent whenever initial failure is followed by eventual success. It is also suggested by the usual ability to recognize that our incorrect approximations are in fact incorrect. As in searching for an object in a cluttered room, we know that it is there, and that we will certainly recognize it when we see it. The problem is not its existence but its availability. (The target word in the previous example, by the way, was *sextant.*)

How can we increase item availability, or, as it were, "encourage the sneeze?" One way is to provide contextual cues or any other hint which cues the category or narrows the search (e.g., giving a word of similar meaning or sound, naming the semantic category, and so forth). Viewed in this way, the verbal rambling of our aphasic patient, or a person in the throes of a TOT state, may be more than a way of occupying time. The utterances accompanying the search may well be intuitive attempts at self-produced category cueing which plays the same role as the hints ordinarily supplied by others.

To Search or Not to Search

Sometimes, memories seem to pour forth in a spontaneous rush of associations. At other times, such as in the TOT state, recall seems more a process of active search. In the former case recall is rapid and effortless. In the latter case it is slow, sometimes conscious, and often nothing short of hard work. The fact is, however, that this seemingly great disparity may well be more apparent than real. A growing trend in memory research is to view the process as one of search in both cases. The feeling of spontaneity in recall may be an erroneous one, induced by rapidity and lack of conscious effort. This difference in speed and awareness may obscure the fact that it is no less a search (cf. Oldfield & Wingfield, 1965).

These thoughts raise a legitimate question. How does one decide when a search is worth initiating? Surely not *any* question will automatically prompt an exhaustive search of the sum total of all our knowledge. The memory process must logically include some procedures for analyzing questions and for determining the likelihood that we in fact have any knowledge of the relevant information. Lindsay and Norman (1972, pg. 376) illustrate this point with the following series of five graded questions. You will see the sense in which they are "graded" as you read through and try to answer them.

1. What was Beethoven's telephone number? (No search initiated. Beethoven died before telephones were invented.)
2. What was Hemingway's telephone number? (No search initiated. He undoubtedly did have a telephone, but we know we don't know what it was.)
3. What is the telephone number of the White House?[1]
4. What is the telephone number of your best friend?
5. What is your telephone number?

As we scan these questions, our own intuition assures us that some stage of preliminary analysis must occur prior to, or as part of, the search process.

Part of the answer lies in an organized memory system where subsets such as "telephone numbers" can be isolated and exclusively searched. Memory storage and retrieval, however, do not exist in a vacuum. Other knowledge can be brought to bear to facilitate the search. In this case it is the abstraction of "knowing what we know." In other cases, such as those discussed by Barlett, it is relevant information from other sources which can inhibit recall which in isolation would be knowingly incorrect or incomplete. The details of how this interaction actually operates remains probably the single largest challenge currently facing memory research.

Recall Versus Recognition

One noticeable feature of the TOT state is the recognition that the initial approximations are incorrect, even though the correct response is still elusive. This phenomenon is obviously not unique to the TOT state. It is one example of a larger principle which holds in all phases of memory research. Tests of recognition memory almost always yield higher scores than tests of free recall (see Chapter 7).

The principle that recognition is easier than recall underlies not only the comment, "I'll know it when I see it," but also some students' apparent preference for multiple-choice examinations over short-answer or essay tests. Interestingly, people can occasionally recognize this principle in themselves but mistake it for a unique personal trait. Indeed, we sometimes even hear it offered as a special virtue: "I often forget people's names, but I *never* forget a face." What they are really saying, is that recognition ("knowing" a face when you see it) is easier than recall (remembering the name that goes with it).

The reasons for the advantage of recognition situations over free recall become readily apparent when memory is viewed as a search. To put it

---

[1] The telephone number of the White House is (202)456-1414.

bluntly: recognition is usually more successful simply because it offers less opportunity for failure. Specifically, recognition situations limit the area of search by limiting the number of possible alternatives (Davis, Sutherland & Judd, 1961; Field & Lachman, 1966). That is one factor; another is that they often supply partial cues which directly aid recall (McNulty, 1965).

Compare these two methods of interrogating memory. First, free recall: "Who was the first person to make extensive use of nonsense syllables in the study of rote learning and memory?" If the answer is not readily available, try the same question through recognition. "Was it (a) Hull, (b) Ebbinghaus, (c) Thorndike, (d) Bartlett?" As long as we know that one of these answers is correct, our room for error is clearly reduced. No less important, being able to see the alternatives can allow utilization of remembered characteristics which in themselves were insufficient for free recall. One could, for example, distinguish the correct answer as "Ebbinghaus" by simply remembering that it was a German name, a long name, or that it ended in something like "house."

Free recall is thus a more rigorous test of retention than recognition. As we have seen, however, the difference is not an inherent one, but one of degree. One can narrow the gap between the two by offering hints which reduce the range of posssible alternatives in free recall. Similarly, the demands of recognition memory can be increased by simply enlarging the range of alternatives. The police do this as they test a witness' recollection by bringing in a large number of suspects for an identification lineup. The more similar in appearance the individuals, the more demands are put on memory task. The same principle applies to the multiple-choice test when the alternatives are made to appear as similar as possible, and when the final alternative is the now familiar, "none of the above."

PARADOXICAL RECOGNITION.   Let us return to that earlier question of how one knows when a search of memory is worthwhile, and when it is not. One accompaniment of recognition is that difficult to articulate, but almost tangible, feeling of familiarity one often gets when confronted by a stimulus known to have been encountered in the past. One can, for example, pass persons on the street and know with certainty that we have seen them somewhere before. Where we have seen them, what their names are, how we know them; all of this can elude us. But the feeling of familiarity and of "recognition" is nevertheless strong. When it occurs, this alone is sufficient to encourage the search.

There is a related phenomenon, sometimes called "paradoxical recognition" or déjà vu. Déjà vu, which literally means "already seen," can best be described as an erroneous feeling of familiarity for scenes or events which in fact have *not* been experienced before. The effect can at times be so strong that one can feel not only that the scene has been experienced before, but that it is almost possible to know with certainty what is going to happen next. Indeed, many occultists have mistaken a feeling of déjà vu for "precognition."

Little is known about déjà vu except that in normal individuals it most frequently occurs in states of extreme fatigue, and that it seems to be associated with spontaneous neural discharges in the temporal lobe of the brain.

SUMMARY

The effectiveness of contextual cues in recall illustrates the organized character of long-term memory. Recall can often be facilitated by giving associations, cueing a conceptual category, or in some other way narrowing the field of search.

One approach to the study of organization was that of Bousfield, who analyzed the nature of associative clustering in recall; the way in which persons tend to recall together items which are conceptually related. Later studies suggested that search through memory ordinarily proceeds from category to category, with individual items retrieved through their category membership. This is sometimes referred to as a "content addressable" memory store.

The so-called TOT state ("tip of the tongue"), illustrates the important distinction between items which may be truly lost from memory and those which are present in memory but temporarily inaccessible. An intriguing mystery associated with the TOT state is our common ability to know that an incorrect response is not the desired one, even though the correct response remains unavailable.

The view of memory as a search process largely explains the usual advantage of recognition memory over free recall. Recognition situations, such as multiple-choice examinations, limit the search by limiting the number of possible alternatives. Further, the presence of the alternatives can supply partial cues to aid recall and allow utilization of remembered characteristics which, in themselves, would not be sufficient for free recall.

In Search of the Mind's Eye

THE NATURE OF "MENTAL IMAGERY"

Psychologists have often been accused of hiding even the simplest of everyday phenomena behind terminology which seems more to obscure than to clarify. On occasion, the nonpsychologist can gain some measure of revenge by using "psychological" terms which seem to have meaning to almost everyone except psychologists. One favorite is the "nervous breakdown."

Other star performers in this category are a range of terms all related to a common idea: *mental images, mental pictures,* or simply, "seeing with the *mind's eye.*" What are mental images, how do they work, and where are they located? Part of the problem, and the reason for some resistance to these terms in psychology, is one of definition. Briefly, "mental imagery" implies especially vivid, detailed memories of stimuli and events which seem almost perceptual in character. Asked to picture their living room at home, most people describe a very real sensation of "seeing" the room, almost as if some picture or "image" were visually reconstructed in memory.

The concept of mental imagery has been in the psychological literature for almost 100 years, but it has so defied understanding that many psychologists have been inclined either to ignore it or to outright deny its existence. The behaviorists of the 1940s and 1950s, for example, considered reports of mental imagery as "linguistic fictions" or "ghosts." However commonly we talk about seeing things in the mind's eye, the argument has been that describing memory sensations "as if" they were mental images may be only confusing inadequate verbal description with what may, or may not, be reality. There is in no literal sense, a mind's eye.

The linguistic philosopher, Gilbert Ryle, was as blunt as could be: there are, in his words, "no such objects as mental images" (Ryle, 1949, pg. 254). The following observation, then, should be regarded more as one of quiet despair than of paronia:

> It would be an exaggeration to say that there was a conspiracy against mental images. But 'campaign' would not be too strong a word. The author of a recent account admits, with disarming candor, that to be able to dispose of mental images would be 'a clear case of good riddance' (Hannay, 1971, pg. 19).

The systematic study of mental imagery began with Sir Francis Galton's published account of questionnaires on imagery which he distributed to over 100 students, artists, and statesmen of his day (Galton, 1880). He simply asked his respondents to conjure up a mental picture of their morning's breakfast table and to answer a series of specific questions about these images. One of the most important findings was that the request to form a "mental picture in the mind's eye" did in fact have meaning to almost all of the respondents. That is, *almost* all the respondents. Most reported memory images as clear and detailed as if they had the scene in front of them. But some reported having no imagery at all. This latter group all felt they could certainly given an excellent *verbal* description from memory, but in no sense did they feel they experienced "mental pictures" as they thought about it. Interestingly, one of this latter group was a well-known artist of his day.

Beyond the fact that most (but not all) people experience some form of mental imagery, surprisingly little light has been shed on the phenomenon since Galton's day. We can, however, summarize some points on which there seems to be general agreement. (1) Most people do report mental imagery of some sort and accept their imagery as a true mental event, rather than as simply a metaphorical way of describing an indefinable experience of detailed memory. (2) The character of the imagery people report shows surprisingly little variation. Visual imagery is by far the most common form, but smaller numbers stress auditory or sometimes tactile imagery as well. Even those who rank auditory images as their primary mode usually report having some visual imagery as well (Richardson, 1969, pg. 50). (3) Imagery seems a matter of voluntary control, and reconstruction of images often requires some effort. At the same time, radar operators working for long periods, long-distance drivers, and aircraft pilots on high altitude level flights are occasionally troubled by uncontrolled mental (usually visual) images which can be vivid enough to be mistaken for reality (Holt, 1964). (4) Finally, people tend to take their own forms of imagery for granted and often express surprise to discover that not everyone shares their modes of imagery, let alone that some people claim to have no imagery at all.

Imagery and Recall

Gaining an understanding of what imagery is, and how it works, remains a difficult task (cf. Segal, 1971). For example, Penfield (1951) has reported obtaining imagery by electrical stimulation of the temporal lobe of the brain (see Chapter 12). He does not, however, suggest that this is where imagery is primarily located. On the other hand, we do know something about the way in which imagery can facilitate learning and memory.

The use of imagery in memory operates in much the same way as *mediators*, by offering a concrete anchor for learning materials. Lists of easily visualizable nouns such as *cup* or *chair*, for example, are far easier to learn and remember than lists of more abstract words such as *happiness* or *truth* (Paivio, 1969). Visual imagery seems to be an effective form of mediation which is commonly employed in a variety of learning situations. A point which will become more pertinent in the following chapter, however, is that visual memory looses its advantage to verbal memory when sequential order of the materials must also be retained (Bartlett, 1932; Paivio & Csapo, 1969).

We are, nevertheless, still begging the question. To say that instructing subjects to form an "image" facilitates memory, brings us little closer to understanding the form such an image might take. Indeed, perhaps imagery instructions merely lead subjects to form a better, more conceptually organized impression in memory than when no such instructions are given (cf. Anderson & Bower, 1973). For example, Neisser and Kerr (1973) have shown that subjects' own report of the vividness of an image is not always a reliable predictor of recall performance. Similarly, other results raise serious questions about the photographic quality of such images. Although one might expect the amount of visual detail to be important, Nelson, Metzler, and Reed (1974) found little difference in recognition memory for nondetailed line drawings of scenes, detailed drawings, and actual photographs (although all were better than simply verbal descriptions).

Experiments such as these would seem to counter the idea of pictures being stored in memory as vividly detailed copies of what was seen rather than, for example, as more abstract semantic interpretations of the pictures. Indeed, congenitally blind college students given pairs of words which Paivio would consider more concrete and easier to image show the same facilitation of concrete words over abstract ones as found for normally sighted persons (Jonides, Kahn & Rozin, 1975). The nature of the memory coding used by the blind students is not at all clear from this study, but since these students had been blind from birth, it would be hard to argue that it was a "visual" image in any strict meaning of the term. It is certainly the case that, even for normally sighted subjects, we need more objective indices of the existence of imagery beyond subjective reports. Two such attempts have been offered by studies of "picture memory" and "mental rotation."

Studies of "Picture Memory" and "Mental Rotation"

In Chapter 7 we mentioned Shepard's (1967) experiment in which he found amazingly accurate recognition memory for lists of literally hundreds of words and sentences. He was, in fact, also able to show equally high, or higher, recognition scores for *pictures* presented under the same circumstances. Even more impressive results for picture memory were later obtained by Standing, Conezio, and Haber (1970), who presented subjects with a series of 2560 slides (such as pictures of scenic views) for ten seconds each. Scores on a later recognition test showed an astonishing average of between 85 and 93 percent correct. Given results like these, it seems hard to deny the existence of some form of picturelike visual memory. As Klatzky (1975, pg. 225) has observed with some humor, if one picture is worth 1000 words, then to store those pictures as verbal descriptions would have required something like 2.56 million words!

Among the most impressive studies purporting to show evidence for visual memory—as more than a metaphor—are studies of "mental rotation" of simple forms (Shepard & Metzler, 1971; Cooper & Shepard, 1973). Specifically, these studies set out to determine whether subjects can perform as though they had available to them a physical (as opposed to, for example, a verbal) representation of a stimulus in memory.

Subjects were first shown a single letter, such as *R*, followed by a second one which was either that letter, or its mirror image: Я. The subjects' task was to press one button if the second letter was normal; another, if it was a mirror image. There was a catch: the letters were not always presented right side up! The degree of rotation of the letters varied between 0 and 360° such that, for example, subjects had to recognize ↘ as a normal letter simply rotated, but ♂ as a mirror image.

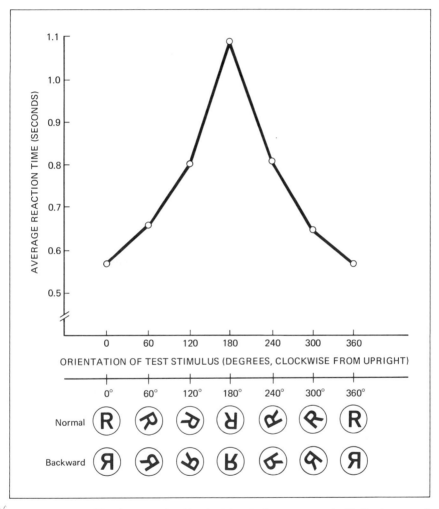

Figure 10.5   The time required to decide whether a presented letter is normal or backward, as a function of the degree of rotation of the test stimulus from the vertical. Examples of normal and backward versions of the stimuli in various degrees of rotation are shown below the graph. (*Source:* L. A. Cooper and R. N. Shepard, Chronometric studies of the rotation of mental images. In: W. G. Chase (ed.), *Visual Information Processing*, figs. 2 & 5, pp. 95 & 103. New York: Academic Press, 1973. Reprinted by permission of the publisher.)

Their results are summarized in Figure 10.5 in terms of the average reaction time to making the decision, as a function of the degree of rotation of the letters. (Examples of normal and reversed letters in various rotations are shown below the graph.) The results caused no small flurry in the imagery debate. The greater the angular distance between the letters' orientation and true vertical, the longer were the reaction times. To put it another way, the time required to decide whether a letter was normal or reversed was an almost exact function of the amount of rotation in degrees that would be necessary to bring it to the vertical (either clockwise or counterclockwise, depending on which is the shorter route).

These results were widely interpreted as evidence that the subjects must have "mentally rotated" the figures to their upright position before making their decision. It would indeed seem hard to ascribe these results to anything but the existence of an ability to store and retain (and even rotate) a picturelike, visual memory image.

While a number of other studies have postulated support for detailed imagery of a visual character (e.g., Shepard & Chapman, 1970; Frost, 1972), the notion still seems to defy logic. For example, if such images were duplicative representations of each and every visual experience, then the number of such "pictures" would have to be nearly infinite (Pylyshyn, 1973).

The current status of imagery research, like the existence of imagery itself, is still a matter of heated controversy. Thus, some believe that memory holds both visual information, which produces the effects of imagery, and a second memory system which is primarily linguistic in nature (Paivio, 1971; 1975); others favor the idea of an abstract memory code which is neither visual nor linguistic (Anderson & Bower, 1973), or, more properly, which contains elements of both (Potter & Faulconer, 1975). All we can say with any degree of confidence at this time is that so-called mental imagery is something less than a literal "picture" seen with the "mind's eye," and surely something more than simply a "linguistic fiction."

However poorly understood, mental imagery is a very normal, common phenomenon. There is another form of imagery which, by contrast, is statistically quite rare and causes considerable excitement when it is encountered. This form is referred to as *eidetic imagery,* or by the more popular but erroneous name of "photographic memory."

EIDETIC IMAGERY

Every four years, American television viewers renew their acquaintance with that mysterious figure which now hovers behind every presidential election: the electronic computer. Its role in the election coverage is simply to tabulate the state-by-state returns as they come in and, as a little bonus, to venture some predictions based on the votes counted to that point. So effective has this operation become that one may be forgiven for the feeling that it is the computer itself which is doing the voting or, in the very least, quietly controlling the outcome of the election.

In the presidential election of 1932, listeners to one radio station in the United States were enthralled to hear state-by-state returns rapidly tabulated by a human computer: a Polish stage performer who billed himself variously as "The Lightning Calculator" or, more modestly, as "The Calculating Genius."

We know little of this extraordinary individual except for a brief report by two psychologists who were later able to interview him and to watch some of his stage performances (Bousfield & Barry, 1933). He could memorize a five-by-five matrix of digits at one glance, and then reproduce the numbers in any sequence requested. He claimed to know the value of π to 200 decimal places, and the logarithms of the numbers 1 to 100 to seven places. His attraction to the radio station was that he could also add three and four place numbers more rapidly than any of the mechanical adding machines of the day.

Part of his "trick," if we can call it that, was a highly developed ability to maintain visual images of almost photographic quality for long periods. Like most people with eidetic imagery (from the Greek *eidētikos*, which implies "identical" or "duplicative"), it was in fact far from photographic in character. However unusual his memory, it still showed the full array of omissions, distortions, and influences of past experience as in normal memory. Shown a column of figures to memorize, he claimed the numbers appeared in his memory as if on a blackboard, and *written in his own handwriting*. He could remember a list of 200 numbers, but only one group of six figures could "stand out clearly" at any one time. The capacity, detail, and striking visual quality of his memory, however, clearly set it far apart from ordinary memory.

Eidetic imagery is a fairly rare event. It is also more frequently encountered in children than in adults. In one early study, G. W. Allport (1924) tested sixty 11-year-old English children using a series of pictures for memory. The stimuli were richly detailed picture book illustrations, each shown to the children for 35 seconds and then removed from view.

Of the 60 children tested, a number showed a vividness of recall which went beyond the normal range of memory ability. One of the pictures, for example, showed a village street with the German word *Gartenwirtschaft* lettered on a sign over a doorway. Along with an amazing number of other details, 30 of the children reported "seeing" the lettered sign in memory. Of this 30, 3 were able to spell out the full word correctly, while a further 7 missed only two of the sixteen letters. As an encore, these same 10 children showed they could give the letters of *Gartenwirtschaft* from left to right, or from right to left, with equal facility. The picture, you will recall, was very detailed, and was shown for only 35 seconds. None of the children spoke German. Any notion that they simply memorized the word is out of the question—at least in any sense that we would ordinarily use the term "memorize."

How does eidetic imagery differ from the more ordinary mental imagery previously discussed? First and foremost, of course, is the almost photographic vividness of detail exhibited by eidetic recall. Stromeyer and Psotka (1970) employed stimuli known as "random dot stereograms" (Julesz, 1964). These are sets of two patterns of large numbers of randomly arranged dots. When viewed alone, they both appear to be identical and meaningless. However, when they are viewed simultaneously through a stereoscope, one picture to each eye, a particular three-dimensional pattern suddenly stands out from a common background. Stromeyer and Psotka used these patterns to test the ability of a 23-year-old woman known to have eidetic ability. In this case, the two patterns were not presented simultaneously. They were presented sequentially; one of the two patterns was presented for a period to the subject's left eye, and some time later the second pattern was presented to the right eye. They report that the subject was actually able to "see" the three-dimensional pattern even when the two presentations were separated by intervals as long as several hours!

Such eidetic imagers are extremely rare, and Stromeyer and Psotka's report ended with a plea for information as to where they might find other such individuals.

Second, eidetic images, unlike mental images, are usually not reported as occurring "in the head." Eidetic imagers typically report "seeing" their images as if they were projected on a wall or, for some, on the back of their eye lids. Indeed, one frequently observes patterned eye movements by eidetic imagers during recall, just as if they were scanning such a projection.

A final characteristic of eidetic imagery is the frequent use of the present tense in describing such a scene. Again, it is just as if it were being viewed directly. Here is an extract from an eidetic child recalling a previously seen picture from memory: "I can see the yellowish ground . . . (the girl's dress) is green. It has some white spots on it." (Haber, 1969). Eidetic imagery is reminiscent of the afterimages one gets when looking at a bright light and turning away quickly. Afterimages, however, are a retinal phenomenon, while eidetic imagery clearly is not. In addition, eidetic images can be reconstructed weeks (Doob, 1965) or years later (Luria, 1960). A good review of recent work on eidetic imagery can be found in Gray and Gummerman (1975).

Estimates of the number of people who have eidetic imagery varies widely, depending on the rigor of one's criteria. Hunter (1964) estimates its occurrence as between 1 to 10 percent of the adult population, and from 50 to 60 percent of children under 12. Teasdale (1934) estimated its frequency as 12.5 percent of 11-year-olds, 8.3 percent of 12-year-olds, 5.8 percent of 13-year-olds, and 2.1 percent by the age of 14 or 15 years. Whatever the actual frequency, it is certainly the case that the ability declines as children

get older (Haber & Haber, 1964). Few of these children, we should emphasize, even approach the range of ability of our "Calculating Genius" of
1932. Rather, they are unique in their above average ability to report minute detail and in the especially vivid visual character of their recollections.
Beyond this ability, persons with eidetic imagery can seem quite ordinary as
regards intelligence, personality traits, and other skills.

There have been reports that eidetic imagery is encountered with
greater than expected frequency in brain-damaged and retarded children
(Siipola & Hayden, 1965; Freides & Hayden, 1966). Its appearance in such
children, who are often unusually poor in linguistic ability, and the fact that
it becomes less and less common in normal children as they get older, may
not be a coincidence. Specifically, some have speculated that eidetic imagery may be a more primitive, preverbal form of memory, which atrophies as
linguistic skills in oral and written expression become increasingly emphasized in school (Richardson, 1969, pg. 40). Although this remains speculation, some support for the idea can be seen in observations such as Haber's
(1969) that children with eidetic imagery tend not to use it when they are
encouraged to verbalize details of a scene they are to memorize.

It may be, both in eidetic and in ordinary imagery, that people simply
tend to use a visual analogy in trying to describe for others a vivid and detailed memory which they themselves do not fully understand. Lest this
possibility tend to trivialize what is in fact an extraordinary phenomenon,
let us close with a report by A. R. Luria, who regularly tested a Moscow
newspaper reporter with this ability over a 20-year period (Luria, 1960;
1968). Here is Luria's account of the man's attempt to recall a list of words
shown to him briefly many years before. As you read it, note the intriguing
use of very normal contextual cues and associations in the retrieval process.

> [His] behavior was always the same. He closed his eyes, raised his finger,
> slowly wagged it around and said: 'Wait . . . when you were dressed in a
> gray suit . . . I was sitting opposite you in a chair . . . that's it!'—and then
> and there quite rapidly he reproduced without hesitation the information
> which had been given to him many years before. The observer got the im-
> pression that [he] was rather 'reading through' the material than 'reproducing'
> it (for he acted as though the list was present in front of him), and that here
> there was no more cause for amazement than in the case when a man reads a
> book lying in front of him (Luria, 1960, pg. 82).

SUMMARY

Current views of long-term memory owe their beginnings to the work of
Sir Frederick Bartlett who produced the first, and perhaps the clearest, ex-
position of the dynamics of retention and recall. According to Bartlett, ac-

curacy of recall may well be the exception rather than the rule. As new information is assimilated in memory, it is mapped onto organized but everchanging conceptual systems referred to as schemata. This interaction may simplify the original input, or transform some of its characteristics to fit existing knowledge and belief. The interaction is dynamic and may result in the modification of the schemata themselves.

Interpretation and modification of an experienced event can occur at all three stages in the sequence of learning: input, storage, or retrieval. For these reasons, Bartlett and others have seen normal memory as more reconstructive than reproductive. This implies a certain creative quality to memory, where eventual recall is influenced not only by other knowledge, but is also guided by a sense of internal logic.

Current trends are to view recall as analogous to a process of active search through a conceptually organized memory system. Contextual cues and other aids to recall, facilitate the process by identifying relevant categories or otherwise limiting the area of search. The "tip of the tongue" phenomenon, or TOT state, offers some support for this view. It also raises the concept of alternative retrieval strategies which may be used in gaining access to information which is present in memory but temporarily unavailable to retrieval.

While these and other studies have built a fairly systematic picture of memory storage and retrieval, considerable work is still needed to fit this picture with some levels of phenomenological experience. One case in point is the little understood concept of mental imagery—an especially vivid, detailed memory, frequently of a visual character. Mental images, like the statistically rarer eidetic imagery, may well raise issue with the more usual emphasis on the verbal character of human memory. It is certainly the case that the earlier view of memory as simply the reproduction of learned associations is as counter to the trend of modern research as it is to our own intuitions.

chapter 11

Causes of Forgetting and Theories of Memory

The previous chapter looked closely at the structure and characteristics of long-term memory. For most of us, however, our real concern is not so much how we remember, but why we forget. Specifically, we would like to know what causes forgetting, and what, if anything, can be done to retard the process.

The present chapter looks at this question under three main headings. The first section deals with the causes of forgetting, and the historical conflict between the belief that memory decays simply with the passage of time, versus loss as a consequence of active interference from other learning.

The second section returns to our earlier discussion of the "bottleneck" of stimulus input, with a closer look at the nature of short-term memory and its implications for more permanent memory storage.

The final section deals with the practical question of whether memory can in fact be improved, and, in the light of current views of memory function, how this might be accomplished.

What Causes Forgetting?

There is a legendary anecdote about a professor of ichthyology who claimed that every time he learned the name of a new student, he forgot the name of a fish. This is more than another story about an absent-minded professor. It introduces the question of whether ordinary forgetting results simply from the passage of time, or whether forgetting is due primarily to interference from other memories in an increasingly crowded memory store (Ceraso, 1967). These two points of view have been argued back and forth for a number of years under the names of *spontaneous trace decay* versus the *interference* theory of forgetting.

SPONTANEOUS TRACE DECAY

Plato, interestingly enough, was one of the earliest proponents of the decay theory of forgetting. Plato likened the initial formation of a memory trace to the fresh imprint of a seal on a block of wax. Wax gradually loses its shape over time, and no imprint on its surface can remain clear indefinitely. First there will be a loss of sharp detail, then a complete fading of the entire pattern beyond recognition. The life of the imprint can be extended by cutting the initial trace as deeply as possible, or by periodically restamping the image whenever it starts to fade.

The analogy is a clear one. Each learning experience is recorded by the formation of a semipermanent *memory trace* in the nervous system. The stronger the initial learning, the "deeper" will be the trace, and the longer it will last before fading. Periodic recall or reuse of the memory reactivates and strengthens the trace in much the same way as ordinary rehearsal. Frequent utilization represents the necessary "restamping" of the imprint to keep it alive and clear. With disuse, and the passage of time, the trace fades beyond recognition and the memory is lost.

The idea that memories fade spontaneously with time may seem reasonable but it is surprisingly difficult to prove. Indeed, the theory might have faded completely—at least for psychologists—had it not been "restamped" by Thorndike (1913) with his laws of effect and exercise (Chapter 5). You will recall his argument that learning represents a connection, or bond, between a stimulus and response. The connection will be maintained only so long as it is exercised (and exercised only so long as it is followed by pleasurable consequences). Failure to exercise the connection through practice leads to a gradual weakening of the bond; and with its disuse, forgetting occurs.

Since the days of Pavlov and his recognition of spontaneous recovery, however, few people have seen extinction as simply a process of passive decay. Even for lower animals, points of view have ranged from active "unlearning" to "inhibition"; the latter suggests that associations are not so much lost as blocked from response.

What is the case in human memory, and why does passive decay seem unlikely to many psychologists? No one could deny that recall accuracy generally diminished with the passage of time. The question is, whether it is the passage of time itself, or something that happens during this time, which actually causes the forgetting.

The alternative to spontaneous decay is that forgetting is due to active interference from other learning. In other words, the more time that passes between learning and recall, the greater will be the opportunity for such interference to occur.

Jenkins and Dallenbach (1924) felt that one way to break out of this obviously circular argument might be to compare the retention scores for volunteers following a period of sleep to their scores for a similar period of normal waking activity. The passage of time would be the same. The difference, they argued, would be in the likelihood of external interference from new learning.

Their results are summarized in Figure 11.1, and show precisely the expectations of interference theory. While the waking curve shows a steady decline in retention over an eight-hour period, the "noninterference" sleep curve, does not. After some forgetting during the first two hours, there is virtually no loss from that point to the end of the test period. Indeed, even that initial loss might have been due to interference before the subjects were fully asleep. Their conclusion was that interference from new experience, not time decay, is the primary cause of forgetting.

The Jenkins and Dallenbach study has been replicated many times (with more than the two subjects used in that early study) with essentially similar results (Ekstrand, 1967; Dillon, 1970; Barret & Ekstrand, 1972). It also sparked analogous studies with lower animals (rats and insects) that used interference-preventing techniques ranging from freezing and chemical anesthesia to physical immobilization (Hunter, 1932; Russell & Hunter, 1937; Minami & Dallenbach, 1946).

It is certainly the case that the so-called sleep studies were hardly definitive proof for an interference theory of forgetting, any more than they completely negated the possibility of spontaneous decay. On the one hand, the results of such sleep studies vary to some extent with the learning materials employed (Newman, 1939). On the other hand, there is still much we

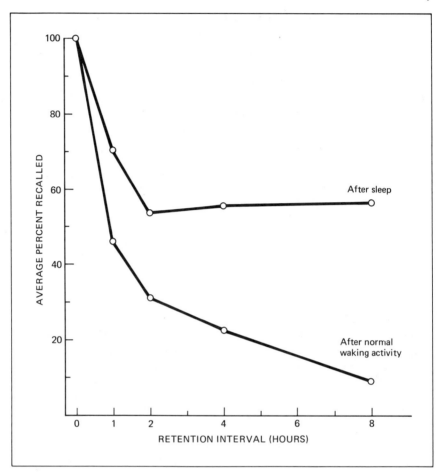

Figure 11.1   Average retention curves for two subjects over an eight-hour period occupied either by sleep or by normal waking activity. (*Source:* Data from J. G. Jenkins and K. M. Dallenbach, Oblivescence during sleep and waking. *American Journal of Psychology*, 1924, 35:605–612.)

do not know about the level of mental activity during sleep, and there is always the possibility that some subjects could have kept their scores high by engaging in unconscious rehearsal during presleep periods.[1]

Nevertheless, Jenkins and Dallenbach's conclusion caught the fancy of many students of learning and memory: ". . . forgetting is not so much a

---

[1] These experiments raise the practical question of whether there may be a special advantage to study just before sleep. Unfortunately, any benefits to retention would be partially offset by the inefficiency of study late at night. Further, these benefits would be limited to the brief period just after waking, and would soon be negated by interference from subsequent daily activity. A special advantage to study before sleep would occur only if the reduced forgetting were combined with a return to the study task refreshed and alert soon after waking (Hunter, 1964).

matter of decay of old impressions and associations as it is a matter of the interference, inhibition, or obliteration of the old by the new" (Jenkins & Dallenbach, 1924, pg. 612). Their results were consistent enough with the predictions of interference theory to have prompted a flurry of research activity directed toward the understanding of this somewhat mysterious process.

INTERFERENCE THEORY

The subject of memory is rife with analogies. While Plato had talked of decay theory and wax, McGeoch (1932) introduced modern interference theory with the news that iron girders only appear to rust with the passage of time. The cause of rust is of course an active chemical process (oxidation), which merely requires some time to take its full effect. So too, McGeoch argued, forgetting many not be caused by the passage of time. The actual cause may be an equally invisible, but equally active process: competition or interference from other memory traces.

Although it is common to speak of interference as a single theory, there are in reality two distinct classes of interference and a range of theories to explain their effects.

Types of Interference

The most noticeable form of interference is the detrimental effect of new learning on the retention of older memories. This form of "backward" interference is referred to as *retroactive inhibition* (RI). It is the type of interference considered by the sleep study of Jenkins and Dallenbach; the kind which presumably plagues our forgetful ichthyologist. In laboratory settings, effects of RI are typically studied with the following paradigm.

Step 1	Step 2	Step 3	Step 4
Control group	Learn list 1	Rest	Test list 1
Interference group	Learn list 1	Learn list 2	Test list 1

If RI has occurred, the second group will show significantly poorer retention of list 1 than the control group. This paradigm is a common way of comparing the relative interference of different kinds of learning materials (see Chapter 7).

If RI were the only source of interference, memory loss might not be as rapid as it is. There is also interference from prior learning on the retention of newer material. This "forward" acting interference is referred to as *proactive inhibition* (PI). It is illustrated in the following paradigm.

Step 1	*Step 2*	*Step 3*	*Step 4*
Control group	Rest	Learn list 2	Test list 2
Interference group	Learn list 1	Learn list 2	Test list 2

When PI is present, the interference group will show significantly poorer retention of list 2 than the control group.

While logically distinct, RI and PI in everyday forgetting ordinarily form two sides of the same coin of interference. Indeed, even in the laboratory, it is sometimes hard to isolate their independent effects unless we have very strict control over all prior learning of the subject (Underwood, 1957).

Theories of Interference

How does interference work to cause forgetting? The numerous points of view on this subject fall into four general categories of explanation.

1. RESPONSE COMPETITION. When McGeoch (1932; 1942) first stressed the importance of interference in memory, he took the view that new memories tend to supress or block the recollection of the old. To put it simply, there may be very little "forgetting" as such. Rather, failures in memory are the result of competition between responses, and interfering items are recalled in place of the desired ones. We know the experience of trying to recall the name of an old friend, only to have the name of someone else we knew at about the same time keep coming to mind. While perhaps oversimplified, this is the essence of the competition hypothesis. The unavailable name has not been erased from memory; it is being blocked from response by the more available one.

2. UNLEARNING. While recollections may show initial intrusions of one or more competing responses, such confusions tend to decrease with sufficient practice. Yet, even when potentially competing responses become differentiated from the desired ones, the desired responses can nevertheless remain unavailable. The so-called unlearning theory of interference sees these initial confusions as just one part of the total interference process. Prior to the differentiation of the old and new items, the earlier traces become weakened, and forgetting of the preempted responses does indeed occur. The learning of the new material, in other words, cause an "unlearning" of the old (Melton & Irwin, 1940).

3. RESPONSE AVAILABILITY. Our discussion of memory as a search process also has a counterpart within interference theory. One version is that of Ceraso (1967) who likens interference to neither the "blocked channel" of McGeoch nor the "fading canvas" of Melton and Irwin. Rather, he sees in-

terference as causing an "unsuccessful hunt" for the desired item. The effect of new learning is to clutter an already overcrowded memory store. The more crowded with similar materials, the broader any search in memory must be, and the less accessible will some of the items become.

4. QUALITATIVE CHANGE.   A final view of interference is based on the interactive nature of normal memory. New memories confused with older ones render a composite picture that bears little resemblance to either. What appears as "forgetting" may in reality be distorted traces, which go unrecognized in recall. Davis and Sinha's (1950) study involving Brueghel's painting, and Bartlett's (1932) more general views on the reconstructive nature of memory, are illustrative.

Summary: Decay and Interference

Few people now attribute forgetting over the long term to spontaneous decay of unused traces simply with the passage of time. Forgetting is seen as a more active process, with interference between traces as the primary cause of forgetting. Not a single theory, "interference" is an umbrella term which includes at least four different views of the process. They can be summarized as *blocking* (response competition), *erasure* (unlearning), *crowding* (response availability), and *mixing* (qualitative change) theories of interference.

Faced as we are with four different theories of interference, we confront the inevitable question of which one is correct. There is certainly considerable merit to each, and the full picture of forgetting is surely complex enough to encompass them all. For example, in the previous chapter we saw that qualitative change, represented by the work of Bartlett, and the theory of response availability, in the context of memory as a search process, are really complimentary aspects of memory rather than opposing, mutually exclusive theories.

The theories of response competition and unlearning, however, began their existence in deep antagonism to each other. The proponents of each of these two theories remained unconvinced by the arguments of the other, and each side looked for definitive experiments to prove the correctness of its position. It is worth a slight detour to look briefly at some of these experiments.

A SAMPLING OF THE EVIDENCE: THE MYSTERIOUS "FACTOR X"

McGeoch's (1932; 1942) theory of response competition is not an unreasonable explanation of forgetting. Most simply, it postulates that forgetting is not due to a failure of retention, but to a competition between responses that results in new learning blocking the recall of the old. The effect of this will be seen in the common tendency to inadvertently recall more recently learned items in place of the desired, earlier ones. No one could deny that this frequently happens. As we have seen, however, Melton and Irwin (1940) became convinced that this was only part of the interference story. Here is the experiment that led to this conviction.

The Melton and Irwin Experiment

The experiment began by having a group of subjects memorize a list of 18 CVC nonsense syllables through the method of serial anticipation. Once these had been learned, the subjects were given a second list of 18 different CVCs to memorize. While the first list was always practiced for 5 trials, some subjects practiced the second list for 5, 10, 20, or 40 trials. The interest of the experiment was to examine retention of the items from the first list, as the degree of learning of the second one was increased. In short, their goal was to build up retroactive inhibition as a prelude to explaining its operation.

Figure 11.2 shows the results of the experiment as they were originally

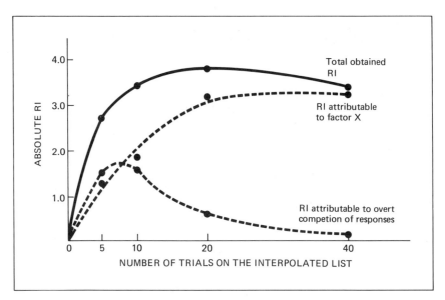

Figure 11.2 Relationship between amount of retroactive inhibition (RI) and the degree of learning of the interpolated material, showing the presumed distribution of the sources of the overall loss of recall accuracy. "Factor X" was interpreted as loss due to "unlearning" of first-list responses. (*Source:* A. W. Melton and J. M. Irwin, The influence of degree of interpolated learning on retroactive inhibition and the overt transfer of specific responses. *American Journal of Psychology*, 1940, 53: fig. 3, pg. 198. Copyright © 1940 by Karl M. Dallenbach. Reprinted by permission of The University of Illinois Press.)

reported by Melton and Irwin (1940). Look first at the top curve on the graph, labeled "total obtained RI." This represents the overall decrease in recall accuracy of the first-list items as a function of the amount of practice of the items on the second list. (The reason this is shown as an increasing function is simply because Melton and Irwin chose to represent the drop in recall as an increase in RI. These are really two ways of saying the same thing.)

The lowest curve on the graph, shown as a dotted line, was intended as a measure of the contribution of *response competition* to the total obtained RI. It shows the relative frequency with which subjects erroneously gave items from the second list in their attempt to recall items from the first list. This curve reflects the essense of the competition hypothesis.

Melton and Irwin recognized that items from the second list might block recall of the first list without necessarily being erroneously given as overt responses. Nevertheless, they argued that this "competition" curve should at least be parallel to the total RI curve; it should show a continual rise over the course of the first 20 trials before reaching its peak. In fact, the RI attributable to competition of responses reaches its peak after only 5 to 10 trials, and then falls sharply. Presumably, competition did occur initially, but then became less important as further practice on the second list eliminated these confusions. Yet the curve of total RI continues to rise!

Obviously, there must have been a second factor at work contributing to the total RI. To measure its effect, Melton and Irwin plotted a third curve representing the difference between total RI and the amount attributable to response competition. They labeled this second, mysterious factor as "Factor X." What is Factor X? As we have already seen, Melton and Irwin explained it as an unlearning of the first-list responses as a consequence of the learning of the second list.

Over the years since that first study, other writers were to add support to the theory (e.g., Briggs, 1954), some of them viewing the unlearning process as analogous to *extinction* in lower animal conditioning, as we discussed it in Chapters 4 and 5 (Underwood, 1948; Postman, 1953; Melton, 1961). However, one nagging problem still remained: were the items from the first list actually erased from memory or did responses from the second list continue to block them even though they no longer appeared as overt intrusions? Barnes and Underwood (1959) took a more direct attack on the question of the fate of first list associations.

The Barnes and Underwood Experiment

This experiment employed the *A-B*, *A-C* paradigm, as described in Chapter 7. Subjects first learned a list of paired-associates consisting of a CVC and a noun, such as *DAX-book, LIM-chair*, etc. Once these had been memorized, they were given a second list consisting of the same CVC stimulus members, but this time combined with a new set of nouns; e.g., *DAX-*

shoe, LIM-boy, etc. The second list was practiced for 1, 5, 10, and 20 trials. At the end of each set of trials, subjects were given the stimulus CVCs and asked to give, if possible, *both* sets of associated words. The percentage of responses subjects were able to give from each of the two lists would be taken as a measure of their association strength in memory.

Let us pause for a moment and look at their logic. According to the competition theory, learning a second list in an RI paradigm hurts recall of the first list associations by creating a confusion between responses, such that the person tends to erroneously recall the second set of associations in place of the desired first set. The first set of associations, however, remain intact in memory. By asking subjects to try to recall *both* sets of responses (and allowing up to two full minutes to do so), Barnes and Underwood hoped to avoid the effects of response competition inhibiting the recall of the first-list responses. According to the unlearning explanation, of course, the learning of the second list would actually cause a weakening of first-list associations such that, even under these circumstances, the first-list responses could not be recalled.

Barnes and Underwood's results, shown in Figure 11.3, are in good

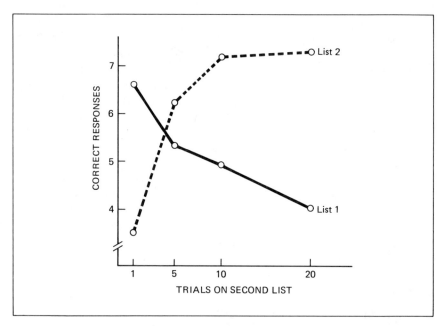

Figure 11.3 Availability of List 1 and List 2 responses, using the MMFR technique, as a function of the amount of practice on List 2. (*Source:* J. M. Barnes and B. J. Underwood, Fate of first-list associations in transfer theory. *Journal of Experimental Psychology*, 1959, 58: fig 1, pg. 101. Copyright 1959 by the American Psychological Association. Reprinted by permission.)

agreement with the unlearning hypothesis. As the second set of associations (list 2) received more and more practice, so the ability to recall the first set of associations (list 1) decreased. The first-list responses, in other words, seemed progressively to become lost from memory.

Unlearning: Further Developments

The Barnes and Underwood experiment did not end the debate between proponents of competition versus unlearning. The trend of the debate, however, began to shift from attempts to prove one theory or the other in the original forms in which they were presented by McGeoch and by Melton and Irwin. As research continued, the dividing line between the two began to blur.

For example, Postman and Stark (1969) repeated the Barnes and Underwood experiment, this time using a multiple-choice recognition test to measure retention. This less demanding test of memory showed virtually *no loss* of the first-list items, even after learning of the second list. Since, in the recognition test, the subjects were given the response items and did not have to find them in memory, it seemed to Postman and Stark that the first-list responses had not been unlearned, or extinguished, so much as having become inaccessible to the usual methods of recall. However, Postman and Stark did not opt for the competition theory, at least in the form in which it was originally given by McGeoch. Instead, they spoke in terms of a "selection bias" which changes gradually over the course of learning, not in terms of individual associations, but in terms of entire sets of responses. Indeed, the development of the theory began to resemble more closely the theory of *response availability* than either "competition" or "unlearning" in their original forms.

At this point the picture becomes exceedingly complex, and we may have already strained the reader's patience beyond the point of endurance. For those whose appetites have been wetted by this controversy, we can recommend good reviews of the research and theory by Postman and Underwood (1973) and by Anderson and Bower (1973, chap. 5).

INTERFERENCE IN PERSPECTIVE: EPISODIC VERSUS SEMANTIC MEMORY

In assessing these theories of forgetting, it is important to recognize that the evidence has related almost exclusively to rote learning of meaningless materials. Like Ebbinghaus, these theorists felt that their problems were complex enough without having to deal also with the vagaries of "meaning" and conceptual learning.

Before leaving this topic, we should highlight an important distinction between *episodic* and *semantic memory* (Tulving, 1972). In a sense, long-term memory contains two kinds of information. Episodic memory holds a more or less faithful record of our experiences in the context in which they occurred. Semantic memory, on the other hand, holds our organized linguistic and conceptual knowledge in their broadest sense. It includes the meaning of words, rules of grammar, and all other rules, such as those necessary for mathematical computations, the solution of problems, and so forth. By way of example, a person's memory of the events of his or her own high school graduation would represent episodic memory, while the knowledge of what a graduation *is* would be held in semantic memory.

If we adopt Tulving's distinction, we can see the limited ground on which these theories of interference have been tested. When we deal with the learning (or forgetting) of such materials as CVCs or lists of words, we are dealing almost exclusively with episodic memory. If you were given a list of words to remember, you might forget which words were on the list (episodic memory), but it is unlikely that you would ever forget the meanings of the words themselves (semantic memory). It becomes clear, then, that memory research in the future must concentrate on a further question: not merely the viability of the theories purely as logical constructs, but also their applicability and generality to ordinary memory as a whole. Readers interested in several theoretical treatments of semantic memory can find good discussions in a number of sources (Collins & Quillian, 1969; Rumelhart, Lindsay & Norman, 1972; Anderson & Bower, 1973; Smith, Shoben & Rips, 1974; Meyer & Schvaneveldt, 1976).

MOTIVATED FORGETTING

One final source of forgetting stands apart from both trace decay and interference theories. This is not because it is any less viable, but because it is restricted only to the loss of certain types of memories; those with negative emotional content which, in a sense, we would rather not remember. Referred to under the general heading of *motivated forgetting*, this can run the range from a temporary forgetting of an unpleasant appointment to the complete blocking of materials which threaten strongly held beliefs about ourselves or others.

Attitude, Belief, and the "Sleeper" Effect

During World War II, when propaganda and counterpropaganda crisscrossed the world to a degree unparalleled in the past, psychologists became blinded by a flash of the obvious. People resist persuasion not only through confidence in their own position but by literally forgetting the arguments of the would-be persuader. One case in point was a study in which

procommunist and anticommunist students were exposed to factual literature supporting either one side or the other. The result was not merely a
lack of persuasion. Later tests showed that each of the groups remembered
far more of the arguments which favored their beliefs than those which opposed them (Levine & Murphy, 1943).

Our own experience suffers enough from such examples of selective forgetting that we need not belabor the point. We need mention only that
these effects of attitude are not necessarily specific to retention; they may in
fact operate at the level of initial learning as well. It would not be surprising, for example, if we attend to, think about, and rehearse primarily those
items which are consistent with our own beliefs and attitudes.

Retention can also be influenced by the source of a communication. For
example, one is less likely to remember the arguments of, or be persuaded
by, persons of low credibility or likability. An interesting wrinkle is the so-
called sleeper effect, which is traceable at least in part to the memory process itself. While the argument of a low credibility communicator may have
little immediate impact, the sought change in attitude can sometimes occur
days or weeks later (Hovland, Lumsdaine, & Sheffield, 1949; Hovland, Janis
& Kelley, 1953). Regrettably, most of us know some individual, whether a
close associate or a public figure, whose ideas, opinions, or purported facts
would be disbelieved (ignored) precisely because they come from that person. The ideas themselves may be good; we may "coincidentally" be heard
making the very same arguments ourselves sometime later without any notion of where we originally heard them. It would seem that the ideas lie
dormant (hence, the "sleeper" effect) and emerge as the argument itself is
disassociated in memory from its source. Paradoxically, it is only when we
forget the source that we remember the argument; as often as not, we assume it to be our own.

Repression

An integral part of Sigmund Freud's (1856–1939) elaborate model of
personality dynamics was the then shocking notion that one may block from
awareness those memories likely to produce severe anxiety, guilt, or conflict. Freud saw this blocking, or *repression*, as one of several *defense mechanisms* of the ego. He won both praise and enmity with one of its
implications. While unavailable to conscious recall, repressed memories
may still exert profound influence on personality development, motivation,
and, potentially, mental disorder.

Freud saw evidence for repression in certain revealing free associations
and in those slips of the tongue, or "Freudian slips," one is prone to make
from time to time. Most controversial was his argument that repressed
memories can also appear disguised in a symbolic form to further the protection. A son with repressed hostility toward his father, for example, might

disguise it by expressing these feelings against other symbols of authority
(Hall & Lindzey, 1957, pg. 49).

However much Freud's notion of repression may have upset some of his
contemporaries, the system itself contains (slightly disguised) elements of
modern interference theory: blocking of responses, unavailability to search,
and qualitative distortion. The essential difference is in the selectivity of its
operation.

Within limits, repression is a normal and at times helpful protective device. Unfortunately, some individuals make overabundant use of the protective aspects of repression. They remain tragically immune to all
criticism, even self-criticism (Byrne, 1961). These so-called repressors, for
example, might reply to questions about school by citing some excellent
grades or test scores. That these are in fact islands of success in a sea of failure seems overlooked. At the other extreme are so-called sensitizers, who
are overly aware of their weaknesses and failings. One may have to probe
behind repeated confessions of failure to discover that their overall performance is generally excellent.

Repression in psychoneurotic personalities can take the form of *disso-
ciative neuroses,* where individuals may block whole areas of memory in
order to eliminate conflict or anxiety. In extreme cases, this can result in
temporary amnesia, or a *fugue state* (literally: "to flee"). All memories related to personal identity are lost to recollection. More general knowledge,
such as language, social customs, and motor skills are only rarely lost.

SUMMARY

Early in the history of memory research, psychologists began to doubt
the likelihood that memories spontaneously fade with the passage of time
and disuse. The early "sleep studies" of Jenkins and Dallenbach (1924) gave
support to the notion that forgetting is ordinarily due to active interference
from other learning. This interference may either take the form of old
learning interfering with the acquisition of new learning (proactive inhibition) or new learning interfering with the retention of the old (retroactive
inhibition).

While interference as the prime cause of forgetting received early acceptance, the specific mechanisms of interference still remain a matter of
dispute. The four major theories of interference were described as response
competition, unlearning, response availability, and qualitative change.

Motivated forgetting refers to specific forgetting of materials which are
personally threatening, embarrassing, or unpleasant. The best known form
of motivated forgetting is based on Freud's notion of repression as a defense
mechanism of the ego. Repression, however, does not stand as an independent "theory" of forgetting and can, to an extent, be understood in terms of

existing interference theories: the blocking of responses, unavailability to search, and qualitative change.

Short-Term Memory

In Chapter 2 we referred to the "bottleneck" of stimulus input, and the notion that incoming information must first be held in the transient form of short-term memory prior to becoming a part of more permanent, long-term memory. That is to say, some information may be lost before it even becomes registered in long-term memory.

If short-term memory (STM) is defined as how much a person can recognize and recall a few seconds or minutes after a single presentation, there is ample evidence that its span is limited, and that it decays rapidly without rehearsal. One implication of this is that some apparent forgetting may be due not to loss from long-term memory (whether through time decay or interference) but to a failure in initial acquisition.

For material to be retained with any degree of permanence, it must first be apprehended and then held in short-term memory long enough for its transfer to long-term memory. Teachers (and parents) have been known to call this the "in-one-ear-and-out-the-other" phenomenon. The child has heard what was said and can repeat it back. But ten minutes later—nothing. Why does some material seem never to survive the transient store of STM? A comparative study of STM in groups of different age and intelligence levels can offer some insights.

THE CAPACITY OF STM

The modern recognition of the limited capacity of STM is usually attributed to psychologists such as Donald Broadbent (1958), who emphasized the advantages of STM as a "buffer" to limit stimulus input, or George Miller (1956), who summarized its capacity as 7 ± 2 "chunks" of information (see Chapter 2). As it happens, the concept is quite old. The first experimental studies of STM appeared in 1887, conducted by the British psychologist J. Jacobs. While lacking the modern idiom, Jacob's understanding of the limits of STM is nonetheless clear. As he observed, "It is obvious that there is a limit to the power of reproducing sounds accurately. Anyone can say 'Bo' after once hearing it: but few would catch the name of the Greek statesman M. Papamichalopous without need of repetition" (Hunter, 1964, pg. 56).

Jacob's notion of "few people" must obviously exclude other Greeks for whom Papamichalopous might be as familiar as Massachusetts is to an

American. Since the apparent span of STM will clearly depend on one's familiarity with the stimuli, comparative studies employ easily controlled materials such as nonsense syllables or random strings of digits. The frequently quoted average span of seven (plus or minus two) items is an artificially "pure" figure. It is based on standardized procedures such as repeating back lists of digits spoken in a rapid monotone, after a single hearing.

STM and Age

Large scale norms show a fairly reliable relationship between age and the average span of STM. At 2½ years, the span averages two digits, increasing to three by age 3, four by age 4, five by age 7, and six by age 10. Increases beyond this point come more slowly, typically leveling out at about seven digits by the mid-teens. Beyond age 30 there is often a slight decline, with the span shrinking back to about 6 digits by the mid-fifties (Hunter 1964).

Surprisingly, these differences in memory span are apparently not due to different forgetting rates once the material has been learned. The differences seem to relate almost entirely to coding and rehearsal strategies which become progressively more sophisticated as children get older (Belmont & Butterfield, 1969). Older children attend better to relevant stimulus cues during presentation, encode or "chunk" the materials more efficiently during acquisition, and make increasingly effective use of active verbal rehearsal during retention. In short, it is not so much that the "size" of STM grows with age, as it is that children begin to make more effective use of this limited capacity. Similarly, the slight decline in late middle age can be traced to a decline in this efficiency.

Research on children's memory offers a dramatic illustration of the importance of active subject involvement during acquisition. For example, we can reduce adult span closer to that of children by simply speeding up the rate at which materials are presented. This acts to deny the adults time during presentation to exploit their advantage of superior encoding and rehearsal skills (Murray & Roberts, 1968). How these skills develop is a fascinating and only recently appreciated subject of study. It is clear that increases in memory span from kindergarten to, for example, fifth grade, exactly parallel an increased use of spontaneous verbal rehearsal (Flavell, Beach & Chinsky, 1966). Similarly, instructing reluctant nursery children to actively rehearse during acquisition can lead to a significant improvement in memory performance (Kingsley & Hagen, 1969).

STM and Intelligence

As the span of STM increases with age, there is also a rough relationship between memory span and general intelligence level (cf. Wechsler, 1949).

And precisely the same factors of *attention, encoding,* and *rehearsal* strategies during acquisition seem to be involved in these differences (Belmont & Butterfield, 1969, pg. 60). Retarded children typically show poor attention to stimuli during learning (Zeaman & House, 1963), coupled with a disinclination to actively rehearse the materials once they have entered STM. Significant increases in memory span result by giving these children more time for acquisition (O'Connor & Hermelin, 1965) and encouraging them to use verbal rehearsal (Belmont & Butterfield, 1971).

This general finding of a disinclination, rather than a disability, for active rehearsal suggests a potential value to training retarded children in the use of rehearsal. As in the case of age differences, the answer seems to lie primarily, if not entirely, on active involvement in acquisition, rather than in retention once the materials have been learned.

Organization and the Span of STM

If active rehearsal and organization bring such dramatic improvements in the span of STM for normal and retarded children, one might ask if something could not be done to improve the span for normal adults. This is ordinarily not the case, since most normal adults are already adept at these principles of organized rehearsal. The tendency to organize, or "chunk," materials into coherent groups for rehearsal is probably well established by early adolescence. One illustration is our ability to encode individual letters into sound patterns and words, thus changing a capacity of 7 items (isolated letters) into 35 items (if the letters form seven 5-letter words). The upper limit of seven "chunks" in STM remains the same; efficiency in coding simply maximizes its effectiveness. As we will see later, the usual form of coding in STM is primarily auditory. This explains why experiments often show deaf subjects to have poorer STM performance than persons with normal hearing. But when the stimuli used are especially amenable to visual encoding, the deaf do as well—or even better—than the normally hearing (Blair, 1957; Olsson & Furth, 1966; Withrow, 1968–1969).

The recognition and use of relationships in acquisition come with education, experience, and, hence, familiarity with the class of stimuli to be remembered. If one were willing to devote the next 50 days to repeated memorization of random digits, for example, one might increase the memory span from the usual 7 or 8 to as many as 15 digits without error (Martin & Fernberger, 1929). On the other hand, we would not expect to see practice at this specific ability to increase memory capacity in general. The only positive transfer might be general principles such as the importance of concentration, grouping when possible, and so forth. (The improvement in this example apparently comes from subjects learning to treat 15-digit lists as if they are composed of three groups of five digits each.)

The ability to rapidly encode incoming information can lead to a variety of impressive performances. One thinks of chess players who can recount a past game on an almost move-by-move basis. With their knowledge of the "language" of chess (allowable moves and familiar sequences), they are remembering not isolated moves but *patterns* of play, as logically coherent to them as the sequence t-h-e to a reader of English.[2]

A breakdown in the ability to rapidly organize input has just the opposite effect. This is frequently the case in elderly persons, where difficulties in rapid organization slows comprehension (Welford, 1958) and reduces the use of mediators in learning (Hulicka & Grossman, 1967). Together with an increased susceptibility to interference from other activity, these factors account in large measure for what only appears as a problem of retention. Early memories would be relatively unaffected by these problems. Frequent claims by the elderly of especially vivid early memories may well be an exaggeration prompted by the contrast they experience between those memories and their diminished ability in handling recently acquired information.

FORGETTING IN STM

Material which is of interest will ordinarily be rehearsed, thought about, and hence retained in long-term memory. Rehearsal plays an important role for this retention. Without it, some have argued, information in STM can be expected to decay *in as little as 18 seconds.*

This is almost an impossible notion to test on oneself, since thinking about the fate of the material in STM virtually insures its unconscious rehearsal! It is, as we said in Chapter 2, hard to "not rehearse." Peterson and Peterson (1959) solved the problem by presenting subjects with two sets of materials in succession. The first was an item for memory, such as a nonsense syllable. The second was a three-digit number, such as "347." Subjects were required to retain the memory material, while at the same time counting backward from the number by threes (347, 344, 341, 338 . . .). When this routine is repeated for various retention intervals, the result is dramatic. Retention drops from 100 percent immediately after presentation to virtually zero after a mere 18 seconds (see Figure 11.4).

The interpolated task, incidentally, need not be backward counting, so long as it occupies the person enough to prevent rehearsal. With young children or the handicapped, counting forward by ones has exactly the same effect (cf. Shallice & Warrington, 1970).

The question is whether the counting simply prevents rehearsal, thus

---

[2] For an impressive analysis of memory virtuosity in chess players, some of whom can hold numerous "blindfold" games simultaneously, the interested reader is referred to Alfred Binet's classic account, now available in English translation (Simmel & Barron, 1966).

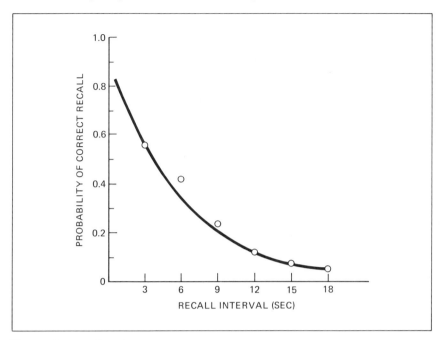

Figure 11.4 Recall accuracy over an 18 second period when subjects were prevented from rehearsing by having to count backward during the retention interval. (*Source:* L. R. Peterson and M. J. Peterson, Short-term retention of individual verbal items. *Journal of Experimental Psychology,* 1959, 58: fig. 3, pg. 195. Copyright 1959 by the American Psychological Association. Reprinted by permission.)

allowing the STM trace to decay with the passage of *time,* or whether it provides a source of active interference which is the actual cause of the memory loss. We are thus faced with exactly the same question we confronted in long-term memory, but this time in the context of STM. We know that it is difficult to retain a telephone number in a room full of voices or to retain the last sentence of a rapid-fire lecturer who offers no pause from one sentence to the next. Do these cases represent interference in a manner analogous to long-term memory (Melton, 1963; Reitman, 1971), or are they primarily distractors which prevent rehearsal and allow time decay to take its natural course (Broadbent, 1958; Brown, 1958)?

Nancy Waugh and Donald Norman (1965) designed an ingenious experiment to test the independent effects of time and interference in STM. They had subjects memorize lists of spoken digits heard either at a fast rate of presentation (four digits per second), or at a slow one (one digit per second). Each list had a special number at the end, a "probe" digit, which was always a repetition of some other digit in the list. The task was not to recall the entire list, but simply to name the digit which had followed the first oc-

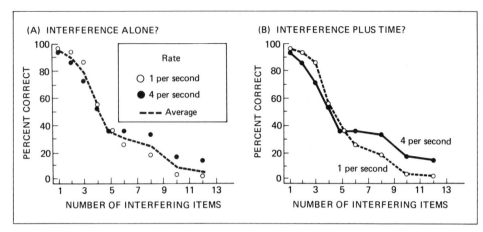

Figure 11.5   Percentage of digits reported correctly as a function of the number of interfering items and rate of presentation. Left-hand panel (*A*) shows single, average curve, as reported by Waugh and Norman (1965). Right-hand panel (*B*) shows same data with separate curves plotted for fast and slow rates of presentation. (*Source:* N. C. Waugh and D. A. Norman, Primary memory. *Psychological Review*, 1965, 72: fig. 1-c, pg. 91. Copyright 1965 by the American Psychological Association. Reprinted by permission.)

currence of the probe in the list. For example, the list might be: 178269157493241—5. The probe is the digit 5, and the correct response would be the name of the following digit—7.

Their logic was straightforward. If *interference* is the primary cause of loss in STM, the more items that come between the probed digit and the probe itself, the poorer should be the retention. For example, in the above list, we could change the probe digit from 5 to 3, to reduce the amount of interference, or to 6, to increase it. If *time* is the crucial factor, the number of interfering items might still have an apparent effect, since the greater the number of interfering items, the greater would be the elapsed time necessary for retention. The direct test would be in the two different presentation rates; the faster rate should show better retention since it offers less time for memory to decay.

As so often happens, the results were not as definitive as one might have hoped. The left-hand panel (A) of Figure 11.5 shows Waugh and Norman's results as they were originally reported. As you examine the figure, it is clear that the probability of recalling a particular digit decreases systematically with the number of intervening digits. Is this due to the increase in interference these intervening digits represent, or is it due to the fact that the larger the number of "interfering" items, the greater will be the passage of time required for retention? Waugh and Norman saw their answer in the very similar scores for both fast and slow rates of presentation. To emphasize the small (if any) effect of time, they plotted a single curve midway between the two sets of scores. Their conclusion was inescapable; the greater the number of interfering items, the poorer will be the probability of recall. Thus, as in long-term memory, interference stands as the prime (or only) cause of loss from STM.

Other writers, however, were impressed more by the difference between the fast and slow rates than by their similarities (e.g., Broadbent, 1971). The right-hand panel (B) of Figure 11.5 emphasizes this difference by showing the same set of data points, but this time with separate functions drawn for the fast and for the slow rates. As Broadbent interpreted these results, they seemed to imply that rate of presentation, and hence amount of elapsed time, does have an effect on retention. Specifically, items presented at a slower rate have an advantage immediately after presentation, since more time is allowed between each digit for its recognition and encoding. Once encoded in STM, however, there seems to be a slight advantage for the faster presentations. If correct, this would indicate that while interference does take a major toll in STM, there is also an effect of time; the less time an item has been in STM, the greater the likelihood that it will be recalled.

In summary, the Waugh and Norman experiment could be interpreted as showing independent effects of both time and interference in the rapid loss from unrehearsed STM, although the effects of time appear relatively small. While the issue is not fully closed, and additional evidence for a possible role of time decay in STM has subsequently appeared (e.g., Reitman, 1974; Crowder, 1976, pp. 178–182), it is safe to say that the majority view continues to favor interference as the primary cause of forgetting in STM, just as it is presumed to be in long-term memory.

Interference in STM

Numerous studies have shown that rehearsal in STM is ordinarily of a verbal form, regardless of the mode in which materials are originally presented. For example, when letters of the alphabet are presented visually, confusion errors in recall are still predominantly acoustic. The letters Q, F are more likely to be misremembered as their "sound-alikes," U, X, than as their look-alikes, O, E (Conrad, 1964; Wickelgren, 1965).

This tendency toward verbal rehearsal seems so uniform that many have felt that this is more than simply an efficient or convenient form of STM encoding: it might in fact be a necessary one. From our discussion of iconic memory, and other research, one might conclude that visual impressions cannot be retained for more than a fleeting instant after presentation, such that materials *must* be encoded verbally for retention beyond that point. Although there may be many representational systems possible, to include a visual short-term memory (see "picture memory" in Chapter 10), considerable evidence suggests that auditory encoding in STM is frequently pre-

dominant, if not obligatory (cf. Posner & Keele, 1967; Posner, Boies, Eichelman & Taylor, 1969; Wingfield, 1973). Considerable research suggests
that while interference may operate in both long- and short-term memory,
the nature of interference in STM is primarily acoustic, while interference
in long-term memory is primarily semantic (Baddely & Dale, 1966; Adams,
1967).

McGeoch's rusting girder analogy for the interplay of time and interference in long-term memory is equally appropriate for the similar interaction
in STM. Only the type of interference would be different. Perhaps an even
better analogy for the interaction would be the effects seen if one placed a
bar of metal in a jar of acid (Posner, 1963; 1967). While the decay itself
would result from the effects of the acid, the longer the bar remained in the
solution, the greater would be the total deterioration. Also, the more concentrated the acid solution, the more rapid would be the decay. While this
"acid bath" theory is only a metaphor, it seems an apt one for summarizing
the issue. Forgetting STM is caused primarily by interference (the "acid"),
which requires time to operate. In addition, the more similar the interfer-
ring stimuli are to the remembered items (the "strength" of the acid), the
more rapidly they will decay. While the acid bath theory tells us little about
how interference operates—the structure of the "acid," as it were—its intrinsic appeal is considerable (Cermak, 1972).

ARE THERE TWO KINDS OF MEMORY?

STM is, first and foremost, a description of one aspect of behavior. It
refers to the observable characteristics of memory storage for the brief period after an experience before it can be transferred into long-term memory. One could broaden the concept of STM to include the temporary
holding of freshly retrieved information from long-term memory.

Consider the task of giving the names of the last five presidents of the
United States in alphabetical order. This requires first, that the names be
retrieved from long-term memory, and then held temporarily until they are
correctly ordered for response. A similar operation applies in mental arithmetic, where one temporarily retains intermediate sums or a formula
freshly retrieved from long-term memory. This implies a dual role of STM
as an initial stage in the sequence of learning and as a "working memory."
This broader notion of STM is a viable one to the extent that the same previously described limitations of span, susceptibility to interference, and
rapid decay without rehearsal continue to apply.

Whether STM is conceptualized in broad terms or in narrow ones, it remains a descriptive convenience. Like Freud's *superego*, it names a class of
behaviors that are distinctive enough to warrant a label without the necessary implication that they have a distinct physical (i.e., neurophysiological)
reality. As there is no little box in the brain labeled "superego," so there is

no little box labeled "STM." Indeed, even on a descriptive level, some have been reluctant to accept STM as a special form of memory, distinct from long-term memory. One could view STM and long-term memory as simply two ends of a single memory continuum; both are susceptible to interference and differ only in the degree of stability through repetition (Melton, 1963).

For some years, however, the trend has been to take quite seriously the notion that STM and long-term memory represent two distinct forms of memory, each with a different functional state in the nervous system. The beginnings of this view are lost to history, but it surely must have been given impetus when, in 1887, a Russian physician named S. S. Korsakoff claimed to have isolated a specific disorder of STM function associated with chronic alcoholism. Now known as *Korsakoff's syndrome*, it is thought to arise from destruction of brain tissues in and around the *mammilary body* and the *hippocampus* (Barbizet, 1963). Whether the destruction arises from toxic effects of the alcohol, or from a dietary deficiency accompanying the alcoholism, remains at issue. The behavioral picture, however, is tragically clear.

A patient with Korsakoff's syndrome cannot retain information for more than a few seconds. He may forget that he has just asked the time, or that he has just asked your name. If he has a clean breakfast tray in front of him, he may "remember" that he has eaten, but not what he has had. Remove the tray, and he may forget that he has eaten at all.

This is a defect which prevents transfer of traces into long-term memory. It makes problem solving impossible, since the patient cannot retain subprocesses long enough to utilize them in a solution. Nor can he easily sustain a normal conversation, since he may literally forget what he has just said. By contrast, long-term memory can remain unaffected, and patients may show accurate recall of events which occurred prior to the onset of the illness. Zangwill (1950) reports one Korsakoff patient who was asked to draw a picture of a person riding on a bus. The result was a strikingly accurate drawing. But what it showed was a bus which was then a full decade out-of-date: a style current before the onset of the patient's ten-year illness. As Zangwill noted, this recollection would be an impressive feat, even for a person without brain pathology.

Memory Consolidation

Once we begin to look for it, there are numerous instances which suggest the existence of a transient, easily disrupted STM trace, versus a more durable, permanent form of storage for long-term memories. *Retrograde amnesia* is one example. It refers to a temporary disruption of normal brain activity which effectively erases all memory for events just prior to the incident, without a concomitant loss of earlier memories. A person recovering from *concussion* following head injury, for example, may retain no memory of the immediate events leading up to the accident. After recovery, the individual may remember approaching the intersection, or stepping off a curb—then nothing, until he or she recalls waking up in an ambulance on the way to the hospital (Russell, 1959). The experiences must surely have registered in STM, but their transfer to long-term memory had been prevented. Short-term retrograde amnesias can also follow the temporary disruption of normal brain activity associated with *epileptic seizures*, or the use of *electroconvulsive shock* as treatment for selected forms of mental disorder (Cronholm & Lagergren, 1959).

Numerous researchers see recent experience as first forming a transient, easily disrupted trace in the nervous system. This trace requires a certain amount of time for "consolidation" into a more permanent structural change in the brain. Concussion, shock, or seizure act to disrupt this transient short-term trace before memory consolidation has had a chance to take place. This general notion of a transient store preceding the formation of a more durable trace has led to *dual-trace*, or *consolidation*, theories of memory (cf. Hebb, 1949; Glickman, 1961; McGaugh, 1966). In short, what began as merely a descriptive convenience may well turn out to have a physical reality in the nervous system (see Chapter 12).

STM or "Levels" of Processing?

Nevertheless, many questions about this hypothetical distinction must be answered, and only recently has some of the traditional evidence for the distinction been called into question (Wickelgren, 1974). For example, many theorists tend increasingly to stress the dynamic nature of memory processing; a dynamism which they feel is lost in the "boxes" of the traditional flow-chart, or structural models, of the STM–long-term memory distinction. As traditionally presented, we have seen how such models speak of "transferring" information from one memory store to another or allowing for the strengthening or "consolidation" of the trace with rehearsal and a lack of interruption.

Part of the problem, as noted by Reynolds and Flagg (1977) who reviewed this work, is that one gets very different estimates of the capacity of STM as the materials to be remembered are "chunked" in various ways. The range of five to nine spoken of earlier can actually be as low as three (Baddeley, 1970; Murdock, 1972). The apparent capacity can also be as high as 20, if, for example, we are dealing with words that form sentences. However we explain chunking, it would necessarily seem to imply a more dynamic interaction between the storage of recently acquired information (i.e., STM) and the knowledge necessary for its chunking (i.e., knowledge which presumably resides in long-term memory).

To meet these problems, theorists such as Craik and Lockhart (1972) have begun to argue that differences in "levels" of processing may be a better characterization of memory activity over the course of time than the earlier views of STM and long-term memory as distinct memory stores. If the traditional distinction is seen as more than a convenient shorthand for degrees of memory processing, then, to Craik and Lockhart, it is a shorthand that has perhaps outlived its usefulness.

The notion of *levels of processing* implies that materials continually undergo varying degrees of analysis in memory as they are attended to, thought about, and thus given a greater or lesser depth of analysis through meaningful connection with knowledge already in memory. In Chapter 7 we saw how one can give "meaning" to almost any material, even materials as unfamiliar as CVC nonsense syllables. Why are "meaningful" materials (words, sentences, and so forth) easier to learn and retained longer? We could speak of the facilitating effects of "anchors" for retention. We could also say that their advantage lies in the likelihood that they will be processed to a "deeper" level more successfully, and faster, than unfamiliar materials of little lasting relevance to the subject. Retention for materials might thus be a direct function of the depth of processing, or degree of analysis, they have received. The amount of attention allocated (see Chapter 2), their compatibility with existing cognitive structures, and the amount of time available for processing the new materials, would all contribute to retention strength. Indeed, it might be argued that the well-documented effects of uninterrupted rehearsal benefit retention to the extent that they allow opportunity for a more complete level of analysis.

The concept of levels of processing is another attempt to describe, in a more sophisticated way, memory operations over the course of time. While still subject to development and debate (cf., Craik & Tulving, 1975; Morris, Bransford & Franks, 1977), it is an approach with the virtue of being closer to the spirit of Bartlett's earlier thoughts on memory than the structural models of STM as they are frequently presented.

As a working hypothesis, however, the STM long-term memory distinction has proven itself to be of considerable value. It's future utility, one ventures to speculate, may well rest on a recognition that while the character of memory storage is very different for short-term and for long-term memories, one may have to reject the notion of any artificial separation which the use of the terms might at first seem to imply. Readers interested in pursuing these issues are encouraged to read Craik and Lockhart's (1972) original paper as well as the excellent introductory review of subsequent developments offered by Reynolds and Flagg (1977).

THREE KINDS OF MEMORY?

Some researchers have in fact isolated a third form of memory in addition to that we have described as STM and long-term memory. This has been characterized as a fleeting, unanalyzed, sensory "echo" of a stimulus for a very brief period just after its receipt. With a presumed duration of well under a few seconds, these sensory stores hold visual or auditory information just long enough for it to be analyzed for registration in STM. The visual store is sometimes referred to as *iconic memory*, and its auditory counterpart as *echoic memory* (Neisser, 1967).

While important to our theoretical understanding of the total perceptual-memory system, these forms of sensory memory can be demonstrated only in the laboratory under tightly controlled experimental conditions.

Iconic Memory

The existence of iconic memory was first reliably demonstrated by George Sperling (Sperling, 1960; Averbach & Sperling, 1963) in the course of studies very much like those used for estimating the span of STM. Subjects were visually presented with letters of the alphabet (e.g., 9 or 12 letters) and were asked to report as many of them as possible from memory. Unlike ordinary STM studies, Sperling flashed these letters very briefly, so that, for example, nine letters were shown in a single presentation lasting only 50 milliseconds (0.05 seconds). With this brief exposure, only about four or five letters could typically be reported.

It occurred to Sperling, however, that even this brief exposure might have allowed his subjects to "see" more letters than they were able to report. That is, perhaps they saw all nine letters, but by the time they had spoken aloud the first four or five, they had "forgotten" the rest. We put "forgotten" in quotations, because we know that four or five letters, and the brief time it takes to speak them, is well within the capacity of STM. But, Sperling wondered, suppose there is another, very brief memory, for recent visual experience which has a larger capacity, but shorter duration than ordinary STM. To investigate this possibility, Sperling introduced a technique referred to as "partial report."

In the partial report technique, subjects see nine letters arranged in three rows of three letters each. The letter array is presented for 50 milliseconds and then, after a specified interval, subjects hear a signal tone of either high, medium, or low frequency. They are told that if they hear a high tone they should report the three letters of the top row, and if it is a low tone they should report the bottom row. The results showed that no matter which row they were told to report, they averaged nearly 100 percent correct. Remember that the tone signal was not given until *after* the display terminated.

From these results, Sperling inferred that his subjects must have seen all nine letters, but that they were stored in some sort of "sensory memory" which decays so rapidly that the information fades by the time the first four or five letters have been reported in the usual "whole report" technique. By varying the delay of the signal tone, Sperling was able to estimate the duration of this sensory memory as something under one second.

While some experiments have put its duration at closer to ¼ second (Averbach & Coriell, 1961; Haber & Standing, 1969) or slightly over one second (Mackworth, 1962, 1963), the notion of what Neisser was later to call iconic memory is now widely accepted.

Why does this iconic memory exist? It takes time to analyze any visual stimulus, and without the existence of this fleeting visual "icon," the visual information would last only as long as it was actually before our eyes. The icon, in other words, gives us a little edge on the rapidly changing visual environment; it lets us "see" the stimulus for just a bit longer for it to be properly identified for rehearsal in ordinary STM.

Echoic Memory

There is a similar need for brief sensory storage of auditory information. For example, we are all familiar with the experience of hearing a garbled message, perhaps over a bad telephone line, and being able to mentally "play it again," so as to try different interpretations of what was heard. The same need can be felt when listening to a speaker with a foreign accent.

On a more technical level, speech itself is a sound pattern which is constantly changing over time, and no single instant of this acoustic signal is sufficient for complete identification. To "hear" the pattern, it is logically necessary to have some way of temporarily holding large enough "pieces" of the sound in some sort of memory, so as to determine this pattern (see Wingfield, 1977, for a fuller discussion).

Most of the evidence for the existence of echoic memory (the auditory counterpart of iconic memory) comes from studies of selective attention in simultaneous listening, as discussed in Chapter 2. One well-known example is a study by Moray, Bates, and Barnett (1965), who used a procedure quite analogous to Sperling's partial report technique.

Subjects heard four different messages presented simultaneously from four separate stereophonic loudspeakers placed around them. The speakers were sufficiently far apart that localization of each of the four messages was fairly easy, and, as we know from Chapter 2, subjects would have no trouble repeating the message from any one of the four speakers, while "filtering out" the other three; that is, provided they know in advance which speaker to attend to.

In one condition, subjects heard four different rapidly spoken letters of the alphabet from each of the four speakers. Moray and his colleagues knew that subjects would not be able to report all 16 letters, which clearly exceeds the ordinary span of STM. Could it be, however, that they could "hear" more letters when they were actually presented than they were later able to report? The question is analogous to the one asked by Sperling in the context of vision, and their solution was an adaptation of his partial report technique. The signal for partial report was in the form of a flashing light which indicated which of the four loudspeaker's messages was to be reported. Even though the signal light came on only *after* the message had terminated, recall accuracy for the four letters from any one speaker was extremely good. As in the case of Sperling's visual studies, the subjects seemed to be able to tap into a sensory "echo" of the auditory information which continued to be available to the subject for a very brief period after the stimulus itself was no longer present.

Since Moray, Bates, and Barnett gave the partial report signal one second after the messages ended, they knew that this echoic memory must last at least that long. Darwin, Turvey, and Crowder (1972), for example, put its duration as at least two seconds, but less than four seconds, while Guttman and Julesz (1963; Julesz & Guttman, 1963) estimate its duration as closer to one second. As in the case of iconic memory, however, the existence of some sort of auditory sensory memory, "echoic memory," has received wide acceptance.

SUMMARY

Short-term memory (STM) is traditionally defined as the amount of information a person can recognize and recall after a single presentation without the benefit of extensive practice. The capacity of STM is usually placed at about 7 ± 2 items of information (digits, letters, or words), but its capacity can be extended if the material can be organized or "chunked" into coherent categories. For example, a memory span of 7 letters can be increased to 35 if the letters form seven 5-letter words.

STM decays rapidly without rehearsal, with estimates ranging up to a duration of about 18 seconds. Like long-term memory, interference seems to be the prime cause of forgetting in STM. Research has tended to emphasize the role of acoustic interference in STM, as opposed to semantic interference in long-term memory.

The distinction between STM and long-term memory served as a descriptive convenience for many years, and is still common in research literature. The notion of levels of processing, on the other hand, stresses the dynamic character of memory, and offers an alternative way to view the acquisition and storage of information over the course of time.

Numerous writers have postulated the existence of an additional form of memory store of an even briefer duration than STM. This is viewed as a fleeting, unanalyzed visual or auditory echo of sensory input (referred to as iconic and echoic memory, respectively) which lasts just long enough for registration of the stimulus in STM.

On Improving Memory

Up to this point we have discussed the character and structure of long-term retention, views on the causes of forgetting, and the limitations on input imposed by short-term memory. One product of this discussion should be an awareness that forgetting is neither a disease, a sign of weakness, nor (invariably) an indication of indifference to the materials. It is a natural phenomenon which follows certain laws and has predictable consequences. And not all of these are bad. We should, in the very least, see forgetting in both ourselves and others with renewed patience and understanding.

Having reached this point, we are bound to ask whether memory can be improved, and whether our understanding of its strengths and limitations can be translated into practical steps to this end.

CAN MEMORY BE IMPROVED?

The question of memory improvement is legitimate and deserves more than the psychologist's usual "yes-no-and-maybe" reply. As it happens, all three answers are correct, depending on what one means by memory improvement. Let us begin with the "no" of memory improvement; then we will move on to the "maybe" and the "yes."

"No": The "Pink Pill" Approach

The answer most of us would like to hear is that there is some technique, some exercise, which can bring about a general improvement in memory. Ideally, it should (1) operate in all situations, and (2) require as little personal effort as possible: some metaphorical "pink pill" as an all purpose cure-all for forgetting.

The seventeenth century was an exciting time in this regard; "cures" for forgetting were abundant. Among the more exotic were a variety of herbal treatments (especially cinnamon), the advice to wear a cap made of beaver skin, or to anoint the head and spine monthly with drops of castor oil (Hunter, 1964). Whatever benefits these might have, they would not seem to extend to improving memory.

The sophistication of the twentieth century has produced its own reports of pending remedies for the forgetful. This time they take the form of occasional newspaper articles with titles like, "Pills to Improve Memory?" As often as not, they turn out to be a science editor's daydreams or the report of mild stimulants whose action on the nervous system duplicates several cups of black coffee or, better still, a good night's sleep.[3]

Learning Latin was once thought to be an invaluable exercise of the intellect which would directly facilitate all other learning and retention. Learning Latin may be valuable and perhaps even less uncomfortable than anointing the head with castor oil (the author has been reluctant to try either), but the only specific transfer we can readily demonstrate is to the learning of other Latin-based languages.

"Maybe": Practice at Memorizing

A more contemporary version of the advice to learn Latin rests on the belief that memory is a skill that, like any other, can be improved by exercise. Thus, we find recommendations to practice memorizing whatever, whenever, and wherever one can: serial numbers on dollar bills, labels on medicine bottles, street names as you walk your dog, and so forth.

Practice at memorizing stands as one of the "maybes" of memory improvement. And probably for the same indirect reason that led others to the claims for learning Latin. The fact is that memorizing is not a direct exercise of some specific faculty of "memory" in a way analogous to a weight lifter exercising his muscles. That is, unless the analogy includes not only the weight lifter strengthening his muscles (the false part of the analogy), but also the discovery of ways the task can be accomplished more efficiently.

There are benefits to practice at memorization, but these occur only when the activity is accompanied by self-analysis and self-discovery about the act of memorizing itself. When this happens, the benefits of practice (or learning Latin) can be very real. Without it, sheer repetitive practice at memorizing for its own sake is of little use. This thought brings us to the "yes" of memory improvement.

"Yes": Self-Analysis and Learning to Learn

The notion of *self-discovery* in memory improvement rests on the important principle that the key to better memory lies in more effective learning in the first place (Hunter, 1964). This is where the majority of "memory" problems originate. And the key to effective learning lies in the ability to become objective, self-critical observers of our own learning ca-

---

[3] Generally speaking, stimulants (caffein, amphetamine, nicotine, strychnine, picrotoxin) administered close to the time of learning do facilitate acquisition and memory, while nervous system depressants (alcohol, nitrous oxide, chlorpromazine) impair learning and memory (Wickelgren, 1974). Their effects, including their harmful ones, however, are still under investigation and are not at all well understood.

pabilities and strategies. This includes both an ongoing self-diagnosis of our current learning habits, and an experimental approach to discovering ways they may be improved.

SELF-ANALYSIS.   Suppose someone sets out to memorize a poem, in the hope that this itself will improve memory. The fact is that memorizing a series of poems does not ordinarily make the learning of each successive poem faster or easier (Norman, 1969). Indirectly, however, a great deal of transferrable knowledge can be learned.

Through an objective appraisal of our own approach to learning, it is possible to experiment with, and to discover, those techniques of study which work best for us as individuals. We can determine the relative advantages of recitation or periodically recopying from memory. We can experiment with whole versus part learning, the use of mediators, associations, and imagery. We can verify the benefits of distributed over massed practice and discover which schedules of pacing seem most viable. (Concentrated study is "work" and, as such, is constrained by physical stamina and general health.) Finally, we can learn general principles of study, such as the value of attentiveness and concentration. As valuable as it may be to read about the importance of these factors in a textbook, it is quite another thing to discover their validity yourself, and to adapt them to your own needs and abilities.

The benefits of practice at memorizing, in other words, come from concentrating as much on *how* as on *what* we are learning. An exercise in memorizing can become an exercise in self-discovery that, in turn, can lead to the development of improved learning techniques. The benefits of a memory exercise will be doubled if the recitation of the learned material is followed by a critical discussion of what went on during the memorizing activity itself.

IMPORTANCE OF ORGANIZATION

If we devote enough time to listening to people's complaints about poor memory, it becomes apparent that their problems relate less to material they find personally interesting than to those common "memory chores" that all of us reluctantly must engage in from time to time. Why are some of these chores (typically they involve rote memory) more difficult than others? The answer should become clear if we briefly review the reasons why interesting material is traditionally easier both to learn and remember than materials which are not.

First, because the material is interesting (we usually mean potentially relevant), we pay close attention to it when it is presented. Second, we think about it and give it active rehearsal. Third, interesting (relevant) material, almost by definition, relates to things we already know. Usually, this is precisely why it is interesting. This relation to preestablished schemata gives the material ready organization and an anchor for retention. Finally, its very interest and relevance insures its repeated reuse once learned. This in turn supplies the repetition which reduces the likelihood of forgetting.

As we said, when the question of memory improvement is raised, it is invariably in the context of materials we do *not* find interesting; where there is no clear relation to existing schemata. In other words, we lack precisely the three key factors present in the learning of interesting materials: *attention, organization,* and *repetition.* Of these three keys, it is the turning of the middle one, organization, which frequently causes the other two to follow.

In formal education, one usually thinks of the curriculum designer or the teacher as having the responsibility of organizing the material for presentation. While educational theories and rationales may differ, the emphasis on organization in learning maintains a central position.

From the S-R approach, Skinner, for example, stressed acquisition of complex information through learning a sequence of specific elements. *Programmed learning* is the well-known child of this concept (Taber, Glaser & Schaefer, 1965). Often, however, the particular sequences found in many programs are only intuitively derived, and may, in fact, not be the best ones. Gagné's (1970) approach to sequencing is to begin with a consideration of the final goal to be achieved. Through this comes specification of the requisite skills necessary for its attainment and the specific subskills necessary to attain each of these. Mathematics and science seem particularly amenable to this approach. But what of civics? Do we begin with the president and congress and move progressively through state to local government? Or do we move the other way? And what of subjects which seem to have no clear sequence at all? A social studies unit on Sweden, for example, might cover its history, government, climate, industry . . . but it is hard to get agreement on which should logically come first.

Ausubel has approached the problem of organization in learning through what he calls *advance organizers* (cf. Ausubel & Robinson, 1969). These are sets of ideas that aid the student both in organizing knowledge he or she may already have and in facilitating the organization of material to be acquired. The concept is a nice application of our notion of schemata in memory, with the difference that these organizers are taught in a systematic way for specific materials, rather than evolving naturally through experience. The use of advance organizers seems to have the most marked success with slower students. This may indirectly imply that better students are already adept at exploiting the advantages of organizing materials for learning (Travers, 1973).

On an individual level, organization becomes the first step in the learning task itself, and numerous books with titles like *How to Improve Your Memory* or *How to Study* are replete with advice (cf. Morgan & Deese, 1957; Weinland, 1957; Mace, 1962; Cermak, 1975). Their essence can be summarized in terms of three steps to be taken at the start of any study session (Hunter, 1964, pp. 312–313). These steps embody most of the principles we have discussed to this point. (1) *Survey the task:* Think about the learning requirements for the specific materials, the study methods to be used, and the circumstances for recall. (2) *Organize the materials:* Organize the materials into some coherent structure, even if it means rearranging their order. See how the components relate to each other and how together they relate to existing knowledge. (3) *Repeat what has been learned:* Rehearsal during initial learning is necessary, but not sufficient, to insure adequate retention. Periodic review and reuse inhibits forgetting. Make a conscious effort to refresh the material by using it whenever the occasion arises. If the occasion does not arise naturally, *make* it arise.

Contrary to what might be expected from our discussion of retroactive and proactive inhibition, learning ability and memory do not decrease as we acquire more and more knowledge. This hardly disproves the potency of RI and PI effects in forgetting. Rather, it shows how our increasing ability to organize material into existing cognitive structures can outweigh these effects of interference. Readers especially interested in the functions of organization of knowledge as they apply to school learning are referred to Klahr (1976).

PLANS, IMAGES, MEDIATORS, AND MNEMONICS

Mnemonic systems are specially designed sets of associations used for the learning and retention of specific sets of materials. So powerful can these mnemonics be, they were considered in medieval times as among the "magic arts." They are today commonly taught in courses on memory improvement; they serve as the backbone of stage performers who make their livelihood through displays of memory virtuosity.

A mnemonic (from *Mnemosyne*, the Greek goddess of memory) is hardly magic. It is a preestablished *plan* for the organization of learning materials—an advance organization of *mediators* and *images* to which learning materials can be easily attached. In other words, they work as a memory aid precisely as they mimic natural organizational schemata ordinarily associated with meaningful material.

Mnemonics: An Illustration

One of the better-known tricks of stage performers, often called *mne-monists*, is to begin their show by asking the audience to name various objects around the theater by number. They might call out, for example, "one-your microphone," "two-that *Exit* sign," "three-front row, end seat," and so forth. After several dozen number-object combinations, the whole matter is apparently dropped, and the mnemonist moves on to the main performance. After perhaps an hour has elapsed, he reminds the audience of that earlier exercise and asks them now to shout their numbers in any order they want. With appropriate theatrical fanfare, he now reproduces perfectly the name of each and every object as its number is called.

The trick, of course, is a particular mnemonic specially designed for the purpose. It combines both rhyme and imagery and is an excellent illustration of what mnemonics are, and how they work. Hunter (1964) took a scaled-down version into the laboratory to see how easily the trick could be acquired. He began with only ten number-object combinations, such as one-SUGAR, two-DAFFODIL, three-BOAT, four-TIGER, etc. Each number-object pair was read aloud once at a steady rate for memory.

Most people will try to learn the sets through the cumulative rehearsal of association chaining. They repeat the first word, then the first and second word, then the first three words . . . by the time five or six sets have been presented, they find it impossible to recite the full list before the next item arrives. Some people will try to integrate the words into a story. Others appear to count off the words on their fingers. Two things become apparent. First, people predictably try to recall the words in the same manner they tried to learn them. Some try to reproduce the chain; others reconstruct their story; still others look studiously at their fingers. The second thing is that none of these methods are up to the task.

In Hunter's demonstration, a second group of students, given the same list of ten number-object pairs, after one hearing was able to reproduce it forward, backward, or in any order desired. Here is how the students did it. The first step is to learn what has now become a rather well-known rhyme (cf. Miller, Galanter, & Pribram, 1960; Norman, 1969; Cermak, 1972)

One is a bun, two is a shoe, three is a tree, four is a door, five is a hive, six is sticks, seven is heaven, eight is a gate, nine is wine, ten is a hen.

As Hunter's novice mnemonists learned the rhyme, they were instructed to picture each object as vividly as possible. Beginning with "one is a bun," they were to think of not just any bun, but a particular one, picturing its shape, color, and kind of icing.

The rhyme is the mnemonic and here is how it is used as a number-object list is presented. When a number-object pair was presented, they were to think of that numbered object in the rhyme and relate the two as vividly as possible. "Suppose the first word is petrol (gasoline). See *your* particular bun covered in petrol, reeking petrol, swimming in a can of petrol, belching flames like a petrol-bun. The more outrageously odd the relation, the better" (Hunter, 1964, pg. 288). As each object was presented, Hunter's subjects would relate it in a similarly vivid way to the correspondingly numbered object in the rhyme. It sounds easy, and it is.

Types of Mnemonics

The above illustration makes three important points about mnemonics in general. First, they not only work, but work so well as to often startle the user. Second, they are totally arbitrary and inappropriate for any other purpose than rote reproduction. Finally, any mnemonic is specific to a particular kind of memory task and no other. For this latter reason, there are a variety of different types of mnemonics and innumerable variations for specific tasks (cf. Miller, Galanter & Pribram, 1960; Hunter, 1964; Yates, 1966). Three of the most commonly used mnemonics are based on *rhyme, imagery*, and *mediated association.*

RHYME.   Rhyming is a useful way of connecting unrelated material when sequencing is important. "Thirty days hath September . . ." is one example, and the rule *"i* before *e*, except after *c"* is another. The rhyme not only cues the elements, but any missing item noticeably disrupts the sequence.

If a rhyme is good, a rhyme with a little melody is even better. Probably the best known example of all has echoed down school corridors for longer than we dare try to calculate. It is the way children commonly learn the letters of the alphabet. It exploits every memory device possible. The rhyme divides the 26 letters into three chunks, each chunk with two elements, each element with two units, and each unit with one to four letters (Norman, 1976, pg. 117):

[(*ab-cd*) (*ef-g*)]   [(*hi-jk*) (*lmno-p*)]   [(*qrs-tuv*) (*w-xyz*)].

It is a beautiful example of chunking, to keep the elements within the span of STM, and rhyming, to give sequential structure to the subspan chunks.

IMAGERY.   The "one is a bun" mnemonic is a specialized use of rhyme, combined with visual imagery. Another mnemonic system for the same task dispenses with the rhyme but is equally powerful. The trick is to learn a preestablished set of objects which look like numbers: one-CANDLE; five-HAND; eight-EYEGLASSES, and so forth. Once this is done, any list of number-object pairs can be handled by fitting each of the items to the mnemonic. If one of the items is five-NECKLACE, one could picture a necklace wrapped around a hand. For eight-CUP, picture eyeglasses floating in a cup of coffee. As Hunter and others suggest, the more vivid and outrageous the imagery, the better.

MEDIATED ASSOCIATION.   Finding mediators to relate arbitrary associations is probably the most common of all memory aids. We can remember that stalagmites come from the ground, while stalactites hang from the ceiling. In the language of mediation:

> stalagmites→g→ground; stalactites→c→ceiling

Examples of such mnemonics are plentiful in the early school years. Children remember the spelling of *principal* versus *principle,* by convincing themselves that "your princi*pal* is your pal." Or that the numerator is the top part of a fraction because it contains the letter *u* as in "up." (The denominator begins with *d* as in "down.")

Should We Teach Mnemonics?

Many people hold surprisingly strong views on the use of mnemonics in the classroom. The disagreement superficially seems to be one of semantics. Proponents see them as useful aids to memory; opponents see them as an undesirable crutch. The fear on the part of this latter group centers on the ability of mnemonics to create effective retention in the absence of conceptual understanding. Indeed, their use can obscure conceptual relationships that actually exist. We could teach that the numerator, with its *u,* is "up." Alternatively, we could say that the numerator enumerates, or *numbers,* the portions in a fraction, while the denominator denominates, or *names,* its size.

There is one interesting justification for encouraging the use of mnemonics. They can give students a dramatic object lesson in their own potential abilities for learning and retention. Many students take the very view of memory we rejected at the outset of the previous chapter. They see memory as a passive sponge which quickly becomes saturated with too much learning and can hold no more. Mnemonics are a particularly striking way of showing students that they are the masters of their own fate in learning. They can *control* the way they learn and remember. In short, their use can not only give them new confidence in their capabilities but serve as an object lesson on the value of organization and active involvement in learning. This in itself, is no small lesson to learn.

SUMMARY

The question of memory improvement has a longer history than the scientific study of memory itself. Current views suggest that improvement in memory rests almost entirely on improvement in techniques of learning.

First, it is imporant to attend to the material; second, to give it organization; and third, to rehearse the material as much as possible.

   Mnemonics are specially designed sets of associations to give organization to otherwise unconnected material. Such mnemonic techniques include the use of rhyme, imagery, and mediated associations. Mnemonics
can be a powerful aid to memory since they can be said to mimic the natural organizational schemata ordinarily used in the learning of meaningful
material.

part five

The Biological Basis and Readiness for Learning

chapter 12

The Biological Basis of Learning and Memory

It could be argued that all of us know how a television set works, even though few of us understand the mysteries of its internal wiring circuits. We know its *operating principles:* which knob turns it on and controls the volume, how to adjust the focus, and so forth. In a similar way, we can know a great deal about the processes of human learning and memory without understanding the internal "wiring" of the brain.

This chapter is about the brain and its presumed function in learning and memory. The subject of our inquiry, by the way, is something less than inspiring in appearance. It is roughly spheroid in shape, soft to the touch, a dull pinkish gray in color; in the adult it weighs, on average, some three pounds. It is living tissue and depends for its survival on constant nourishment from the blood stream. It is also the seat of human intellect, motivation, and learning.

Logic tells us that learning must cause some physiological changes in the brain and, because we can retain what we have learned, that these changes must be relatively permanent. Our task in understanding these changes, however, is not easy. Not only is the subject matter by its nature complex, but much of what we need to know about brain function in learning has yet to be discovered. The more primitive functions of the human brain, those we share with lower animals, are far better understood than the symbolic activities of the brain which are either largely or wholly unique to man. In other words, more is known about the brain's reception of light and sound and the control of motor movements than is known about its role in complex learning, memory, and thought.

The knowledge we do have has not come easily. It reflects the slow and steady development of neurology over a period spanning 100 years, combined with an almost frenetic pace of activity made possible by developments in biochemistry within the past two decades.

Our goal in this chapter is to review some of these developments, to look briefly at the techniques of study in modern neuropsychology, and to consider the future directions in which they may lead.

THE BRAIN IN LEARNING AND MEMORY

The premise that learning and memory are represented by physiological changes in the brain raises two fundamental questions. The first question is concerned with *where* in the human brain learning takes place. Does learning affect the entire brain as a whole, or is the handling of different kinds of experience located in different parts of the brain which are especially devoted to these functions? For example, is speech centered in one area, reading ability in another, and memory for music in a third?

To explore this question, we will look briefly at the anatomy of the human brain and the techniques which have been used to explore the primary functions of its various areas. This discussion will focus on both the functional differences between the left and the right hemispheres of the brain and the consequences of brain injury to learning and other cognitive functions.

The second question addresses *the nature* of the physiological changes in the brain in the course of learning. Are these changes primarily represented by electrical activity, chemical activity, or both? To answer this question, we will have to look briefly at the structure of microscopic brain cells and at their interaction in the course of brain activity. We will also review some current speculations regarding the operation of these cells, and patterns of cells, in the storage of memory.

The first question, under the title *cerebral localization,* asks *where* learning takes place. The second question, under the title *neurophysiology of learning and memory,* asks *how.*

Cerebral Localization

The early history of neurology reflected a seesaw battle between those who believed that specific intellectual activities took place in different, specialized areas of the brain, and those who thought brain activity was surely more general and diffuse. This metaphorical seesaw was never in balance. Beginning in the late nineteenth century, the two sides tended to be either all the way up or all the way down, rocking almost rhythmically with alternate decades.

Certainly the most extreme position on specific localization of function was seen in what came to be called the field of *phrenology* (Gall & Spurzheim, 1810). The *phrenologists*, through a rather mysterious chain of inference, claimed to have discovered the very exact locations of different intellectual functions and personality traits in the human brain. Figure 12.1 reproduces an early phrenological "map" of the brain. As you can see, their view of functional localization was very exact indeed.

The phrenologists, incidentally, would use this "map" in conjunction with feeling the unique irregularities on people's heads. The expert would feel the location of the bumps and grooves, refer to the "map" showing the particular characteristics believed to underlie those areas, and then would pronounce upon the person's strengths and weaknesses in those characteristics ("friendship," "self-esteem," etc.).

Feeling the bumps on people's heads, alas, has given way to less exotic techniques for personality assessment. Clinical psychology and psychiatry felt ready to trade the erroneous overcertainty of phrenology for the recognized uncertainties of such devices as the Rorschach, the thematic apperception test (TAT), and the Minnesota Multiphasic Personality Inventory (MMPI). At the same time, the increasingly sophisticated field of neurology began to amass a great body of data on brain function. Localization of function within the brain there may be, but not quite in the way in which it was seen by the phrenologists.

At the height of the phrenology movement (roughly, the 1830s), there existed over 17 journals devoted to its study and propagation. The last one died—of poor readership—in Philadelphia in 1911 (Robinson, 1973, pg. 50).

Modern research in brain function has led to very different conclusions from those of the early phrenologists. As we will see, certain functions do seem to be associated with various areas of the brain, although they are much broader functions than those envisaged by the phrenologists. The critical point, however, turns on the way the term "localized" is used today. The brain operates as a dynamic whole: no single part of the brain is devoted to any single cognitive activity in a self-contained way. Functions are

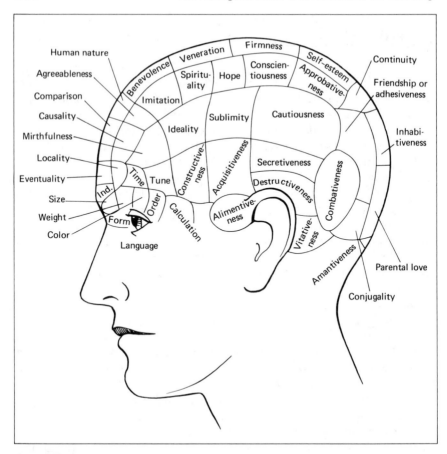

Figure 12.1 A phrenological "map" showing ideas of specific localization of various personality traits and cognitive functions. (*Source:* G. A. Miller, *Psychology: The Science of Mental Life.* New York: Harper & Row, 1962, pg. 252. Reprinted by permission.)

said to be *localized* only in the sense that certain areas of the brain are thought to be especially critical to these functions.

METHODS OF LOCALIZING FUNCTION

The bulk of modern brain research has been conducted with lower animals and has made vital contributions to our understanding of the general functions of the brain, as well as indicating promising directions for human brain research. Common techniques for the study of brain function in lower animals include experimental surgery, in which different portions of the brain are selectively damaged or removed, implanting microelectrodes into the brain tissue to record its electrical activity, and initiating activity by direct electrical stimulation of the brain.

Human brain research is obviously more restricted and has relied almost entirely on studies involving patients with some damage or disease of the brain who are seen in the course of medical treatment. As such, the interests and benefit of the individual patient are held to be of paramount importance. Whenever research is conducted, or data collected, it is done with the express permission of the patient and is primarily the outcome of procedures which would ordinarily be conducted for the patient's own benefit.

1. Brain Injury

By far the greatest single source of information about localization of brain function does not in fact involve surgical intervention or experimental treatment of the patient at all. These are studies of patients who have sustained damage to certain portions of the brain and have consequently suffered some loss or debility of cognitive function. Many of these patients have incurred penetrating head wounds, due either to war injury or traffic accident. Others have suffered cerebrovascular accidents (strokes), where destruction or interruption of function has resulted from insufficient blood supply to the brain due to a blood clot or rupture of a blood vessel.

Such studies are essentially correlational. One observes the impairment of some function (e.g., speech, reading, etc.) and then attempts to relate it to the specific area of the brain known to be damaged. However exacting, this method of neuroanatomical research still involves a high degree of inference. Identifying an area of the brain invariably associated with a loss of a particular cognitive function does not tell us whether that function is directly *controlled* from that area, or whether that area is simply important to its execution. The accumulation of data is necessarily slow and may require the examination of literally hundreds of patients before even such inferences can be made with any statistical confidence (cf. Russell & Espir, 1961).

2. Neurosurgery

Some limited information can come to light from surgeons' reports following operations to alleviate cases of neurological disease which can be treated surgically, such as removal of a tumor, or some forms of epilepsy. In this case we hope to relate the recovery of some function to the site of the operation (cf. Penfield & Roberts, 1959).

These two methods, analyzing the effects of accidental brain damage and the results of neurosurgery, represent the traditional sources of most localization data. More recently, a number of additional techniques have been added to this short list. Some of them were originally developed as clinical tools to aid the diagnostic task of the neurologist or neurosurgeon. Over the years, however, they have added considerably to our knowledge of normal brain function. The final three categories are examples of such procedures.

3. Sodium Amytal

For reasons we will see later, surgery to either one hemisphere or the other can produce differential effects on a patient's language behavior after the operation. For this reason, it can be an advantage for the surgeon to know in advance how a particular patient might react following interference with the ordinary functioning of either of the two hemispheres.

Injection of *sodium amytal* into the *carotid artery* of the neck has the effect of temporarily depressing the function of a single hemisphere for a short period before its effects wear off. The carotid arteries, the principal source of blood supply to the brain, cross within the neck such that injection into the artery on the left side of the neck will temporarily render the right hemisphere nonfunctional, and injection into the right artery has the same effect on the left hemisphere. Testing psychological performance before the effects of the injection wear off can thus give some indication of the independent functions of the two hemispheres (Wada & Rasmussen, 1960). For the researcher metaphorically looking over the surgeon's shoulder, the results of the technique can add to our theoretical knowledge of brain function and cognitive activity (cf. Lansdell, Purnell & Laskowski, 1963).

4. Evoked Potentials

A much less traumatic technique for the study of brain function involves an application of the familiar electroencephalograph (EEG) ordinarily used clinically for neurological examinations. It was long ago discovered (in the 1920s) that neural activity is normally accompanied by the presence of tiny charges of electric current which arc through the cortex as thousands upon thousands of brain cells activate each other in infinitely changing patterns. Neurologists soon learned that this activity could be monitored by placing small electrodes on the surface of the scalp and amplifying these waves for visual display on an oscillograph. In this way abnormal brain activity such as found with epilepsy or brain damage could be recognized, and its location pinpointed in the brain.

In research use, various numbers of electrodes are placed on the scalp of healthy persons to record electrical activity ("potentials") in different parts of the brain caused ("evoked") when the person receives different types of stimuli, such as sounds, visual stimuli, or speech. One can thus determine which areas of the brain show the greatest amount of activity in response to these various types of stimuli and hence draw some inferences about localization of function within the cortex. There have been a number of interesting applications of this technique, especially ones involving the use of linguistic and nonlinguistic stimuli (cf. Wood, Goff & Day, 1971).

5. Electrical Stimulation

A final technique was originally developed in the 1950s as a way for neurosurgeons to map cortical function and so to reduce the likelihood of inadvertently operating on an area of the brain which might interfere with such functions as speech or memory. The procedure begins after the area of the cortex awaiting surgery has been revealed by removing a portion of the skull bone. The surgeon touches a small electrode to various spots on the exposed brain surface and observes the behavioral effects of mild electrical stimulation to these areas. Stimulating one area might cause a particular part of the body to move, stimulating another area might affect another part, while stimulating a third area may stop the patient's speech in the middle of a sentence. In this way, one can systematically map the behavior function of the areas in and around the diseased region prior to surgical intervention.

The patient, by the way, is fully conscious throughout this procedure, having received only a local anesthetic. This is possible because the brain itself has no pain receptors, such that brain stimulation is accompanied by little or no discomfort (Penfield & Roberts, 1959).

These and other studies have supplied considerable information about the localization of function within the human brain and about those areas especially important to various aspects of cognitive function. As, for example, Lenneberg (1967, pp. 54–66) has pointed out, each of these techniques has some limitations, and their results must be treated with caution. Taken together, however, they have built up a fairly clear picture of organization within the brain. As we describe some of the findings, it should become clear that the erroneous specificity of phrenology is well and truly behind us.

THE CEREBRAL CORTEX

The human brain, or *cerebrum*, is constructed as two physically identical halves, known as *hemispheres*. Except for size, coloring, and texture, the two cerebral hemispheres look strikingly like the two connected halves of a shelled walnut. The outer surface of the hemispheres is called the *cortex*. Like the surface of a walnut, it is irregular and somewhat wrinkled in appearance. These "wrinkles" in the cortex are referred to as *convolutions*, and they exist for a very logical reason. The cortex is importantly involved in intellectual and voluntary control. For this reason, there is a clear advantage in having as large a surface area as possible—but not too large a head. The simplest way to fit a large surface area into a small space is to crumple it, rather like crumpling a piece of paper. Hence the convolutions: a way of getting the largest possible surface area into the smallest possible space.

Figure 12.2 shows a rough sketch of the brain as seen from the left side (the right side would look essentially the same). The irregular lines drawn on the side of the hemisphere are intended to represent some of the ridges and crevices of the convolutions. The ridges are called *gyri;* the crevices are called *fissures* or *sulci.*

As an aid to referring to specific areas of the brain, the cortex is descriptively divided into four major areas, called *lobes.* The area from the frontmost part of the brain in Figure 12.2 up to the *central fissure* is known as the *frontal lobe.* The area just to the rear of the central fissure and above the *lateral fissure* is the *parietal lobe.* The area below this is the *temporal lobe.* The rearmost portion of the cortex beyond the parietal and temporal lobes is referred to as the *occipital lobe.* The same four lobes are represented on the right hemisphere.

Also shown in the illustration is a structure below and to the rear of the main body of the brain, appropriately called the *hindbrain.* Three components of the hindbrain are shown in the illustration. These are the *cerebel-*

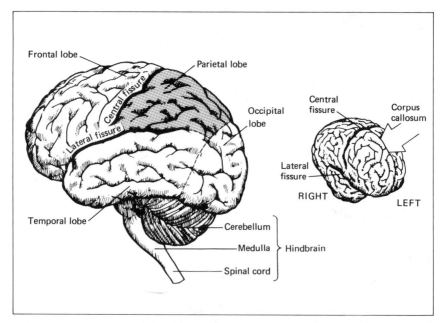

Figure 12.2   Sketch of the left hemisphere of the human brain showing major cortical areas and hindbrain. (*Right:* Perspective drawing of brain showing location of *corpus callosum* lying within the brain connecting the two hemispheres.)

lum which is important to the smoothness of motor coordination, the *medulla* which mediates breathing and heart rate, and the top of the *spinal cord* which continues down the spine to carry nerve fibers to and from the brain to the body as a whole. An important element not shown in the drawing is the *corpus callosum.* This is a thick sheet of tissue which connects the two hemispheres and carries both nourishment and interconnecting nerve fibers between them (see insert, Figure 12.2).

This very brief tour of the human brain has been restricted to the outer surface, or cortex, since this is the part of the brain most directly involved in intellectual and cognitive function. The interior portions of the brain, underneath the outer cortical layer, also contain several structures relevant to learning. These include the *reticular activating system* (RAS), which is crucial to cortical arousal and attention, and the *limbic system,* which is involved in emotion and motivation. In addition, studies have shown that damage to the temporal lobe and associated structures such as the *hippocampus* (located beneath the cortex underlying the temporal lobe) may impair the ability to consolidate short-term into long-term memory (Milner, 1965; 1966). It has been suggested that while short-term memory may involve such subcortical areas, the formation of long-term memory takes place in the cortex itself (Paolino & Levy, 1971).

LOCALIZATION OF FUNCTION WITHIN THE CORTEX

With a possible minor exception to be noted later, there are no obvious physical differences in appearance between the left and the right hemispheres of the brain. They are roughly the same size, share the same degree of convoluted appearance, and so forth. Indeed, for virtually all functions in lower animals, and for many functions in the human, both hemispheres operate identically. They operate, however, in a slightly complicated way. Each hemisphere controls the *opposite* side of the body. Referred to as *contralateral control,* this means that sensation from, and control of, the left arm, left hand, left leg, et cetera, is located in the right hemisphere, while the right side of the body is controlled by the left hemisphere. For example, if we were to see paralysis of the right arm or leg following some damage to the brain, we could infer immediately that the injury must have been to the left hemisphere.

The source of voluntary motor control of body movement lies in a vertical strip just forward of the central fissure in the frontal lobes (*region 1a* in Figure 12.3). The functional mapping of this so-called motor strip or motor cortex is probably as detailed as any area of the brain. The corresponding centers for the movement of the hands, feet, fingers, and toes are all known to almost pinpoint accuracy within the motor strip. The centers in the motor strip of the left hemisphere for control of the body's right side have

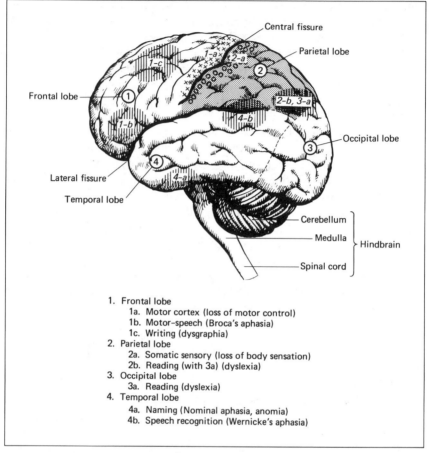

1. Frontal lobe
   1a. Motor cortex (loss of motor control)
   1b. Motor-speech (Broca's aphasia)
   1c. Writing (dysgraphia)
2. Parietal lobe
   2a. Somatic sensory (loss of body sensation)
   2b. Reading (with 3a) (dyslexia)
3. Occipital lobe
   3a. Reading (dyslexia)
4. Temporal lobe
   4a. Naming (Nominal aphasia, anomia)
   4b. Speech recognition (Wernicke's aphasia)

Figure 12.3 Sketch of the left hemisphere of the human brain showing major cortical areas and a summary of localization data for persons with left hemisphere dominance.

their exact counterparts in the right hemisphere for control of the body's left side.

For effective motor learning and skilled performance, the brain must receive constant sensory feedback from the fingers, limbs, and so forth, as they are in movement. This feedback is integrated in the so-called somatic sensory areas of the brain, located in the parietal lobes just to the rear of the central fissure (*region 2a*). As in motor control, the sensory pathways also follow the contralateral principle. The left parietal lobe receives sensory feedback from the right side of the body, and the right parietal lobe receives feedback from the left.

Vision is primarily centered in the rear portion of the occipital lobes (*region 3*), although in this case the simple principle of contralaterality presents a rather more complicated picture. The left half of the visual field of both eyes send fibers to the occipital lobe of the right hemisphere, while the right visual field of both eyes sends fibers to the occipital lobe of the left hemisphere. Thus, damage to the occipital lobe of, say, the right hemisphere would *not* cause complete blindness to either the left or the right eye. Rather, the person would lose vision from the left half only of *both* eyes. (This visual problem is medically termed a *hemianopia*.)

The temporal lobes of the two hemispheres (*region 4*) are involved in hearing. Interestingly, while there are nerve pathways from each ear to both hemispheres, the contralateral fibers are far more efficient. That is, while either hemisphere's temporal lobe can "hear" signals from either ear, when sounds are simultaneously delivered to both ears, the left hemisphere is more sensitive to sounds from the right ear while the right hemisphere is more sensitive to sounds from the left ear (cf. Milner, Taylor & Sperry, 1968; Zurif, 1974).

In addition to these localized functions, there are also noncommitted areas of the brain, such as large portions of the frontal lobes (*region 1*), which contain association fibers from all areas of the brain, allowing the cortex to operate as a whole. Personality, temperament, and emotional control are dependent on mechanisms in the frontal lobes; at least, these characteristics may become disturbed if either one or both frontal lobes become damaged or destroyed (Espir & Rose, 1970, pg. 9). The frontal lobes have also been traditionally associated with the powers of abstract thought (Goldstein, 1950). On the other hand, we must be cautious of the popular view that intelligence (or "personality") is actually located in this single area of the human brain. Intellectual function depends on the integration of activity from the whole of the cerebral cortex. The frontal lobes are probably critical only in respect of their important role in this integration.

Cerebral Dominance

While all of the functions previously described (body control, vision, hearing) are represented contralaterally in both hemispheres, it became apparent toward the end of the nineteenth century that some higher mental functions in the human are not represented equally in both hemispheres. The most important of these functions are language and verbal ability.

For virtually all right-handed people, recognition and production of language, speech, and verbal ability (to include verbal memory) is located in the *left hemisphere*. This includes such language-related functions as reading and writing. In other words, damage to certain areas of the left hemisphere of right-handed persons will disturb these functions, while damage to the same areas of the right hemisphere will not. For this reason, we refer to the left hemisphere as being the *dominant* one in right-handed persons. There is also some evidence that the dominant hemisphere may be slightly larger and may contain more nerve cells than the nondominant hemisphere (Espir & Rose, 1970, pg. 21).

The early recognition of left-hemisphere dominance in right-handers, combined with a knowledge of the general principle of contralaterality, led early workers in neurology to the erroneous conclusion that speech in the left-hander must therefore be in the right hemisphere. Later research was to show that this rather neat conclusion was, in fact, incorrect.

We now know that the left hemisphere is dominant for virtually all right-handed people, and that it is also the dominant hemisphere for most left-handers as well.[1] The most conservative estimates suggest that well over half of all left-handers also have speech located in their left hemisphere, with only a minority of left-handers having dominance (speech) in their right hemisphere. This has been confirmed by most of the techniques previously described: surgery and electrical stimulation (Penfield & Roberts, 1959), the results of brain injury (Russell & Espir, 1961), and intracarotid arterial injection (Milner, Branch & Rasmussen, 1964). For that smaller proportion of left-handers who do have right-hemisphere dominance, all of the functions of the left hemisphere are located in their right hemispheres, and vice versa.

ON BEING LEFT-HANDED.   Left-handers account for only about five to ten percent of the population and, assuming left-hemisphere dominance for all right-handers and for most left-handers, we can see that right-hemisphere dominance is statistically a very rare event. Other than being rare, and the fact that these individuals may suffer language impairment following right- (but not left-) hemisphere lesions, right-hemisphere dominance has no major significance on behavior.

However clear the facts of handedness and cerebral dominance, there is much about the relationship which is not yet fully understood. We know that left-handers are presently in the minority, and evidence from prehistoric cave drawings suggests that this has always been so (Espir & Rose, 1970, pg. 21).

Infants show little particular preference for either one hand or the other until about the age of 9 or 10 months when speech first begins. However, it is not until the age of 2 years, and the first peak of postnatal neurological maturation, that hand preference appears with any regularity, and this development increases only gradually with age until handedness becomes more or less firmly established between 4 and 5 years of age.

While most of the adult population shows clear preference for either the

[1] There are rare exceptions to the rule of left-hemisphere dominance for right-handed persons. These cases are usually attributed to left-hemisphere brain damage in early childhood, and a consequent takeover of function by the ordinarily nondominant right hemisphere.

right or the left hand, there are varying degrees of laterality, some people being more strongly right handed than others. We should not assume from this that laterality for speech is necessarily less complete in these individuals. Many of these "partial right-handers" may in fact be normally left-handed persons who have been conditioned by societal pressure to learn some skills with their right hand. Similarly, it is generally believed that true ambidexterity, the ability to use either hand equally well, is quite rare. Most cases can be attributed to probable left-handers who have accommodated to a right-handed world by developing fine motor skill with their right hand, while not losing skill with their left.

We are moved to speak on behalf of the left-handers of the world, a group singularly victimized over the decades. They have been forced to use right-handed tools, like scissors, to restring their guitars and, not so many years ago, even forced by ill-advised parents and teachers to learn to write with their right (wrong) hand. Even when allowed to write with the left hand, they were often still made to tilt their writing paper to the left instead of to the right as one should do if left handed. This of course leads to the most awkward of hand positions in order to produce the obligatory right-hand slant to cursive writing. The term for the left hand, *sinistral,* and the word *sinister* have the same Latin root.

How does the individual left-hander know whether his or her left or right hemisphere is dominant? As we have seen, the odds are that it is the left. The only sure way of knowing is by testing for language disturbance following injection of sodium amytal (a painful and dangerous procedure), or by observing the results of brain damage. It is better to live with the uncertainty.

Lateralized Function of the Left Hemisphere

The dominant (usually left) hemisphere is generally involved in speech, and damage to that side of the brain can bring about *aphasia*, a language disorder caused by brain damage (Russell & Espir, 1961; Luria, 1970). A unique feature of aphasia is the frequent selectivity in the nature of the functions disturbed. That is, damage to different areas of the left hemisphere can produce selective disturbances in the production of speech, the recognition of speech, or disturbances in reading or writing, while the other functions remain relatively intact. Indeed, it is intriguing to encounter early references to aphasialike symptoms in the perspective of modern neuropsychology. For example, in the Roman times of A.D. 30, Valerius Maximus described a learned Athenian who lost his memory for letters after being struck on the head by a stone, while in the first chapter of the Gospel according to Saint Luke we can read of Zacharias who lost the power of speech but could still manage to write (Espir & Rose, 1970, pg. 24).

The first clear reference to the localization of a particular language function in the left hemisphere came in 1861 when a French physician named Pierre-Paul Broca reported autopsy results of a patient who, among other problems, showed a severe language disturbance following a brain injury. Broca found a lesion in the lower, posterior portion of the left frontal lobe and identified this area as the center for speech production (*region 1b* in Figure 12.3). As Broca charmingly put it, ". . . on parle avec l'hémisphère gauche" . . . we speak with the left hemisphere.

EXPRESSIVE APHASIA.   Severe brain damage can lead to a loss of the ability to formulate the neural programming necessary to perform motor acts. We are speaking here of voluntary, integrated control, and not of simple paralysis. That is, the same motor movements which cannot be performed voluntarily can be performed in isolation or accidentally. The patient seems to have no difficulty in formulating the idea of the act but finds himself or herself incapable of executing it. For example, the patient may have difficulty in dressing in the morning. He or she may attempt to put an arm through a trouser leg or button a shirt with the wrong buttons. In trying to light a cigarette, the patient may put the match to his or her mouth instead of to the end of the cigarette. In testing situations, copying block designs may be exceedingly difficult.

In all of the above situations, we are referring to problems not primarily involving language function, and the source of the damage would most likely be in the nondominant, right hemisphere. When the difficulties take the form of interference with language or verbal skills, however, the lesion is invariably in the left hemisphere. Such cases are referred to as *expressive aphasia.*

The damage to the lower, posterior portion of the left frontal lobe reported by Broca was just one such form of expressive aphasia. Patients with damage to this region ("Broca's aphasia") can use spontaneous speech only with conscious effort and often with considerable hesitation. For these patients, recognition and comprehension of speech is superior to language production and could, in principle, be relatively undisturbed. Broca's aphasia is commonly referred to as a selective disorder of word finding or speech production. We should, however, use the terms *word* and *speech* with caution. The problem is more one of "language" than "speech" in the sense that one occasionally hears of deaf persons who have lost the ability to produce sign language after receiving damage to Broca's area in the left hemisphere. For this reason, many writers have preferred to speak of aphasia in the more abstract sense of a disturbance in *symbolic* function rather than specifically as a speech disorder (cf. Goldstein, 1948).

Expressive aphasia can take other, more specific forms than a disturbance of speech production, depending on where in the left hemisphere the damage occurs. The inability to retrieve from memory the names of objects, sometimes referred to as *nominal aphasia* or *anomia,* has been traced to deep lesions of the left temporal lobe (*region 4a* in Figure 12.3) (cf. Newcombe, Oldfield, Ratcliff & Wingfield, 1971). Intriguingly, while finding the name of an object is exceedingly difficult for these patients, perceptual recognition of objects usually creates no special difficulty. For example, if shown a picture of a piano, the patient might immediately mime playing it, or tell you "it's a thing musicians play." Only the name itself seems elusive. Similar to normal "retrieval" problems as discussed in Chapter 10, these patients usually recognize their errors and can recognize the correct name when they hear it.

Damage to an area in the upper part of the left frontal lobe (*region 1c*) can produce a selective disturbance in writing ability or spelling (*dysgraphia*). Other expressive language problems associated with specific lesions in the dominant hemisphere include an inability to construct grammatical sentences, such as confusing articles and conjunctions (*syntactic aphasia*), a difficulty in doing mathematical calculations (*acalculia*), or sometimes, in employing the normal stress and rhythm patterns which ordinarily accompany fluent speech (*dysprosody*).

Clearly, all of these functions are interrelated as, for example, when a person's difficulty with arithmetic calculations can be traced to an inability to produce the symbols necessary for the calculation. In this case, the problem could be primarily one of word finding (anomia) rather than of acalculia. The following example illustrates the mix of expressive disorders as they may conspire to prevent the simple act of writing a letter from dictation. The patient was a 48-year-old army sergeant who had incurred damage to areas of the frontal and parietal lobes of the left hemisphere as a result of war service in Korea (Eisenson, 1957, pp. 441–442). The dictated material was:

Dear————————:
   I am a patient at ————————— Hospital. I was injured in Korea. When I am well enough to return to duty, may I have my old job back.
                                                                                        Thank you.

The patient wrote:

Dear A.J.
   I am a patent. At ————————— navy hoptile. at. I want hurt Korea when I hurtmeit to duat. May I hurt made open down. Beause.
                                                                                        Thand you.

RECEPTIVE APHASIA.   Damage to certain areas of the brain can also cause difficulties in the ability to interpret sensory information in a meaningful way.[2] This might include a selective difficulty in the interpretation of vis-

---

[2] This general receptive problem is sometimes referred to as *agnosia*, a term first used by Sigmund Freud (1891) who made a number of significant contributions to neuropsychology before his interests shifted to the study of personality and the development of psychoanalytic theory.

ual, auditory, or tactile information, depending on where the cortical damage has occurred. When the difficulty takes the form of an interference with language-related ability it is referred to as *sensory* or *receptive aphasia*.

The most noticeable form of receptive aphasia is a difficulty in recognizing or discriminating the sounds of speech. Once called "word deafness," the source of this difficulty was traced by Karl Wernicke in 1874 to damage to the posterior third of the temporal lobe and sometimes the adjacent area of the parietal lobe in the left hemisphere ("Wernicke's area": *region 4b* in Figure 12.3). The disorder involves difficulties in interpreting heard speech, even though the mechanisms of hearing and hearing acuity per se remain intact. While the speech itself may be heard with no difficulty, it no longer seems to the patient to have meaning. In some cases they can recognize the sounds they hear as speech, but its analysis in terms of words and phrases is difficult. In more severe cases, heard speech may seem to the patient to be little more than a jumble of sounds.

In spite of this difficulty in the understanding of spoken verbal materials, the perception of music and other nonspeech sounds is ordinarily quite normal (Geschwind, 1970; Goodglass, 1972).[3]

This form of receptive aphasia, sometimes referred to as *Wernicke's aphasia*, often takes its toll in speech production as well. Unlike persons with Broca's aphasia, these patients are less likely to recognize their errors since their comprehension difficulty can include the monitoring of their own speech as well as the speech of others. Unaware that their speech makes little sense, they may talk excessively (*logorrhea*), and they may show the disturbance of inflexion, stress, and rhythm associated with *dysprosody*. In extreme cases, their speech may be little more than a meaningless jumble of words.

Visual agnosia is a parallel inability to interpret symbolic visual stimuli, whether pictures, maps, or written words. Even though equipped with normal vision and intelligence, patients show considerable difficulty in recognizing objects and knowing their use. The problem is one of sensory interpretation and not of memory. For example, the patient may readily recognize an object by touch if he or she is allowed to feel it with the eyes closed. The damage is usually found in the occipital lobes or the fibers leading to them.

The most notable case of language related visual agnosia is that of *dyslexia*, a specific inability to read or to interpret visual symbolic material. Once called "word blindness," the damage is usually in the adjacent areas of the parietal and occipital lobes of the left hemispheres (*regions 2b and 3a* in Figure 12.3). For some dyslexic patients, letters may be difficult or impossible to distinguish, with confusions common between similar looking letters

---

[3] An inability to recognize melody due to brain damage is called *sensory amusia* and is associated with damage to the corresponding area in the right temporal lobe (Milner, 1962).

like *b* and *d*, or *g* and *q*. For others, individual letter recognition may be relatively unimpaired, but the letters seem to have little meaning as linguistic symbols. That is, they may recognize letters in isolation but be totally unable to give them meaning as they combine to form words.

Functions of the Nondominant Hemisphere

When the left hemisphere is dominant, the right hemisphere is involved in a variety of cognitive skills unrelated directly to language. Primarily, these include recognition for visual, spatial, and tactile sensation of a nonverbal character (Paterson & Zangwill, 1944; Piercy, 1964). For example, while memory for verbal materials can be disturbed by lesions in the left hemisphere, cases of right-hemisphere lesions often show difficulty with nonverbal, unfamiliar visual forms (Kimura, 1963).

Samuels, Butters, and Fedio (1972), working with postsurgery patients, have offered evidence for visual memory being mediated by the right parietal lobe, while damage to either temporal lobe can produce deficits in auditory memory. Their work, and that of others (e.g., Zurif & Ramier, 1972), however, stresses a distinction between the type of auditory material and the hemisphere in which it is primarily processed. Specifically, syntactic-semantic aspects of language seem to be processed in the left temporal lobe, while nonspeech, or semantically meaningless sounds, may be processed in the right. This is consistent with other studies which show the right ear (left hemisphere) to be more sensitive to detecting speech, while the left ear (right hemisphere) is more sensitive to detecting music and other nonspeech signals (Kimura, 1961, 1964; Shankweiler, 1967; Studdert-Kennedy & Shankweiler, 1970).

To say that music or patterned melody is processed in the nondominant hemisphere is generally correct. However, the full picture is obviously much more complex. For example, the processing of melodic pattern associated with the emotional sounds of speech has been shown to be lateralized in the right hemisphere (King & Kimura, 1972), while the melodic stress pattern of intonation which aids syntactic analysis and recognition of speech may be handled in the left hemisphere (Zurif, 1974). Thus, while primary processing areas can be localized to a good degree within the cortex, the ordinary processing of ongoing speech (and music) most probably involves very much of a global effort throughout the cortex.

"SPLIT-BRAIN" SURGERY. Perhaps nothing gives as dramatic an illustration of the functional contrast between the two hemispheres as reports of the peculiar effects which can be observed when the two hemispheres of the brain are surgically isolated by severing the corpus callosum.

This is a rather drastic and rare operation. It has, however, proven quite successful for certain forms of very severe epilepsy which have resisted alle-

viation by medication or other forms of treatment. These are cases in which
a seizure may begin in one hemisphere and rapidly spread to the other, until
the entire brain is involved in a generalized seizure. The hope of this operation was that severing the corpus callosum would act as a sort of "fire
break" to at least confine the effects of the seizure to the one hemisphere in
which it begins. As it happens, this so-called split-brain operation proved
even more successful than anticipated. Not only are the seizures confined to
one hemisphere, but there is an overall reduction in their severity. It would
appear that isolating the two hemispheres prevents them from reciprocally
exciting each other back and forth across the corpus callosum in what
would ordinarily be a snowballing build-up of the effects of the seizure.

In spite of the drastic nature of this operation, postoperative patients
appear normal and healthy in every regard. It is only when they are given
tests specifically designed to reveal the consequences of a loss of communication between the two hemispheres that the anomaly becomes apparent.
Here are just a few examples.

If a split-brain patient is blindfolded and allowed to touch an object,
such as a pair of scissors, with the left hand (whose signals go to the nonlinguistic right hemisphere), the patient can easily recognize the object. He or
she may indicate this by using gestures to illustrate its use or by later picking out the object from among others by feeling each in turn. But the patient is completely unable to give its name or in any other way say what it
is. This is because the right hemisphere is denied its usual access across the
corpus callosum to the linguistic store of the left hemisphere. If at this
point, however, the patient is allowed to touch the object with the right
hand (whose sensory information goes to the left hemisphere), he or she is
immediately able to give the correct name.

We have already noted that the right hemisphere is superior to the left
for determining spatial relations and for the recognition of nonlinguistic visual and auditory patterns. We can also see this effect in the performance of
split-brain patients. They will make numerous mistakes if they try to use the
right hand (left hemisphere) to copy patterns with colored blocks or to
complete a jigsaw puzzle. When allowed to use the left hand (right hemisphere), however, such tasks are relatively easy. Indeed, there are reports of
patients sometimes having trouble in keeping the left hand from automatically correcting the mistakes being made by the right hand (cf. Sperry,
1964; Gazzaniga, 1970).

BRAIN DAMAGE AND LEARNING

Leaving aside such homilies as whether old dogs can or cannot learn
new tricks, it is certainly the case that learning is more rapid during youth
than in old age, and that memory is at its keenest during adolescence and

young adulthood. Part of the answer lies in very real changes in the brain which accompany the normal aging process. These changes include a progressive loss of brain calls from the cortex which, in middle age, can amount to the loss of as many as several thousand per day (Espir & Rose, 1970, pp. 61–65).

This sounds frightening until we remember that we have some 10 billion or so brain cells to start with, such that the proportionate loss is gratifyingly low. In fact, only in exceptional cases is the deterioration of brain tissue over a lifetime sufficiently rapid to produce a noticeable effect on overall intellectual function. Such cases are referred to as *senile dementia* and can, in the extreme, result in a generalized deterioration of all aspects of cognitive function including intelligence, memory, and personality.

The overall intellectual debilitation of senility is thus quite different from the effects of specific brain damage resulting from accident or disease in an otherwise healthy individual. As we have seen, such specific damage typically leads to a loss of specific function in the absence of a generalized intellectual impairment. As such, the problems associated with aphasia, and kindred disorders of language and perceptual ability, are not directly ones of learning and memory. On the other hand, we cannot hope to see effective learning in a patient with, for example, sensory aphasia, for whom verbal or written language becomes unintelligible. However debilitating, it would nevertheless be incorrect to refer to aphasia as a disorder of learning per se.

Aphasia in the adult typically involves the *loss* of some function the person was known to have previously possessed. The nature of the loss may therefore be fairly clear, and its recovery, when this does occur, can be systematically plotted. In the case of aphasia in young children, where such abilities have yet to be acquired, however, the consequences of brain damage can seem more diffuse, and their effects on learning ability can be quite severe.

Brain Damage in Children

The issue of brain damage in infancy or early childhood presents a considerably more complex picture than it does in the adult. This is true both in terms of diagnosis and in classification of the disorder. This difficulty applies not so much to older children who have incurred accidental brain injury after some years of schooling. These cases produce essentially the same forms of functional loss as in the adult, and the major difference is only that prognosis for recovery of function is generally much better for children than for adults.

The real difficulty in classification and diagnosis is in cases of so-called congenital aphasia, where the damage was incurred either before, during, or shortly after the birth itself. Such damage could be associated with injury during the delivery or with initial difficulties in breathing at the moment of birth. Temporary deprivation of oxygen (*anoxia*) can result in destruction of brain tissue.

Damage which in the adult might result in specific loss of function, may, in this case, be translated into either a mild or severe *learning* disorder related to abilities involving these functional areas. For example, dyslexia in this case would not be a loss of reading skills but a difficulty in their acquisition. A further complication can be the spread of what might in principle be a limited debility to include difficulties in related areas as well. The most obvious example might be that of a primarily dyslexic child who would consequently also show difficulties with spelling and other skills which depend on some minimal development of reading ability.

A frequent accompaniment of brain damage in both children and adults is a sometimes severe limitation on attention span. Brain damaged children often show unusual difficulties in focal concentration for long periods and are very easily distracted. In extreme cases, such distractability can be a serious impediment to learning, as in the so-called hyperactive or hyperkinetic child, who may literally be in constant motion throughout a school day.

There is a need for caution. Attentional disorders and learning difficulties are often the direct result of early brain damage. The appearance of such difficulties in an individual child, however, should not in itself lead one to automatically assume brain damage without supportive evidence. The issue of learning disorders related to brain damage is complex and will be treated in greater detail in the following chapter.

SUMMARY

Contrary to the views of the early phrenologists, there is no one place in the brain for memory, for learning, or for particular mental faculties. The brain is a complex, interconnective network of nerve cells and fibers which requires an adequate blood supply, oxygen, vitamins, et cetera. When these requirements are restricted, or brain tissue is subjected to damage from accident or disease, these cells will be destroyed. The result will be an impairment of normal brain function.

As we shall see later, brain cells have reached such a point of specialization that they have lost the power of regeneration. Once damaged, they can neither replace nor repair themselves. Recovery of cognitive function following brain damage does occur, but for this to happen, other parts of the brain must take over the function of the injured part. Whether this takeover occurs in the cortical areas surrounding the affected area, or whether it occurs in the corresponding region of the opposite hemisphere, it is clear that the chances for complete recovery are greater for children than for adults. This "plasticity" of the young brain seems to be replaced by increasing functional specialization within the cortex as a result of age, experience, and, most probably, the development of language.

A systematic study of deficits caused by damage to different areas of the brain has led to a fairly sophisticated "mapping" of cognitive function within the cortex. The primary area for vision is located in the occipital lobes, and that for hearing is in the temporal lobes. Motor programming is centered in the so-called motor strip in the frontal lobes, just forward of the central fissure. The receptive area for the integration of sensory feedback from body and muscle movements is located in the parietal lobes, just to the rear of the central fissure.

Functional control of the brain is said to be contralateral, in that the left hemisphere deals with sensory information and motor functions of the right side of the body, while the right hemisphere controls the left side of the body.

The human brain shows the feature of cerebral dominance. Language, and language related functions (speech production and recognition, reading, writing, and verbal memory) are located in the left hemisphere for all right-handed persons and for most left-handers. This is said to be the dominant hemisphere. For these individuals, the nondominant right hemisphere is primarily concerned with nonverbal functions such as the recognition of complex visual forms, memory for nonverbal stimuli, and perhaps for the recognition of music. For that small proportion of left-handers whose right hemisphere is dominant, these functions are reversed.

Aphasia is the general term given to language disorders due to brain damage; they are roughly divided into expressive or receptive disorders depending on the primary source of difficulty. These deficits of central cognitive function can occur in the absence of either motor paralysis of the muscles of speech or a general impairment of hearing or intellectual function.

Where Is Learning?

Where then is "learning" in the human brain? Learning and the capacity for thought are closely tied to memory for names, words, and language, which seem to be stored in the cortex, primarily in the region of the temporal lobe of the dominant hemisphere. Memory for motor and sensory skills is generally thought to be mediated within the frontal and parietal lobes of both hemispheres. These general observations, while correct, could nevertheless be misleading for two reasons.

First, the nature of the data on which these conclusions are based involves a high degree of inference. That is, we can say with some confidence that a particular area of the brain (e.g., Broca's area in the left hemisphere) is important to a certain function (e.g., motor-speech production). At least this function is disturbed following damage to that area. But to say that integrity of an area is critical for a certain function is not the same as saying that the function is "located" there (certainly not in the sense that the early phrenologists used the term).

Second, to the extent that our "mapping" studies are valid, they should not imply an isolation of function within the indicated areas. The key to neural control of cognitive activity is in the interaction of activity from all areas of the cortex. For example, in the normal brain, simply learning to write the letter A involves both hemispheres, the interaction of visual, motor, and sensory association areas of the brain, and access to memory of both a verbal and a visual nature. Cognitive activity, in short, is very much a global effort.

This brief sampling of neuropsychological research may nevertheless give the reader some indication of the sorts of results obtained as one attempts to map the cortex for the localization of cognitive function. It should be clear that certain areas of the brain are of primary importance for certain activities. It should also be clear that they may be nothing more than this—areas of "primary importance." The real breakthrough—one which is still far in the future—will occur only as we understand how these various areas of the brain interact and work together as a dynamic whole.

No matter how successful these efforts prove to be, however, they will not directly answer the second of the two questions we posed: not only *where* learning takes place within the cortex, but *how* it occurs. The answer to this question lies within the cortex, and in the action of the microscopic nerve cells themselves.

Neurophysiology of Learning and Memory

The heart of mental activity within the cortex is a consequence of the activity of some 10 billion or so individual brain cells, called *neurons.* Figure 12.4 shows a simplified drawing of the basic elements of a typical neuron. The term "typical" is used as neurons, which can be seen in detail with the aid of an electron microscope, come in various shapes and sizes. The tightly packed neurons in the cortex have relatively short fibers, while those carrying impulses to the arms and legs, so-called motor neurons, have relatively long ones.

STRUCTURE OF THE NEURON

Each neuron (nerve cell) consists of a nucleus within a cell body, which keeps the neuron alive and nourished and is instrumental in generating nerve impulses from the cell. Two types of fibers extend from the cell body.

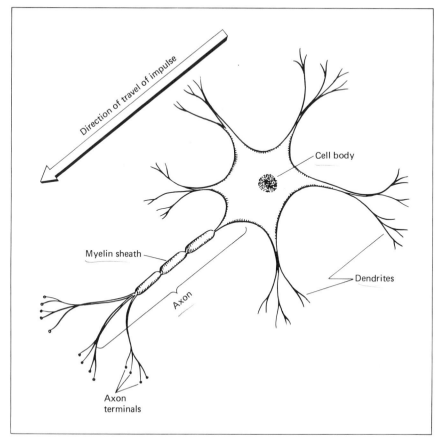

Figure 12.4 Simplified diagram of a *neuron*. Cell receives stimulation through *dendrites* which carry impulse to cell body. Chemical change at cell body generates a new impulse which travels down the *axon* to *axon terminals* where a chemical ''transmitter'' is released to excite neighboring cell. Arrow shows direction of travel of impulse along neuron.

One set of fibers, called *dentrites*, receives stimulation from neighboring neurons and conducts those impulses to the cell body. The other is a longer single fiber called the *axon*, which conducts nerve impulses from the cell to other neurons or, in the case of the motor neurons just mentioned, to muscles throughout the body to initiate movement.

Axons are frequently covered by a thin layer of fatty tissue called a *myelin sheath.* Although reminiscent of insulation on a wire, its presence actually facilitates more rapid movement of impulses along the axon. References to "gray matter" and "white matter" in the brain, incidentally, come from the color of the closely packed cell bodies, which are normally gray, and their extending myelin covered axons, which bundled together appear white.

The neurons of the brain are rather unusual in two respects. First, among all cells in the body, they are so specialized that once damaged they are lost forever. Damaged neurons can neither replace nor repair themselves, nor can they be surgically repaired. Fortunately, with several billions of them in the brain, a fair number can be lost due to accident or disease and their function taken over by other neurons. Exactly how this is done, however, still remains somewhat of a mystery. What is clear is that recovery of lost function following brain damage is far more hopeful in children than in adults.

A second extraordinary thing about the neuron is the simplicity of its operation. Neurons are capable only of being excited by neighboring neurons and of, in turn, stimulating others. That is, as it were, their entire role in life. To put it bluntly, but correctly, the basis of all intellectual activity, including memory, thought, and learning, is fundamentally a consequence of these billions of microscopic nerve cells in the brain, activating or "firing" each other in different orders and combinations. The translation of this reality into the experience of cognitive activity truly defies imagination.

THE NERVE IMPULSE

There are some who believe in the existence of mental telepathy or, as it used to be called in the days of vaudeville, "mind reading." Serious students of this probably nonexistent phenomenon occasionally argue that although admittedly mysterious, it could be scientifically possible. The brain, after all, does give off some very slight electrical activity which can be detected and recorded with suitably sensitive equipment. The electroencephalograph (EEG) used in neurological examinations does just this. Perhaps, they argue, such electrical patterns might also be picked up by other, especially sensitive, brains.

Nerve activity, as it happens, is partly electrical. It is also, however, largely chemical or, more properly, *electrochemical*. In brief, nerve impulses are conducted between neurons in the following way. A neuron receives stimulation from a neighboring neuron through one of its dendrite branches. The nerve impulse, in the form of an electrical potential, travels along the dentrite toward the cell body where it makes contact with the cell wall. This contact induces a chemical change within the cell body that, in turn, acts to generate another electrical potential that now travels away from the cell body via the axon to make contact with the dendrite of a neighboring cell. And so the process is repeated from cell to cell.

The term "make contact" with a neighboring cell may be misleading; the axon of one neuron and the dendrites of others are in fact not actually in physical contact. Separating them are microscopic gaps known as *synapses*. This synaptic gap must be crossed by the impulse in order to excite the neighboring neuron. At this point the process again becomes chemical. As the nerve impulse reaches the end of the axon, a specific chemical, such as *acetylcholine* (ACh), is released by the axon endings into the synaptic gap. It is the presence of this chemical "transmitter substance" which allows the signal to cross the synapse from one neuron to another. As soon as the impulse is passed, a second substance, *acetylcholinesterase* (AChE), is released into the synapse. AChE is an enzyme which rapidly breaks down the ACh and thus terminates the impulse transmission and prevents repeated firing of the cells.

The nature of these transmitter substances and their chemical inhibitors is still under active investigation. While we have illustrated the process with one of them, *acetylcholine*, there are other known transmitter substances which include *norepinephrine* and also *serotonin*. Interneuron activation, however, is now recognized to be primarily chemical, and earlier notions of neural transmission as a "spark" jumping from the axon of one nerve cell to the dendrite of another is no longer given much emphasis.

What happens when a neuron becomes activated? The answer is that it will in turn either activate one or a number of neighboring neurons, or it will not. That is, a neuron can only be in one of two states. It is either "firing" (being activated by other neurons and stimulating still others), or it is at rest. The strength of the impulse does not vary.

This limited "on" or "off" state of the neuron is sometimes referred to as the "all-or-none law" of neural activity. While the *strength* of a nerve impulse is always the same, however, its *rate* of firing can, and does, vary a great deal. It may range from very slow bursts of activity to extremely rapid volleys of repeated firing as fast as 1000 impulses per second. The rate of firing of a neuron carries a great deal of information, although the exact "code" underlying these patterns has yet to be fully broken.

The traveling time of a nerve impulse from neuron to neuron is fast, but it does take time. For example, it has been calculated that about 20 to 30 milliseconds (1 millisecond = one-thousandth of a second) is required for an impulse to travel from the finger tips to the cortex through the many synaptic crossings which are involved. Or, to put it another way, nerve impulses can travel at about 250 miles per hour.

It was such calculations, incidentally, that led Lashley to reject the notion of S-R chaining as a viable explanation of skilled motor performance (see Chapter 6). Thus, if we think of a pianist initiating finger movements on a note-by-note basis, a minimum of 20 to 30 milliseconds would be required for the information to go from the finger tips to the cortex, plus another 20 to 30 milliseconds for a signal to return to the fingers to produce the next note—a total of 40 to 60 milliseconds. Since an expert pianist can play sequences of notes separated by much less than 40 to 60 milliseconds, Lashley realized that some form of higher-order planning of organized programs of movement had to be involved. (For a good discussion of temporal patterning in motor programs, see Lenneberg, 1967.)

MEMORY: SOME SPECULATIONS

However complex, the basis of motor movement and of mental activity must be a consequence of the pattern of activation of these billions of microscopic neurons as they are either on or off, exciting or not exciting neighboring neurons. Logically, the physiological basis of learning and memory must center on specific changes in the pattern of neural activity which accompanies experience. It must also be clear that whatever these changes are, they must be understood in terms of the surprisingly limited "all-or-none" simplicity of the operation of the neurons.

We should recognize at this point that the problem is one of such complexity that we can only begin to understand how this may actually be accomplished within the brain. Nevertheless, the alternatives are narrow, and we can describe some reasonable, if tentative, speculations.

Reverberation, Cell Assemblies, and Phase Sequences

An early and provocative view was put forward some years ago by the Canadian psychologist, D. O. Hebb (1949; 1966). Admittedly in the absence of much real evidence, Hebb argued the logical likelihood that particular sensory experiences and mental activities must be represented in the brain as particular combinations of neurons firing in different and unique sequences. A particular motor act, like writing the letter A, or a thought process like performing multiplication, would each involve its own groups of neurons and orders of firing within the groups. The number of different hypothetical sequences required for the neural representation of the full complex of cognitive activity would of course stagger the imagination. At the same time, the total number of different possible combinations of activation sequences among some 10 billion neurons is no less staggering!

At the basis of the theory is the idea that the same sequence of neurons might be activated whenever the same sensory experience is encountered or the same cognitive act performed. Repeated experience, and hence reactivation of the same cell sequence, might act to facilitate the transmission of impulses across the synapses of the member neurons of the set.

In principle, such facilitation might reach the point where a particular pattern could almost be said to be "wired in"; the activation of any neuron in the sequence being sufficient to activate the entire pattern. "Wired in" should not be taken literally as implying, for example, that the dendrites and axons of a series grow together so as to eliminate the synapses (although this was once erroneously believed). The synaptic gaps remain; the facilitation would be in the ease of electrochemical transmission across the still existent gaps.

Hebb described such a developing pattern as a *reverberating circuit*. A simple way to view this might be as a circulating, "closed loop" system in which the impulse continues to the end neuron in the sequence where it in turn reactivates the first one. This repeated, circular firing (reverberation) would thus keep the trace alive for some period before the activity faded, and the "memory" was lost (see Figure 12.5).

No task or sensory experience would be simple enough to consist of just one sequence of neurons but might instead involve a number of related reverberating circuits. Hebb referred to such a "sequence of sequences" as a *cell assembly*. He further suggested that this larger organization of a cell assembly might also involve the same closed-loop principle as its constituent reverberating circuits. Cell assemblies might in turn be organized into even larger hierarchies, called *phase sequences*, also organized in a closed-loop fashion.

A schematic representation of such a phase sequence is illustrated in Figure 12.6. The diagram shows the major phase sequence composed of a number of cell assemblies, and these in turn are comprised by a number of reverberating loops. Although Hebb stressed the development of new neural connections in learning, the process might also involve the dropping out or disconnection of irrelevant ones (cf. Rosenzweig & Møllgaard, 1972).

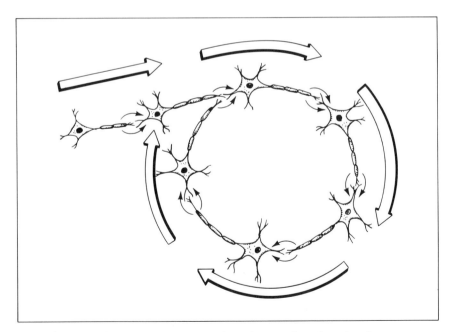

Figure 12.5   Schematic representation of a reverberating circuit.

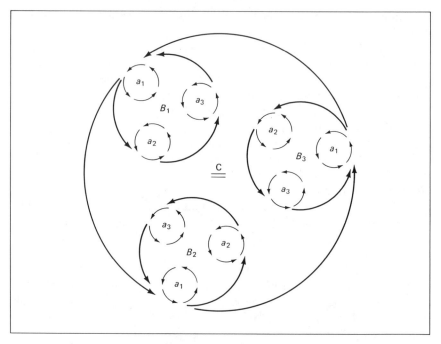

Figure 12.6   An idealized drawing of a phase sequence. The *phase sequence* (*C*) is composed of an organization of *cell assemblies* (B_1, B_2, B_3), each cell assembly in turn consisting of individual *reverberating circuits* (a_1, a_2, a_3).

In spite of the simplicity of the diagram, and of our description, such a development of sequences might potentially build to the point of involving thousands upon thousands of individual cells. A full network of phase sequences, with some of their elements shared with other sequences representing associated activities or similar operations, would culminate, at least in principle, in that elusive butterfly we call "thought."

Trace Consolidation

Hebb viewed the reverberating activity as a fairly unstable, transient representation of experience in the nervous system. Not only would such activity die away unless reinforced by rehearsal, but it would be immediately terminated if the reverberation were disrupted by some external agent such as electroconvulsive shock (ECS). It might also be interrupted through interference from some different, but closely related, mental activity. The concept of reverberation, in other words, has the general characteristics of, and is one view of, the neurological basis of what we have been referring to descriptively as short-term memory.

If transient reverberating activity represents short-term memory, then more permanent learning would have to involve an equivalently more permanent facilitation of impulse transmission within well-rehearsed sequences. Moreover, this process will occur only if (1) there is a sufficient repetition of neural activity within the particular sequence, and (2) the activity is allowed to continue without disruption of the trace. Hebb referred to this general process of stabilizing a trace into long-term memory as *consolidation,* a term already encountered in the previous chapter.

The basic principle that learning and memory are based on the development of more effective contacts between neurons is in fact almost as old as the discovery of the synapse itself (Tanzi, 1893). Insight into the possible mechanisms of memory consolidation, however, had to await fairly recent developments in biochemical theory and technique.

Experimental studies with lower animals had already shown that a strong electric shock delivered to an animal's brain soon after learning would destroy the memory for the task. It is only recent experience that is affected, however. If a sufficient period of time is allowed to elapse between the learning and the shock, recall is relatively unimpaired. This particular finding is reliable, although there is still some disagreement about the exact time interval necessary (Chorover & Schiller, 1966; Kopp, Bohdanecky & Jarvik, 1966; McGaugh, 1966).

This interval has been viewed by some as representing the time required for consolidation to take place. After this period, the trace is represented in some more durable form than self-actuating reverberation and can thus withstand the effects of the shock.

One possibility is that consolidation comes about through the gradual substitution of temporary reverberation by a more permanent *chemical change* within the relevant cell bodies themselves. As this idea goes, it would be the structure of this chemical change which in all future events "tells" the neurons which of their neighbors to stimulate when activated. This presumably would be directly accomplished by the release of a transmitter substance into the appropriate synapses.

RNA and Memory

The search for the chemical source within the neuron representing long-term memory has a certain headline quality about it, which has not gone entirely unnoticed by the popular press ("Memory Pills to Replace Schools and Textbooks?"). To suggest that this is a foolish overreaction to very tentative and limited findings makes the work on which it is vaguely based no less exciting nor, for that matter, the headlines any less entertaining.

The search has largely centered on a complex protein substance called *ribonucleic acid* (RNA), a close relative of the more famous *deoxyribonu-*

cleic acid (DNA). Both DNA and RNA are compounds which occur in an infinite number of forms and are found in all living cells. DNA has a very stable chemical structure. It is extremely resistant to change from environmental effects, barring the intervention of such agents as X rays and other forms of radiation. DNA, as most people now know, is the essential component of the *genes*, and it is DNA which carries the coded "memory" of inherited characteristics within a species. It is DNA which "remembers" that human infants should be born with two legs, not eight.

The related RNA, which controls the production of certain proteins in the cells, is much less stable. Unlike DNA, its chemical structure can be potentially altered through environmental effects or experience.

A possible role for changes in cell RNA in learning came through early reports, such as those of Hydén, that found that rats taught a balancing trick showed changes in the proportion of different kinds of RNA in the parts of their brains that receive fibers from the semicircular canals that control balance (Hydén & Egyházi, 1962; Hydén, 1967). Such findings were quickly followed by other reports from various laboratories showing systematic increases in RNA synthesis in the brain following a variety of simple learning tasks in lower animals.

One current line of thought is that changes in the chemical structure of RNA might underlie long-term retention. RNA, acting through the synthesis of specific proteins, might determine the appropriate production of transmitter substance released by neurons into their synapses. This in turn would facilitate the transmission of impulses to other neurons. RNA, in other words, might carry individual memory, just as DNA carries species memory.

We can perhaps summarize one view of memory storage in the following way. Newly arrived information is held in the temporary form of electrochemical reverberating activity among cell sequences (e.g., reverberating circuits, cell assemblies, phase sequences). Without disruption, continued reactivation of the cell sequences will produce a chemical change in the RNA structure of these neurons. Prior to this time, as we have seen, the short-term memory trace is relatively unstable and easily disrupted by electric shock or other interference. Once the cell chemistry has been altered, however, shock no longer disrupts the memory. The storage is now presumably chemical in nature.

This it should be emphasized, is speculation, not fact. Nevertheless, it would be intriguing to consider what would happen to retention if, after consolidation has taken place, some drug were injected into an animal to inhibit the activity of RNA. One such drug is an antibiotic, *puromycin*, which is thought to inhibit protein synthesis by RNA. In fact, it has been shown that injection of puromycin soon after an animal has learned a task (i.e., prior to consolidation) has little effect. Injection after some time has elapsed since learning, and consolidation has presumably taken place, does indeed appear to cause the animal to "forget" the learned task (Agranoff, Davis &

Brink, 1955; Flexner, 1968). We should point out that these studies have been carried out on rats and goldfish—warning enough of their tentative nature. (The interested reader can find a good review and collection of research papers on this subject in, for example, McGaugh & Herz, 1972.)

Memory Transfer

We cannot leave this subject without mentioning the most widely known, and perhaps the most controversial, studies connected with the physiological basis of memory. These have been reports of alleged "memory transfer" from one animal to another. It was primarily these studies which brought some newspapers into the picture with fanciful predictions that taking an "RNA pill" derived from a professor's brain might eventually eliminate the need for schools and college. Students may have been delighted at the suggestion; scientists working in the field were horrified.

The beginnings of this research centered on the lowly *planarian*, a tiny water-dwelling flatworm whose only claim to fame up until that time seemed to be that if cut in half each end would readily regenerate a new head (or tail). Also, it is cannibalistic. To a flatworm, nothing tastes quite as good as another flatworm.

In a typical early experiment, a group of planaria would be conditioned to curl up whenever a bright light was shined on them by reinforcing the light with shock. Once trained, these planaria were mashed up and fed to another group of planaria with no previous experience with this learning. As a control, another group were fed the remains of other planaria without such training.

The initial reports were that the planaria who had eaten the trained worms were able to learn (or relearn ?) the task faster than those who had eaten the untrained ones. Presumably, it was argued, some trace of the original learning had been "transferred" from one animal to another (McConnell, 1962). These studies were rapidly followed by others which reported that by simply extracting RNA from trained flatworms and injecting it into untrained ones, one could produce essentially the same positive effects on performance (Zelman, Kabot, Jacobson & McConnell, 1964).

A heated controversy soon erupted, based both on theoretical grounds and on the objection that such findings were often hard to replicate (e.g., Bennett & Calvin, 1964). While some workers have been unable to produce the effect, others have reported consistently reliable transfer even in animals as high on the phylogenetic scale as the rat (cf. Byrne, 1970; Fjerdingstad, 1971). When successful, it should be noted, injection of RNA from a trained animal into an untrained one does not typically lead to the recipient animal immediately demonstrating the donor animal's knowledge. Rather, it seems to evidence some "savings" in learning the task, requiring less time to do so than animals without the benefit of RNA transfer.

Studies of interanimal transfer are still far from conclusive. They have typically involved very restricted forms of learning, such as passive avoid-ance, where some form of punishment is involved. While some studies may suggest that "something" is being transferred from one animal to another, it is as yet hard to say whether this "something" is in fact specific memory. No less important, there is no generally accepted explanation on a biochemical level of how a transfer of specific memory might take place, even if it were readily demonstrable.

As exciting and provocative as these studies may be (and they are), it would appear, in other words, that the teacher's job is not in jeopardy. At least, not yet.

DRUGS AND BEHAVIOR

As we have seen, the human brain represents a complex interaction among some 10 billion neurons with a delicate and ever-changing chemical structure. We have also seen how this careful balance can be upset through interference in the chemical activity of protein synthesis, electroconvulsive shock, and physical injury to the brain tissues themselves.

Direct chemical intervention in the nervous system in everyday life is of course as common as the use of alcohol, tobacco, and coffee. Although not usually thought of in the context of "drugs" (whether legal or illegal), they really are, and their effects on the nervous system are no less real.

The use of various drugs in psychotherapy has been with us for some time. Drugs have, for example, been used to control the major mood swings from severe depression to inappropriate elation which can accompany some forms of psychosis. Tranquilizing drugs have seen wide use (and peri-odic wide abuse) for treatment of symptoms of severe disturbances such as schizophrenia. Similarly, milder drugs have been developed which can aid the basically healthy individual to cope with a temporary period of unusual stress or anxiety.

Drug effects on learning have a shorter history and remain very much in the experimental stages. For example, some research has involved excitant drugs like *pentylenetetrazol* and *strychnine sulphate*, which have been in-jected into lower animals with a view to stimulating neural activity asso-ciated with learning and memory (McGaugh & Krivanek, 1970). Such studies, it should be emphasized, are highly exploratory and have been re-stricted to use with lower animals.

Chemical control related to learning in humans has been limited pri-marily to dietary control in cases of metabolic dysfunction associated with certain forms of mental retardation (see Chapter 13), and to the use of drugs in experimental treatment of the extremely distractible or "hyperactive" children mentioned earlier in this chapter. This latter use offers a good il-lustration of the complexity of the issues involved.

The drugs used in the treatment of hyperactivity, such as *methylpheni-date* and *dextroamphetamine,* are typically considered as excitatory or stimulant drugs when given to adults. When administered to hyperactive children, however, they seem to have the paradoxical effect of an opposite reaction, significantly enhancing sustained attention and the control of impulsive behavior (Douglas, 1974). This curiosity of a paradoxical effect, combined with inadequate knowledge of their long-term effects, has indicated both a need for further research and caution in their routine use.

In spite of these complexities, one can offer some general observations regarding drug effects and learning (Wickelgren, 1974). Generally speaking, drugs which act as central nervous system depressants (e.g., alcohol, nitrous oxide, and chlorpromazine) can impair the establishment of long-term memory consolidation when administered shortly before, during, or after a learning experience in humans (Steinberg & Summerfield, 1957; Goodwin, Othmer, Halikas & Freemon, 1970) and in animals (Johnson, 1969; Leukel, 1957). Central nervous system stimulants (e.g., caffeine, amphetamine, nicotine, strychnine, and picrotoxin) can facilitate long-term learning and memory when administered close in time to the learning experience (McGaugh & Dawson, 1971).

When one thinks of drug effects on behavior, however, one usually thinks of the widespread use of illegal drugs or, perhaps, the equally widespread abuse of legal ones. While these drugs have only an indirect effect on learning and retention, they offer a dramatic illustration of the relative ease with which the delicate chemical balance of the nervous system can be upset. The effects of four classes of drugs, *stimulants, sedatives, tranquilizers,* and *hallucinogens,* are especially illustrative.

Stimulants can be found in a variety of forms, some as mild as the *caffeine* in coffee, tea, and many cola-flavored soft drinks. Operating to chemically increase the excitability of neurons throughout the nervous system, it is the consequence of this stimulation that gives the psychological "lift" to a cup of coffee. Examples of much stronger stimulants include various *amphetamine* compounds with such trade names as Benzedrine, Dexedrine, and Methedrine. Ordinarily prescribed to prevent sleepiness, depress the appetite, or to serve as psychological antidepressants, they are known to operate on the *reticular activating system* (RAS), which, as already described, controls the level of activation and arousal of the cerebral cortex. The specific action of the amphetamines is thought to derive from their chemical similarity to the naturally occurring neural transmitter substances, and their action on the RAS comes about either because they mimic these transmitters, or because they cause their spontaneous release. When abused, amphetamines can cause inappropriate euphoria and manic, antisocial behavior.

The opposite effects are found with so-called sedative drugs, such as the *barbiturates,* which include phenobarbital (Luminal), pentobarbital (Nembutal), secobarbital (Seconal) and thiopental (Pentothal). Sedatives operate to depress central nervous system activity through their chemical action on the RAS. Their effect is to produce drowsiness or sleep. Potentially dangerous in themselves, sedatives can be especially so if taken with *alcohol*, which is also a depressant. (While it may seem to be a stimulant to the user, alcohol is a depressant of the central nervous system which operates on the inhibitory mechanisms of the brain. This produces the paradoxical effect of apparent activation associated with a loss of self-restraint, mood swings, and difficulties in concentration, learning, and memory).

Tranquilizers, such as *chlorpromazine* (Thorazine), have seen wide use in the treatment of certain forms of psychosis. Properly used, they are intended to stabilize the patient's behavior sufficiently to allow for the conduct of psychotherapy or in some cases to allow for a release from hospital and outpatient treatment which might not ordinarily be possible. Milder tranquilizers, such as *meprobamate* (Miltown, Equanil), have also been developed for the relief of milder anxieties and tension, while patients suffering from chronic depression can sometimes be helped with drugs called *monoamine oxidase inhibitors* (Marplan, Nardil, Parnate). These latter drugs are thought to operate by raising the level of the naturally occurring neural transmitter substances *serotonin* and *norepinephrine*.

Marijuana is distinguishable from other hallucinogens such as LSD and mescaline in being far less potent, not altering consciousness to the same degree, and not leading to an increased tolerance to the drug dosage. Nevertheless, the effects of its most active chemical ingredient, *tetrahydrocannabinol* (THC), on the nervous system are far from understood. Effects of the drug include reports of heightened sensory experience, a free flowing of ideas, joyousness, tranquility, and a generalized sense of well-being.

For the interested reader, excellent introductory summaries of major drug effects can be found in a variety of sources such as Morgan and King (1971, pp. 673–678). The particular effects of any drug, however, are highly influenced by what are known as *drug-environment interactions*. That is, while the chemical action of a drug may be determined, its behavioral effects are always less predictable. For example, the effects of any drug can vary not only from one person to another, but can be widely different in the same individual at different times. Taken in one setting or psychological mood, the effects might be pleasant; in another, they might be disastrous. Even the mildest drugs can sometimes have very serious consequences when taken by psychologically unstable users (cf. Zinberg & Robertson, 1972). These variables, commonly referred to as effects of "set and setting," simply highlight the complexity of interaction between physiological change and subjective experience.

SUMMARY

The key to all mental activity, including learning and memory, lies in the action of some 10 billion microscopic brain cells called neurons. Neurons consist of a cell body which keeps the cell alive and nourished, dendrite fibers which carry impulses from neighboring neurons to the cell body, and an axon fiber which transmits impulses away from the cell body to other neurons.

The axon of one neuron and the dendrites of others are separated by tiny gaps called synapses, with activation of neighboring neurons accomplished through release of a chemical transmitter substance which allows the impulse to travel across these synaptic gaps. Such transmitter substances include acetylcholine, norepinephrine, and serotonin, along with their chemical inhibitors which terminate impulse transmission once the neighboring cells have been stimulated.

An early attempt to conceptualize the physiological basis of learning and memory was that of D. O. Hebb, who saw learning represented by the facilitation of different sequences of neuronal stimulation, in the form of new "pathways" of impulse travel among preexisting neurons. Short-term memory could be represented as the transient formation of reverberating circuits which are highly susceptible to interference and require time for consolidation into long-term memory.

A current view of memory consolidation sees the formation of long-term traces as a consequence of chemical changes within the neurons themselves, causing a cell to "remember" its position in a particular neuronal sequence. The physiological basis of memory is thus seen as primarily chemical, brought about by changes in the structure of ribonucleic acid (RNA) within the cell bodies which controls the formation of specific proteins to regulate synaptic transmission.

Two approaches taken to investigate the role of RNA in memory have been studies attempting to demonstrate the *transfer* of specific memory from one animal to another, and the use of protein inhibitors to explore the nature and time span of memory consolidation. This research has been accompanied by an increased understanding of drug effects as they operate to mimic neural transmitter substances or in other ways upset the delicate chemical balance within the brain.

chapter 13

Readiness
for Learning

We earlier defined learning as a relatively permanent change in behavior or knowledge due to practice or experience. This means that the individual must experience, and internalize, the realities and events of his or her world. In some cases, internalization of experience may take the form of stored associations. In others, it takes the form of abstracted, potentially generalizable principles to guide future behavior and future learning.

The purpose of learning theory is to specify, and to explain, the necessary preconditions for learning. We have attempted to do this, in terms of an understanding of the varieties of learning and systems of reward, the elements of practice, the nature of internal representation in memory, and so forth. For learning to occur, however, the stage must be set both by motivational factors and by intellectual capability. Let us be clear. While the intelligent 6-year-old in one classroom is learning to tell time, learning to read and spell, and perhaps conducting rudimentary scientific experiments, success for a mentally retarded child in another classroom may simply be the ability to recognize his or her coat from among others when it is time to go home. The principles of learning in both cases may be quite similar. The difference lies in intellectual capability which will determine both the *rate* of learning and the ultimate *level* of ability each can be expected to attain. That there are children (and adults) with severe learning difficulties is a fact it does us no good to ignore. For this reason, it would be wrong to leave the topic of learning and memory without looking, however briefly, at the character and nature of some of these learning problems.

READINESS FOR LEARNING

The end of the nineteenth century saw the beginnings of a welcomed change in society's attitude toward the mentally retarded. From a sad history of educational neglect, ridicule, and even torture came the recognition that retardation is nothing more or less than slowness of learning in an otherwise healthy individual. While medical research began a still unfinished search for prevention, psychology turned its attention to early detection and the design of programs for remedial education. Part of this effort led to the development of formal tests of intelligence, the so-called IQ test, developed originally for the early discovery of children who would later need special help in their education. As these tests developed in sophistication, however, there also developed misconceptions about what such tests could and could not do. The most common of these are: (1) that IQ test scores *are* intelligence; that IQ is an index of innate intellectual potential representing a fixed property of the individual which remains unchanged over life, or (2) that such tests merely evaluate educational achievement over a rather limited range and have little use in predicting future potential. Misapplied, these tests can potentially do more harm than good.

Which of these statements is correct? What is the meaning of the IQ, and how were these tests originally developed? One purpose of this chapter is to look at these questions and at the interaction between intelligence and learning.

As we examine the nature of intelligence, even in the normal child, it becomes apparent that intellectual skill grows with age. Some have seen this as simply reflecting an accumulation of learning upon which more complex intellectual skills can be built. This is true. Others, however, have emphasized the necessity for what might be called *developmental readiness* for certain types of learning. This is the notion that older children can undertake learning tasks impossible for younger ones because of differences in nervous system maturation which are analogous to the more obvious differences in their physical structures (Gagné, 1970, pg. 279). One version of this latter view is counter to intelligence as a "commodity"; a single property one acquires more of with time. Attributed largely to the work of Piaget (1952), this view suggests that differences in mental maturity lead not only to differences in the ease with which information can be acquired, but to differences in the logical conclusions children of different ages will draw from this information.

In the final section of this chapter we will look at a very special issue, that of children whose age, intelligence, and motivation would all seem to predict success in the classroom, but who, nevertheless, show unusual difficulties in learning. These problems will be addressed under the current description of "specific learning disabilities."

Development of the IQ Test and the Concept of ''Mental Maturity''

In 1904, the school authorities of Paris, France, formally instituted a landmark study into the special problems encountered by the school system in dealing with the slow-learning child. At that time a major cause for concern was the child who might have to endure months or years of frustration and failure in the ordinary classroom; a classroom equipped neither to deal with nor indeed to recognize his or her special learning difficulties. The desire, then, was to devise some means of reliably detecting children with potential learning disabilities so as to make available to them from the very beginning the special help they might need.

Their search for the person to organize this study ended with the selection of one of France's foremost psychologists, Alfred Binet (1857–1911). This selection, in turn, began the search for what later would be called the "intelligence test." It cannot be too highly stressed that Binet's intention was *not* to develop a test to distinguish between subtle differences in abilities among average or brighter children. This was to appear very much later as a preoccupation of American education, and to become a subject of heated controversy among psychologists, educators, and nonprofessionals alike. Binet's goal was only to easily and reliably determine those children whose intelligence or learning abilities were sufficiently below that of the average classroom child so as to require special educational help.

Binet, working with a psychiatrist named Theophile Simon (1873–1961), attempted to define intelligence in terms of a large collection of traits such as memory, imagery, attention, and comprehension. Some of his proposed traits, "aesthetic appreciation," "moral ideas," and "will power," now not only border on the archaic but are virtually untestable. Luckily, Binet's final approach was more pragmatic. If his task was to discover children who would be likely to have trouble with school achievement, then he would choose those abilities which seemed to be important to this limited sphere of endeavor. In a real sense, then, "intelligence" testing began in the absence of any formal, generally accepted definition of intelligence. It was tied specifically to school achievement.

Binet and Simon's first test, published in 1905, contained some 30 questions and problems, such as recognizing objects in pictures, remembering lists of digits, defining abstract words, and so forth. Here was the goal behind their test:

> The fundamental idea of this method is the establishment of what we shall call a measuring scale of intelligence. This scale is composed of a series of tests of increasing difficulty, starting from the lowest intellectual level that can be observed, and ending with that of normal intelligence. Each group in the series corresponds to a different mental level (Binet & Simon, 1961, pg. 92).

The concept was simple, but central to the later development of intelligence testing. To Binet, just as the child grows in physical maturity with passing years, so he or she grows mentally. His or her capability for handling new concepts and dealing with abstractions could be viewed as growing in a systematic, developmental sequence not dissimilar to growth in physical maturity. In short, Binet spoke of the development of "mental maturity" with age. Based on this notion, Binet's test was devised to determine a child's *mental age* (MA), that is, to place his or her abilities relative to those of other children of various ages.

His test was organized by arranging the 30 test items in ascending order of difficulty. He determined this empirically, by testing large numbers of children and rearranging the items according to the number of children, at different ages, who were able to pass each item. By 1911, there had been two revisions of the test, leading to an increase in the number of items, and a systematic classification of these items in terms of subtests according to age. Based on tests conducted with large numbers of children between the ages of 3 and 13, an item was assigned to a particular "age level" if it could be passed by the majority of children of that age, but not by younger children.

As the test was eventually used, a particular child's mental ability would be measured against these preestablished norms. For example, if a child was able to pass all of the items passed by most 7-year-olds, and half of the items passed by 8-year-olds, he or she could be said to have a "mental age" of 7 years, 6 months.

In fact, the test was somewhat cruder than the apparent exactness of Binet's scoring method. Nevertheless, it did prove to be a workable method of comparing the abilities of one child to another, in order to determine those whose scores were sufficiently below normative standards to warrant special help in school. Binet, incidentally, originally avoided use of the term "mental age" because of its specific developmental implications. He preferred the more neutral term of "mental level" (Wolf, 1973).

THE STANFORD-BINET TEST

By 1916, Binet's ideas and a sample of his test had crossed the Atlantic where both were given close attention by an American psychologist, Lewis Terman of Stanford University. There, Terman and his colleagues translated the test into English, further modified it, and then standardized the scoring for American school children. This test, further revised in 1937, 1960, and 1972, came to be called the *Stanford-Binet Intelligence Scale,* named by Terman jointly for its historical originator and for the university where the American version was developed. It was, and in revised form still is, one of the more widely used intelligence tests in the United States.

Like the original, the American version consists of a series of increasingly more difficult subtests, each representing an increasingly higher age level. Here are some examples from the test, given in ascending order of difficulty: Identifying parts of the body (year 2); copying a circle (year 3); repeating a simple sentence after one hearing (year 5); explaining verbal absurdities like, "A man had flu twice. The first time it killed him, but the second time he got well quickly" (year 8); defining abstract words such as *pity* and *curiosity* (year 12) (Terman & Merrill, 1960).

Like the original Binet test, the Stanford-Binet retained as its primary measure what was hoped to be the educationally useful estimate of a child's mental age. For predictive purposes, however, many felt the need for a single index of intelligence which would not systematically increase as the child grew older. The bright child at age 6 will invariably also be a bright child at age 8, age 10, and so on. What was clearly needed, they felt, was a "brightness ratio"; an index that would remain relatively constant as the child grew older and his or her mental abilities increased. For this purpose, the Stanford-Binet test adopted the simple expedient of expressing a child's MA as a function of his or her chronological age (CA). Given by the following formula, the world now had the *intelligence quotient,* or IQ. (The purpose of multiplying by 100 was simply to eliminate the decimal point.)

$$IQ = \frac{mental\ age\ (MA)}{chronological\ age\ (CA)} \times 100$$

For example, if an 8-year-old child could pass all of the items passed by the average 8-year-old, his or her IQ would be $8 \div 8 \times 100$, or 100. In this way, 100 was taken as the "average" IQ. Similarly, if a child of 7 were able to pass these same items, his or her IQ would be above average

$(IQ = 8 \div 7 \times 100 = 114)$. A child of 9 who received the same score would have an IQ below average $(IQ = 8 \div 9 \times 100 = 89)$.

Beginning with the 1960 revision, the authors of the Stanford-Binet supplied tables for computing IQ which more exactly adjusted test score for age. While no longer a "quotient" in the strict meaning of the word, the term IQ was retained because of its familiarity with the general public.

FURTHER DEVELOPMENT OF IQ TESTING

For a test to maintain its validity, it must be subjected to routine revision, as has the original Stanford-Binet. Other tests, however, also became available over the years to answer specific criticisms of the Stanford-Binet test or to meet special needs (such as testing large numbers of people at one time). By 1968, Anastasi (1968, pp. 638–641) was able to list some 56 different tests purporting to measure intellectual, motor, or social development.

Among the most important of these new tests were the *Wechsler Adult Intelligence Scale* (WAIS), the *Wechsler Intelligence Scale for Children* (WISC) for ages 7 to 16, and most recently the *Wechsler Preschool and Primary Scale of Intelligence* (WPPSI) for ages 4 to 6½ (Wechsler, 1955; 1972). The WAIS, WISC, and WPPSI added the very useful feature of separating subtests not by age group but by the kinds of abilities tested. One category, the "verbal" scale, includes such subtests as vocabulary, comprehension, and memory span; a second category, the "performance" scale, attempts to examine abilities less influenced by purely verbal skills. Subtests on this scale include assembling shapes to form patterns, discovering the incomplete parts in a picture, and ordering comic strip pictures in the correct sequence to tell a logical story. The Wechsler tests thus have available not only subtest scores but a calculation of two separate IQ scores. These are the verbal IQ (VIQ) and the performance IQ (PIQ). If desired, the two scores can be combined into a single IQ score which, in practice, usually correlates quite highly with the Stanford-Binet IQ.

TEST SCORE VALIDITY

The intention of intelligence tests remains an attempt to estimate intellectual potential in order to aid schools in placing children in educational settings appropriate to their abilities. Along with other indicators, such as teachers' judgments and knowledge of the adequacy of educational preparation, they have shown themselves to be a *generally* useful predictor of academic ability. The controversy referred to earlier stemmed to a large degree from the many misuses of the test. The most common of these is the naive assumption that an IQ score *is* a child's intelligence.

The makers of these tests share with their critics the realization that many factors can contribute to an invalid IQ score. For example, a child's test score can be heavily influenced by both educational background and attitude when the test is taken. A child may be ill during testing, he or she may be frightened, misunderstand the instructions, work poorly under pressure, or for a variety of reasons feel resentful in the testing situation. Similarly, a child easily frustrated, or not convinced of the importance of the test, can sometimes give up, failing to complete test items actually within his or her capability. For these reasons, the scoring sheets for both the Stanford-Binet and the Wechsler tests have a space on the form for the examiner to note such contingencies and to question the validity of the reported score. Unfortunately, some examiners may fail to do this. More often, the score alone is transferred to a child's school file without the examiner's accompanying reservations.

Other criticisms of the test have frequently been voiced. For example, stories or pictures portraying typical suburban middle-class family scenes may alienate a child from a low-income, inner-city home. Exclusive representation of physical features of a single racial type in test illustrations may have a similar effect on members of an ethnic minority. Finally, there are objections to the perpetuation of sex stereotypes in test content, such as a consistent portrayal of male doctors and executives, and female nurses and secretaries (Anastasi, 1976, pg. 59).

A final consideration relates to the stability of IQ test scores over time. When we look at average scores for large numbers of children, we do tend to find relative stability, in the sense that such scores remain fairly constant as the children grow older and are retested at later ages. (This claim must, however, be qualified for the younger ages, where IQ scores are often poor predictors of adult or older childhood scores.) Again, on average, there is a fairly high correlation between test performance and a child's ability to handle concepts in formal educational settings. On an individual level, however, test scores from one testing session to another can easily fluctuate by as much as 5 to 15 points (Bayley, 1970). Among the factors influencing such shifts (up or down) can be changes in family conditions, adoption into a foster home, severe illness, or introduction to a remedial program (Anastasi, 1976, pg. 329). Indeed, changes in IQ score by as much as 50 points for an individual are not unknown (Honzik, Macfarlane & Allen, 1948). For these reasons, many express caution regarding the predictive value of the IQ test, except for the widest extremes. They may, at best, be indicative of the *present* level of intellectual functioning of the child at the time the test was given (Travers, 1973, pg. 228).

Into this mixture was also thrown a heated controversy regarding possible racial differences in IQ (Jensen, 1969). These particular studies, and those which followed, tended to create as much heat as light, becoming for a time a political football to be kicked back and forth by extreme views.

(See Loehlin, Lindzey & Spuhler, 1975, for a review of this issue.) If nothing else, the argument was to further shake the credibility of the IQ tests themselves and IQ testing in general.

These problems unfortunately do not exhaust the potential misuses and misunderstandings of IQ testing. A more subtle problem relates to the way knowledge of a child's IQ can erroneously influence both parental and teacher expectations regarding the child's potential ability. In a tragically circular way, this can become a self-fulfilling prophecy, as we shall see later in this chapter.

SUMMARY

The modern IQ test stems historically from the work of Alfred Binet in Paris who devised a simple test of "mental maturity" to detect children who would be in need of special help when they began school.

The first major American intelligence test was the Stanford-Binet Intelligence Scale which introduced the notion of the intelligence quotient (IQ). This reports a child's mental age (MA) as a ratio of his or her chronological age (CA), with an IQ of 100 representing average intelligence.

Later developments included the Wechsler Adult Intelligence Scale (WAIS), the Wechsler Intelligence Scale for Children (WISC), and the Wechsler Preschool and Primary Scale of Intelligence (WPPSI). These three tests report separate IQ scores for purely verbal ability (VIQ) and for other abilities less influenced by verbal skills, which are expressed as a performance IQ (PIQ).

The modern IQ test is not a perfect device and can at best serve only as an approximation for the placement of a child's ability relative to others of the same age. The test score (as distinct from a child's "intelligence") is heavily influenced by language ability, cultural and educational background, and the child's physical and psychological state when taking the test. We must also recognize that it may be influenced by the competence of the person administering the test.

Given these variables, interpretation of an IQ score for any particular child must be put in perspective along with other sources in estimating a child's true educational potential. It is easy to condemn IQ testing when a teacher recognizes a child in his or her class as being above average in ability, but is reluctant to give the child more challenging assignments because of a low IQ score found in the child's school file. The teacher, in this case, is wrong not to question the validity of the IQ score and to locate the source of the incongruity. The assumption that IQ *is* intelligence is a naive interpretation of a single test result, and it is this that deserves the condemnation.

The Nature of Intelligence

What is intelligence? Attempts to find a simple definition have included "the ability to think abstractly" (Stoddard, 1943), "the ability to apply past experience to the solution of new problems" (Goddard, 1946), and "the capacity to act purposefully, think rationally, and deal effectively with the environment" (Wechsler, 1944). For many of us, the most intelligent person is simply the one who agrees with us the most. Intelligence, like "integrity," is a trait far easier to recognize when seen than to define formally.

It will not be our intention to add to the existing list of inadequate definitions. Rather, we will explore some dimensions of the problem which would have to form the basis for an adequate definition.

INTELLIGENCE: ONE, TWO, OR MANY FACTORS?

One dimension of the question was raised by the opposing views of Charles Spearman (1927) and L. L. Thurstone (1938, 1941). The question they asked was surely the most fundamental. Is intelligence a single trait; or should one speak of intelligence in the plural as a collection of separate, distinct abilities, each with its own potential level?

The single-factor idea of intelligence is probably the earliest view, and had its most influencial proponent in the British psychologist Charles Spearman (1927). Spearman recognized that people often show some variability in tests which measure such factors as mathematical ability, verbal fluency, and so forth. Nevertheless, he became impressed with the generally high relationship between one area of ability and another in most persons. That is, he believed he saw a "general intelligence" baseline, along which these minor fluctuations of special abilities lie.

Spearman put forth his ideas as the *g-factor theory* of intelligence. All of us, he argued, show a *general intelligence* (*g*) *factor* which, in his view, represents "true" intelligence. This g-factor underlies performance in all spheres of intellectual endeavor. The "bumps" on this g-factor baseline, a relative superiority in, for example, verbal, mathematical, or artistic ability, he referred to as *special abilities* (*s*). In essence, the usually high correlation one sees between subtests on an intelligence test would indicate the existence of the g-factor, while the fact that such correlations are typically less than perfect would support the existance of s-factors.

A contrary view was taken in the United States by Louis Thurstone (1938). While Spearman placed his stress on general intelligence, Thurstone was more impressed by individuals' variability from one aspect of intelligence to another. Thurstone used a statistical technique known as *factor analysis*, which works in the following way. He began by giving large numbers of people various tests consisting of a variety of different kinds of tasks and problems. He then determined the degree to which performance on one type of task was predictive of performance on others. For example, one might find that if a person is exceptionally good at solving anagrams, he or she might also be especially good at thinking of rhyming words or giving words drawn from a single category. On the other hand, such performance might have only a low correlation with, for example, mathematical ability. Factor analysis is simply a mathematical technique which discovers correlations, or a lack of them, between test items.

On the basis of these studies, Thurstone characterized intelligence not in terms of a single, general factor, but as composed of seven *primary mental abilities*—seven separate, distinct intellectual capacities. As we implied earlier, one might, in principle, excel in some and be poor in others. He identified these seven primary abilities as: (1) *verbal comprehension* (vocabulary, reading comprehension, the ability to see verbal analogies), (2) *word fluency* (producing words from a single category, rhymes, solving anagrams), (3) *space* (visualizing spatial relations for rotated figures, recognizing geometric relationships), (4) *memory* (rote memory for paired-associates, memory for sentences), (5) *number* (mathematical reasoning, the ability to do computations and work with numbers), (6) *perceptual speed* (recognizing visual details quickly, rapidly noting similarities and differences between pictures), and (7) *general reasoning* (discovering rules underlying sequences of events).

The exact number of primary mental abilities would have to vary with the rigor of one's definition. Guilford (1967), for example, completed a factor analytic study which suggested some 120 different factors, divided into three major categories (the contents, operations, and products of thought). The important point of Thurstone's view, however, is the composition of intelligence as sets of separate abilities, rather than as a single factor of general intelligence.

When Thurstone later developed specific tests for each of his primary abilities, he often found fairly high correlations between subtest scores. He thus had to argue that these abilities, while formally distinct, might well be interrelated (Thurstone & Thurstone, 1941). It is hard to hide the irony of the conflicting views of Spearman's g-factor (plus special abilities) and Thurstone's seven primary mental abilities. Both begin with essentially the same data—a high, but imperfect, correlation between test scores for various abilities—and each used the same facts as proof of his position.

Which of the two views is correct? As we have seen, modern intelligence tests reflect the influence of both. Their test items incorporate a wide variety of abilities (Thurstone), summarized by a single overall score (Spearman), expressed as the IQ. The Wechsler tests in particular, with their separate subtest scores and verbal and performance IQ measures, come closest to the spirit of Thurstone's position. The controversy remains one of explaining the nature of intelligence once it is measured.

Some have argued that young children show Spearman's g, while older children and adults develop the various abilities stressed by Thurstone. Still others have formed various compromise solutions, such as the view that large numbers of specific abilities (Spearman's s-factors) cluster into a smaller number of Thurstone-like primary abilities, with each of these abilities ultimately resting on the baseline of a Spearman g-factor. We can feel confident that a really good definition of intelligence will remain elusive for some time to come. It seems likely that such a definition will have to employ a more sophisticated analysis of cognitive operations of individuals than is currently represented by existing tests of intelligence. (Interested readers are referred to Hunt, Frost, and Lunneborg, 1973, and Sternberg, 1977, for the beginnings of such an approach.)

COGNITIVE DEVELOPMENT

Whether one takes a Spearman or Thurstone view of intelligence, mental age is generally used as an estimate of overall intellectual level which increases systematically with chronological age. For the brighter child, mental maturity grows faster than for the average; for the retarded child, it grows more slowly. General learning ability and the types of problems a child can handle are based on the particular level of mental development at which the child happens to be.

Does increasing mental maturity represent simply a quantitative growth in ability as a child acquires more vocabulary, accumulates more experience, and increases his or her span of attention? Is it correct to assume that the young child is just a "slower" or "more limited" learner than the older child or adult? Or could it be that increases in mental age bring with them major *qualitative* changes in intelligence; that intelligence develops progressively through *stages*, each with its own system of logic? This is a second dimension of the problem of intelligence; one which is critical to our understanding of the learning process.

Consider the following scenario. A mother enters the room just as her young son swats his baby sister on the back of the head, perhaps with his favorite teddy bear or perhaps merely with gusto. Parents have been known to forget that punishing violence with violence in the young child may in fact be counterproductive. She delivers a small swat to the back of the little boy's head, accompanied by the comment, "There, now you can see how it feels."

The mother, of course, does not merely wish to punish the child (or vent her anger). She wishes also to teach him an object lesson by reinforcing the learning with a little understanding, letting the "punishment fit the crime" (or rationalizing her guilt over her anger). We share an implicit assumption that the child will associate the hitting of his sister on the head with his being hit on the head himself: "There, now you can see how it feels." This is simple reciprocity: recognizing the equivalence of the actions you take against others with actions taken against you.

Leaving aside the broader implications of the parental response, let us look more closely at the logic underlying this situation. The child may well be confused. He is not confused about being hit—that he can understand, if only on a stimulus-response level. He is confused by the accompanying remark, "see how it feels." The child is confused, and the mother is confused at his confusion. To the child, the two acts seem to have no logical connection. (He may even attempt to discover the connection with his sister should the mother again leave the room.)

If the child were able to articulate his confusion, it might go something like this: "When my mother hits me, I feel it here, on the back of my head. When I hit my baby sister, I feel it here, on my hand. Why should the two feel the same?"

We are now confronted by a fundamental question. Is this child's logic simply an immature version of the parent's, or is it in fact a rather strict, formal logic that differs from the parent's by the absence of a specifiable principle—"reciprocity"?

The Development of Intelligence

In the Paris laboratory of Theophile Simon, Binet's collaborator in the development of the intelligence test, worked a young Swiss psychologist named Jean Piaget (1896–). The year was 1920, and Piaget's assignment was hardly challenging. His task was to translate into French a number of reasoning tests previously developed in Britain and to develop normative data on French school children in the form of the average age at which each of the test items could be passed by most children (Ginsburg & Opper, 1969).

Piaget's frustration with his assignment began to appear from the very beginning. In standard intelligence testing, one's primary interest is naturally in the child's ability to produce the correct response to a given task or problem. By contrast, Piaget became fascinated by the character of the *errors* children made. Some erroneous responses were very common among children, and different kinds of errors seemed to be typical of children at different ages. In short, he became less interested in whether children could or could not solve a particular reasoning problem, and more interested in what he saw as the logical structure underlying their errors. Why could children at certain ages solve some kinds of problems and not others? Binet's notion of a single dimension of mental age, or mental maturity, seemed too simple an answer. Piaget raised the question of whether this "maturity" dimension of intelligence could not be better understood as a series of stages, each accompanied by a unique logical structure which, in turn, would lead a child to very different conceptual approaches to problems.

Piaget came to the conclusion that older children were not just "brighter" than younger ones; they seemed to think in a qualitatively different way and to use different methods in problem solving. Excited by this possibility, Piaget returned to his native Switzerland to establish his own laboratory in Geneva. He would dedicate the remainder of his career to the study of cognitive development in young children.

Piaget's experience with standard intelligence testing in Paris had convinced him that one could lose considerable information due to children simply misunderstanding a tester's instructions. (Standardized tests typically have an "official" set of instructions which must be used with all children.) Instead, Piaget, borrowing interview techniques from psychotherapy, used the flexibility and relative informality of this less-structured situation to vary the form of problems given to children when it seemed appropriate and to talk with them about their solutions.

As an example of Piaget's approach, we can begin with a 5-year-old child seated before a table with two ordinary, identical drinking glasses, *a* and *b* (see Figure 13.1). We fill the first one, *a*, with milk and ask the child to look carefully at the glass. Let us say it reaches a height of three inches. We then pour exactly the same amount of milk into the second glass, *b*, and ask the child if the amount of milk in the two glasses is the same. Most children will immediately agree that they are. This first step establishes that the child has a sense of the concept of quantity and of the meaning of the words "same" and "different."

Step 2, illustrated in the lower half of Figure 13.1, represents the actual test. We now pour the milk from the second glass, *b*, into a third one, *c*, which is very much taller and thinner. The quantity of milk is of course the same, even though the height it reaches in the glass has doubled. The child is now asked whether the third glass, *c*, holds the same amount of milk as the first glass, *a*. Our experimental subject at the age of 5 may well respond that the third glass has more.

Why is this so? It might be that the child simply thinks that *amount* or *quantity* means *height*. We could test this by asking the child what he or she thinks would happen if we were to pour the milk back into the second glass, *b*, again. How high would it go? The child may well point to a level higher than it originally was in the second glass. There does seem to be more than a misunderstanding of the words used. Some conceptual knowledge seems to be lacking in this child that is not lacking in older children.

An older child of, say, 8 or 9 will not only respond "the same" during the second stage of the experiment, but may do so with mild surprise that such a foolish question would even be asked. Of course they are the same! There is a natural law regarding the constancy or *conservation* of quantity of a liq-

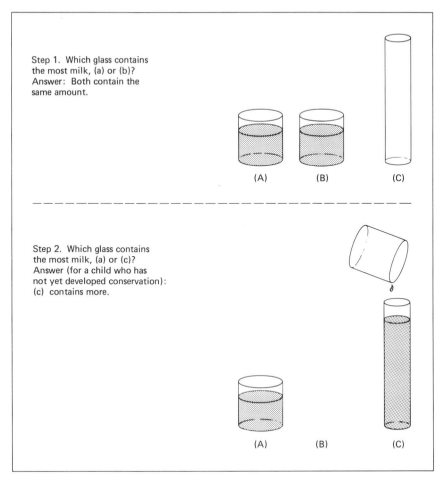

Step 1. Which glass contains
the most milk, (a) or (b)?
Answer: Both contain the
same amount.

(A)   (B)   (C)

Step 2. Which glass contains
the most milk, (a) or (c)?
Answer (for a child who has
not yet developed conservation):
(c) contains more.

(A)   (B)   (C)

Figure 13.1 Piaget's conservation problem. The concept of *conservation*, that the quantity of a liquid remains the same regardless of the shape of the container, does not develop until the *concrete operations* stage of intelligence.

uid, regardless of any change in its shape due to changing the shape of its container. And the older child knows this.

How can we distinguish between the conceptual operations of the younger and the older child? To Piaget, the difference lies in their respective stages of conceptual development. In this case, the older child has developed the principle of conservation, aided and abetted by the ability to look simultaneously at more than one dimension of a problem (the height and the width of the glass), rather than at just a single dimension (the height of the glass). The important point is that Piaget's emphasis is *not* on whether to score the child as "correct" (i.e., giving the adult response) or "incorrect" (giving a response that an adult would not give). Rather, he would emphasize viewing the problem from the framework of the child and discovering the basis underlying the child's "wrong" answer.

In this example, the correctness of the response is not arbitrary. The amount of milk is the same. Here is another example, not taken from Piaget, where the correctness of the answer is less absolute. Look at the five letters below. (1) Which letter should follow in the sequence? (2) Should the letter go on the top or the bottom line? and (3) Why?

$$A \quad E$$
$$BCD$$

If you need help, here is more of the sequence:

$$A \quad EF$$
$$BCD$$

You may still be unsure or feel that more than one answer is possible. Here is more of the sequence.

$$A \quad EF$$
$$BCD \quad G$$

The "correct" answer is *G* on the bottom line, followed by *H* and *I* on the top line. Why? The top line contains letters with all straight lines, and the bottom line has letters with curves in them.

When one give this allegedly "correct" solution to adults, one typically gets a heated argument in return. But now give the same problem to a child up to the age of 9 or 10. You will probably not only get the "correct" solution immediately, but get it with a startling degree of certainty and lack of recognition of ambiguity in the problem. To the child, the solution is obvious. If the pun can be forgiven, it is *childishly* obvious!

This example introduces a central problem in education. At what age is a child "ready" to handle algebra or formal grammar (each sentence is composed of a subject and a predicate or a noun phrase and a verb phrase), or, at an even lower level, the concepts of quantity and number? The notion of "readiness" generally implies that there is an optimal point to introduce new kinds of learning to a child; below this point the learning may not be possible (and above it the learning may be less efficient).

Piaget's research and tentative conclusions are quite involved, and many of his specific suggestions are a matter of some controversy. The interested reader is encouraged to take advantage of the fact that many of Piaget's writings have been translated into English and are now readily available in the United States (Piaget, 1965; Piaget & Inhelder, 1967; Inhelder & Piaget, 1969).

Piaget outlined four major stages in the growth of conceptual intelligence, some with numerous substages. Each stage marks the evolution of the child's conceptual approach to the world and allows forms of solutions to problems not possible in the earlier stages.

Stages in the Development of Intelligence

1. SENSORIMOTOR STAGE (birth to 2 years).   It is difficult to characterize the intelligence of children early in life, both because their preverbal behavior can seem diffuse, and because their relative lack of fine motor coordination can make some abilities difficult to test.

The *sensorimotor* stage begins with primitive reflexes, such as sucking motions to pressure on the cheek, and proceeds to the appearance of alert attention to the source of sounds and smiling in response to the parents and to friendly voices. Between 4 and 8 months of age there is an increased interaction with the environment, manifested by imitative gestures and repeated actions which bring about interesting consequences.

At 8 to 12 months children begin to demonstrate a primitive "problem-solving" ability, such as purposefully removing an obstacle to get at a favorite toy. Even such a simple activity as this, however, is built on an even more fundamental discovery. The child has developed the concept of *object constancy:* the knowledge that objects continue to exist even when they are out of sight. Prior to this time, the reappearance of a hidden object might be greeted with surprise, just as if it had ceased to exist and was then magically recreated for the child's own amusement.

From 12 to 18 months sees progressively more purposeful experimentation with the environment, an increase in trial-and-error behavior, and the beginnings of true goal-directed behavior. For example, we begin to see children invent unique solutions, such as turning a large toy sideways to slip it through a narrow opening.

To Piaget, the origins of intelligence lie in the acquisition of these perceptual and manipulative experiences, accompanied by neuromotor maturation necessary for increased control and self-direction of behavior. As the child develops these skills throughout the sensorimotor period, they in turn make possible the transition into the next stage of development.

2. PREOPERATIONAL THOUGHT (2 to 7 years).   This stage shows the development of symbolic functioning, the ability to anticipate the consequences of actions, and to show the beginnings of truly planned behavior. The child's mental development during this period is as amusing and amazing as a young colt's first attempts to run—by the time we recover from laughter at seeing it trip over its own feet, it is running as smoothly as a thoroughbred. The child's conceptual mistakes can be amusing, but they do not mark "failure." They are reflections of progressively more sophisticated conceptual abilities being pushed to their very limits.

During the preoperational period we see the growth of language—not merely names for objects, but sentences. The child begins to learn how to ask questions, how to make requests and demands, and how to assert statements of truth. While at times impressive, preoperational children's thinking is nevertheless limited by its *egocentricity*. All aspects of the world are seen only in relation to themselves, and they cannot imagine that their point of view is not shared by others. Like the fish being the last to discover water, the child may not even see his or her point of view *as* a point of view. Their understanding of the world is, for them, an inherent, existential reality. Brown (1965, pg. 220) cites a representative example. If a child walking away from his or her house is asked to point toward home, he or she will quite correctly point to the rear. When asked to do this on the return trip, however, he or she may *still* point to the rear. In the terms of the child, the house, once left behind, conceptually remains to the rear. In the same way, preoperational children often seem unable to clearly explain things to other people. They fully assume that others know in advance everything that is to be explained.

We opened this discussion of conceptual development with the notion of "reciprocity": seeing the equivalence between your own actions and parallel actions taken by others against you ("There, now you can see how it feels!"). It is the egocentricity of the preoperational child which Piaget saw as the stumbling block to this logical connection. Reciprocity precisely requires that the child readily shift from his or her point of view to that of another and to compare the two. Without the concept of reciprocity, and its underlying prerequisite, there can be no justice in letting the "punishment fit the crime."

All learning and concept formation during this period is necessarily built on this limited conceptual structure. There is insurmountable conflict, for example, in the notion that one's mother could also be the daughter of another mother. There is also a tendency to confuse dreams with reality and to assume that everything that moves must be alive. This includes clouds, trains, or the wind. The child firmly believes that flowers feel pain and emotion and wonders exactly how ants get married.

Piaget referred to the attribution of life and consciousness to all moving objects as *animism*. It maintains throughout the preoperational stage, only gradually becoming limited to objects which move of their own accord, before finally becoming limited to members of the animal kingdom. What the child understands by "alive," of course, is another matter. The concept would certainly appear to mean less to them than it does to an adult (Klingensmith, 1953).

The preoperational stage is a very special time for parents. The child sees their values and beliefs as fundamental realities of existence. The parents have always been there, as all-perfect beings, and always will be. The names "mommy" and "daddy" are not arbitrary labels, but part of the parents' very essense. In general, names of objects are assumed to be as much a part of the objects as any of their physical properties. Piaget referred to this as *nominal realism.* A "blackboard," the child will tell you, is called a "blackboard" because you write on it.

3. CONCRETE OPERATIONAL THOUGHT (7 to 11 years). Piaget's third major stage, concrete operations, represents a qualitative leap in the child's ability to handle logical operations and abstractions. Egocentricity is reduced, and the child shows greater ability to consider other people's points of view. Similarly, objects can now be simultaneously classed into more than one category. The notion that the child's mother could also be a daughter, a niece, and an aunt, no longer represents a logical dilemma.

Especially noticeable in this stage is an improved facility in understanding trial-and-error problems, predicting the outcomes of events, and using an adultlike logic in approaching intellectual activities. The evolving contrast between preoperational and concrete operational modes can be illustrated with another of Piaget's examples.

In one room we build a tower of blocks on a low table, show it to the child, and then ask him or her to build a tower of the same height on a table in another room. The task is made purposely difficult by separating the two rooms so that both towers cannot be viewed simultaneously, using tables of different heights, and using smaller blocks for the second tower to prevent the child from simply counting them.

The approach of early preoperational children is usually limited to running rapidly back and forth between the rooms as the building progresses, attempting to keep the height of the two towers "in the mind's eye." Later in the preoperational stage, we begin to see a developing attempt to use a third object as a comparator. This begins in a very limited way, with the child trying to measure off the height on his or her arm, or holding the two hands the correct distance apart (running quickly between rooms before the hands change position; an unsuccessful "preoperational" behavior we have seen many adults use).

Late in the preoperational stage, children will look for a true third-object comparator, such as a stick or long piece of wood. There nevertheless seems a fixed limit to what is possible. The use of a measuring device may only occur to the child if it bears some similarity to the objects being compared. A third tower of blocks, if available, is more likely to be used than a stick, and a stick only if its length is approximately the same as the height of the tower. If it is not, the child may consider its use inappropriate, irrelevant, or confusing.

Emergence of the "correct" solution typically does not appear until the stage of concrete operations. Only now will we see children spontaneously measuring off the height of one of the towers part way up on a long stick or taking repeated measures with a short one, in the form of the tower's height being "two-and-a-half sticks" high.

Piaget's point in this demonstration is an important one. At this stage of conceptual development, the correct solution is as obvious to the child as it is totally out of the reach of children below this level. While one stage merges into the next, development seems to be marked by qualitatively discontinuous milestones of conceptual ability which determine not merely which operations are more likely, but which operations are possible.

The development of conservation makes its slow emergence during this period; the child learns to shift his or her attention to various dimensions of a problem (such as height *and* width of a container) rather than to concentrate on only the most salient perceptual attribute (the height).

A prerequisite for the learning of arithmetic also develops during this stage. It is the understanding that adding two apples and three apples is essentially the same problem as adding two cars and three cars, even though "cars cannot be eaten." The child will also be able to tell you that eight coins laid closely together contain the same number as when the same coins are widely separated in a long line. It may seem like a small achievement, but these demonstrations signal the child's development of the concept of *number,* as independent of both the objects counted and their spatial relations.

4. FORMAL OPERATIONAL THOUGHT (from 11 years on). In spite of the impressive development of problem-solving skills, the concrete operations stage is still marked by a relative lack of abstraction and a concentration on concrete qualities. The child's conceptual horizons extend only to the "here and now" of objects and events.

The final, "adult" stage of developing intelligence, *formal operations,* begins to emerge at about the age of 11 or 12. It is signaled by the ability to think in abstract terms replacing a dependence on manipulation of objects physically present in the environment. Thinking is guided by reason, hypothesis, and the ability to follow logical propositions. Alternative outcomes can be envisaged from hypothetical situations. Thought is possible not only about what is but also about what might be.

While formal operations thus represents the final stage of cognitive development, learning and mental growth of course continue beyond adolescence where formal operational thought begins to appear. What these studies intend to say is that these ages complete the development of those cognitive processes upon which this future learning will be built.

IMPLICATIONS FOR EDUCATION

Piaget's research on the dynamics of cognitive development introduced an important new dimension to the study of intelligence. It also sparked sharp controversy about both the generality of his specific findings and how these stages might develop through the child's interaction with the environment. For example, Piaget placed great emphasis on the importance of physical manipulation of objects for conceptual development, especially during the sensorimotor period; yet Bower (1966) has claimed to see the development of size constancy in infants as young as 5 weeks old, in spite of their very limited manipulative activities. In addition, claims are often made for the appearance of some conceptual abilities much earlier than Piaget had thought. For example, when the stimuli are especially meaningful to children, conservation of quantity may appear before the concrete operational stage (Mussen, Conger & Kagan, 1974).

It is equally important, however, to note two factors which Piaget's work does *not* emphasize. First, his theories of conceptual development deal with *sequences* of development rather than individual differences in the rate at which these stages may be attained by different children. Second, Piaget's stress throughout is on *capability* rather than performance. That is, he has concentrated less on what children might do in a formal testing situation and more on what they are potentially capable of doing under the right circumstances. To do otherwise would be to open his work to the same pitfalls and criticisms of standardized intelligence tests which he hoped so much to avoid.

In spite of Piaget's own caution in this regard, it was inevitable that many workers became interested in whether some stages might not be bypassed entirely, or at least their sequence accelerated, through special training. Piaget has humorously referred to this proposition as "the American question." It is, he says, the one point invariably raised whenever he visits the United States (Elkind, 1970, pg. 24).

Piaget does not categorically deny the possibility of limited acceleration through the stages with special training. Fundamentally, however, he believes that the attainment of each stage rests directly on reaching an appropriate level of biological maturation, or "readiness." In practical terms, this means that until maturational readiness has been established, no amount of experience or training will see the child through to a higher stage. Once this readiness period is at hand, however, appropriate learning and experience is necessary for the potential ability to be realized.

The "American question," as Piaget put it, and its answer are still a subject of controversy. Experiments attempting to teach concepts, such as conservation of quantity, before a child would ordinarily be "ready" have met with mixed success. Some have claimed that it is possible; others claim that it is not (cf. Glaser & Resnick, 1972). In fairness to both sides, it should be said that few would deny the importance of either maturation or learning experience for determining the order and timing of the developmental stages. The argument relates primarily to how much weight should be assigned to each.

The question of readiness, the central theme of this chapter, is generally recognized in education. There may well be readiness periods for certain kinds of learning; that is, there may be stages of conceptual development when certain kinds of skills will be more readily acquired than at other times. Unfortunately for the educator, a careful reading of Piaget will not tell the teacher (or parent) specifically what kinds of conceptual problems can (or cannot) be handled by children at different ages. While Piaget does report average ages for the development of some important concepts, the list is not exhaustive and the ages are not to be taken as norms in the strict sense. He offers them primarily as examples to illustrate more general notions of *sequences* in conceptual development.

In short, Piaget has not made a point of the potential applications of his work to formal education. Numerous implications can nevertheless be found (cf. Ginsburg & Opper, 1969, pp. 218–230).

1. A major point must be that there are limits to what a child can learn at different stages of conceptual development. We have seen, for example, that below the ages of 7 or 8, children tend to center on only limited amounts of information at any one time. Reinforced by a tendency toward egocentricity of thought, these children find great difficulty taking into account more than one point of view at a time.

2. Even when children can handle subtle mental operations, they still reason best about objects and events which are immediately present. Remote possibilities inherent in a situation can easily remain unappreciated. For example, below the formal operational period, children learn best from concrete activities. Activity and physical manipulation of objects, in other words, is preferable to purely verbal instruction at younger ages.

3. Whatever training is offered to a child, it will inevitably be understood by the child in terms of his or her own conceptual structure. One might attempt to teach a preoperational child about *inertia,* or some other abstract notion more properly associated with the formal operational stage; yet, no matter how innovative the teaching method, the teacher's instruction will necessarily be mapped onto the child's existing cognitive schemata. Whatever it is the child may have learned about inertia, it may bear little relation to what the teacher thinks has been imparted (Ginsburg & Opper, 1969).

4. One should not rely too heavily on "norms" to determine a particular child's conceptual ability. This must be discovered on a trial-and-error basis, using essentially the same experimental-exploratory approach taken by Piaget himself. The teacher thus becomes a detective, unravelling clues to the child's world, as the child sees it, and then presenting the world in ways the child can understand.

Perhaps it is too much to expect all, or even most, teachers to have the subtle insight of a Piaget. Indeed, even if they did, one wonders if it could be routinely displayed in a classroom of 20 or more boisterous children. The lessons to be drawn from Piaget's work are probably less tangible. Certainly, two points high on any list would be a renewed appreciation for the logic of the child and a redefinition of "success" as an adequate response in terms of the child's own, not the adult's, conceptual framework.

SUMMARY

The previous section has addressed two dimensions of the nature of intelligence. The first of these is whether intelligence is a single, unitary trait or is composed of a number of distinct abilities. The former view was expressed by Spearman, who described intelligence in terms of a single factor, a general intelligence, or g-factor, upon which may rest any number of special abilities, or s-factors.

The opposing view was held by Thurstone, who saw intelligence as composed of seven separate and distinct primary mental abilities. He argued that, in principle, one might excell in some primary abilities and be poor in others. In practice, the two theories make surprisingly similar predictions, and modern intelligence testing reflects a combination of both views.

The second dimension is whether the development of intelligence is a gradual, quantitative growth along a single continuum, or whether intelligence progresses through a series of qualitatively different and more or less definable stages. The latter view was taken by Piaget, who saw a transformation with age in the nature of the logical structure of children, rather than simply a quantitative improvement in ease of learning.

Piaget identified these stages as the sensorimotor stage (birth to 2 years), preoperational thought (2 to 7 years), concrete operational thought (7 to 11 years), and formal operational thought (from 11 years on). He argued that each stage could be recognized by certain bench marks of conceptual learning, reflecting a combination of readiness through biological maturation, and exposure to the necessary experience in the environment.

Intelligence and Learning

As we have seen, there are many limitations to IQ tests as measures of intellectual potential. Further, even when they are valid, effective learning is influenced by many other factors. In Chapter 3, for example, we looked at motivational factors which can retard performance even in the most intellectually gifted. On the other side of the coin is the fact that many "retarded" persons with good social adequacy, who live in a protective or supportive environment, can function in society with a fair degree of success.

These are the "ands" and "buts," the necessary qualifications to any simple statement about intelligence and learning. Having asserted this caution, the fact remains that learning in the mentally retarded, the person of average intelligence, or the educationally gifted will be markedly different.

THE RANGE OF INTELLECT

Figure 13.2 shows an approximation to the results one would theoretically get if IQ measures were obtained from a large, random sample of the population. The graph shows the relative proportion of people (the vertical axis of the graph) who would achieve various IQ scores (shown on the horizontal axis). Most people would score at or around the "average" IQ range of between 90 and 110. As we move to the right and to the left of this point we see smaller and smaller proportions receiving the more extreme scores of 120, 140, and so on at the higher end, and 90, 80, or 70, at the lower end. (The shape of this curve, referred to as a *normal distribution,* or *bell curve,* is common to a large number of biological and psychological characteristics. For example, the distribution of a population's height, weight—or length of hair—would follow the same general form).

For descriptive purposes, different ranges of intelligence are denoted. IQ ranges of 110 to 119 (18 percent of the population) are referred to as "high average," IQs of 120 to 139 (11 percent of the population) are referred to as "superior," and IQs above 140 (1 percent of the population) are referred to as "very superior." In a similar way, IQ ranges below the mean are distinguished as "low average" for IQs between 80 and 89 (15 percent of

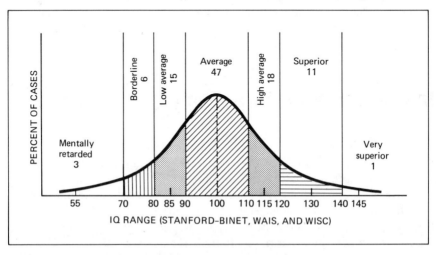

Figure 13.2   Descriptive classification of IQ ranges showing the approximate proportion of persons who would fall into each range in a large sample.

the population), "borderline" for IQs between 70 and 79 (6 percent of the population), and "mentally retarded" for IQs below 70 (3 percent of the population).

The implications of the bell curve are clear. For each person with an IQ above 110 (the rough average of those completing high school successfully), or 120 (the approximate average of college graduates), there is an equal number of people whose intelligence is sufficiently below average that special educational help is required for even moderate school success.

The question of education for the intellectually gifted, those with IQs above 130 or 140, remains a problem of pressing concern. Many of these children find ordinary school work boring, fail in college, or are unable to find vocational fulfillment (Oden, 1968). These children have been educationally neglected in the past because of the assumption that, because of their superior abilities, they will be able to fend for themselves.

The concern of our present discussion, however, is that group on the lower end of the scale who manifestly cannot fend for themselves; those whose learning abilities are so limited that special training, or often a sheltered environment, is a societal necessity.

Mental Retardation

Defining mental retardation can never be precise, since individual differences in motivation, personality, and educational opportunity can yield very different levels of performance for different individuals of the same presumed potential. What definitions there are tend to be statistical, selecting some cutoff point on the IQ range below which one is considered retarded. Figure 13.2 shows the conventional definition of the retarded as those in the lowest 3 percent of the population, whose IQ scores are below 70. By this definition, something over 6 million Americans would be considered mentally retarded; a figure to be compared with the 7 million or so Americans now attending college or university on a full-time basis.

This is a fairly conservative definition. Some classifications have considered an IQ of 84 or below as representing some degree of retardation. This definition takes in 16 percent of the population, or some 32 million Americans.

The causes of mental retardation are beyond the coverage of this text, there being well over 100 different causes, or *etiologies*, so far identified. These causes include genetic defects, physical damage to the brain due to traumatic injury, disease, or lack of oxygen during birth (anoxia), exposure to toxic agents such as lead poisoning or overexposure to radiation, or to a variety of maternal diseases such as syphilis or German measles (rubella).

These causes, for which a physical impairment can be established, are referred to as *organic* disorders. They generally account for that smallest proportion in the very severe ranges of retardation. Three of the better-known organic disorders are discussed below.

DOWN'S SYNDROME. Once referred to as "mongolism," children with *Down's syndrome* have been born with an extra chromosome (47 instead of the usual 46). The effect is typically an extremely low IQ, often below 30, along with recognizable physical characteristics.

The cause of the syndrome has not been fully established, although it has been linked to the possibility of a defective *ovum* (egg cell) in the mother. The most important single variable seems to be the mother's age. The chances of a woman in her twenties having a child with Down's syndrome is 1 in 2000. For a woman in her forties, however, the risk factor increases to 1 in 50 (Koch, Fishler & Melnyk, 1971, pp. 117–118). Because of the attendant physical deficiencies and poor health, as many as 60 percent of these children fail to survive beyond the age of 10. Recent developments have now raised the possibility of detecting the presence of a fetus with Down's syndrome before birth.

PHENYLKETONURIA. Advances in biochemical research have isolated a whole "family" of genetic, metabolic disorders that can lead, if untreated, to severe retardation. While these are inherited disorders, they are carried by a recessive gene trait and thus may appear only rarely in a given family line.

The best-known of these disorders is *phenylketonuria* (PKU), a failure of the body system to metabolize *phenylalanine,* an ordinarily harmless substance occuring naturally in many foods. The PKU infant is born without retardation; damage to the brain occurs only as unmetabolized phenylalanine builds up to toxic levels in the body. Estimated to occur in some 1 in 10,000 live births, it can be detected by a simple urine analysis, and the retardation either prevented or reduced by placing the child immediately on a special diet of food with low phenylalanine content (cf. Berman, Waisman & Graham, 1966).

CRETINISM. So-called cretinism, which results in physical abnormalities and severe retardation, has been traced to a bodily failure to metabolize *thyroxine* (a hormone produced by the thyroid gland), or to a hormonal disorder that decreases normal secretion of thyroxine. Like PKU, it is usually an inherited disorder, although it can also be caused by environmental factors such as an iodine deficiency in the mother's diet before the baby's birth. Like PKU, it can be detected early and treated, in this case by administration of a thyroid hormone which can be effective in reducing the degree of retardation.

The great majority of the retarded, however, some 75 percent of the cases, have yet to be attributed to any single, known, organic cause. These cases are sometimes referred to as *cultural-familial* retardation. Such retardation, typically in the milder ranges, often occurs in members of the same family. As the term implies, it may be partly attributable to a lack of environmental stimulation ("cultural") and/or to some inherited component ("familial"). In other words, the appearance of low ability in the offspring of retarded parents could imply either explanation.

Behavioral Correlates of Retardation

An earlier classification of degrees of retardation used now archaic terms: "moron" for those with IQs ranging from 50 to 70; "imbecile" for those with IQs from 25 to 49; and "idiot" for those with IQs below 25. The gradual introduction of these terms into popular usage, and the attendant loss of their original meanings, necessitated the introduction of new, more descriptive, terminology. Today we refer to these general degrees of retardation as, respectively, "mild" or "educable," "moderate" or "trainable," and "severe" or "profoundly retarded."

Although considerable variation in ability can be expected, one can offer a general picture of the expected levels of performance for various degrees of retardation (Kisker, 1964).

MILD RETARDATION (IQ 53 to 69). These children, about 89 percent of those considered retarded, usually develop normal sensorimotor function and, without early screening, can often spend several years in school before the true degree of retardation is discovered. These years of failure and unnecessary humiliation by attempting to compete in the ordinary classroom without special help was just the motivation that led to Binet's search for an early screening device.

We can expect these children to develop social and academic skills to the level of the average sixth-grader, with their intellectual abilities corresponding to a mental age of 8 to 12 years. However, they will be slow in attaining this level, probably reaching it only by their late teens. While ordinary high school subjects would probably be beyond their ability, they would benefit from a modified program along with special educational help. With good vocational training, there is a fair chance for meaningful employment, although guidance and supervision would be necessary if unexpected events are likely to occur.

MODERATE RETARDATION (IQ 36 to 52). These children, representing about 6 percent of the retarded population, can usually be detected much earlier through evident slowness in motor and speech development. They can be expected to reach fourth grade level, or a mental age of approximately 6 to 8 years. Their learning will be quite slow, and they may not reach this level until their late teens. Special education would be required throughout their school years.

As adults, they may be able to learn some unskilled or semiskilled occupations, provided supervision is available in case a departure from routine should be encountered.

SEVERE RETARDATION (IQ 20 to 35). Speech, language, and motor development in these children will be markedly slow, and only rudimentary communication skills can be expected to develop. These children, representing about 3.5 percent of the retarded population, can reach mental age levels of only 3 to 6 years. Ordinary classroom performance, such as learning to read and write, would be beyond their ability. With extensive training, appropriate health habits can be expected, but self-support as adults can only be expected with complete supervision.

PROFOUND RETARDATION (IQ below 20). These children, about 1.5 percent of the retarded population, have limited capacity in sensorimotor areas, and show little benefit from training. They rarely exceed a mental age of 3. While limited motor and speech development might be possible, nursing care on an almost around-the-clock basis may have to be provided.

IQ IN PERSPECTIVE

Mental retardation, by definition, represents a slowness of learning. This is true both in terms of the rate of mental growth and the level one can expect the child to achieve. The mechanisms of learning and retention seem, in all essential regards, to follow the same principles as we have presented them in previous chapters. The retarded individual's level of performance will be dependent on factors such as motivation, systematic reinforcement, and so forth. They are limited in their speed of learning, and limited in their level of conceptual learning, especially as linguistic deficiencies contribute to this learning. (See O'Connor and Hermelin, 1963, for a good discussion of this interaction in the retarded.)

On the other hand, we have seen that persons in the ranges of mild retardation can attain a good degree of vocational adequacy and, with the proper support, contribute meaningfully to their own and to their community's welfare. As Baldwin and Baldwin (1974) note, a limited ability in formal school situations need not necessarily imply an equivalent disability in social or nonacademic functioning. Most workers in the field of special education for the retarded now agree that one must distinguish between formal test scores and social effectiveness, with overall assessment of ability giving weight to both factors.

In careful balance, then, intelligence testing can be of considerable value in preparing educational help for those in need. It is at this point that a final caution regarding such testing should be mentioned. One needs to guard against the dangers of an erroneous assessment of a child's ability adversely influencing teacher and parental expectation regarding the child's true potential.

Pygmalion in the Classroom

In a well-known series of studies, teaches were given false information regarding the IQ scores of children in their classrooms or fictitious test scores indicating that certain carefully specified students showed unusual potential for intellectual growth, due to "bloom" that year. Although none of this was true, and nothing was in fact special about the indicated students, the prophecy seemed to become fulfilled. Not only did the teachers' belief that these children showed exceptional promise influence school grades, but increases in actual IQ scores were also observed (Rosenthal & Jacobsen, 1968).

The explanations underlying this self-fulfilling prophecy are complex, especially as the teachers in such studies typically deny treating these children any differently or even remembering which of the children were indicated as the "bloomers." One factor may be that teachers tend to pay special attention to those children which they believe have more academic promise (Rothbart, Dalfen & Barrett, 1971). There is, however, more to the reported growth than that. It is also likely that the teachers *expect* more from these children, and that these expectations are somehow communicated to those children. This, in turn, would influence the children's own levels of aspiration and confidence in their own ability.

Some aspects of Rosenthal's findings have been questioned on methodological grounds, and subsequent follow-up studies have found IQ scores more resistant to change through teacher expectation than measures of purely academic achievement (Thorndike, 1968; Baker & Crist, 1971). Nevertheless, Rosenthal's general conclusions are inescapable, and the role of social expectation on the performance of school children is well documented (Baldwin & Baldwin, 1974).

It becomes apparent, then, that IQ testing, or any other method of assessment, could lead to the special help the slow-learning child needs. Misunderstood by the ill-informed, it could just as easily lead to an erroneous lowering of expectations and prevent the child—retarded or otherwise—from meeting his or her true potential. Because of these, and other misunderstandings and consequent misuse, it may be inevitable that one of two things must happen. We must either (1) eliminate IQ scores altogether from children's school files, or (2) educate both parents and teachers as to the limitations of inference which can be drawn from a single IQ score. In all candor, it is hard to say at this time which of these two alternatives is likely to occur sooner.

SPECIFIC LEARNING DISABILITIES

Mental retardation is obviously only one factor that will impose limits on a child's expected rate of learning. To any list of potential obstacles we would also have to add severe emotional disturbances, hearing and visual deficits, environmental disadvantage, and general health impairment (Swets, 1974, pp. 1–2).

There is a final group of children who also show mild to severe learning difficulties. They are perhaps the most misunderstood of all, since the nature of their problem is diagnosed largely by exclusion. That is, they appear average or above average in intelligence, show no sensory impairment, no severe emotional disturbances, and no health or environmental disadvantage. They are often shifted from one "expert" to another for diagnosis and rediagnosis. This is because, for no obvious reason, they do not learn normally in the classroom.

These children are commonly referred to as having *specific learning disabilities* (LD). They seem to have little in common, except for some difficulty, mild or severe, in understanding or using spoken or written language, which in turn may manifest itself in poor ability to learn to read, write, spell, or do mathematical calculations. Some children may show difficulties in all of these areas; others may show a deficit in only one or a few areas, such as reading or mathematical achievement.

The problems of these LD children have not been helped by the proliferation of terms and implied diagnoses which began to flood the literature once these problems became recognized: *perceptual handicaps, brain injury, minimal brain dysfunction, dyslexia, developmental aphasia,* and so forth. Many of these terms derive from the fact that LD children share symptoms with persons known to have brain damage (see Chapter 12). That is, a child or adult incurring brain injury following an accident frequently shows specific learning or performance deficits in the absence of general intellectual impairment. Other typical symptoms include problems of attention and often a marked discrepancy between verbal and performance IQs on the WISC or WAIS (the PIQ for these patients is typically higher than the verbal scale). As we have seen, dyslexia (reading disability) and aphasia (a more general language deficit), for example, are medical terms which specifically relate to impaired function following known brain injury.

The fact is, however, that most LD children show no clear indication of brain injury in standard neurological examinations (no evidence of anoxia at birth, abnormal EEG readings, gross neurological signs, etc.). For this reason, it has become increasingly common to place the weight of the LD diagnosis on the behavioral and education picture presented by the child, rather than the earlier concentration on what was often a vain search for indications of a presumed organic etiology.

Recognition of the LD Child

Johnson and Mykelbust (1967) give a good account of the educational picture of the LD child. Unlike the retarded child, who is uniformly below age level across all aspects of academic ability, the LD child typically shows a good (often very high) IQ, combined with marked discrepancies in performance from one subject area to another. For example, the child may be average or above average in overall class performances, while his or her level in mathematics or reading may be a full year or two below grade level.

Admittedly, many of these cases are due to frankly poor teaching, either present or past. Further, the diagnostic picture may be muddied by the interdependence of skills in the higher school grades. Reading difficulties, for example, will bring down the performance level in all academic subjects which require reading skill. Usually, however, we see the learning difficulty accompanied by other indicative signs such as the previously mentioned discrepancy between verbal and performance IQs on the WISC (the two scores are usually quite similar in most children). We may also see problems with fine motor coordination, poor visual memory, and, perhaps, an unusual degree of distractability or uncontrolled activity (hyperactivity or hyperkinetic behavior) (Strauss & Lehtinen, 1947).

Given the present state of knowledge concerning LD (it is a classic case of the more we have learned, the less we realize we know), the term should not imply a diagnostic or etiological category so much as a description of a class of behaviors related to learning (Torgesen, 1975). The fact to bear in mind is that LD children are a very heterogeneous group, often failing to show the kind of common symptoms which might indirectly lead us to a more complete understanding of the problem. The most common LD problem, that of specific reading disabilities, illustrates this point.

DYSLEXIA: A CASE STUDY.   Whether uniquely susceptible to learning difficulties, the most easily recognizable problem, or because it includes so many processes (visual, spatial, linguistic), some 70 to 80 percent of all recently published work on LD has centered on the failure or unusual difficulty of otherwise normal children to learn to read (Torgesen, 1975).

Sometimes called *dyslexia,* the possibility of a specific reading disability was recognized as early as 1898 (Hinschelwood, 1917). It has been related to subtle organizational and integrative disturbances at a neurological level (Bender, 1958; Critchley, 1970); hence the popularity at one time of the expression, "minimal brain dysfunction." There may be involvement of perceptual problems, not in visual acuity but in the form of difficulties in perceptual integration of the sensory information (cf. Hallahan & Cruickshank, 1973). Although not universal, this idea was sufficiently common to have led at one time to the use of the term "Perceptually handicapped." There is also some evidence that poor readers have a reduced span of short-term memory (Johnson, 1957; Katz & Deutsch, 1967).

The problem of heterogeneity, however, defies any simple symptom classification for the dyslexic child. Attention is a problem in some dyslexic children, but not in others. Some show difficulty in letter recognition; some, in letter reversals, such as confusing b and d, or g and q; still others can read isolated letters successfully but cannot integrate them into words. Further, while studies of reading programs designed to teach single words and paragraph reading show some children to learn at much slower rates than others, the shapes of the learning curves themselves are quite uniform (Camp, 1973). In other words, the learning process for fast and slow learners might itself be quite similar.

In spite of the many uncertainties surrounding dyslexia and other specific learning disabilities, a number of remedial programs have been at least partially successful. Many of these programs attempt to exercise the specific deficits thought to be involved. Some programs, for example, purport to teach such specific skills as "perception," "attention," "visual memory," and so forth.

On the other hand, others feel that, in light of our poor understanding of the problem, the best approach may be the most direct one. This approach stresses instruction and practice in regular academic skills directly, rather than trying to train abilities which may in fact be irrelevant to what may or may not be the child's problem. As Torgesen puts this position:

> Such an approach seems realistic at the present time because it does not depend too heavily on unproven assumptions about the importance of specific abilities for performance in school, or the effectiveness of current diagnostic techniques in identifying which children are deficient in those abilities (Torgesen, 1975, pg. 414).

Disability Not Inability

The question of LD in general, just like its best studied form, dyslexia, thus remains an area of considerable controversy. Brain injury, or brain "dysfunction," may well be the cause in some cases, but not in others, just as we know the symptoms to vary from one child to another. As we have seen, uncertainties of etiology have been matched by disagreement as to the best methods of remediation. In fact, great strides are being taken toward these ends, and it may well be that, as in many other problems, what appears as a single disorder may be a series of similar appearing, but quite distinct, difficulties, implying more than one source of difficulty, and more than one system of remediation.

The increasingly wide recognition of the problem of specific learning disabilities, while not yet supplying many definitive answers, has nevertheless had a positive impact on the school experience of children with LD. Without this recognition, many of these children were being mistaken as "slow," "lazy," or "unmotivated." Indeed, the hyperactivity and distractability which often accompanies these difficulties can easily resemble extreme disinterest.

It is not too surprising, therefore, that one often finds that the correct recognition of the problem brings about positive effects even before special education programs are initiated. The parents', teacher's, and indeed the *child's* knowledge that he or she does have ability, and that there are reasons for his or her difficulties, can itself yield a constructive change in attitude toward the problem. This recognition of a disability to overcome, as opposed to some notion of an inability to learn, can often yield a true Pygmalion in the classroom.

SUMMARY

Any large scale population sample will typically show a bell-shaped, or normal, distribution in the range of intelligence. That is, we can expect to find the greatest number of persons having IQs falling roughly within the range of "average" intelligence, with progressively fewer and fewer numbers having scores in the extreme ranges, either above or below this average.

A common convention defines mental retardation as the lowest 3 percent of the population having IQs below 70. This group, in turn, is loosely categorized as mildly retarded (IQ 53–69), moderately retarded (IQ 36–52), severely retarded (IQ 20–35), and profoundly retarded (IQ below 20).

The possible causes of mental retardation are many, such as the organic defects associated with brain damage, Down's syndrome, phenylketonuria, and cretinism. These organic causes are primarily associated with the very small proportion of retarded persons falling into the severe and profound categories. For the great majority of the retarded, so-called cultural-familial retardation, however, no physical defect is evident, and they usually represent the milder ranges of retardation.

Specific learning disabilities refer to those children whose general intelligence level, level of motivation, and educational background would all predict success in learning, but who, nevertheless, show selective difficulties in such areas as reading, writing, or mathematics. The most common of these is dyslexia, a specific disability in reading.

SUMMARY: READINESS FOR LEARNING

The present chapter has examined the issue of readiness for learning; the recognition that there are levels below which some skills cannot be mastered, regardless of the excellence of instruction, or the richness of available experience. We considered several dimensions of these limitations. These included the effects of intelligence on learning, attempts to define and measure intelligence, and Piaget's pioneering efforts to understand the dynamics of its growth.

As there must be levels below which some skills cannot be mastered, so there may also be upper limits beyond which some skills may become increasingly more difficult to acquire. There may well be an upper bound to some optimal, critical readiness period. On the one hand, there may be a fear of wasting our time and risking frustration by presenting some materials too soon. On the other hand, there is a corresponding fear of missing educational opportunity by withholding some instruction past the point of some hypothetical "readiness" period.

Many factors might contribute to this notion of readiness for learning. Readiness for any skill, such as reading, depends not only on the child's level of intellectual growth, but also on his or her readiness in terms of neuromotor control and motivation. Further, a highly distractable or hyperactive child may be ready to learn to read in regard to these factors but may yet be unready to function successfully in learning situations under ordinary conditions.

When is any given child ready for reading, for mathematics, or any other important skill? What prerequisite capacities and prior learning is necessary? Certainly, normative data gathered from surveys of success at various ages can offer some broad guidelines. But these norms are of little help in determining the point at which any individual child is most ready for, say, reading. In spite of continuing efforts to develop tests of reading readiness, the best rule of thumb still seems to be that readiness is a post hoc phenomenon. When the child has successfully begun to learn to read we know that he or she must surely have been ready!

To begin instruction too soon may lead to frustration along with failure and may effectively "turn off" many children for the future. At the same time, if we have made a single mistake in modern education, it is perhaps that we have been too cautious. In this regard we might well take a cue from "readiness" in language acquisition. Parents do not faithfully consult normative data for acquisition of the first word and start talking to the child for the first time between 9 and 11 months. They begin early, chatting to the infant virtually from the moment of birth. Somewhere along the line, the level of readiness for sound discrimination, motor control of the speech mechanism, intellectual integrity, and so forth do develop. While we do not know in advance when these readiness periods will reliably occur, the stimulation is nevertheless there when the child does in fact become "ready." The comparative success children as a whole experience with language acquisition as opposed to reading skills may well carry its own implications.

We opened this book with frank awe at the cognitive and learning capabilities of young children. We marveled at their curiosity, their excitement in discovery, and the eagerness that characterizes so much of their learning. We saw in the work of Piaget a renewed appreciation for the logic of even the very young child. What seems to be "failure" in the reasoning of children turns out often to mark a carefully defined notion of success. From our experience with retarded children, we can say that, while the rate of learning may be drastically slower, the excitement of learning and of discovery is in no way diminished for these children.

In short, we end this survey of theories and mechanisms of human learning and memory with no less awe of human capability, nor less optimism in its potential, than when we began. There is still much of the mystery to unravel.

References

Adams, J. A. (1954) Psychomotor response acquisition and transfer as a function of control-indicator relationships. *Journal of Experimental Psychology*, 48:10–14.

Adams, J. A. (1967) *Human Memory.* New York: McGraw-Hill.

Adams, J. A. (1971) A closed-loop theory of motor learning. *Journal of Motor Behavior*, 3:111–149.

Adams, J. A. (1976) *Learning and Memory. An Introduction.* Homewood, Ill.: Dorsey Press.

Adams, R. L. & Phillips, B. N. (1972) Motivational and achievement differences among children of various ordinal birth positions. *Child Development*, 43:155–164.

Adamson, R. E. (1952) Functional fixedness as related to problem solving: A repetition of three experiments. *Journal of Experimental Psychology*, 44:288–291.

Agranoff, B. W., Davis, B. E. & Brink, J. J. (1955) Memory fixation in the goldfish. *Proceedings of the National Academy of Sciences*, 54:788–793.

Ainslie, G. W. (1974) Impulse control in pigeons. *Journal of the Experimental Analysis of Behavior*, 21:485–489.

Allport, G. W. (1924) Eidetic imagery. *British Journal of Psychology*, 15:99–120.

Alper, T. G. (1973) The relationship between role orientation and achievement motivation in college women. *Journal of Personality*, 41:9–31.

Ammons, R. B. (1956) Effects of knowledge of performance: A survey of tentative theoretical formulation. *Journal of Genetic Psychology*, 54:279–299.

Anastasi, A. (1968) *Psychological Testing.* 3rd ed. New York: Macmillan.

Anastasi, A. (1976) *Psychological Testing.* 4th ed. New York: Macmillan.

Anderson, J. R. & Bower, G. H. (1973) *Human Associative Memory.* Washington, D.C.: V. H. Winston & Sons.

Ardrey, R. (1961) *African Genesis.* New York: Dell.

Argyris, C. (1964) *Integrating the Individual and the Organization.* New York: Wiley.

Atkinson, J. W. (1954) Exploration using imaginative thought to assess the strength of human motives. In: M. R. Jones (ed.), *Nebraska Symposium on Motivation.* Lincoln: University of Nebraska Press.

Atkinson, J. W. (1958) *Motivation in Fantasy, Action, and Society.* New York: Van Nostrand.

Atkinson, J. W. & Feather, N. T. (eds.) (1966) *A Theory of Achievement Motivation.* New York: Wiley.

Attneave, F. (1959) *Applications of Information Theory to Psychology.* New York: Holt, Rinehart and Winston.

Ausubel, D. P. (1968) *Educational Psychology: A Cognitive View.* New York: Holt, Rinehart and Winston.

Ausubel, D. P. & Robinson, F. C. (1969) *School Learning: An Introduction to Educational Psychology.* New York: Holt, Rinehart and Winston.

Averbach, E. & Coriell, A. S. (1961) Short-term memory in vision. *Bell System Technical Journal,* 40:309–328.

Averbach, E. & Sperling, G. (1963) Short-term storage of information in vision. In: C. Cherry (ed.), *Fourth London Symposium on Information Theory.* London: Butterworth.

Babich, F. R., Jacobson, A. L., Bubash, S. & Jacobson, A. (1965) Transfer of learning to naive rats by injection of ribonucleic acid extracted from trained rats. *Science,* 149:656–657.

Baddeley, A. D. (1970) Estimating the short-term component in free recall. *British Journal of Psychology,* 61:13–15.

Baddeley, A. D. & Dale, H. C. A. (1966) The effect of semantic similarity on retroactive inhibition in long- and short-term memory. *Journal of Verbal Learning and Verbal Behavior,* 5:417–420.

Bahrick, H. P. & Bahrick, P. D. (1964) A re-examination of the inter-relations among measures of retention. *Quarterly Journal of Experimental Psychology,* 16:318–324.

Baker, J. P. & Crist, J. L. (1971) Teacher expectancies: A review of the literature. In: J. D. Elashoff & R. E. Snow, *Pygmalion Reconsidered.* Worthington, Ohio: Charles A. Jones.

Baldwin, C. P. & Baldwin, A. L. (1974) Personality and social development of handicapped children. In: J. A. Swets & L. L. Elliott (eds.), *Psychology and the Handicapped Child.* DHEW Publication No. (OE) 73-05000, 169–185. Washington, D.C.: Government Printing Office.

Bandura, A. & Walters, R. H. (1959) *Adolescent Aggression.* New York: Ronald Press.

Barbizet, J. (1963) Defect of memorizing of hippocampal-mammillary origin: A review. *Journal of Neurology, Neurosurgery, and Psychiatry,* 26:127–135.

Barnes, J. B. & Underwood, B. J. (1959) "Fate" of first-list associations in transfer theory. *Journal of Experimental Psychology* 58:97–105.

Barrett, T. R. & Ekstrand, B. R. (1972) Effects of sleep on memory. III. Controlling for time-of-day effects. *Journal of Experimental Psychology,* 96:321–327.

Bartlett, F. C. (1932) *Remembering: An Experimental and Social Study.* London: Cambridge University Press.

Bayley, N. (1970) Development of mental abilities. In: P. Mussen (ed.), *Carmichael's Manual of Child Psychology,* vol. 1, pp. 1163–1209. New York: Wiley.

Becker, W. C., Madsen, C. H., Arnold, R. & Thomas, D. R. (1967) The contingent use of teacher attention and praise in reducing classroom behavior problems. *Journal of Special Education,* 1:287–307.

Beebe-Center, J. G., Rogers, M. S. & O'Connell, D. N. (1955) Transmission of information about sucrose and saline solutions through the sense of taste. *Journal of Psychology,* 39:157–160.

Belmont, J. M. & Butterfield, E. C. (1969) The relations of short-term memory to development and intelligence. In: L. P. Lipsett & H. W. Reese (eds.), *Advances in Child Development and Behavior,* vol. 4, pp. 29–82. New York: Academic Press.

Belmont, J. M. & Butterfield, E. C. (1971) Learning strategies as determinants of memory deficiencies. *Cognitive Psychology,* 2:411–420.

Bender, L. (1958) Problems in conceptualization and communication in children with development dyslexia. In: P. M. Hoch & J. Zubin (eds.), *Psychopathology of Communication.* New York: Grune & Stratton.

Bennett, E. L. & Calvin, N. (1964) Failure to train planarians reliably. *Neuro-Sciences Research Program Bulletin,* vol. 2 (July-August).

Berko, J. (1958) The child's learning of English morphology. *Word,* 14:150–177.

Berkowitz, L. (1969) *Roots of Aggression: A Re-examination of the Frustration-Aggression Hypothesis.* New York: Atherton.

Bergquist, E. H. (1972) Role of the hypothalamus in motivation: An examination of Valenstein's reexamination. *Psychological Review, 79:542–546.*

Berlyne, D. E. (1960) *Conflict, Arousal and Curiosity.* New York: McGraw-Hill.

Berlyne, D. E. (1966) Curiosity and exploration. *Science,* 153:25–33.

Berman, P., Waisman, H. & Graham, F. (1966) Intelligence in treated phenylketonuric children: A developmental study. *Child Development,* 37:731–747.

Berry, M. F. (1969) *Language Disorders of Children: The Bases and Diagnoses.* Englewood Cliffs, N.J.: Prentice-Hall.

Bexton, W. H., Heron, W. & Scott, T. H. (1954) Effects of decreased variation in the sensory environment. *Canadian Journal of Psychology,* 8:70–76.

Bilodeau, E. A. & Bilodeau, I. McD. (1961) Motor-skills learning. *Annual Review of Psychology,* 12:243–280.

Binet, A. & Simon, T. (1905) Sur la necessite d'establir un diagnostic scientifique des etats inferieurs de l'intelligence. *L'Anee psychologique,* 11:191–244.

Binet, A. & Simon, T. (1961) The development of intelligence in children. In: J. Jenkins & D. G. Paterson (eds.), *Studies in Individual Differences.* Englewood Cliffs, N.J.: Prentice-Hall.

Bjork, R. A. & Jongeward, R. H. (1975) Rehearsal and mere rehearsal. Unpublished manuscript cited in D. A. Norman (1976) *Memory and Attention. An Introduction to Human Information Processing,* pg. 119. New York: Wiley.

Black, J. W. (1951) The effects of delayed side-tone upon vocal rate and intensity. *Journal of Speech and Hearing Disorders,* 16:56–60.

Blair, F. X. (1957) A study of the visual memory of deaf and hearing children. *American Annals of the Deaf,* 102:254–263.

Blakemore, C. (1976) A child of the moment. *The Listener,* 96 (December): 705–708.

Blanchard, E. B. & Young, L. B. (1973) Self-control of cardiac functioning: A promise as yet unfulfilled. *Psychological Bulletin,* 79:145–163.

Blodgett, H. C. (1929) The effect of the introduction of reward upon maze performance in rats. *University of California Publications in Psychology,* 4:113–134.

Bloom, B. S. (ed.) (1956) *Taxonomy of Educational Objectives.* Handbook One: Cognitive Domain. New York: McKay.

Bloom, L. (1970) *Language Development: Form and Function in Emerging Grammars.* Cambridge, Mass.: M.I.T. Press.

Bloom, L. (1971) Why not pivot grammars? *Journal of Speech and Hearing Disorders,* 36:40–50.

Boakes, R. A. & Lodwick, B. (1971) Short term retention of sentences. *Quarterly Journal of Experimental Psychology,* 23:399–409.

Bobrow, S. A. & Bower, G. H. (1969) Comprehension and recall of sentences. *Journal of Experimental Psychology,* 80:455–461.

Bolles, R. C. (1975a) *Theory of Motivation.* 2nd ed. New York: Harper & Row.

Bolles, R. C. (1975b) *Learning Theory.* New York: Holt, Rinehart and Winston.

Boucher, J. L. (1974) Higher processes in motor learning. *Journal of Motor Behavior,* 6:131–138.

Bourne, L. E. (1971) *Human Conceptual Behavior.* Boston: Allyn & Bacon.

Bourne, L. E. & Archer, E. J. (1956) Time continuously on target as a function of distributed practice. *Journal of Experimental Psychology,* 51:25–32.

Bourne, L. E. & Bunderson, C. V. (1963) Effects of delay of informative feedback and length of postfeedback interval on concept identification. *Journal of Experimental Psychology,* 65:1–5.

Bourne, L. E. & Guy, D. E. (1968) Learning conceptual rules: I. Some interrule transfer effects. *Journal of Experimental Psychology,* 76:423–429.

Bourne, L. E. & Haygood, R. C. (1959) The role of stimulus redundancy in concept identification. *Journal of Experimental Psychology,* 58:232–238.

Bourne, L. E. & Haygood, R. C. (1961) Supplementary report: Effect of redundant relevant information upon the identification of concepts. *Journal of Experimental Psychology,* 61:259–260.

Bousfield, W. A. (1953) The occurrence of clustering in the recall of randomly arranged associates. *Journal of General Psychology,* 49:229–240.

Bousfield, W. A. & Barry, H. (1933) The visual imagery of a lightning calculator. *American Journal of Psychology,* 45:353–358.

Bousfield, W. A., Cohen, B. H. & Whitmarsh, G. A. (1958) Associative clustering in the recall of words of different taxonomic frequencies of occurrence. *Psychological Reports,* 4:39–44.

Bower, G. H. & Clark, M. C. (1969) Narrative stories as mediators for serial learning. *Psychonomic Science,* 14:181–182.

Bower, T. G. R. (1966) The visual world of infants. *Scientific American,* 205:80–92.

Bowlby, J. (1958) The nature of the child's tie to his mother. *International Journal of Psychoanalysis,* 39:350–373.

Braine, M. D. S. (1963a) The ontogeny of English phrase structure: The first phase. *Language,* 39:1–13.

Braine, M. D. S. (1963b) On learning the grammatical order of words. *Psychological Review,* 70:323–348.

Bransford, J. D., Barclay, J. R. & Franks, J. J. (1972) Sentence memory: A constructive vs. interpretive approach. *Cognitive Psychology,* 3:193–208.

Bransford, J. D. & Franks, J. J. (1971) The abstraction of linguistic ideas. *Cognitive Psychology,* 2:331–350.

Brehm, J. W. (1962) Motivational effects of cognitive dissonance. In: M. R. Jones (ed.), *Nebraska Symposium on Motivation.* Lincoln: University of Nebraska Press.

Briggs, B. E. (1954) Acquisition, extinction, and recovery functions in retroactive inhibition. *Journal of Experimental Psychology,* 47:285–293.

Broadbent, D. E. (1952) Speaking and listening simultaneously. *Journal of Experimental Psychology,* 43:267–273.

Broadbent, D. E. (1954) The role of auditory localization in attention and memory span. *Journal of Experimental Psychology,* 47:191–196.

Broadbent, D. E. (1958) *Perception and Communication.* London: Pergamon Press.

Broadbent, D. E. (1971) *Decision and Stress.* London: Academic Press.

Broadhurst, P. L. (1957) Emotionality and the Yerkes-Dodson law. *Journal of Experimental Psychology,* 54:345–352.

Brown, B. L. (1970) Stimulus generalization in salivary conditioning. *Journal of Comparative and Physiological Psychology,* 71:467–477.

Brown, J. (1958) Some tests of the decay theory of immediate memory. *Quarterly Journal of Experimental Psychology,* 10:12–21.

Brown, J. S. (1961) *The Motivation of Behavior.* New York: McGraw-Hill.

Brown, R. (1956) Language and categories. In: J. S. Bruner, J. J. Goodnow & G. A. Austin, *A Study of Thinking,* pp. 247–312. New York: Wiley.

Brown, R. (1958) How shall a thing be called? *Psychological Review,* 65:14–21.

Brown, R. (1965) *Social Psychology.* New York: Free Press.

Brown, R. (1970) The first sentences of child and chimpanzee. In: R. Brown (ed.), *Psycholinguistics,* pp. 208–231. New York: Free Press.

Brown, R. (1973) *A First Language: The Early Stages.* Cambridge, Mass.: Harvard University Press.

Brown, R. & Bellugi, U. (1964) Three processes in the child's acquisition of syntax. In: E. H. Lenneberg (ed.), *New Directions in the Study of Language,* pp. 131–161. Cambridge, Mass.: M.I.T. Press.

Brown, R. & Fraser, C. (1963) The acquisition of syntax. In: C. N. Cofer & B. S. Musgrave (eds.), *Verbal Behavior and Learning,* pp. 158–197. New York: McGraw-Hill.

Brown, R. & Hanlon, C. (1970) Derivational complexity and order of acquisition in child speech. In: J. R. Hayes (ed.), *Cognition and the Development of Language.* New York: Wiley.

Brown, R. W. & McNeill, D. (1966) The "tip of the tongue" phenomenon. *Journal of Verbal Learning and Verbal Behavior,* 5:325–337.

Brownfield, C. A. (1965) *Isolation: Clinical and Experimental Approaches.* New York: Random House.

Bruce, D. J. (1964) The analysis of word sounds by young children. *British Journal of Educational Psychology,* 34:158.

Bruce, D. & Cofer, C. N. (1967) An examination of recognition and free recall as measures of acquisition and long-term retention. *Journal of Experimental Psychology,* 75:283–289.

Bruner, J. S. (1966) *Toward a Theory of Instruction.* Cambridge, Mass.: Harvard University Press.

Bruner, J. S., Goodnow, J. J., & Austin, G. A. (1956) *A Study of Thinking.* New York: Wiley.

Bruner, J. S. & Olver, R. R. (1963) The development of equivalence transformations in children. In: J. C. Wright & J. Kagan (eds.), *Basic Cognitive Processes in Children. Monographs of the Society for Research in Child Development,* 28 (2, Serial No. 86).

Bryan, W. L. & Harter, N. (1899) Studies on the telegraphic language: The acquisition of a hierarchy of habits. *Psychological Review,* 6:345–375.

Bugelski, B. R. (1971) *The Psychology of Learning Applied to Teaching.* 2nd ed. New York: Bobbs-Merrill.

Burstein, K. R., Epstein, S. & Smith, B. (1967) Primary stimulus generalization of the GSR as a function of objective and subjective definition of the stimulus dimension. *Journal of Experimental Psychology,* 74:124–131.

Butler, R. A. (1953) Discrimination learning by rhesus monkeys to visual exploration motivation. *Journal of Comparative and Physiological Psychology,* 46:95–98.

Butler, R. (1954) Curiosity in monkeys. *Scientific American,* 190:18, 70–75.

Byrne, D. (1961) The repression-sensitization scale: Rationale, reliability, and validity. *Journal of Personality,* 29:334–349.

Byrne, W. L. (ed.) (1970) *Molecular Approaches to Learning and Memory.* New York: Academic Press.

Camp, B. W. (1973) Learning rate and retention in retarded readers. *Journal of Learning Disabilities,* 6:65–71.

Carmichael, L., Hogan, H. P. & Walter, A. A. (1932) An experimental study of the effect of language on the reproduction of visually perceived form. *Journal of Experimental Psychology,* 15:73–86.

Ceraso, J. (1967) The interference theory of forgetting. *Scientific American,* 217:117–124.

Cermak, L. S. (1972) *Human Memory: Research and Theory.* New York: Ronald Press.

Cermak, L. S. (1975) *Improving Your Memory,* New York: Norton.

Chapanis, A. (1954) The reconstruction of abbreviated printed messages. *Journal of Experimental Psychology,* 48:496–510.

Cherry, E. C. (1953) Some experiments on the perception of speech with one and with two ears. *Journal of the Acoustical Society of America,* 25:975–979.

Cherry, E. C. & Taylor, W. (1954) Some further experiments on the recognition of speech with one and with two ears. *Journal of the Acoustical Society of America,* 26:554–559.

Cherry, E. C. (1957) *On Human Communication.* Cambridge, Mass.: M.I.T. Press.

Chomsky, N. (1957) *Syntactic Structures.* The Hague: Mouton.

Chomsky, N. (1959) Verbal behavior (A review). *Language,* 35:26–58.

Chomsky, N. (1965) *Aspects of a Theory of Syntax.* Cambridge, Mass.: M.I.T. Press.

Chomsky, N. (1968) *Language and Mind.* New York: Harcourt Brace Jovanovich.

Chorover, S. L. & Schiller, P. H. (1966) Reexamination of prolonged retrograde amnesia in one-trial learning. *Journal of Comparative and Physiological Psychology,* 61:34–41.

Clayton, K. N. (1964) T-maze choice-learning as a joint function of the reward magnitude of the alternatives. *Journal of Comparative and Physiological Psychology,* 58:333–338.

Cofer, C. N. (1966) Some evidence for coding processes derived from clustering in free recall. *Journal of Verbal Learning and Verbal Behavior,* 5:188–192.

Cofer, C. N. (1973) Constructive processes in memory. *American Scientist,* 61:537–543.

Cofer, C. N., Chmielewski, D. L. & Brockway, J. P. (1975) Constructive processes and the structure of human memory. In: C. N. Cofer (ed.), *The Structure of Human Memory,* pp. 190–203. San Francisco: Freeman.

Cohen, B. D., Kalish, H. I., Thurston, J. R. & Cohen, E. (1954) Experimental manipulation of verbal behavior. *Journal of Experimental Psychology,* 47:106–110.

Collins, A. M. & Quillian, M. R. (1969) Retrieval time from semantic memory. *Journal of Verbal Learning and Verbal Behavior,* 8:240–247.

Coltheart, V. (1971) Memory for stimuli and memory for hypotheses in concept identification. *Journal of Experimental Psychology,* 89:102–108.

Conrad, R. (1964) Acoustic confusions in immediate memory. *British Journal of Psychology,* 55:75–84.

Cooper, L. A. & Shepard, R. N. (1973) Chronometric studies of the rotation of mental images. In: W. G. Chase (ed.), *Visual Information Processing,* pp. 75–176. New York: Academic Press.

Corteen, R. S. & Wood, B. (1972) Autonomic responses to shock-associated words in an unattended channel. *Journal of Experimental Psychology,* 94:308–313.

Cotler, S. B., Applegate, G., King, L. W. & Kristal, S. (1972) Establishing a token economy program in a state hospital classroom: A lesson in training student and teacher. *Behavior Therapy,* 3:209–222.

Crafts, L. W., Schneirla, T. C., Robinson, E. E. & Gilbert, R. W. (1950) *Recent Experiments in Psychology.* 2nd ed. New York: McGraw-Hill.

Craik, F. I. M. & Lockhart, R. S. (1972) Levels of processing: A framework for memory research. *Journal of Verbal Learning and Verbal Behavior,* 11:671–684.

Craik, F. I. M. & Tulving, E. (1975) Depth of processing and the retention of words in episodic memory. *Journal of Experimental Psychology; General,* 104:268–294.

Craik, F. I. M. & Watkins, M. J. (1973) The role of rehearsal in short-term memory. *Journal of Verbal Learning and Verbal Behavior,* 12:599–607.

Crespi, L. P. (1942) Quantitative variation of incentive and performance in the white rat. *American Journal of Psychology* 55:467–517.

Critchley, M. (1970) *The Dyslexic Child.* Springfield, Ill.: Thomas.

Cronholm, B. & Lagergren, A. (1959) Memory disturbances after electroconvulsive therapy. *Acta Psychiatrica Neurologia Scandinavica* 34:283–310.

Crossman, E. R. F. W. (1959) A theory of the acquisition of speed-skill. *Ergonomics,* 2:153–166.

Crowder, R. G. (1976) *Principles of Learning and Memory.* Hillsdale, N.J.: Lawrence Erlbaum Associates.

Dallett, K. & Wilcox, S. G. (1968) Contextual stimuli and proactive inhibition. *Journal of Experimental Psychology,* 78:475–480.

Darwin, C. T., Turvey, M. T. & Crowder, R. G. (1972) An auditory analogue of the Sperling partial report procedure: Evidence for brief auditory storage. *Cognitive Psychology,* 3:255–267.

Davis, C. M. (1939) Results of the self-selection of diets by young children. *Canadian Medical Association Journal,* 41:257–261.

Davis, D. R. & Sinha, D. (1950) The effect of one experience upon the recall of another. *Quarterly Journal of Experimental Psychology,* 2:43–52.

Davis, R., Sutherland, N. S. & Judd, B. R. (1961) Information content in recognition and recall. *Journal of Experimental Psychology,* 61:422–429.

Deese, J. (1964) *Principles of Psychology.* Boston: Allyn & Bacon.

Delgado, J. M. R. & Hamlin, H. (1960) Spontaneous and evoked electrical seizures in animals and in humans. In: E. R. Ramey & D. S. O'Doherty (eds.), *Electrical Studies in the Unanesthetized Brain.* New York: Harper & Row.

Delgado, J. M. R., Roberts, W. W. & Miller, N. E. (1954) Learning motivated by electrical stimulation of the brain. *American Journal of Psychology,* 179:587–593.

DeNike, L. D. (1964) The temporal relationship between awareness and performance in verbal conditioning. *Journal of Experimental Psychology*, 68:521–529.

Denny, N. R. (1969) Memory and transformations in concept learning. *Journal of Experimental Psychology*, 79:63–68.

DeRivera, J. (1959) Some conditions governing the use of cue-producing response as an explanatory devise. *Journal of Experimental Psychology*, 57:299–304.

Deutsch, J. A. & Deutsch, D. (1963) Attention: Some theoretical investigations. *Psychological Review*, 70:80–90.

Deutsch, J. A. & Deutsch, D. (1967) Comments on "Selective attention: Perception or response?" *Quarterly Journal of Experimental Psychology*, 19:362–363.

Digman, J. M. (1959) Growth of a motor skill as a function of distribution of practice. *Journal of Experimental Psychology*, 57:310–316.

Dillon, D. J. (1970) Intervening activity and the retention of meaningful verbal materials. *Psychonomic Science*, 19:369–370.

DiVesta, F. J. (1974) *Language, Learning, and Cognitive Processes*. Monterey, Calif.: Brooks/Cole.

Dodd, D. H., Kinsman, R. A., Klipp, R. D. & Bourne, L. E. (1971) Effect of logic pretraining on conceptual rule learning. *Journal of Experimental Psychology*, 88:119–122.

Dominowski, R. L. (1965) Role of memory in concept learning. *Psychological Bulletin*, 63:271–280.

Doob, L. W. (1965) Exploring eidetic imagery among the Kamba of Central Kenya. *Journal of Social Psychology*, 67:3–22.

Douglas, V. I. (1974) Sustained attention and impulse control: Implications for the handicapped child. In: J. A. Swets & L. L. Elliot (eds.), *Psychology and the Handicapped Child*. DHEW Publication No. (OE) 73-05000 pp. 148–168. Washington, D.C.: Government Printing Office.

Duncker, K. (1945) On problem-solving. *Psychological Monographs*, 58, no. 270.

Ebbinghaus, H. (1913) *Memory: A Contribution to Experimental Psychology*. Translated by H. A. Ruger & C. E. Bussenius. New York: Teachers College, Columbia University. (Originally published by Leipzig: Altenberg, 1885).

Eimas, P. D. (1974) Auditory and linguistic processing of cues for place of articulation for infants. *Perception and Psychophysics*, 16:513–521.

Eimas, P. D., Siqueland, E. R., Jusczyk, P. & Vigorito, J. (1971) Speech perception in infants. *Science*, 171:303–306.

Eisenson, J. (1957) Aphasia in adults: Classification and examination procedures. In: L. E. Travis (ed.), *Handbook of Speech Pathology*, pp. 436–449. Englewood Cliffs, N.J.: Prentice-Hall.

Ekstrand, B. R. (1967) Effect of sleep on memory. *Journal of Experimental Psychology*, 75:64–72.

Elkind, D. (1970) *Children and Adolescents: Interpretive Essays on Jean Piaget*. New York: Oxford University Press.

Ellis, H. C. (1972) *Fundamentals of Human Learning and Cognition*. Dubuque, Iowa: Brown.

Engel, B. T. (1974) Comment on self control of cardiac functioning: A promise as yet unfulfilled. *Psychological Bulletin*, 81:43.

Epstein, S. & Burstein, K. R. (1966) A replication of Hovland's study of stimulus eneralization to frequencies of tone. *Journal of Experimental Psychology*, 72:782–784.

Epstein, W. (1961) The influence of syntactic structure on learning. *American Journal of Psychology*, 74:80–85.

Epstein, W. (1962) A further study of the effect of syntactic structure on learning. *American Journal of Psychology*, 75:121–126.

Eriksen, C. W. (1954) Multidimensional stimulus differences and accuracy of discrimination. USAF, WADC Technical Report no. 54-165.

Eriksen, C. W. & Hake, H. W. (1955) Absolute judgments as a function of the stimulus range and the number of stimulus and response categories. *Journal of Experimental Psychology*, 49:323–332.

Espir, M. L. E. & Rose, F. C. (1970) *The Basic Neurology of Speech*. Oxford: Blackwell.

Estes, W. K. (1960) Learning theory and the new "mental chemistry." *Psychological Review*, 67:207–223.

Feigenbaum, E. A. & Simon, H. A. (1962) A theory of the serial position effect. *British Journal of Psychology*, 53:307–320.

Field, W. H. & Lachman, R. (1966) Information transmission (I) in recognition and recall as a function of alternatives (K). *Journal of Experimental Psychology*, 72:785–791.

Fitts, P. M. (1964) Perceptual-motor skill learning. In: A. W. Melton (ed.), *Categories of Human Learning*. New York: Academic Press.

Fjerdingstad, E. J. (ed.) (1971) *Chemical Transfer of Learned Information*. Amsterdam: North Holland Publishing Company.

Flavell, J. H., Beach, D. R. & Chinsky, J. M. (1966) Spontaneous verbal rehearsal in a memory task as a function of age. *Child Development*, 37:283–299.

Fleishman, E. A. & Parker, J. F. (1962) Factors in the retention and relearning of perceptual-motor skill. *Journal of Experimental Psychology*, 64:215–226.

Flexner, L. B. (1968) Dissection of memory in mice with antibiotics. *American Scientist*, 56:52–57.

Fodor, J. & Bever, T. G. (1965) The psychological reality of linguistic segments. *Journal of Verbal Learning and Verbal Behavior*, 4:414–420.

Fodor, J. A., Bever, T. G. & Garrett, M. F. (1974) *The Psychology of Language*. New York: McGraw-Hill.

Foot, M. (1973) *Aneurin Bevan 1945-60*. London: Davis-Poynter.

Freides, D. & Hayden, S. D. (1966) Monocular testing: A methodological note on eidetic imagery. *Perceptual and Motor Skills*, 23:88.

French, E. G. & Thomas, F. H. (1958) The relation of achievement to problem-solving effectiveness. *Journal of Abnormal and Social Psychology*, 56:45–48.

French, J. D. (1957) The reticular formation. *Scientific American*, 196:54–60.

Freud, S. (1891) *Zur Auffassung der Aphasien*. Leipzig and Vienna: Franz Deuticke. Translated by E. Stengel. *On Aphasia, a Critical Study*. New York: International Universities Press.

Friebergs, V. & Tulving, E. (1961) The effect of practice on utilization of information from positive and negative instances in concept identification. *Canadian Journal of Psychology*, 15:101–106.

Frost, N. (1972) Encoding and retrieval in visual memory tasks. *Journal of Experimental Psychology*, 95:317–326.

Gagné, R. M. (1965) *The Conditions of Learning.* New York: Holt, Rinehart and Winston.

Gagné, R. M. (1969) Context, isolation and interference effects on the retention of facts. *Journal of Educational Psychology,* 60:408–414.

Gagné, R. M. (1970) *The Conditions of Learning.* 2nd ed. New York: Holt, Rinehart and Winston.

Gagné, R. M. & Wiegand, V. K. (1970) Effects of subordinate context on learning and retention of facts. *Journal of Educational Psychology,* 61:406–409.

Gall, F. J. & Spurzheim, G. (1810) *Anatomie et physiologie du systeme nerveux en général et du cerveau en particulier.* Paris: Schoell.

Galton, F. (1880) Statistics of mental imagery. *Mind,* 5:300–318.

Garcia, J., Ervin, F. R. & Koelling, R. A. (1966) Learning with prolonged delay of reinforcement. *Psychonomic Science,* 5:121–122.

Gardner, R. A. & Gardner, B. T. (1969) Teaching sign language to a chimpanzee, *Science,* 165:664–672.

Garner, W. R. (1953) An informational analysis of absolute judgments of loudness. *Journal of Experimental Psychology,* 46:373–380.

Garrett, M. F., Bever, T. G. & Fodor, J. (1966) The active use of grammar in speech perception. *Perception and Psychophysics,* 1:30–32.

Gazzaniga, M. S. (1970) *The Bisected Brain.* Englewood Cliffs, N.J.: Prentice-Hall.

Geschwind, N. (1970) The organization of language in the brain. *Science,* 170:940–944.

Gewirtz, J. L. & Baer, D. M. (1958) Deprivation and satiation of social reinforcers as drive conditions. *Journal of Abnormal and Social Psychology,* 57:165–172.

Ginsburg, H. & Opper, S. (1969) *Piaget's Theory of Intellectual Development: An Introduction.* Englewood Cliffs, N.J.: Prentice-Hall.

Glanzer, M. & Dolinsky, R. (1965) The anchor for the serial position curve. *Journal of Verbal Learning and Verbal Behavior,* 4:267–273.

Glaser, R. & Resnick, L. B. (1972) Instructional psychology. *Annual Review of Psychology,* 23:207–276.

Glasser, W. (1969) *Schools Without Failure.* New York: Harper & Row.

Glaze, J. A. (1928) The association value of nonsense syllables. *Journal of Genetic Psychology,* 35:255–269.

Gleitman, H. (1955) Place learning without prior performance. *Journal of Comparative and Physiological Psychology,* 48:77–79.

Gleitman, H. (1963) Place learning. *Scientific American,* 209:116–122.

Glickman, S. E. (1961) Perseverative neural processes and consolidation of the neural trace. *Psychological Bulletin,* 58:218–233.

Glucksberg, S. & Danks, J. H. (1969) Grammatical structure and recall: A function of the space in immediate memory or of recall delay? *Perception and Psychophysics,* 6:113–117.

Glucksberg, S. & Danks, J. H. (1975) *Experimental Psycholinguistics: An Introduction.* Hillsdale, N.J.: Lawrence Erlbaum Associates.

Glucksberg, S. & Weisberg, R. (1966) Verbal behavior and problem solving: Some effects of labeling in a functional fixedness paradigm. *Journal of Experimental Psychology,* 71:659–664.

Goddard, H. H. (1946) What is intelligence? *Journal of Social Psychology,* 24:51–69.

Goldman-Eisler, F. (1961) Hesitation and information in speech. In: C. Cherry (ed.), *Information Theory*. London: Butterworth.

Goldman-Eisler, F. (1964) Discussion and further comments. In: E. H. Lenneberg (ed.), *New Directions in the Study of Language*, pp. 109–130. Cambridge, Mass.: M.I.T. Press.

Goldman-Eisler, F. (1968) *Psycholinguistics: Experiments in Spontaneous Speech*. New York: Academic Press.

Goldman-Eisler, F. & Cohen, M. (1970) Is N, P, and NP difficulty a valid criterion of transformational operations? *Journal of Verbal Learning and Verbal Behavior*, 9:161–166.

Goldstein, K. (1948) *Language and Language Disturbances*. New York: Grune & Stratton.

Goldstein, K. (1950) Prefrontal lobotomy: Analysis and warning. *Scientific American*, 182:44–47.

Goodglass, H. (1972) Discussion paper on cortical functioning. In: J. H. Gilbert (ed.), *Speech and Cortical Functioning*. New York: Academic Press.

Goodnow, R. E. (1954) Utilization of partially valid cues in perceptual identification. Ph.D. dissertation, Harvard University.

Goodwin, D. W., Othmer, E., Halikas, J. A. & Freemon, F. (1970) Loss of short-term memory as a predictor of the alcoholic "blackout." *Nature*, 227:201–202.

Gray, C. R. & Gummerman, K. (1975) The enigmatic eidetic image: A critical examination of methods, data, and theory. *Psychological Bulletin*, 82:383–407.

Greene, J. (1972) *Psycholinguistics*. Baltimore: Penguin Books.

Greenspoon, J. & Brownstein, J. A. (1967) Awareness in verbal conditioning. *Journal of Experimental Research in Personality*, 2:295–308.

Gregory, R. L. (1966) *Eye and Brain*. London: World University Library.

Grether, W. F. (1938) Pseudo-conditioning without paired stimulation encountered in attempted backward conditioning. *Journal of Comparative Psychology*, 25:91–96.

Griggs, R. A. (1974) The recall of linguistic ideas. *Journal of Experimental Psychology*, 103:807–809.

Gross, C. G. (1968) General activity. In: L. Weiskrantz (ed.), *Analysis of Behavioral Change*, pp. 91–106. New York: Harper & Row.

Guilford, J. P. (1967) *The Nature of Human Intelligence*. New York: McGraw-Hill.

Guthrie, E. R. (1935) *The Psychology of Learning*. New York: Harper & Row.

Guthrie, E. R. (1952) *The Psychology of Learning*. Rev. ed. New York: Harper & Row.

Guthrie, E. R. (1959) Association by contiguity. In: S. Koch (ed.), *Psychology: A Study of a Science*, vol. 2. New York: McGraw-Hill.

Guttman, N. (1953) Operant conditioning, extinction, and periodic reinforcement in relation to concentration of sucrose used as reinforcing agent. *Journal of Experimental Psychology*, 46:213–224.

Guttman, N. & Julesz, B. (1963) Lower limits of auditory periodicity analysis. *Journal of the Acoustical Society of America*, 35:610.

Guttman, N. & Kalish, H. I. (1956) Discriminability and stimulus generalization. *Journal of Experimental Psychology*, 51:79–88.

Haber, R. N. (1969) Eidetic images. *Scientific American*, 220:36–44.

Haber, R. N. & Haber, R. B. (1964) Eidetic imagery I: Frequency. *Perceptual and Motor Skills,* 19:131–138.

Haber, R. N. & Standing, L. G. (1969) Direct measures of short-term visual storage. *Quarterly Journal of Experimental Psychology,* 13:83–84.

Hake, H. W. & Garner, W. R. (1951) The effect of presenting various numbers of discrete steps on scale reading accuracy. *Journal of Experimental Psychology,* 42:358–366.

Hall, C. S. & Lindzey, G. (1957) *Theories of Personality,* New York: Wiley.

Hallahan, D. P. & Cruickshank, W. M. (1973) *Psycho-educational Functions of Learning Disabilities.* Englewood Cliffs, N.J.: Prentice-Hall.

Halliday, M. S. (1968) Exploratory behavior. In: L. Weiskrantz (ed.), *Analysis of Behavioral Change,* pp. 107–126. New York: Harper & Row.

Hammond, K. R. (1955) Probabilistic functioning and the clinical method. *Psychological Review,* 62:255–262.

Hanawalt, N. G. & Demarest, I. H. (1939) The effect of verbal suggestion in the recall period upon the reproduction of visually perceived form. *Journal of Experimental Psychology,* 65:6–11.

Hanfmann, E. (1941) A study of personal patterns in an intellectual performance. *Character and Personality,* 9:315–325.

Hannay, A. (1971) *Mental Images—A Defence.* New York: Humanities Press.

Harlow, H. F. (1949) The formation of learning sets. *Psychological Review,* 56:51–65.

Harlow, H. F. (1950) Performance of catarrhine monkeys on a series of discrimination reversal problems. *Journal of Comparative and Physiological Psychology,* 43:231–239.

Harlow, H. F. & Zimmerman, R. R. (1959) Affectional responses in the infant monkey. *Science,* 130:421–432.

Hayes, K. J. (1950) Vocalization and speech in chimpanzees. *American Psychologist,* 5:275–276.

Haygood, R. C., Sandlin, J., Yoder, D. J. & Dodd, D. H. (1969) Instance of contiguity in disjunctive concept learning. *Journal of Experimental Psychology,* 81:605–607.

Head, H. (1926) *Aphasia.* Cambridge University Press.

Heath, R. G. & Mickle, W. A. (1960) Evaluation of seven years' experience with depth electrode studies in human patients. In: E. R. Ramey & D. S. O'Doherty (eds.), *Electrical Studies in the Unanesthetized Brain.* New York: Harper & Row.

Hebb, D. O. (1949) *The Organization of Behavior.* New York: Wiley.

Hebb, D. O. (1966) *A Textbook of Psychology.* 2nd ed. Philadelphia: Saunders.

Hebron, M. E. (1966) *Motivated Learning.* London: Methuen.

Heidbreder, E. (1946) The attainment of concepts: I. Terminology and methodology. *Journal of General Psychology,* 35:173–189.

Heidbreder, E. (1947) The attainment of concepts: III. The process. *Journal of Psychology,* 24:93–138.

Herman, L. M., Beach, F. A., Pepper, R. L. & Stalling, R. B. (1969) Learning set formation in the bottlenose dolphin. *Psychonomic Science,* 14:98–99.

Heron, W., Doane, B. K. & Scott, T. H. (1956) Visual disturbances after prolonged perceptual isolation. *Canadian Journal of Psychology,* 10:13–18.

Herrnstein, R. J. & Boring, E. C. (1965) *A Source Book in the History of Psychology.* Cambridge, Mass.: Harvard University Press.

Hilgard, E. R. (1951) The role of learning in perception. In: R. R. Blake & G. V. Ramsey (eds.), *Perception: An Approach to Personality*, pp. 95–120. New York: Ronald Press.

Hilgard, J. R. (1932) Learning and maturation in pre-school children. *Journal of Genetic Psychology*, 41:36–56.

Hinshelwood, J. (1917) *Congenital Word-Blindness*. London: H. K. Lewis.

Hockey, R. (1969) Noise and efficiency: The visual task. *New Scientist*, 42: 244–246.

Hoebel, B. G. & Teitelbaum, P. (1962) Hypothalamic control of feeding and self-stimulation. *Science*, 135:375–377.

Holt, R. R. (1964) Imagery: The return of the ostracized. *American Psychologist*, 19:254–264.

Homans, G. C. (1961) *Social Behavior: Its Elementary Forms*. New York: Harcourt Brace Jovanovich.

Honzik, M. P., Macfarlane, J. W. & Allen, L. (1948) The stability of mental test performance between two and eighteen years. *Journal of Experimental Education*, 17:309–324.

Hovland, C. I. (1937) The generalization of conditioned responses with varying frequencies of tone. *Journal of General Psychology*, 17:125–148.

Hovland, C. I. (1938) Experimental studies in rote-learning theory. III. Distribution of practice with varying speeds of syllable presentation. *Journal of Experimental Psychology*, 23:172–190.

Hovland, C. I., Janis, I. L. & Kelley, H. H. (1953) *Communication and Persuasion*. New Haven: Yale University Press.

Hovland, C. I., Lumsdaine, A. A. & Sheffield, F. D. (1949) *Experiments on Mass Communication*. Princeton University Press.

Hovland, C. I. & Weiss, W. (1953) Transmission of information concerning concepts through positive and negative instances. *Journal of Experimental Psychology*, 45:175–182.

Howe, M. J. A. (1972) *Understanding School Learning: A New Look at Educational Psychology*. New York: Harper & Row.

Huggins, A. W. F. (1968) Delayed auditory feedback and the temporal properties of speech materials. *Zeitschrift für Phonetik, Sprachwissenschaft und kommunikationsforschung*, 21:54–60.

Hulicka, I. M. & Grossman, J. L. (1967) Age-group comparisons for the use of mediators in paired-associate learning. *Journal of Gerontology*, 22:45–51.

Hull, C. L. (1920) Quantitative aspects of the evolution of concepts. *Psychological Monographs*, 28, no. 1 (Whole no. 127).

Hull, C. L. (1943) *Principles of Behavior*. Englewood Cliffs, N.J.: Prentice-Hall.

Hull, C. L. (1951) *Essentials of Behavior*. New Haven: Yale University Press.

Hull, C. L. (1952) *A Behavior System*. New Haven: Yale University Press.

Hulse, S. H. (1973) Reinforcement contrast effects in rats following experimental definition of a dimension of reinforcement magnitude. *Journal of Comparative and Physiological Psychology*, 85:160–170.

Hulse, S. H., Deese, J. & Egeth, H. (1975) *The Psychology of Learning*. 4th ed. New York: McGraw-Hill.

Hunt, E., Frost, N. & Lunneborg, C. (1973) Individual differences in cognition: A new approach to intelligence. In: G. Bower (ed.), *The Psychology of Learning and Motivation*, vol. 7. New York: Academic Press.

Hunt, E. B. & Hovland, C. I. (1960) Order of consideration of different types of concepts. *Journal of Experimental Psychology*, 59:220–225.

Hunter, I. M. L. (1964) *Memory*. Baltimore: Penguin Books.

Hunter, W. S. (1932) The effect of inactivity produced by cold upon learning and retention in the cockroach, *Blatella germanica*. *Journal of Genetic Psychology*, 41:253–266.

Hydén, H. (1967) Behavior, neural function and RNA. *Progress in Nucleic Acid Research*, 6:187–218.

Hydén, H. & Egyházi, E. (1962) Nuclear RNA changes of nerve cells during a learning experiment in rats. *Proceedings of the National Academy of Sciences*, 48:1368–1372.

Inhelder, B. & Piaget, J. (1969) *The Early Growth of Logic in the Child*. New York: Norton.

Jacobs, J. (1887) Experiments on "prehension." *Mind*, 12:75–79.

Jacobson, A. L., Babich, F. R., Bubash, S. & Jacobson, A. (1965) Differential approach tendencies produced by injection of ribonucleic acid from trained rats. *Science*, 150:636–637.

Jakobson, R., Fant, C. G. & Halle, M. (1963) *Preliminaries to Speech Analysis: The Distinctive Features and their Correlates*. 2nd ed. Cambridge, Mass.: M.I.T. Press.

Jenkins, J. G. & Dallenbach, K. M. (1924) Oblivescence during sleep and waking. *American Journal of Psychology*, 35:605–612.

Jenkins, J. J. (1963) Mediated associations: Paradigms and situations. In: C. N. Cofer & B. S. Musgrave (eds.), *Verbal Behavior and Learning*, pp. 210–245. New York: McGraw-Hill.

Jensen, A. R. (1969) How much can we boost I.Q. and scholastic achievement? *Harvard Educational Review*, 39:1–123.

Johnson, D. J. & Myklebust, H. R. (1967) *Learning Disabilities: Educational Principles and Practices*. New York: Grune & Stratton.

Johnson, F. N. (1969) The effects of chlorpromazine on the decay and consolidation of short-term memory traces in mice. *Psychopharmacologia*, 16:105–114.

Johnson, M. K., Bransford, J. & Solomon, S. (1973) Memory for tacit implications of sentences. *Journal of Experimental Psychology*, 98:203–205.

Johnson, M. S. (1957) Factors related to reading disability. *Journal of Experimental Education*, 26:1–26.

Johnson, N. F. (1965) The psychological reality of phrase structure rules. *Journal of Verbal Learning and Verbal Behavior*, 4:469–475.

Johnston, W. A. & Heinz, S. P. (1974) It takes attention to pay attention. Paper presented at the meeting of the Psychonomics Society, Boston, Mass., November, 1974.

Jonides, J., Kahn, R. & Rozin, P. (1975) Imagery improves memory for blind subjects. *The Bulletin of the Psychonomic Society*, 5:424–426.

Julesz, B. (1964) Binocular depth perception without familiarity cues. *Science*, 145:256–262.

Julesz, B. & Guttman, N. (1963) Auditory memory. *Journal of the Acoustical Society of America*, 35:1895 (Abstract).

Kagan, J. (1966) Developmental studies in reflection and analysis. In: A. H. Kidd & J. L. Rivoire (eds.), *Perceptual Development in Children*. New York: International Universities Press.

Kagan, J. & Kagan, N. (1970) Individual variation in cognitive processes. In: P. H. Mussen (ed.), *Carmichael's Manual of Child Psychology*, vol. 1. 3rd ed. New York: Wiley.

Kahneman, D. (1973) *Attention and Effort*. Englewood Cliffs, New Jersey: Prentice-Hall.

Kalish, H. L. (1965) Behavior therapy. In: B. Wolman (ed.), *Handbook of Clinical Psychology*, pp. 1230–1253. New York: McGraw-Hill.

Kanfer, F. H. (1968) Verbal conditioning: A review of its current status. In: T. R. Dixon & D. L. Horton (eds.), *Verbal Behavior and General Behavior Theory*, pp. 245–290. Englewood Cliffs, N.J.: Prentice-Hall.

Kantowitz, B. H. & Knight, J. L. (1976) On experimenter-limited processes. *Psychological Review*, 83:502–507.

Kaufman, E. L., Lord, M. W., Reese, T. W. & Volkmann, J. (1949) The discrimination of visual number. *American Journal of Psychology*, 62:498–525.

Katz, P. A. & Deutsch, M. (1967) Auditory and visual functioning and reading achievement. In: M. Deutsch (ed.), *The Disadvantaged Child*. New York: Basic Books.

Kazdin, A. E. (1975) *Behavior Modification in Applied Settings*. Homewood, Ill.: Dorsey Press.

Kazdin, A. E. & Polster, R. (1973) Intermittent token reinforcement and response maintenance in extinction. *Behavior Therapy*, 4:386–391.

Keele, S. W. (1973) *Attention and Human Performance*. Pacific Palisades, Calif.: Goodyear.

Keele, S. W. (1975) The representation of motor programmes. In: P. M. A. Rabbitt & S. Dornic (eds.), *Attention and Performance* V, pp. 357–365. New York: Academic Press.

Keele, S. W. & Archer, E. J. (1967) A comparison of two types of information in concept identification. *Journal of Verbal Learning and Verbal Behavior*, 6:185–192.

Kelleher, R. T. (1956) Discrimination learning as a function of reversal and nonreversal shifts. *Journal of Experimental Psychology*, 51:379–384.

Kelleher, R. T. (1957) Conditioned reinforcement in chimpanzees. *Journal of Comparative and Physiological Psychology*, 50:571–575.

Keller, F. S. (1958) The phantom plateau. *Journal of Experimental Psychology*, 1:1–13.

Kellogg, W. N. & Kellogg, L. A. (1933) *The Ape and the Child*. New York: McGraw-Hill.

Kendler, T. S. (1964) Verbalization and optional reversal shifts among kindergarten children. *Journal of Verbal Learning and Verbal Behavior*, 3:428–433.

Kendler, T. S. & Kendler, H. H. (1959) Reversal and nonreversal shifts in kindergarten children. *Journal of Experimental Psychology*, 58:56–60.

Kendler, H. H. & Kendler, T. S. (1962) Vertical and horizontal processes in problem solving. *Psychological Review*, 69:1–16.

Kendler, T. S., Kendler, H. H. & Wells, D. (1960) Reversal and nonreversal shifts in nursery school children. *Journal of Comparative and Physiological Psychology*, 53:83–88.

Kennedy, A. & Wilkes, A. (1968) Response-time at different positions within a sentence. *Quarterly Journal of Experimental Psychology*, 20:390–394.

Kimble, G. A. (1961) *Hilgard and Marquis' "Conditioning and Learning."* Englewood Cliffs, N.J.: Prentice-Hall.

Kimmel, H. D. (1974) Instrumental conditioning of autonomically mediated responses in human beings. *American Psychologist,* 29:325–335.

Kimura, D. (1961) Cerebral dominance and the perception of verbal stimuli. *Canadian Journal of Psychology,* 15:166–171.

Kimura, D. (1963) Right temporal-lobe damage. *Archives of Neurology,* 8:264–271.

Kimura, D. (1964) Left-right differences in the perception of melodies. *Quarterly Journal of Experimental Psychology,* 16:355–358.

King, F. L. & Kimura, D. (1972) Left-ear superiority in dichotic perception of vocal nonverbal sounds. *Canadian Journal of Psychology,* 26:111–116.

Kingsley, P. R. & Hagen, J. W. (1969) Induced versus spontaneous rehearsal in short-term memory in nursery school children. *Developmental Psychology,* 1:40–46.

Kintsch, W. (1975) Memory for prose. In: C. N. Cofer (ed.), *The Structure of Human Memory,* pp. 90–113. San Francisco: Freeman.

Kintz, B. L., Foster, M. S., Hart, J. O., O'Malley, J. J., Palmer, E. L. & Sullivan, S. L. (1969) A comparison of learning sets in humans, primates, and subprimates. *Journal of General Psychology,* 80:189–204.

Kisker, G. W. (1964) *The Disorganized Personality.* New York: McGraw-Hill.

Klahr, D. (ed.) (1976) *Cognition and Instruction.* Hillsdale, N.J.: Lawrence Erlbaum Associates.

Klatzky, R. L. (1975) *Human Memory: Structures and Processes.* San Francisco: Freeman.

Klingensmith, S. W. (1953) Child animism: What the child means by "alive." *Child Development,* 24:51–61.

Knapp, R. R. (1965) Relationship of a measure of self-actualization to neuroticism and extraversion. *Journal of Consulting Psychology,* 29:168–172.

Koch, R., Fishler, K. & Melnyk, J. (1971) Chromosomal anomalies in causation: Down's syndrome. In: R. Koch & J. C. Dobson (eds.), *The Mentally Retarded Child and his Family: A Multidisciplinary Handbook.* New York: Brunner/Mazel.

Koch, S. & Daniel, W. J. (1945) The effect of satiation on the behavior mediated by a habit of maximum strength. *Journal of Experimental Psychology,* 35:167–187.

Kopp, R., Bohdanecky, Z., & Jarvik, M. E. (1966) Long temporal gradient of retrograde amnesia for a well-discriminated stimulus. *Science,* 153:1547–1549.

Kraeling, D. (1961) Analysis of amount of reward as a variable in learning. *Journal of Comparative and Physiological Psychology,* 54:560–565.

Krueger, W. C. F. (1929) The effects of overlearning on retention. *Journal of Experimental Psychology,* 12:71–78.

Krueger, W. C. F. (1930) Further studies in overlearning. *Journal of Experimental Psychology,* 13:152–163.

Kurtz, K. H. & Hovland, C. I. (1956) Concept learning with differing sequences of instances. *Journal of Experimental Psychology,* 51:239–243.

Lack, D. (1965) *The Life of the Robin.* London: Witherby.

Lansdell, H., Purnell, J. K. & Laskowski, E.J. (1963) The relation of induced dysnomia to phoneme frequency. *Language and Speech,* 6:88–93.

Lashley, K. S. (1951) The problem of serial order in behavior. In: L. A. Jeffress (ed.), *Cerebral Mechanisms in Behavior: The Hixon Symposium.* New York: Wiley.

Laughlin, P. R. (1968) Conditional concept attainment as a function of if factor complexity and then factor complexity. *Journal of Experimental Psychology,* 77:212–222.

Lazlo, J. I. (1967) Training of fast tapping with reduced kinesthetic, tactile, visual, and auditory sensations. *Quarterly Journal of Experimental Psychology,* 71:764–771.

Leeper, R. (1951) Cognitive processes. In: S. S. Stevens (ed.), *Handbook of Experimental Psychology,* pp. 730–757. New York: Wiley.

Lefrancois, G. R. (1972) *Psychological Theories and Human Learning: Kongor's Report.* Monterey, Calif.: Brooks/Cole.

Lenneberg, E. H. (1961) Color naming, color recognition, color discrimination: A re-appraisal. *Perceptual and Motor Skills,* 12:375–382.

Lenneberg, E. H. (1967) *Biological Foundations of Language.* New York: Wiley.

Lett, B. T. (1975) Long delay learning in the T-maze. *Learning and Motivation,* 6:80–90.

Leukel, F. A. (1957) A comparison of the effects of ECS and anesthesia on acquisition of the maze habit. *Journal of Comparative and Physiological Psychology,* 50:300–306.

Levin, S. M. (1961) The effects of awareness on verbal conditioning. *Journal of Experimental Psychology,* 61:67–75.

Levine, J. M. & Murphy, G. (1943) The learning and forgetting of controversial material. *Journal of Abnormal and Social Psychology,* 38:507–517.

Lewis, J. L. (1970) Semantic processing of unattended messages using dichotic listening. *Journal of Experimental Psychology,* 85:225–228.

Linden, E. (1974) *Apes, Men, and Language.* Baltimore: Penguin Books.

Lindsay, P. H. & Norman, D. A. (1972) *Human Information Processing: An Introduction to Psychology.* New York: Academic Press.

Lobb, H. & Hardwick, C. (1976) Eyelid conditioning and intellectual level: Effects of repeated acquisition and extinction. *American Journal of Mental Deficiency,* 80:423–430.

Loehlin, J. C., Lindzey, G. & Spuhler, J. N. (1975) *Race Differences in Intelligence.* San Francisco: Freeman.

Loftus, E. F. & Palmer, J. C. (1974) Reconstruction of automobile destruction: An example of the interaction between language and memory. *Journal of Verbal Learning and Verbal Behavior,* 13:585–589.

Logan, F. A. (1960) *Incentive.* New Haven: Yale University Press.

Logan, F. A. (1965) Decision making by rats: Delay versus amount of reward. *Journal of Comparative and Physiological Psychology,* 59:1–12.

London, P. (1975) *Beginning Psychology.* Homewood, Ill.: Dorsey.

Longstreth, L. E. (1970) Tests of the law of effect using open and closed tasks. *Journal of Experimental Psychology,* 84:53–57.

Lorenz, K. (1966) *On Aggression.* New York: Harcourt Brace Jovanovich.

Lorge, I. (1930) Influence of regularly interpolated time intervals on subsequent learning. *Teachers College Contributions to Education,* no. 438.

Lowell, E. L. (1952) The effect of need for achievement on learning and speed of performance. *Journal of Psychology,* 33:31–40.

Luborsky, L. F. (1945) Aircraft recognition: I. The relative efficiency of teaching procedures. *Journal of Applied Psychology,* 29:385–398.

Luh, C. W. (1922) The conditions of retention. *Psychological Monographs,* 31, no. 142.

Luria, A. R. (1960) Memory and the structure of mental processes. *Problems of Psychology,* 1:81–93.

Luria, A. R. (1961) *The Role of Speech in the Regulation of Normal and Abnormal Behavior.* London: Pergamon Press.

Luria, A. R. (1968) *The Mind of a Mnemonist.* New York: Basic Books.

Luria, A. R. (1970) *Traumatic Aphasia.* The Hague: Mouton.

Luria, A. R. & Yudovich, F. Ia. (1959) *Speech in the Development of Mental Processes in the Child.* London: Staples.

Lyons, J. (1970) *Noam Chomsky.* New York: Viking Press.

MacCorquodale, K. (1970) On Chomsky's review of Skinner's *Verbal Behavior. Journal of the Experimental Analysis of Behavior,* 13:83–99.

Mace, C. A. (1962) *The Psychology of Study.* Baltimore: Penguin Books.

MacKay, D. G. (1973) Aspects of the theory of comprehension, memory and attention. *Quarterly Journal of Experimental Psychology,* 25:22–40.

Mackintosh, N. J. (1965) Selective attention in animal discrimination learning. *Psychological Bulletin,* 64:124–150.

Mackworth, J. F. (1962) The visual image and the memory trace. *Canadian Journal of Psychology,* 16:55–59.

Mackworth, J. F. (1963) The duration of the visual image. *Canadian Journal of Psychology,* 17:62–81.

Mackworth, J. F. (1970) *Vigilance and Habituation.* Baltimore: Penguin Books.

MacNeilage, P. F. (1970) Motor control of serial ordering in speech. *Psychological Review,* 77:182–196.

Madsen, C. H. Becker, W. C., Thomas, D. R., Koser, L. & Plager, E. (1970) An analysis of the reinforcing function of "sit down" commands. In: R. K. Parker (ed.), *Readings in Educational Psychology,* pp. 265–278. Boston: Allyn & Bacon.

Maier, N. R. F. (1970) *Problem Solving and Creativity: In Individuals and Groups.* Monterey, Calif.: Brooks/Cole.

Malmo, R. B. (1975) *On Emotions, Needs and Our Archaic Brain.* New York: Holt, Rinehart and Winston.

Marks, L. & Miller, G. A. (1964) The role of semantic and syntactic constraints in the memorization of English sentences. *Journal of Verbal Learning and Verbal Behavior,* 3:1–5.

Marshall, J. (1969) *Law and Psychology in Conflict.* New York: Doubleday (Anchor Books).

Martin, P. R. & Fernberger, S. W. (1929) Improvements in memory span. *American Journal of Psychology,* 41:91–94.

Maslow, A. H. (1954) *Motivation and Personality.* New York: Harper & Row.

Maslow, A. H. (1968) *Toward a Psychology of Being.* 2nd ed. New York: Van Nostrand.

Maslow, A. H. (1970) *Motivation and Personality.* 2nd ed. New York: Harper & Row.

Maslow, B. G. (1972) *Abraham H. Maslow: A Memorial Volume.* Monterey, Calif.: Brooks/Cole.

Massaro, D. W. (1975) *Experimental Psychology and Information Processing.* Skokey, Ill.: Rand McNally.

Mathews, W. A. (1968) Transformational complexity and short-term recall. *Language and Speech,* 11:120–128.

McClelland, D. C. (1955) *Studies in Motivation.* Englewood Cliffs, N.J.: Prentice-Hall.

McClelland, D. C. (1961) *The Achieving Society.* New York: Van Nostrand.

McClelland, D. C., Atkinson, J. W., Clark, R. A. & Lowell, E. L. (1953) *The Achievement Motive.* Englewood Cliffs, N.J.: Prentice-Hall.

McConnell, J. D. (1962) Memory transfer through cannibalism in planarians. *Journal of Neuro-Psychiatry,* 3, Monograph Supplement 1.

McGaugh, J. L. (1966) Time-dependent processes in memory storage. *Science,* 153:1351–1358.

McGaugh, J. L. & Dawson, R. G. (1971) Modification of memory storage processes. *Behavioral Sciences,* 16:45–63.

McGaugh, J. L. & Herz, M. J. (1972) *Memory Consolidation.* San Francisco: Albion.

McGaugh, J. L. & Krivanek, J. (1970) Strychnine effects on discrimination learning in mice: Effects of dose and time of administration. *Physiology and Behavior,* 5:1437–1442.

McGeoch, J. A. (1932) Forgetting and the law of disuse. *Psychological Review,* 39:352–370.

McGeoch, J. A. (1942) *The Psychology of Human Learning.* New York: Longmans, Green.

McGeoch, J. A. & Irion, A. L. (1952) *The Psychology of Human Learning,* 2nd ed. New York: McKay.

McNulty, J. A. (1965) An analysis of recall and recognition processes in verbal learning. *Journal of Verbal Learning and Verbal Behavior,* 4:430–435.

Mehler, J. (1963) Some effects of grammatical transformations on the recall of English sentences. *Journal of Verbal Learning and Verbal Behavior,* 2:346–351.

Meichenbaum, D. H., Bowers, K. & Ross, R. R. (1968) Modification of classroom behavior of institutionalized female adolescent offenders. *Behavior Research and Therapy,* 6:343–353.

Melton, A. W. (1961) Comments on Professor Postman's paper. In: C. N. Cofer (ed.), *Verbal Learning and Verbal Behavior,* pp. 179–193. New York: McGraw-Hill.

Melton, A. W. (1963) Implications of short-term memory for a general theory of memory. *Journal of Verbal Learning and Verbal Behavior,* 2:1–21.

Melton, A. W. & Irwin, J. (1940) The influence of degree of interpolated learning on retroactive inhibition and the overt transfer of specific responses. *American Journal of Psychology,* 53:173–203.

Meyer, D. E. & Schvaneveldt, R. W. (1976) Meaning, memory structure, and mental processes. In C. N. Cofer (ed.), *The Structure of Human Memory,* pp. 54–89. San Francisco: Freeman.

Miller, G. A. (1951) *Language and Communication.* New York: McGraw-Hill.

Miller, G. A. (1952) Finite Markov processes in psychology. *Psychometrika,* 17:149–167.

Miller, G. A. (1956) The magical number seven plus or minus two: Some limits on our capacity for processing information. *Psychological Review,* 63:81–97.

Miller, G. A. (1958) Free recall of redundant strings of letters. *Journal of Experimental Psychology*, 56:485–491.

Miller, G. A. (1962) Some psychological studies of grammar. *American Psychologist*, 17:748–762.

Miller, G. A. & Frick, F. C. (1949) Statistical behavioristics and sequences of responses. *Psychological Review*, 56:311–324.

Miller, G. A., Galanter, E. & Pribram, K. H. (1960) *Plans and the Structure of Behavior.* New York: Holt, Rinehart and Winston.

Miller, G. A. & Selfridge, J. A. (1950) Verbal context and the recall of meaningful material. *American Journal of Psychology*, 63:176–185.

Miller, N. E. (1957) Experiments on motivation. *Science*, 126:1271–1278.

Miller, N. E. (1969) Learning of visceral and glandular responses. *Science*, 163:434–445.

Miller, N. E. & DiCara, L. (1967) Instrumental learning of heart rate changes in curarized rats: Shaping, and specificity to discriminative stimulus. *Journal of Comparative and Physiological Psychology*, 63:12–19.

Miller, N. E. & Dworkin, B. R. (1974) Visceral learning: Recent difficulties with curarized rats and significant problems for human research. In: P. A. Obrist, A. H. Black, J. Brener & L. V. DiCara (eds.), *Cardiovascular Physiology: Current Issues in Response Mechanisms, Biofeedback, and Methodology.* Chicago: Aldine.

Miller, N. E. & Kessen, M. L. (1952) Reward effects of food via stomach fistula compared with those of food via mouth. *Journal of Comparative and Physiological Psychology*, 43:471–480.

Miller, W. & Ervin, S. (1964) The development of grammar in child language. In: U. Bellugi & R. Brown (eds.), *The Acquisition of Language. Monographs of the Society for Research in Child Development*, 29 (1, Serial No. 92).

Milner, B. (1962) Laterality effects in audition. In: V. B. Mountcastle (ed.), *Interhemispheric Relations and Cerebral Dominance.* Baltimore: The Johns Hopkins Press.

Milner, B. (1965) Brain disturbance after bilateral hippocampal lesions. In: P. Milner & S. Glickman (eds.), *Cognitive Processes and the Brain*, pp. 97–111. New York: Van Nostrand.

Milner, B. (1966) Amnesia following operation on the temporal lobes. In: C. W. M. Whitty & O. L. Zangwill (eds.), *Amnesia*, pp. 109–113. London: Butterworth.

Milner, B., Branch, C. & Rasmussen, T. (1964) Observations on cerebral dominance. In: A. V. S. deReuch & M. O'Connor (eds.), *Ciba Foundation Symposium on Disorders of Language*, pp. 200–214. London: Churchill.

Milner, B., Taylor, L. & Sperry, R. W. (1968) Lateralized supression of dichotically presented digits after commissural section in man. *Science*, 161:184–186.

Minami, H. & Dallenbach, K. M. (1946) The effect of activity upon learning and retention in the cockroach. *American Journal of Psychology*, 59:1–58.

Moray, N. (1959) Attention in dichotic listening: Effective cues and the influence of instructions. *Quarterly Journal of Experimental Psychology*, 11:56–60.

Moray, N. (1960) Broadbent's filter theory: Postulate H and the problem of switching time. *Quarterly Journal of Experimental Psychology*, 12:214–220.

Moray, N., Bates, A. & Barnett, T. (1965) Experiments on the four-eared man. *Journal of the Acoustical Society of America*, 38:196–201.

Moray, N. & O'Brien, T. (1967) Signal detection theory applied to selective listening. *Journal of the Acoustical Society of America*, 42:765–772.

Moray, N. & Taylor, A. (1960) Statistical approximations to English. *Language and Speech*, 3:7–10.

Morgan, C. T. & Deese, J. (1957) *How to Study*. New York: McGraw-Hill.

Morgan, C. T. & King, R. A. (1971) *Introduction to Psychology*. 4th ed. New York: McGraw-Hill.

Morris, C. D., Bransford, J. D. & Franks, J. J. (1977) Levels of processing versus transfer appropriate processing. *Journal of Verbal Learning and Verbal Behavior*, 16: 519–533.

Morris, D. (1967) *The Naked Ape*. New York: McGraw-Hill.

Morton, J. (1964) The effects of context on the visual duration threshold for words. *British Journal of Psychology*, 55:165–180.

Moss, H. A. & Kagan, J. (1961) Stability of achievement and recognition seeking behaviors from early childhood through adulthood. *Journal of Abnormal and Social Psychology*, 62:504–513.

Mowbray, G. (1964) Perception and retention of verbal information presented during auditory shadowing. *Journal of the Acoustical Society of America*, 36:1459–1465.

Mowrer, O. H. (1947) On the dual nature of learning—A reinterpretation of "conditioning" and "problem-solving." *Harvard Education Review*, 17:102–148.

Mowrer, O. H. (1950) *Learning Theory and Personality Dynamics*. New York: Ronald Press.

Mowrer, O. H. (1954) The psychologist looks at language. *American Psychologist*, 9:660–694.

Mowrer, O. H. (1960) *Learning Theory and the Symbolic Processes*. New York: Wiley.

Moyer, K. E. & Korn, J. H. (1964) Effects of UCS intensity on the acquisition of an avoidance response. *Journal of Experimental Psychology*, 67:352–359.

Murdock, B. B. (1972) Short-term memory. In: G. H. Bower (ed.), *Psychology of Learning and Motivation*, vol. 5, pp. 67–127. New York: Academic Press.

Murray, D. J. & Roberts, B. (1968). Visual and auditory presentation, presentation rate, and short-term memory in children. *British Journal of Psychology*, 59:119–125.

Murray, H. A. (1938) *Explorations in Personality*. New York: Oxford University Press.

Mussen, P. H., Conger, J. J. & Kagan, J. (1974) *Child Development and Personality*. 4th ed. New York: Harper & Row.

Nabokov, V. (1966) *Speak Memory*. New York: Putnam.

Neisser, U. (1963) Decision-time without reaction-time: Experiments in visual scanning. *American Journal of Psychology*, 76:376–385.

Neisser, U. (1967) *Cognitive Psychology*. Englewood Cliffs, N.J.: Prentice-Hall.

Neisser, U. & Kerr, N. (1973) Spatial and mnemonic properties of visual images. *Cognitive Psychology*, 5:138–150.

Neisser, U. & Weene, P. (1962) Hierarchies in concept attainment. *Journal of Experimental Psychology*, 64:640–645.

Nelson, K. (1973) Structure and strategy in learning to talk. *Monographs of the Society for Research in Child Development*, 38 (1–2, Serial no. 149).

Nelson, K. E., Carskaddon, G. & Bonvillian, J. D. (1973) Syntax acquisition: Impact of experimental variation in adult verbal interaction with the child. *Child Development*, 44:497–504.

Nelson, T. O., Metzler, J. & Reed, D. (1974) Role of details in the long-term recognition of pictures and verbal descriptions. *Journal of Experimental Psychology*, 102:184–186.

Newcombe, F., Oldfield, R. C., Ratcliff, G. G. & Wingfield, A. (1971) Recognition and naming of object-drawings by men with focal brain wounds. *Journal of Neurology, Neurosurgery, and Psychiatry*, 34:329–340.

Newcombe, F., Oldfield, R. C. & Wingfield, A. (1965) Object-naming by dysphasic patients. *Nature*, 207:1217–1218.

Newell, K. M. (1974) Knowledge of results and motor learning. *Journal of Motor Behavior*, 6:235–244.

Newman, E. B. (1939) Forgetting of meaningful material during sleep and waking. *American Journal of Psychology*, 52:65–71.

Nisbett, R. R. (1968) Taste, deprivation, and weight determinants of eating behavior. *Journal of Personality and Social Psychology*, 10:107–116.

Noble, C. E. (1961) Measurement of association value (*a*), rated associations (*a'*), and scaled meaningfulness (*m*) for the 2100 CVC combinations of the English alphabet. *Psychological Reports*, 8:487–521.

Noble, C. E. & McNeely, D. A. (1957) The role of meaningfulness (*m*) in paired-associate learning. *Journal of Experimental Psychology*, 53:16–22.

Norman, D. A. (1969) *Memory and Attention: An Introduction to Human Information Processing.* New York: Wiley.

Norman, D. A. (1968) Towards a theory of memory and attention. *Psychological Review*, 75:522–536.

Norman, D. A. (1976) *Memory and Attention. An Introduction to Human Information Processing.* 2nd ed. New York: Wiley.

Norman, D. A. & Bobrow, D. G. (1975) On data-limited and resource-limited processes. *Cognitive Psychology*, 7:44–64.

Norman, D. A. & Bobrow, D. G. (1976) On the analysis of performance operating characteristics. *Psychological Review*, 83:508–510.

Nowlis, D. P. & Kamiya, J. (1970) The control of EEG alpha rhythm through auditory feedback and the associated mental activity. *Psychophysiology*, 6:476–484.

Nuttin, J. & Greenwald, A. G. (1968) *Reward and Punishment in Human Learning.* New York: Academic Press.

O'Connell, D. C., Turner, E. A. & Onuska, L. A. (1968) Intonation, grammatical structure, and contextual association in immediate recall. *Journal of Verbal Learning and Verbal Behavior*, 7:110–116.

O'Connor, N. & Hermelin, B. (1963) *Speech and Thought in Severe Subnormality.* London: Pergamon Press.

O'Connor, N. & Hermelin, B. (1965) Input restriction and immediate memory decay in normal and subnormal children. *Quarterly Journal of Experimental Psychology*, 17:323–328.

Oden, M. H. (1968) The fulfillment of promise: 40-year follow-up of the Terman gifted group. *Genetic Psychology Monographs*, 77:3–93.

Oldfield, R. C. (1963) Individual vocabulary and semantic currency: A preliminary study. *British Journal of Social and Clinical Psychology*, 2:122–130.

Oldfield, R. C. & Wingfield, A. (1965) Response latencies in naming objects. *Quarterly Journal of Experimental Psychology,* 17:273–281.

Olds, J. (1958) Satiation effects in self-stimulation. *Journal of Comparative and Physiological Psychology,* 51:675–678.

Olds, J. (1961) Differential effects of drive and drugs on self-stimulation at different brain sites. In: D. E. Sheer (ed.), *Electrical Stimulation of the Brain.* Austin: University of Texas Press.

Olds, J. (1962) Hypothalamic substrates of reward. *Physiological Review,* 42:554–604.

Olds, J. & Milner, P. (1954) Positive reinforcement produced by electrical stimulation of septal area and other regions of rat brain. *Journal of Comparative and Physiological Psychology,* 47:419–427.

Olds, J. & Olds, M. (1965) Drives, rewards and the brain. In: F. Barron et al., *New Directions in Psychology,* vol. II. New York: Holt, Rinehart and Winston.

Olds, J., Travis, R. P. & Schwing, R. C. (1960) Topographic organization of hypothalamic self-stimulation functions. *Journal of Comparative and Physiological Psychology,* 53:23–32.

O'Leary, K. D., Kaufman, K. F., Kass, R. & Drabman, R. (1970) The effects of loud and soft reprimands on the behavior of disruptive students. *Exceptional Children,* 37:145–155.

Olsson, J. E. & Furth, H. G. (1966) Visual memory-span in the deaf. *American Journal of Psychology,* 79:480–484.

Orton, S. (1937) *Reading, writing and speech problems in children.* New York: Norton.

Osgood, C. E. (1963) On understanding and creating sentences. *American Psychologist,* 18:735–751.

Osgood, C. E. (1968) Toward a wedding of insufficiencies. In: T. R. Dixon & D. L. Horton (eds.), *Verbal Behavior and General Behavior Theory.* Englewood Cliffs, N.J.: Prentice-Hall.

Oswald, I., Taylor, A. M. & Treisman, M. (1960) Discrimination responses to stimulation during human sleep. *Brain,* 83:440–453.

Paivio, A. (1969) Mental imagery in associative learning and memory. *Psychological Review,* 76:241–263.

Paivio, A. (1971) *Imagery and Verbal Processes.* New York: Holt, Rinehart and Winston.

Paivio, A. (1975) Perceptual comparisons through the mind's eye. *Memory and Cognition,* 3:635–647.

Paivio, A. & Csapo, K. (1969) Concrete image and verbal memory codes. *Journal of Experimental Psychology,* 80:279–285.

Paolino, R. M. & Levy, H. M. (1971) Amnesia produced by spreading depression and ECS: Evidence for time-dependent memory trace localization. *Science,* 172:746–749.

Paterson, A. & Zangwill, O. L. (1944) Disorders of visual space perception associated with lesions of the right cerebral hemisphere. *Brain,* 67:331–358.

Patty, R. A. & Page, M. M. (1973) Manipulations of a verbal conditioning situation based upon demand characteristics theory. *Journal of Experimental Research in Personality,* 6:307–313.

Pavlov, I. P. (1927) *Conditioned Reflexes.* (Translated by G. V. Anrep.) London: Oxford University Press.

Peckstein, L. A. (1918) Whole vs. part methods in learning nonsensical syllables. *Journal of Educational Psychology*, 9:379–387.

Peckstein, L. A. & Brown, F. D. (1939) An experimental analysis of the alleged criteria of insight learning. *Journal of Educational Psychology*, 30:38–52.

Penfield, W. (1951) Memory mechanisms. *Transactions of the American Neurological Association*, 76:15–31.

Penfield, W. & Roberts, L. (1959) *Speech and Brain Mechanisms*. Princeton University Press.

Perin, C. T. (1942) Behavior potentiality as a joint function of the amount of training and degree of hunger at the time of extinction. *Journal of Experimental Psychology*, 30:93–113.

Peterson, L. R. & Peterson, M. J. (1959) Short-term retention of individual verbal items. *Journal of Experimental Psychology*, 58:193–198.

Piaget, J. (1952) *The Origins of Intelligence in Children*. New York: International Universities Press.

Piaget, J. (1965) *The Child's Conception of Number*. New York: Norton.

Piaget, J. & Inhelder, B. (1956) *The Child's Conception of Space*. New York: Norton.

Piaget, J. & Inhelder, B. (1959) *La genèse des structures logiques élémentaires: Classifications et sériations*. Neuchâtel: Delchaux et Niestlé.

Piercy, M. (1964) The effects of cerebral lesions on intellectual function: A review of current research trends. *British Journal of Psychiatry*, 110:310–352.

Pollack, I. (1952) The information of elementary auditory displays. *Journal of the Acoustical Society of America*, 24:745–749.

Pollio, H. R. (1974) *The Psychology of Symbolic Activity*. Reading, Mass.: Addison-Wesley.

Pollio, H. R. & Foote, R. F. (1970) Memory as a reconstructive process. *British Journal of Psychology*, 61:1–5.

Pollio, H. R., Richards, S. & Lucas, R. (1969) Temporal properties of category recall. *Journal of Verbal Learning and Verbal Behavior*, 8:95–102.

Posner, M. I. (1963) Immediate memory in sequential tasks. *Psychological Bulletin*, 60:333–349.

Posner, M. I. (1967) Short-term memory systems in human information processing. *Acta Psychologica*, 27:267–284.

Posner, M. I. (1973) *Cognition: An Introduction*. Glenview, Ill.: Scott, Foresman.

Posner, M. I., Boies, S. J., Eichelman, W. H. & Taylor, R. L. (1969) Retention of visual and name codes of single letters. *Journal of Experimental Psychology*, 79 (1, pt. 2):1–16.

Posner, M. I. & Keele, S. W. (1967) Decay of visual information from a single letter. *Science*, 158:137–138.

Postman, L. J. (1953) Does interference theory predict too much forgetting? *Journal of Verbal Learning and Verbal Behavior*, 2:40–48.

Postman, L. (1962) Repetition and paired-associate learning. *American Journal of Psychology*, 75:372–389.

Postman, L. (1964) Short-term memory and incidental learning. In: A. W. Melton (ed.), *Categories of Human Learning.* New York: Academic Press.

Postman, L. & Stark, K. (1969) Role of response availability in transfer and interference. *Journal of Experimental Psychology*, 79:168–177.

Postman, L. & Underwood, B. J. (1973) Critical issues in interference theory. *Memory & Cognition*, 1:19–40.

Potter, M. C. & Faulconer, B. A. (1975) Time to understand pictures and words. *Nature*, 253:437–438.

Poulton, C. (1971) Skilled performance and stress. In: P. B. Warr (ed.), *Psychology at Work*, pp. 55–75. Baltimore: Penguin Books.

Premack, D. (1965) Reinforcement theory. In: D. Levine (ed.), *Nebraska Symposium on Motivation*, pp. 123–188. Lincoln: University of Nebraska Press.

Premack, D. (1971) Language in the chimpanzee? *Science*, 172:808–822.

Prentice, W. C. H. (1954) Visual recognition of verbally labeled figures. *American Journal of Psychology*, 67:315–320.

Pylyshyn, Z. W. (1973) What the mind's eye tells the mind's brain: A critique of mental imagery. *Psychological Bulletin*, 80:1–24.

Rabbitt, P. M. A. (1967) Time to detect errors as a function of factors affecting choice-response time. *Acta Psychologica*, 27:131–142.

Rabbitt, P. M. A. (1968) Three kinds of error-signalling responses in a serial choice task. *Quarterly Journal of Experimental Psychology*, 20:179–188.

Reed, H. B. (1946) Factors influencing the learning and retention of concepts. I. The influence of set. *Journal of Experimental Psychology*, 36:71–87.

Reitman, J. S. (1971) Mechanisms of forgetting in short-term memory. *Cognitive Psychology*, 2:185–195.

Reitman, J. S. (1974) Without surreptitious rehearsal, information in short-term memory decays. *Journal of Verbal Learning and Verbal Behavior*, 13:365–377.

Rescorla, R. A. (1972) Informational variables in Pavlovian conditioning. In: G. H. Bower (ed.), *The Psychology of Learning and Motivation*, vol. 6, pp. 1–46. New York: Academic Press.

Rescorla, R. A. & Solomon, R. L. (1967) Two-process learning theory: Relationships between Pavlovian conditioning and instrumental learning. *Psychological Review*, 74:151–182.

Rescorla, R. A. & Wagner, A. R. (1972) A theory of Pavlovian conditioning: Variations in the effectiveness of reinforcement and nonreinforcement. In: A. Black & W. F. Prokasy (eds.), *Classical Conditioning II. Current Research and Theory*. Englewood Cliffs, N.J.: Prentice-Hall.

Restle, F. (1957) Discrimination cues in mazes: A resolution of the "Place-vs.-response" question. *Psychological Review*, 64:217–228.

Restorff, H. von (1933) Über die Wirkung von Bereinschbildungen im Spurenfeld. *Psychologische Forschung*, 18:299–342.

Reynolds, A. G. & Flagg, P. W. (1977) *Cognitive Psychology*. Cambridge, Mass.: Winthrop.

Richardson, A. (1969) *Mental Imagery*. New York: Springer-Verlag.

Richter, C. P. (1922) A behavioristic study of the rat. *Comparative Psychology Monographs*, 1:1–55.

Richter, C. P. (1927) Animal behavior and internal drives. *Quarterly Review of Biology*, 2:307–343.

Robinson, D. N. (1973) *The Enlightened Machine. An Analytic Introduction to Neuropsychology*. Encino, Calif.: Dickenson.

Rock, I. (1957) The role of repetition in active learning. *American Journal of Psychology*, 70:186–193.

Rosch, E. H. (1974) Natural categories. *Cognitive Psychology*, 4:328–350.

Rosenthal, R. (1970) Another view of Pygmalion. *Contemporary Psychology*, 15:524.

Rosenthal, R. & Jacobsen, L. (1968) *Pygmalion in the Classroom*. New York: Holt, Rinehart and Winston.

Rosenzweig, M. R. & Møllgaard, K. M. (1972) Negative as well as positive synaptic changes may store memory. *Psychological Review*, 79:93–96.

Rothbart, M., Dalfen, S. & Barrett, R. (1971) Effects of teachers' expectations on student-teacher interaction. *Journal of Educational Psychology*, 62:49–54.

Routtenberg, A. & Lindy, J. (1965) Effects of the availability of rewarding septal and hypothalamic stimulation on barpressing for food under conditions of deprivation. *Journal of Comparative and Physiological Psychology*, 60:158–161.

Rubenstein, H. & Pollack, I. (1963) Word predictability and intelligibility. *Journal of Verbal Learning and Verbal Behavior*, 2:147–158.

Rumelhart, D. E., Lindsay, P. H. & Norman, D. A. (1972) A process model for long-term memory. In: E. Tulving & W. Donaldson (eds.), *Organization and Memory*, pp. 198–246. New York: Academic Press.

Russell, W. R. & Espir, M. L. E. (1961) *Traumatic Aphasia*. London: Oxford University Press.

Russell, R. W. & Hunter, W. S. (1937) The effects of inactivity produced by sodium amytal on the retention of the maze habit in the albino rat. *Journal of Experimental Psychology*, 20:426–436.

Russell, W. A. & Storms, L. H. (1955) Implicit verbal chaining in paired-associate learning. *Journal of Experimental Psychology*, 49:287–293.

Russell, W. R. (1959) *Brain, Memory, Learning*. London: Oxford University Press.

Ryle, G. (1949) *The Concept of Mind*. London: Hutchinson.

Saltz, E. (1961) Response pretraining: differentiation or availability? *Journal of Experimental Psychology*, 62:583–587.

Samuels, I., Butters, N. & Fedio, P. (1972) Short term memory disorders following temporal lobe removals in humans. *Cortex*, 8:283–298.

Savin, H. B. & Perchonock, E. (1965) Grammatical structure and the immediate recall of English sentences. *Journal of Verbal Learning and Verbal Behavior*, 4:348–353.

Sawisch, L. P. & Denny, M. R. (1973) Reversing the reinforcement contingencies of eating and keypecking behaviors. *Animal Learning and Behavior*, 1:189–192.

Schachter, S. (1971a) *Emotion, Obesity, and Crime*. New York: Academic Press.

Schachter, S. (1971b) Some extraordinary facts about obese humans and rats. *American Psychologist*, 26:129–144.

Schaffer, H. R. & Emerson, P. E. (1964) The development of social attachments in infancy. *Monographs of the Society for Research in Child Development*, 29 (3, serial no. 94).

Schein, E. H. (1965) *Organizational Psychology*. Englewood Cliffs, N.J.: Prentice-Hall.

Schrier, A. M. & Stollnitz, F. (eds.) (1971) *Behavior of Nonhuman Primates*, vol. 4. New York: Academic Press.

Schwartz, S. H. (1966) Trial-by-trial analyses of processes in simple and disjunctive concept-attainment tasks. *Journal of Experimental Psychology*, 72:456–465.

Sears, R. R. (1957) Identification as a form of behavioral development. In: D. B. Harris (ed.), *The Concept of Development*, pp. 147–161. Minneapolis: University of Minnesota Press.

Secord, P. F. & Backman, C. W. (1964) *Social Psychology*. New York: McGraw-Hill.

Segal, S. J. (ed.) (1971) *Imagery: Current Cognitive Approaches*. New York: Academic Press.

Sem-Jacobson, C. W. (1959) Effects of electrical stimulation on the human brain. *Electroencephalography and Clinical Neurology*, 11:379.

Sem-Jacobson, C. W. & Torkildsen, A. (1960) Depth recording and electrical stimulation in the human brain. In: E. R. Ramey & D. S. O'Doherty (eds.), *Electrical Studies of the Unanesthetized Brain*, pp. 280–288. New York: Harper & Row.

Shaffer, L. H. & Hardwick, J. (1969) Monitoring simultaneous auditory messages. *Perception and Psychophysics*, 6:401–404.

Shallice, T., & Warrington, E. K. (1970) Independent functioning of verbal memory stores: A neuropsychological study. *Quarterly Journal of Experimental Psychology*, 22:261–273.

Shanab, M. E. & Biller, J. D. (1972) Positive contrast in the Lashley maze under different drive conditions. *Psychonomic Science*, 3:179–184.

Shankweiler, D. (1967) Effects of temporal lobe damage on perception of dichotically presented melodies. *Journal of Comparative and Physiological Psychology*, 62:115–119.

Shannon, C. E. (1948) A mathematical theory of communication. *Bell System Technical Journal*, 27:379–423.

Shannon, C. E. (1951) Prediction and entropy in printed English. *Bell System Technical Journal*, 30:50–64.

Shannon, C. E. & Weaver, W. (1949) *The Mathematical Theory of Communication*. Urbana: University of Illinois Press.

Shapiro D., Schwartz, G. E. & Tursky, B. (1972) Control of diastolic blood pressure in man by feedback and reinforcement. *Psychophysiology*, 9:296–304.

Shatz, M. & Gelman, R. (1973) The development of communication skills: Modification in the speech of young children as a function of the listener. *Monographs of the Society for Research in Child Development* 38 (5, Serial No. 152).

Sheffield, F. D. & Roby, T. B. (1950) Reward value of a non-nutritive sweet taste. *Journal of Comparative and Physiological Psychology*, 43:471–480.

Shepard, R. N. (1967) Recognition memory for words, sentences, and pictures. *Journal of Verbal Learning and Verbal Behavior*, 6:156–163.

Shepard, R. N. & Chapman, S. (1970) Second-order isomorphism of internal representations: Shapes of states. *Cognitive Psychology*, 1:1–17.

Shepard, R. N. & Metzler, J. (1971) Mental rotation of three-dimensional objects. *Science*, 171:701–703.

Siddle, D. A. & Heron, P. A. (1976) Effects of length of training and amount of tone frequency change on amplitude of autonomic components of the orienting response. *Psychophysiology*, 13:281–287.

Siipola, E. M. & Hayden, S. D. (1965) Exploring eidetic imagery among the retarded. *Perceptual and Motor Skills*, 21:275–286.

Simmel, M. L. (1953) The coin problem: A study in thinking. *American Journal of Psychology*, 66:229–241.

Simmel, M. L. & Barron, S. B. (1966) Mnemonic virtuosity: A study of chess players. *Genetic Psychology Monographs*, 74:127–162. (A translation of Alfred Binet's, "Les grandes mémoires: Résumé d'une enquête sur les joueurs d'echecs," originally published in *Revue des deux mondes*, 1893, 117:826–859).

Simon, C. T. (1957) The development of speech. In: L. E. Travis (ed.), *Handbook of Speech Pathology*, pp. 3–43. Englewood Cliffs, N.J.: Prentice-Hall.

Skinner, B. F. (1938) *The Behavior of Organisms*. Englewood Cliffs, N.J.: Prentice-Hall.

Skinner, B. F. (1948a) *Walden Two*. New York: Macmillan.

Skinner, B. F. (1948b) Superstition in the pigeon. *Journal of Experimental Psychology*, 38:168–172.

Skinner, B. F. (1953) *Science and Human Behavior*. New York: Free Press.

Skinner, B. F. (1956) A case history of scientific method. *American Psychologist*, 11:221–233.

Skinner, B. F. (1957) *Verbal Behavior*. Englewood Cliffs, N.J.: Prentice-Hall.

Skinner, B. F. (1971) *Beyond Freedom and Dignity*. New York: Knopf.

Smith, E. E., Shoben, E. J. & Rips, L. J. (1974) Structure and process in semantic memory: A feature model for semantic decision. *Psychological Review*, 81:214–241.

Smith, K. U. & Smith, W. M. (1962) *Perception and Motion: An Analysis of Space-Structured Behavior*. Philadelphia: Saunders.

Smode, A. (1958) Learning and performance in a tracking task under two levels of achievement information feedback. *Journal of Experimental Psychology*, 56:297–304.

Smoke, K. L. (1933) Negative instances in concept learning, *Journal of Experimental Psychology*, 16:583–588.

Snow, C. E. (1972) Mothers' speech to children learning language. *Child Development*, 43:549–565.

Snow, R. E. (1969) Review of Pygmalion in the classroom. *Contemporary Psychology*, 14:197–199.

Sokolov, E. N. (1960) Neuronal models of the orienting reflex. In: M. Brazier (ed.), *The Central Nervous System and Behavior*, pp. 187–276. New York: Josiah Macy, Jr. Foundation.

Sokolov, E. (1963) *Perception and the Conditioned Reflex*. London: Pergamon Press.

Solomon, R. L. & Wynne, L. C. (1953) Traumatic avoidance learning: Acquisition in normal dogs. *Psychological Monographs*, 67, no. 354.

Spearman, C. (1927) *The Abilities of Man*. New York: Macmillan.

Spence, K. W. (1948) The postulates and methods of behaviorism. *Psychological Review*, 55:67–68.

Spence, K. W. (1951) Theoretical interpretations of learning. In: S. S. Stevens (ed.), *Handbook of Experimental Psychology*. New York: Wiley.

Spence, K. W. (1954) Current interpretations of learning data and some recent developments in stimulus-response learning theory. In: *Learning Theory, Personality Theory, and Clinical Research*. The Kentucky Symposium. New York: Wiley.

Spence, K. W. (1956) *Behavior Theory and Conditioning.* New Haven: Yale University Press.

Spence, K. W. (1960) *Behavior Theory and Learning.* Englewood Cliffs, N.J.: Prentice-Hall.

Sperling, G. (1960) The information available in brief visual presentations. *Psychological Monographs,* 74 (Whole no. 498).

Sperry, R. W. (1964) The great cerebral commissure. *Scientific American,* 210:42–52.

Spielberger, C. D. & DeNike, L. D. (1966) Descriptive behaviorism versus cognitive theory in verbal operant conditioning. *Psychological Review,* 73:306–326.

Staats, A. W. (1968) *Learning, Language, and Cognition.* New York: Holt, Rinehart and Winston.

Standing, L., Conezio, J. & Haber, R. N. (1970) Perception and memory for pictures: Single-trial learning of 2560 visual stimuli. *Psychonomic Science,* 19:73–74.

Starr, A. & Phillips, L. (1970) Verbal and motor memory in the amnestic syndrome. *Neuropsychologia,* 8:75–88.

Steer, M. D. & Hanley, T. D. (1957) Instruments of diagnosis, therapy, and research. In: L. E. Travis (ed.), *Handbook of Speech Pathology,* pp. 174–245. Englewood Cliffs, N.J.: Prentice-Hall.

Stein, A. H. & Bailey, M. M. (1973) The socialization of achievement motivation in females. *Psychological Bulletin,* 80:345–366.

Steinberg, H. & Summerfield, A. (1957) Influence of a depressant drug on acquisition in rote learning. *Quarterly Journal of Experimental Psychology,* 9:138–145.

Stennett, R. G. (1957) The relationship of performance level to level of arousal. *Journal of Experimental Psychology,* 54:54–61.

Stern, W. (1938) *General Psychology.* New York: Macmillan.

Sternberg, R. J. (1977) *Intelligence, Information Processing, and Analogical Reasoning: The Componential Analysis of Human Abilities.* Hillsdale, N.J.: Lawrence Erlbaum Associates.

Stoddard, G. D. (1943) *The Meaning of Intelligence.* New York: Macmillan.

Strand, B. Z. (1970) Change of context and retroactive inhibition. *Journal of Verbal Learning and Verbal Behavior,* 9:202–206.

Strauss, A. A. & Lehtinen, L. (1947) *Psychopathology and Education of the Brain-Injured Child.* New York: Grune & Stratton.

Stromeyer, C. F. & Psotka, J. (1970) The detailed texture of eidetic images. *Nature,* 225:346–349.

Studdert-Kennedy, M. & Shankweiler, D. P. (1970) Hemispheric specialization for speech perception. *Journal of the Acoustical Society of America,* 48:579–594.

Suci, G., Ammon, P. & Gamlin, P. (1967) The validity of the probe-latency technique for assessing structure in language. *Language and Speech,* 10:69–80.

Sulin, R. A. & Dooling, D. J. (1974) Intrusion of a thematic idea in retention of prose. *Journal of Experimental Psychology,* 103:255–262.

Swets, J. A. (1974) Introduction. In: J. A. Swets & L. L. Elliot (eds.), *Psychology and the Handicapped Child.* DHEW Publication No. (OE) 73-05000, pp. 1–11. Washington, D.C.: Government Printing Office.

Taber, J., Glaser, R. & Schaefer, H. (1965) *Learning and Programmed Instruction.* Reading, Mass.: Addison-Wesley.

Talland, G. A. (1968) *Disorders of Memory and Learning.* Baltimore: Penguin Books.

Tanzi, E. (1893) I fatti e le induzioni nell' odierna isologia del sistema nervoso. *Rivista sperimentale di freniatria e di medicina legale,* vol. 19.

Teasdale, H. H. (1934) A quantitative study of eidetic imagery. *British Journal of Educational Psychology,* 4:56–74.

Terman, L. M. & Merrill, M. A. (1960) *Measuring Intelligence: A Guide to the Administration of the New Revised Stanford-Binet Tests of Intelligence.* Rev. ed. Boston: Houghton Mifflin.

Thistlethwaite, D. L. (1951) A critical review of latent learning and related experiments. *Psychological Bulletin,* 48:97–129.

Thomson, D. M. & Tulving, E. (1970) Associative encoding and retrieval: weak and strong cues. *Journal of Experimental Psychology.* 86:255–262.

Thorndike, E. L. (1911) *Animal Intelligence.* New York: Macmillan.

Thorndike, E. L. (1913) *Educational Psychology.* New York: Teachers College Press, Columbia University.

Thorndike, E. L. & Lorge, I. (1944) *The Teacher's Word Book of 30,000 Words.* New York: Columbia University Press.

Thorndike, R. (1968) Review of "Pygmalion in the classroom." *American Educational Research Journal,* 5:708–711.

Thurstone, L. L. (1938) Primary mental abilities. *Psychometric Monographs* (Whole no. 1).

Thurstone, L. L. & Thurstone, T. G. (1941) Factorial studies of intelligence. *Psychometric Monographs* (Whole no. 2).

Tighe, T. J. (1964) Reversal and nonreversal shifts in monkeys. *Journal of Comparative and Physiological Psychology,* 58:324–326.

Tinbergen, N. (1969) *The Study of Instinct.* New York: Oxford University Press.

Tolman, E. C. (1938) Determiners of behavior at a choice point. *Psychological Review,* 45:1–41.

Tolman, E. C. (1948) Cognitive maps in rats and men. *Psychological Review,* 55:189–208.

Tolman, E. C. & Honzik, C. H. (1930) Introduction and removal of reward, and maze performance in rats. *University of California Publications in Psychology,* 4:257–275.

Tolman, E. C., Ritchie, B. F. & Kalish, D. (1946) Studies in spatial learning. Part II: Place learning versus response learning. *Journal of Experimental Psychology,* 36:221–229.

Torgesen, J. (1975) Problems and prospects in the study of learning disabilities. In: E. M. Hetherington (ed.), *Review of Child Development Research,* pp. 385–440. University of Chicago Press.

Travers, R. M. W. (1973) *Educational Psychology. A Scientific Foundation for Educational Practice.* New York: Macmillan.

Travis, L. E. (ed.) (1957) *Handbook of Speech Pathology.* Englewood Cliffs, N.J.: Prentice-Hall.

Treisman, A. M. (1960) Contextual cues in selective listening. *Quarterly Journal of Experimental Psychology,* 12:242–248.

Treisman, A. M. (1964a) Selective attention in man. *British Medical Bulletin*, 20:12–16.

Treisman, A. M. (1964b) Effect of irrelevant material on the efficiency of selective listening. *American Journal of Psychology*, 77:533–546.

Treisman, A. M. (1965) Effect of verbal context on latency of word selection. *Nature*, 206:218–219.

Treisman, A. M. (1969) Strategies and models of selective attention. *Psychological Review*, 76:282–299.

Treisman, A. M. & Geffen, G. (1967) Selective attention: Perception or response? *Quarterly Journal of Experimental Psychology*, 19:1–18.

Treisman, A. M. & Riley, J. G. A. (1969) Is selective attention selective perception or selective response? A further test. *Journal of Experimental Psychology*, 79:27–34.

Tulving, E. (1972) Episodic and semantic memory. In: E. Tulving & W. Donaldson (eds.), *Organization of Memory*, pp. 381–403. New York: Academic Press.

Tulving, E. & Gold, C. (1963) Stimulus information and contextual information as determinants of tachistoscopic recognition for words. *Journal of Experimental Psychology*, 66:319–327.

Tulving, E. & Pearlstone, Z. (1966) Availability versus accessibility of information in memory for words. *Journal of Verbal Learning and Verbal Behavior*, 5:381–391.

Underwood, B. J. (1948) Retroactive and proactive inhibition after 5 and 48 hours. *Journal of Experimental Psychology*, 38:29–38.

Underwood, B. J. (1957) Interference and forgetting. *Psychological Review*, 64:49–60.

Underwood, B. J. & Keppell, G. (1962) One-trial learning? *Journal of Verbal Learning and Verbal Behavior*, 1:1–13.

Valenstein, E. S., Cox, V. C. & Kakolewski, J. W. (1970) Reexamination of the role of the hypothalamus in motivation. *Psychological Review*, 77:16–32.

Vigotsky, L. S. (1934) *Thought and Language*. Cambridge, Mass.: The M.I.T. Press.

Vigotsky, L. S. (1939) Thought and speech. *Psychiatry*, 2:29–54.

Vinacke, W. E. (1974) *The Psychology of Thinking*. 2nd ed. New York: McGraw-Hill.

von Frisch, K. (1962) Dialects in the language of bees. *Scientific American*, 207:79–87.

von Frisch, K. (1967) Honeybees: Do they use direction and distance information provided by their dancers? *Science*, 158:1072–1076.

von Wright, J. M., Anderson, K. & Stenman, U. (1975) Generalization of conditioned GSRs in dichotic listening. In: P. M. A. Rabbitt & S. Dornic (eds.), *Attention and Performance V*. London: Academic Press.

Wada, J. & Rasmussen, T. (1960) Intracarotid injection of sodium amytal for the lateralization of cerebral speech dominance. Experimental and clinical observations. *Journal of Neurosurgery*, 17:266–282.

Watson, J. B. & Rayner, R. (1920) Conditioned emotional reactions. *Journal of Experimental Psychology*, 3:1–14.

Waugh, N. C. & Norman, D. A. (1965) Primary memory. *Psychological Review*, 72:89–104.

Wearing, A. J. (1970) The storage of complex sentences. *Journal of Verbal Learning and Verbal Behavior,* 9:21–29.

Wechsler, D. (1944) *The Measurement of Intelligence.* 3rd ed. Baltimore: Williams & Wilkins.

Wechsler, D. (1949) *The Wechsler Intelligence Scale for Children.* New York: Psychological Corporation.

Wechsler, D. (1955) *Manual for the Wechsler Adult Intelligence Scale.* New York: Psychological Corporation.

Wechsler, D. (1972) *Manual: Wechsler Intelligence Scale for Children.* New York: Psychological Corporation.

Weinland, J. W. (1957) *How to Improve Your Memory.* New York: Barnes & Noble Books.

Weinstock, S. (1954) Resistance to extinction of a running response following partial reinforcement under widely spaced trials. *Journal of Comparative and Physiological Psychology,* 47:318–323.

Weir, R. H. (1963) *Language in the Crib.* The Hague: Mouton.

Weiskrantz, L. (1968) Some aspects of attention. In: L. Weiskrantz (ed.), *Analysis of Behavior Change,* pp. 239–267. New York: Harper & Row.

Welford, A. T. (1958) *Ageing and Human Skill.* London: Oxford University Press.

Wells, W. D., Goi, F. J. & Seader, S. A. (1958) A change in product image. *Journal of Applied Psychology,* 42:120–121.

Wenger, M. & Bagchi, B. (1961) Studies of autonomic function in practitioners of Yoga in India. *Behavioral Science,* 6:312–323.

Wenger, M., Bagchi, B. & Anand, B. (1961) Experiments in India on "voluntary" control of the heart and pulse. *Circulation,* 24:1319–1325.

Werner, H. & Kaplan, E. (1950) Development of word meaning through verbal context: An experimental study. *Journal of Psychology,* 29:251–257.

West, L. J. (1967) Vision and kinesthesis in the acquisition of typing skill. *Journal of Applied Psychology,* 51:161–166.

White, R. W. (1959) Motivation reconsidered: The concept of competence. *Psychological Review,* 66:297–333.

Whiting, J. W. M. (1960) Resource mediation and learning by identification. In: I. Iscoe & H. W. Stevenson (eds.), *Personality Development in Children,* pp. 112–126. Austin: University of Texas Press.

Wickelgren, W. A. (1965) Acoustic similarity and intrusion errors in short-term memory. *Journal of Experimental Psychology,* 70:102–108.

Wickelgren, W. A. (1974) Memory. In: J. A. Swets & L. L. Elliott (eds.), *Psychology and the Handicapped Child.* DHEW Publication No. (OE) 73-05000. Washington, D. C.: Government Printing Office.

Wickens, D. D. (1973) Some characteristics of word encoding. *Memory and Cognition,* 1:485–490.

Winch, R. F. (1962) *Identification and its Familial Determinants.* Indianapolis: Bobbs-Merrill.

Wingfield, A. (1967) Perceptual and response hierarchies in object identification. *Acta Psychologica,* 26:216–226.

Wingfield, A. (1973) Effects of serial position and set size in auditory recognition memory. *Memory and Cognition,* 1:53–55.

Wingfield, A. (1975) Acoustic redundancy and the perception of time-compressed speech. *Journal of Speech and Hearing Research,* 18:96–104.

Wingfield, A. (1977) The perception of alternated speech. *Brain and Language*, 4:219–230.

Wingfield, A. & Byrnes, D. L. (1972) Decay of information in short-term memory. *Science*, 176:690–692.

Wingfield, A., & Klein, J. F. (1971) Syntactic structure and acoustic pattern in speech perception. *Perception and Psychophysics*, 9:23–25.

Winkler, R. C. (1971) The relevance of economic theory and technology of token reinforcement systems. *Behavior Research and Therapy*, 9:81–88.

Winterbottom, M. R. (1958) The relation of need for achievement to learning experience in independence and mastery. In: J. W. Atkinson (ed.), *Motives in Fantasy, Action, and Society*, pp. 453–478. New York: Van Nostrand.

Withrow, F. B. (1968–1969) Immediate memory span of deaf and normally hearing children. *Exceptional Children*, 35:33–41.

Wolf, M. M., Giles, D. K. & Hall, R. V. (1968) Experiments with token reinforcement in a remedial classroom. *Behavior Research and Therapy*, 6:51–64.

Wolf, T. H. (1973) *Alfred Binet*. University of Chicago Press.

Wolfe, J. B. (1936) Effectiveness of token rewards for chimpanzees. *Comparative Psychology Monographs*, 12 (Whole no. 60).

Wolpe, J. (1974) *The Practice of Behavior Therapy*. 2nd ed. Elmsford, N.Y.: Pergamon.

Wood, C. C., Goff, W. R. & Day, R. S. (1971) Auditory evoked potentials during speech perception. *Science*, 173:1248–1251.

Woodworth, R. S. & Schlosberg, H. (1954) *Experimental Psychology*. Rev. ed. New York: Holt, Rinehart and Winston.

Yates, F. A. (1966) *The Art of Memory*. University of Chicago Press.

Yerkes, R. M. & Dodson, J. D. (1908) The relation of strength of stimulus to rapidity of habit-formation. *Journal of Comparative Neurology of Psychology*, 18:459–482.

Yntema, D. B. & Trask, F. P. (1963) Recall as a search process. Journal of Verbal Learning and Verbal Behavior, 2:67–74.

Zangwill, O. L. (1950) Amnesia and the generic image. *Quarterly Journal of Experimental Psychology*, 2:7–12.

Zeaman, D. (1949) Response latency as a function of the amount of reinforcement. *Journal of Experimental Psychology*, 39:466–483.

Zeaman, D., & House, B. J. (1963) The role of attention in retardate discrimination learning. In: N. R. Ellis, (ed.), *Handbook of Mental Deficiency*, pp.159–223. New York: McGraw-Hill.

Zelazo, P. R., Zelazo, N. A. & Kolb, S. (1972) Walking in the newborn. *Science*, 176:314–315.

Zelman, A., Kabot, L., Jacobson, R., & McConnell, J. W. (1963) Transfer of training through injection of "conditioned" RNA into untrained worms. *Worm Runner's Digest*, 5:14–21.

Zimbardo, P. G. (1969) *The Cognitive Control of Motivation*. Glenview, Ill.: Scott, Foresman.

Zimbardo, P. G., Cohen, A., Weisenberg, M., Dworkin, L. & Firestone, I. (1969) The cognitive control of experimental pain. In: P. G. Zimbardo, (ed.), *The Cognitive Control of Motivation*, pp. 100–122. Glenview, Ill.: Scott, Foresman.

Zinberg, N. E. & Robertson, J. A. (1972) *Drugs and the Public*. New York: Simon & Schuster.

Zurif, E. B. (1974) Auditory lateralization: Prosodic and syntactic factors, *Brain and Language*, 1:391–404.

Zurif, E. B. & Ramier, A. M. (1972) Some effects of unilateral brain damage on the perception of dichotically presented phoneme sequences and digits, *Neuropsychologia*, 10:103–110.

Zwislocki, J., Maire, F., Feldman, A. S., & Rubin, H. (1958) On the effect of practice and motivation on the threshold of audibility. *Journal of the Acoustical Society of America*, 30:254–262.

indexes

Author Index

Subject Index

81 82 9 8 7 6 5 4